Manufacturing the Muse

MUSIC/CULTURE
A series from Wesleyan University Press
Edited by George Lipsitz, Susan McClary, and
Robert Walser

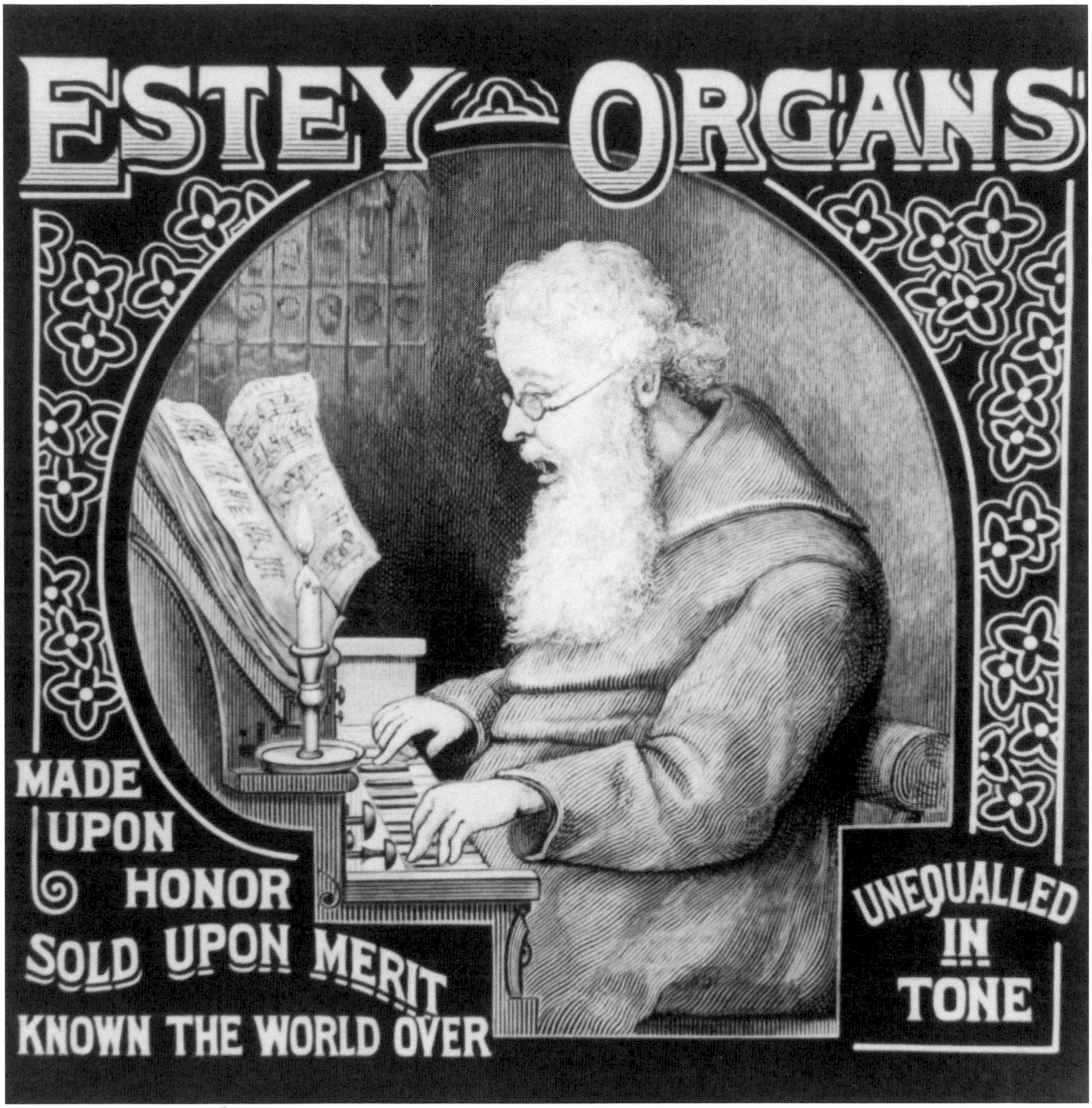
ESTEY ORGANS
MADE UPON HONOR
SOLD UPON MERIT
KNOWN THE WORLD OVER
UNEQUALLED IN TONE

Manufacturing the MUSE

Estey Organs & Consumer Culture in Victorian America

DENNIS G. WARING

WESLEYAN UNIVERSITY PRESS

Middletown, Connecticut

Published by

Wesleyan University Press,

Middletown, CT 06459

© 2002 by Dennis G. Waring

Special thanks to Furthermore,

a program of the J. M. Kaplan Fund,

for funding

Printed in the United States of America

Designed by Richard Hendel

Set in Monotype Bell, Kuenstler, and

Madrone types by B. Williams & Associates

Library of Congress

Cataloging-in-Publication Data

Waring, Dennis, 1945–

Manufacturing the muse : Estey organs &

consumer culture in Victorian America /

Dennis G. Waring.

p. cm.

Includes bibliographical references and index.

ISBN 0-8195-6507-5 (cloth : alk. paper)—

ISBN 0-8195-6508-3 (pbk. : alk. paper)

1. Reed organ—United States—History.

2. Estey Organ Company. 3. Music—

Social aspects—United States—History—

19th century. I. Estey Organ Company. II. Title.

ml597 . w37 2002

786.5'51973—dc21   2002023460

5   4   3   2   1

CONTENTS

ILLUSTRATIONS

Unless otherwise noted, all photos are from the Brattleboro Historical Society and the collection of Harold A. Barry.

TIMELINES

MAPS

DIAGRAMS, CHARTS, AND TABLES

MUSIC SCORES

Preface

Musical instruments have long been a major concern of the music scholar and are of increasing interest to those involved in related cultural studies. The study of musical instruments tells us much about a people and their culture, since it uniquely combines perspectives of anthropology and sociology, history and psychology, science and technology, philosophy and religion, art and craft, and of course, music itself.

In the classic volume *The Anthropology of Music*, the ethnomusicologist Alan Merriam outlines several principles concerning the sociocultural functions of music and implements of music production. He asserts: "The uses and functions of music represent one of the most important problems in ethnomusicology, for in the study of human behavior we search constantly, . . . not only for the descriptive facts, . . . but, more important, for the meaning. . . . We wish to know not only what a thing is, but, more significantly, what it does for people and how it does it."[1] Merriam's list of sociomusical functions includes aesthetic enjoyment, entertainment, communication, symbolic representation, encouragement of conformity to social norms, validation of social institutions and religious rituals, and contribution to the continuity and stability of culture and to the integration of society.[2] These universal constructs are clearly illustrated in the present study.[3]

Because America's history is comparatively short, information regarding the development of music in this country is relatively accessible and reveals much concerning its cultural beginnings and consequent multiethnic interaction. American music bears witness to various sociocultural values, patterns of migration, urbanization, economic development, industrialization, regional diversity, commercialization, and social stratification. More recently, it personifies the effects

Examining a culture's tools and technology can tell us about the group's history and way of life. Similarly, research into the material culture of music can help us to understand the music-culture. The most vivid body of "things" in it, of course, are musical instruments.

Mark Slobin,
Worlds of Music

of an increasingly globalized economy, rapidly changing technologies, and world-wide media and communications networks.

Beyond the study of music per se, the historical progression of musical instrument manufacturing in America is largely undocumented, though it is an area that has periodically attracted scholarly attention.[4] Thus far, organological research, regardless of the culture examined, supports the thesis that the instrument maker or manufacturer has great influence in effecting change within the music process.[5] Though we are generally familiar with the names such of companies as Gibson, Martin, and Fender in guitars; Chickering, Steinway, and Mason & Hamlin in keyboards; and Conn, Selmer, and Yamaha in wind instruments, knowledge of large-scale American instrument manufacture, especially early efforts, is particularly obscure. Yet, a thorough search to identify less-celebrated makers or manufacturers, trace their careers within a cultural context, and evaluate their contributions, is of value. It is, after all, this tradition that forged America's musical instrument industry into a major musical influence in the world today.

This book examines American instrument manufacture during a time when increasing industrialization impacted nearly every aspect of American life. It traces the development of the reed organ in America as exemplified by the life and enterprise of the great nineteenth-century reed organ manufacturer Jacob Estey (figure 1). My story concentrates on a core period from the middle of the nineteenth century, when small reed organs began to filter into the popular mainstream, into the ensuing century, as they began their decline.

The introduction to this volume sets the stage by briefly assessing some of the historical influences that underpinned the development of reed organ manufacture in America.

Part I maps the cultural contexts and iconographic significance of the reed organ in a rapidly changing, consumer-oriented American society. Chapter 1 describes how the Victorian aesthetic was fully indulged through the reed organ and its milieu and details how nineteenth-century advertisers manipulated collective symbols by associating reed organ imagery and the Victorian household with society at large. Chapter 2 examines the Victorian ethos and sensibility and traces the beginnings of popular expression to the music played on reed organs.[6]

Part II, Chapters 3 through 5, focuses on the life and legacy of Jacob Estey and examines his formidable enterprise within its historical and cultural context. The biographical emphasis is intentional. Estey's story, though personal and unique, is paradigmatic of an era of American history: Victorian life in Brattleboro, Vermont, though "local," mirrored the country's mood in general. This segment details how Estey's company epitomized the complex process of manufacturing a musical instrument to fit a cultural mold and how the instrument, in turn, helped Americans further formulate and define themselves through the latter half of the nineteenth century and well into the twentieth.

Figure 1.
Jacob Estey

Acknowledgments

I would like to thank the following people and institutions for their invaluable assistance in the research and preparation of this book. I am forever grateful to Harold and Alene Westover, who first suggested the idea of the Estey saga as a story ripe for the telling. Richard M. Mitchell, a Brattleboro historian and steamship authority, was the first to show me Estey's old pathways. By sharing a lifetime of research and experience, he made history come alive, and this volume is dedicated to his memory. Harold A. (Jeff) Barry, a professional photographer and collector emeritus, likewise made Brattleboro history vividly manifest. Many of the photographs used in this book were selected from his extensive library.

In regard to this work's early stages, I am deeply grateful to David McAllester, Wesleyan University professor emeritus, whose guidance and generosity of spirit on matters ethnomusicological and otherwise have inspired generations of students. Thanks also are due Wesleyan professors Mark Slobin and Neely Bruce for their vast stores of knowledge; Yale University for access to their archive of American music trade journals; the ever-helpful Jerry J. Carbone, head librarian in Brattleboro's Brooks Memorial Library; and Connell Gallagher, curator of the Wilbur Collection at the Bailey-Howe Library, University of Vermont, Burlington; and the Brattleboro Museum and Art Center. I wish to express particular gratitude as well to the Brattleboro Historical Society for providing access to their growing collections (the source of several of this book's illustrations) and to Gerry Gatz, Harriet Ives, and Pauline (Peg) Barry, who were particularly helpful in early preparation and research.

Louise Renaud of Brattleboro, Vermont, eased my labor considerably: "mostly out of curiosity" and in hopes of one day writing a book, she painstakingly combed the old newspapers of her town for years, documenting all information relating to the Estey enterprise. Mrs. Renaud generously gave me access to over five hundred pages of handwritten primary source material.

E. A. Boadway, historian, organist, and organ restorer in Claremont, New Hampshire, provided a portion of the music on the accompanying compact disc and special insight into the quality workmanship and impressive sound of Estey's instruments. He generously helped in the editing of this work and allowed me access to his extensive library and collection of Estey ephemera. Touring the small churches, lodges, and homes around Claremont with Mr. Boadway was virtually a trip back to the nineteenth century. As he played various Estey organs still housed and used at their original locations, the Victorian ambience became irresistible. He also introduced me to Laurence W. Leonard of Laconia, New Hampshire, who let me examine and record several reed, pipe, and player organs that he restored.

Ned Phoenix, of Townshend, Vermont, reed organ restorer, collector, teacher, and all-around musician, contributed considerable time, talent, and knowledge to this project. With his particular expertise in free-reed technology, Mr. Phoenix helped me understand some of the mechanical intricacies (and idiosyncrasies) of the reed organ. He also provided several music selections recorded on the companion compact disc. His insightfulness regarding particular requirements for playing the reed organ properly gave me a new appreciation of subtle aspects of reed organ performance practice. Both Mr. Boadway and Mr. Phoenix have been invaluable informants and tireless editors. Much of the fine-tuned detail of this study is attributable to their technical expertise and prodigious knowledge of reed organ history. Their special contributions to the appendixes are also greatly appreciated.

And my sincere thanks to the good citizens of Brattleboro for their generous hospitality and the Crosby Foundation for funding assistance. The stalwart encouragement and support of John Carnahan and Barbara George have been of special value through the arduous process of updating and revising this work. The firsthand accounts of the Estey employee John Wessel were particularly important in clearing up some confusions in the final years of the Estey history. I am also grateful to Becky Graber, Brattleboro musician and teacher, for volunteering to sing the old songs; Carolyn Halsted, of Middletown, Connecticut, for playing selections from Estey's organ methods; Jack and Nancy Reed of Newfane, Vermont, for performing a selection of Victorian favorites; and Luella Frechette, organist at the First Baptist Church of Brattleboro, for demonstrating the handsome Estey pipe organ housed therein. Selected trade card illustrations are from the Brattleboro collection of William Fleming and from the files of the Brattleboro Historical Society. Thanks to David Schulz for rendering the graphics found in the appendixes.

Mack Sowell, Assistant Vice President for Operations, and Mrs. Annie Coleman, librarian and cataloger for the James E. Cheek Learning Resources Center at Shaw University in Raleigh, North Carolina, helped in my inquiry into the Esteys' involvement with black education after the Civil War.

My appreciation goes as well to Wesleyan Press of Middletown, Connecticut, and its editor in chief, Suzanna Tamminen, whose patient and expert advice helped pull the pieces of this study into a coherent whole. Also Julie Allred of B. Williams & Associates and my copy editor, Barbara Norton, for their painstaking work on the production and editing of this book.

My final and most affectionate gratitude naturally goes to my mother and father, Mary Jane and Oral, and to my brother, George, for their unconditional love and support through the years, and to my grandmother, Lottie Coffin, who lived the Victorian ideal.

Introduction

When people think of "the organ" they picture magnificent pipe organs situated in sanctified surroundings on which notable virtuosi play Bach and Buxtehude. This was not always the case.[1] The late-nineteenth-century informant would have been more likely to specify the reed organ, then the predominant instrument in households and churches across the United States.[2]

Reed organ is a "generic term for keyboard instruments whose sound is produced by freely-vibrating reed tongues . . . and activated by air under either pressure or suction."[3] The reeds are, of course, the central element. There are many determinates of reed pitch and timbre: alloy and temper of the brass, dimensions and configuration of the tongue, and the reeds' physical, acoustic environment (see Appendix E). In addition to the reed organ, other air-blown free-reed instruments, including the accordion, concertina, and harmonica were introduced early in the nineteenth century.

Practically speaking, the reed organ had several features that made it attractive to Americans: it was inexpensive and easy to move, and it required little maintenance. Its simple construction enabled owners to effect their own repairs, and, unlike many of the zithers, guitars, and other popular stringed instruments of the day (including the more elite harpsichord and piano), the reed organ stayed in tune.

Reed organs also stood up well to changes in weather and humidity. Even into the middle of the nineteenth century, pianos' wooden frameworks withstood high-tension strings and the vagaries of the American climate for only a few seasons before developing problems.[4] Since there were no such self-destructive forces at work on a reed organ, about the worst thing that might happen was for a family of mice to take up residence inside it.

The study of musical instruments may be approached from different angles. It may be viewed historically, in terms of origin and development, or culturally, in terms of social uses, functions, and the beliefs and values associated with them. Musical instruments may also be studied as material objects in terms of their technology, with respect to their design and craftsmanship, materials and construction, and musical function.

J. H. Kwabena Nketia,
The Music of Africa

Nonetheless, the reed organ and piano have a long and close association, and many of the factors surrounding the better-known piano's popularity apply equally to its free-reed relative. As early as 1790, the piano was seen by Americans as a symbol of prosperity and refinement and a means to artistic cultivation. Since the development of the piano and its social import have been well documented, I will not reiterate its history except as it sheds light on the present subject.[5]

While a variety of smaller musical instruments became popular in the nineteenth century, the reed organ became an American icon, an accessory of the emerging middle class. In its secular function, it contributed significantly to a budding popular culture in America.[6] In the religious arena, it gained such popularity that around mid-century, the building of small pipe organs was almost abandoned.[7] And for over a half century, the reed organ exceeded even the piano in its popularity as an instrument for domestic music-making.[8]

The reed organ was known by many names throughout the nineteenth century, and an increasing number of patents were taken out by builders and manufacturers trying to popularize the brand name of their latest model. The most common term used in Europe was *harmonium*;[9] its immediate precursor was called the Royal Seraphine or simply seraphine (produced both in Europe and in America). Other common appellations include melodeon (which, in Britain and France, meant accordion), reed organ, parlor organ, American organ, and pump organ.

The Estey Cottage, Salon (figure 2), Drawing Room, and Parlor Organs drew their names from their setting. Likewise the Chapel, Chancel, Church, and Cathedral Organs, which had more reeds and/or keyboards to help fill the volume of larger rooms.[10] The designation of the successful Mason & Hamlin Cabinet Organ, which featured a nonportable, enclosed-case design (without the foldable legs found on earlier models), signified its elevation to the status of domestic furniture for the well-to-do. Further, it was hoped that brand names and descriptive nomenclature such as Aeolina, Euphonion, Melodiflute, Organochordium, Aeolklavier, Organo-Violine, L'Orgue Expressif, Vocalion, Phonorium, and Physharmonika, to name only a few, would catch the fancy of those musical aspirants who depended on pretension as much as talent for social advancement.[11] Indeed, as a symbol of a musically democratic society, the reed organ's success rested on a foundation of amateur, rather than professional, musicianship.

Reed organs were as diverse in size as in name, ranging from early button-keyed, single-manual, lap-top versions to those having two (or sometimes three) manuals and pedal keys and incorporating many sets of reeds, which allowed a greater choice of timbres and pitches.[12] The earlier, small, portable styles could fit on the player's lap or on a table. Larger instruments with more substantial cabinetry came into vogue for those who had parlors (and pocketbooks) sizable

NEW SALON ORGAN.

HEIGHT, 6 ft. 7 in.; LENGTH, 4 ft. 7 in.; DEPTH, 2 ft. 1½ in.   WEIGHT, boxed, 700 lbs.

enough to accommodate them. As the century gathered steam, the more "elegant" models came festooned with Victorian woodwork, brass, and plate-glass mirrors (see Appendix D). The larger styles could also be winded by a separate blowing lever or crank or, later, by a water motor or electric turbine. The Vocalion, distinguished by its exceptionally wide reeds and individual resonating chambers, may well represent the reed organ at the highest stage of its development.[13] The most common American organs, however, had one manual of three to six octaves (divided into bass and treble "halves") and two to five sets of reeds. Their stops opened reed mutes, activated tremolo or Vox Humana vibrato effects, and coupled keys at octaves. A right knee lever controlled swell, and the left dramatically brought on all stops.

Nineteenth-century Americans, including an increasingly affluent middle class and especially those who were residents of smaller rural towns and villages, were naturally attracted to a bargain. A fairly good reed organ could be purchased for $100.00 at a time when a cheap piano cost close to $300.00.[14] The Sears, Roebuck catalogue of 1902 still offered the $22.00 Happy Home Organ, or, for $27.45, customers received a free stool and instruction book with their Acme Queen Parlor Organ.[15] The rather notorious manufacturer Daniel Beatty advertised organs as low as $27.00, but with Beatty and others of his ilk, customers complained that when they arrived at the factory with payment, the model pitched was often out of stock. Not surprisingly, salesmen were quick to offer several alternative styles of more expensive organs that just happened to be on hand.[16]

The reed organ came on the scene at a time when increasing religious liberalism allowed such instruments in the buildings of more and more Protestant denominations. Reed organs were considered highly suitable for Sabbath schools, lecture rooms, vestries, public halls, and especially the numerous small church congregations whose budget or limited space prohibited the purchase of a pipe organ.[17] It was reported that the gifted revival preacher Dwight L. Moody and his musical director, Ira D. Sankey, could sway huge crowds with a small reed organ as their only accompaniment.[18] Because the sound of the reed organ lent itself to religious music, such music became regular fare in homes as well as in churches. In the home, worship and entertainment became closely related; those who owned organs could create the sound of sacred music any time of the week.

The American reed organ and its associated industry did not, of course, suddenly appear from nothingness. Its development is only part of a larger history of instrument making in this country, a history I will now briefly highlight for context and perspective.

A CONCISE HISTORY OF MUSICAL INSTRUMENT

MANUFACTURE IN AMERICA

Though records of professional instrument makers in America exist as far back as 1740, it was not until much later that instrument manufacture gained a firm footing.[19] The 1860 census report claimed: "So unimportant was this branch of industry a half century since, that its products were recorded by the marshal in 1810 only in one state, in which they amounted in value only $17,830, nearly the whole of which was produced in Boston. Now American skill and genius have placed our manufacturers in rivalship with those of Europe on which, for many years, we were dependent for our instruments of music."[20]

Nonetheless, foreign-made instruments, which started being imported commercially in the last decades of the eighteenth century, both supplemented and subverted the meager output of early American builders. As with music and art, Americans looked to Europe first for cultural precedents. Newspaper advertisements such as the following from New York (including the quaint spellings and capitalizations) were not unusual: "Jacob Astor, No. 81, Queen-street, two doors from the Friends Meeting-House, Has just imported from London, An elegant assortment of Musical Instruments, such as piano-fortes, spinnets, piano-forte guittars, guittars, the best of violins, German flutes, clarinets, hautboys, fifes, the best Roman violin strings, and other kinds of strings, music books and paper, and every other article in the musical line, which he will dispose of on very low terms for cash."[21] And at the turn of the century, a government report, "Musical Instruments and Materials of 1900," noted: "The successful manufacture of musical instruments requires a skill on the part of both manufacturers and workmen which is only attained by long experience. For this reason the industries included in this report were slow in establishing themselves in the United States, buyers of musical instruments being for a long period very largely dependent upon foreign manufacture."[22]

Since competition was stiff, it was not unusual to find early efforts that combined instrument making with the manufacture of nonmusical items. Tools and raw materials employed in manufacturing utilitarian items were sometimes adapted to instrument production. A Hartford, Connecticut, advertisement dated June 23, 1800, states: "George Catlin, at head of Prison St., makes almost every kind of musical instrument now in use such as, piano fortes, harpsichords, violin-cellos, guitars, bassoons, clarinets and hautboys of different keys, tenor clarinets, flutes of various kinds, fifes, reeds, etc, etc. Also mathematical instruments, gauging rods . . . sliding Gunter calipers, board and log measures, wood measures on a new scale. Those who favor him with their custom may depend on having their work well done and warranted. A generous allowance to good customers."[23]

Eventually the high cost of importing foreign-made instruments, coupled with the tendency for foreign wooden instruments to degenerate under harsh North American conditions, gave local craftsmen the incentive to begin to develop the commercial potential for building musical instruments. It was difficult, however, to make a living doing so. Fine workmanship requires careful techniques, and it takes a great deal of time to craft instruments using hand tools. Individual makers produced limited numbers of instruments and had to prove that American products were as good as their European counterparts. The search for a salable product and a receptive market often forced instrument makers to change profession, place of work, and residence.[24]

As eastern seaboard populations increased, mostly in Boston, New York, and Philadelphia, so did music-making activity and opportunities for instrument manufacture, especially for piano makers. Those who achieved some success in the business often took in other members of the family or apprenticed workers to increase production. Partnerships were formed to pool financial resources.

The broadening markets that resulted from the coalescing of music-oriented firms forced ambitious manufacturers to rely more and more on mechanized forms of production. Survival depended on finding sources of venture capital, overcoming geographical handicaps for effective distribution, and developing increased entrepreneurial specialization. From the end of the Civil War into the twentieth century, America was committed to progress and economic achievement through industrialized commodification. During this period, instrument manufacture, though still a relatively small sector of the industrial community, reflected many of the trends and developments peculiar to that era. It is instructive to focus for a moment on the production of "instruments of general use," a segment of the industry that expanded dramatically as the nineteenth century progressed.[25]

Though instrument production was limited early on, instruments such as pianofortes, small reed organs, and guitars were generally available to the American buyer by the mid-1800s; smaller instruments such as flutes, clarinets, and bugles were also mostly within the means of musically aspiring but frugal families.[26] And sheet music for singing popular songs could be bought for twenty-five cents a copy.[27] Although instruments for making music were within reach of almost everyone, the majority of them were reserved for use by men only. For most of the nineteenth century, guitar playing was considered too masculine for women; playing the cello and horn blowing were also deemed unladylike. Likewise, minstrel instruments including the fiddle, banjo, bones, and tambourine definitely belonged to the man's world, specifically to the forbidden domain of the "Negro." Even harps, historically the province of women, generally went out of vogue early in the nineteenth century. In the final equation, women were mostly confined to and thus monopolized the keyboard instruments and retained their modesty in the days of long skirts while managing the pedal keys of pipe organs.

Starting around the last quarter of the century, some of these sociomusical strictures began to ease. Guitars, mandolins, and banjos came into vogue and were in great demand as parlor instruments, a movement that culminated in an early-twentieth-century craze for ensembles of plucked chordophones.[28] Enjoyed by both sexes, banjo and mandolin clubs (often with guitars to fill in the lower range) were especially popular on college campuses. Other varieties of folk instruments, such as the Appalachian lap dulcimer in the Southeast and the hammered dulcimer in the upper Midwest, thrived regionally and attracted large local followings.

Though many of these instruments were "ethnically" derived (i.e., "African" banjo, "Italian" mandolin, "Spanish" guitar, "Hawaiian" ukulele, and "Hungarian" dulcimer), as in other areas of American innovation, large doses of Yankee ingenuity were applied to their design and manufacture. This is amply illustrated by such instrument-making pioneers as Orville Gibson, who built mandolin-banjos, cello-banjos, guitar-banjos, harp-guitars, mando-cellos, mandolas, and other unusual instrument hybrids,[29] and by such distributors as Montgomery Ward and Sears, Roebuck & Company, who advertised peculiarities like the Zitho-Harp and the Mandolin-Guitar-Zither ("three instruments combined at the price of one!").[30]

Later, around the 1920s, Americanized versions of the German zither also became popular musical items, particularly for economy-minded individuals or those without formal music education. Tens of thousands of zithers in various bastardized forms were manufactured and sold during this invention-happy period: Ukelins, Pianolins, Pianoettes, Marxophones, Tremoloas, Violin Ukes, Sol-o-lins, Hawaiian Art Violins, and other zithers with zany attachments were tendered through catalogues and door to door.[31] The musical fare arranged for these instruments was a varied repertoire and typically included a hodgepodge of well-known (and less-well-known) favorites. One music collection, *Leisure Hours Folio No. 22*, published by the Zither Music Company of New York, contains a representative selection of pieces: "Aloha Waltz," "Alexander's Ragtime Band," "Break the News to Mother," "Blue Bells of Scotland," "Chop Sticks Waltz," "Home on the Range," "I've Been Working on the Railroad," "Love's Old Sweet Song," "*Merry Widow* Waltz," "Old Black Joe," "Moth and the Flame," "O Suzanna," "Kiss Waltz," "Red Wing," "Stars and Stripes Forever March," and "Whoopee Ti Yi Git Along Little Dogies."[32]

Now found in museums, private collections, and attics, these instruments attest to a fad of some importance. Only the autoharp, a concluding and somewhat more successful manifestation of the zither, reminds us of a day when Americans plucked, bowed, stroked, tapped, and strummed these multi-stringed monsters.[33]

Wind and percussion instruments had their heyday too, though the growth in popularity of brass instruments lagged somewhat behind that of woodwinds until underdeveloped American mines could supply manufacturers with quantities of less expensive metals.[34] The melodeon, because of its brass reeds, was also susceptible to this issue. A market that required a large quantity of wind and percussion instruments was the military bands (fueled especially by the Civil War), which, later in the nineteenth century, were generally supplied by leading musical instrument manufacturers such as the Rudolph Wurlitzer Company.[35]

But it was most likely the civilian band activity that encouraged enterprises such as Graves & Company in Winchester, New Hampshire, and John F. Stratton & Company in New York (originally of Swanzey, New Hampshire) to produce brass and woodwinds full time.[36] Permanent municipal bands, militia and factory

Figure 3.
Brattleboro Military
Band, c. 1890

bands, professional traveling circus and concert bands, and less formal community ensembles, found in towns and villages across America, guaranteed a steady demand for wind instruments (figure 3).[37] On the other hand, bowed instruments generally resisted attempts at mass production until fairly recently. Though one might find a two-dollar mail-order violin or fiddle, the care and judgment required in violin making does not easily accommodate automation. Instead, violin-family instruments were either imported or "folk" versions made by woodworkers who, though often skilled, had little or no formal training in instrument making.[38]

But of all the instruments being manufactured during this period, keyboard instruments were by far the largest enterprise.[39] The reed organ was the answer to Victorian America's craving for aesthetic enrichment and social status through acquisition of manufactured goods.

ANCESTRY OF THE REED ORGAN

Though the reed organ was essentially a creation of nineteenth-century Western culture, the history of the free-reed principle as applied in the reed organ and its organological kin is actually quite ancient. A glimpse into the free reed's arcane past will enlighten us about significant circumstances that led to the reed organ's rise to prominence in America.

One of the oldest and most ubiquitous manifestations of a free-reed instrument is found in the Jew's harp. Despite the difficulty of proving early chronologies of instruments, the ethnomusicologist Curt Sachs, using geographic criteria, places the Jew's harp's arrival during the Neolithic period.[40] Its eventual diffusion to Europe (where it may or may not have influenced reed organ experimentation) dates from the fourteenth century.[41]

The idea of incising a flap or lamella in a hollow reed, one end of which is fixed while the other is left free to vibrate, is different from the principle of a "beating" or "striking" reed which, as in a clarinet, vibrates against the aperture of a mouthpiece, or, in a pipe organ, against a shallot. Though it is probable that cutting flaps in hollow straws, reeds, or bamboo shoots dates from prehistoric times, the earliest written record of an instrument based on the free-reed principle comes from China.[42]

Mythical tales tell of the Chinese sheng (pronounced "sung"; see figure 4),[43] as it was and is still called, as early as 2852 B.C.; the first actual documentation, however, dates from 1100 B.C.[44] Various types of related mouth organs of assorted sizes, still played today, are found throughout Southeast Asia and the Far East.[45] Though such an instrument may seem remote from our subject, it was reported that Ebenezer Goodrich (1782–1841), an early and influential Boston organ builder, made a reed organ around 1809 for the painter Gilbert Stuart, the inspiration for which was a sheng that Stuart had imported as a novelty.[46] The free-reed principle used in the sheng was to inspire other reed organ builders as well as inventors of harmonicas, melodicas, accordions, and concertinas.[47]

During the first half of the nineteenth century, the reed organ idea caught the imaginations of numerous European instrument makers. Innovators in Germany and France made important refinements on the bellows and other mechanisms, and experiments with reeds increased the pitch range. In 1810 the Frenchman Gabriel-Joseph Grenié made an Orgue Expressif, an instrument that allowed players to control dynamics by adjusting the intensity of their treadling. After Grenié came increased experimentation: Voit's Aeolodikon (1820), Haeckl's Physharmonika (1821), Cavaillé-Coll's Poikilorgue (1830), and Dlugosz's Aeolopantalon (1830), to name but a few, attest to heightened activity in the refinement and promotion of free-reed keyboard instruments.[48]

In 1842 François Debain of Paris—given the most credit for successfully bringing the reed organ through its early stages of development in Europe—first used the word "harmonium," a term that was soon universally applied to the European style of reed organ.[49] Financial difficulties forced Debain to sell several of his patents to the French organ manufacturers Jacob Alexandre and Victor Mustel, who made several significant improvements that expanded the harmonium's expressive and tonal qualities.

Not to be outdone, the Englishmen Charles Wheatstone, inventor of the concertina, and John Green, author of the *Concise Instructions for Performance on the Royal Seraphine or Organ* (c. 1833), also worked on constructing improved styles of reed organs in Britain.[50] As a result of such efforts, by the late nineteenth century, the European reed organ was regarded as a serious instrument for serious

Figure 4.
Traditional Chinese
sheng

musicians, a development that prompted many noteworthy composers to write music especially for it.[51] Harmonium courses were even taught at the Paris Conservatoire, at one time by the esteemed César Franck.

Meanwhile, a combination of circumstances prevented the American reed organ from competing for concert status (see Appendix E). Because native composers did not share the artistic heritage common to the European cultural environment, they felt little motivation to develop sophisticated music for the relatively unsophisticated newcomer instrument.[52] Though countless compositions, arrangements, and transcriptions were eventually published for the American reed organ, they were written mostly for a popular audience, especially the home amateur musician.

AMERICAN REED ORGAN MANUFACTURE

Though a limited number of reed organs had found their way into a few American churches and homes early in the century, most records indicate that relatively few seraphines and melodeons were made before the 1840s. Up to 1835 most melodeons used in the United States were imported from France.[53] As with all the early instrument-making enterprises, production and mechanization techniques were virtually unknown, and instruments were made by relatively isolated craftsmen in small shops.

Ebenezer Goodrich is credited with being one of the first makers of reed organs in America. Doubtless there were others, including many immigrants, who experimented with free-reed designs.[54] Surviving United States patent records provide a listing of some of these early builders. Unfortunately, an 1836 Patent Office fire destroyed thousands of records, thus obscuring the exact sequence and rights of invention.

The pioneers, nevertheless, include Aaron M. Peaseley, of Boston, who in 1818 received a patent for the idea of substituting free reeds for pipes in organs. James A. Bazin, of Canton, Massachusetts, and Josiah Bartlett, of Concord, New Hampshire, are best remembered for their lap organs, also commonly called rocking melodeons or elbow melodeons.

Early lap organs, equally playable on a table, had button keys with a range of three or four octaves (figure 5). The keys were mounted directly on a spring-loaded double bellows, allowing the player to activate the instrument with his left forearm or the heel of his left hand while playing. This resulted in a rocking action reminiscent of a boat in a high sea. Lap organs mainly accompanied hymns, typically played slowly and in two parts: melody and bass. The reservoir was small, so playing too many simultaneous notes immediately depleted the wind supply. Other minor annoyances were that the button keys were close together and that the left-hand contortion required to operate the instrument made fast playing awkward.[55]

To alleviate some of this difficulty, special stands were constructed for the lap organ by adding a levered foot pedal with a string attached to the bellows, thus freeing the left hand for playing. But it was Abraham Prescott, another builder from Concord, New Hampshire, who received the first patent for an effective floor-model design.[56] Prescott increased the instrument's range, separated the keyboard from the bellows' motion by reconfiguring the bellows' position, and designed a floor stand with a stable foot pedal to work the bellows, thus allowing greater wind volume and further freeing the player's hands for

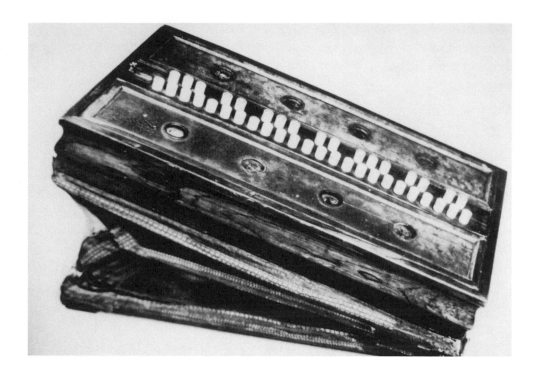

greater facility on the keyboard (figure 6).[57] The first instrument of this type was called a seraphine,[58] which with modifications became the melodeon.[59]

After the mid-1840s melodeon activity quickened, mostly in the Northeast (especially in Boston and Worcester, Massachusetts); in the Midwest, Chicago eventually became a leading center of production. The plant of George A. Prince of Buffalo, New York, acted as a training ground for two important manufacturers: Jeremiah Carhart and Emmons Hamlin. Carhart, a prolific inventor, was for a time credited with inventing the suction bellows system, a technology that became an American standard. Most builders knew that suction bellows had been devised and used by others who predated Carhart's claim, but because of the 1836 Patent Office fire, Carhart was technically the first officially on record and could thus license his innovation to other organ builders.[60]

Emmons Hamlin claimed the distinction of refining a reed voicing technique that rendered the tone "more round, smooth, [and] pipelike." He determined, possibly by accident, that a slight bending, curving, or twisting of reed ends markedly altered the speech and quality of timbre.[61] Other inventors working on the same notion during the time Hamlin made his claim achieved similar results; Riley Burdett also claimed to be the real inventor of the technique. It is probable that it was discovered by various men, working concurrently and without knowledge of each other's work. Coincidences of this kind are not uncommon in the history of invention.[62]

It was this same Hamlin who, in 1855, formed the famous partnership with

Figure 6.
American Seraphine,
c. 1845

Henry Mason in Boston. In 1861 the Mason & Hamlin Organ Company coined the term "cabinet organ" to distinguish their product from "inferior ones of other makers." Cabinet organs (the term eventually became generically applied) featured larger bellows enclosed in fashionable cases that extended to the floor, thus elevating them to the status of furniture. Mechanisms were enlarged and refined and swell effects were improved resulting in a louder and more varied sound. The company held production expenses in check by constructing cases of American woods.

In the second half of the century, small manufacturers in many trades became more concerned with production, standardization, and mechanical improvement, a combination of concerns that which came to be known abroad as the "American System." The concept of division of labor in the service of efficient, mechanized assembly-line production,[63] called the "continuous-process" or "flow" production system, would eventually be adopted for all manner of products, from chewing gum and fountain pens to automobiles and airplanes.[64] In the case of keyboards, factory-minded, production-oriented, business-savvy instrument builders recognized that the reed organ's assembly of keys, couplers, levers, stops, springs, and valves made it a perfect candidate for the production line.[65]

As the industrial pace quickened during the last half of the nineteenth century, manufacture of reed organs became an exceedingly lively industry in New England, contributing significantly to the general development of precision woodworking machinery. In the same way that the construction of Paxton's Crystal Palace Exhibition in London (1851) demanded new building techniques and improved machinery, routing reed cells and other parts of the organ called for highly specialized machinery that could efficiently produce complex shapes, a technology attractive to other industries.[66]

Steam power became a requisite for quantity-oriented factories. Though more expensive than water power, the wheels of production could be regulated and kept turning around the clock when necessary. This level of large-scale production paid off only if the firm could sell in bulk. Reed organ manufacturers began to get involved in all activities related to their instruments—not only the actual manufacturing, but also design development, product promotion and advertising, customer financing schemes, distribution through agents, printing music, publishing periodicals, and setting up educational support systems, including distribution of their own reed organ methods and "instructors." Later I will conduct a detailed investigation of these interrelated areas in regard to Jacob Estey's enterprise.

Moreover, organ manufacturers' efforts were in complete accord with a growing fascination of the American populace for machines. It was said that Mark Twain's attraction to the reed organ was due in part to an enthrallment with mechanical apparatus supposedly endowed with human capabilities.[67] The reed organ, with its hundreds of intricately connected parts, appeared as a triumph of human ingenuity and metaphysically symbolized man's prowess in his continuing quest for control over nature and fate. Ethereality aside, on a practical level, to possess one, particularly one of the latest models, was an emblem of triumphant modernity.[68]

By the last quarter of the century, enterprises such as the Mason & Hamlin Organ and Piano Company, Story & Clark Organ Company, Estey Organ Company, Aeolian Company, W. W. Kimball Company, and Beatty Organ Company—to name but a few of the 247 or so companies extant during this period—systematized their manufacturing processes and capitalized on the reed organ's popularity both here and abroad. During the final decades of the century, every major North American maker (including those in Canada) had European agents.

By this time the harmonium industry in Britain and Europe was under full siege by American manufacturers. In response, many continental harmonium makers hurriedly began production of American organs to compete with the imports. But European builders found it difficult to produce instruments at a lower price than the Americans, a situation made worse by the fact that American import duties hindered retaliation. And one continental correspondent gave another reason for European inefficacy: "the [European] harmonium makers are behind the age, and do not give their instrument such an attractive exterior as the Yankees provide."[69] After so many years of European affronts regarding American aesthetic immaturity, American designers must have enjoyed this observation.

For a time the American reed organ held sway over all other musical instruments of the day. Only the piano and guitar have ever enjoyed such ubiquity. Of the total number of reed organs manufactured in this country, well over a half million of them were made in Brattleboro, Vermont, by the Estey Organ Company. The progression and significance of this amazing feat is the primary subject of this book. Jacob Estey's life, in fact, must stand among the great rags-to-riches stories of nineteenth-century America; in many ways he typifies the heroes found in Horatio Alger's popular novels.[70] Self-made and self-improved, Estey rose to a position of prominence. The name of Estey remains, even after several generations, well known in New England and beyond, for his products not only were placed in countless homes, schools, social clubs, and churches across America, but also were shipped to Asia, Africa, Australia, South America, New Zealand, and seemingly everywhere else—as an Estey promotion declared, "from the far-off pines of Siberia to the golden shores of the Pacific." Though the company has been defunct for nearly half a century, thousands of Estey's organs are still actively collected, restored, maintained, and in use today.

Reed Organ Contexts

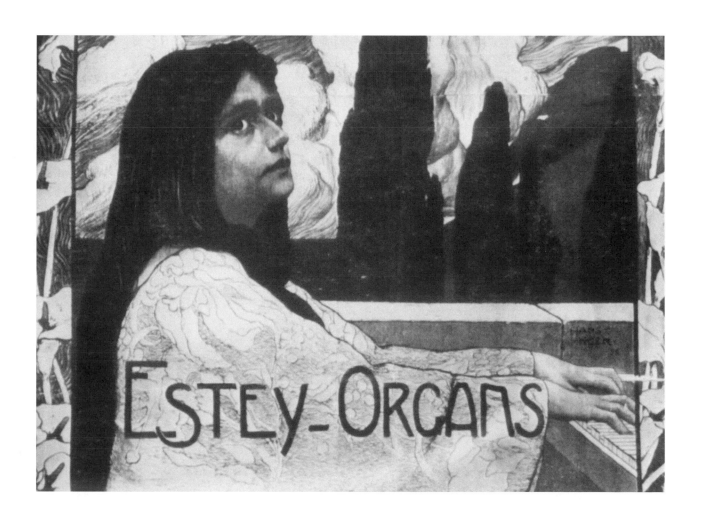

The Reed Organ and the Victorian Image

One of many outstanding features of the Victorian age was rapid expansion in the production, commodification, and proliferation of material goods; the more ostentatious, the better.[1] A glance through any pre-twentieth-century Estey company catalogue immediately impresses one with the extremely ornate, architecturally inspired styles of reed organ cabinetry. This was a clear reflection of a general trend in the decorative arts, from about 1840 to 1900, both in America and abroad. Many stylistic influences converged during this time, first one taking the lead, then another; in retrospect it is clear that the dominant stylistic mode after Greek Revival was Gothic Revival. Later, a whole conglomeration of styles came under the "Victorian" rubric.[2] It is said that Victoriana has no true distinguishing feature to call its own; yet few people have difficulty identifying Victorian styles. The pieces are so distinctive that they could not possibly be mistaken for anything else.[3]

Domestically speaking, the period was generally characterized by what might now be considered a breakdown in formal furniture arrangement: walls, windows, and floors were covered with figured paper, heavy drapery, and patterned, imitation oriental carpets. Other decor constituted a generous use of arches, vaults, clustered columns, mirrors, jigsaw ornament, and other architectural embellishment. As one authority observed, it was "the kind of opulence that would appeal to an ambitious and at the same time socially insecure clientele," namely, middle-class Americans on the ascent.[4] "Novelty was demanded, but connoisseurship was lacking. Ideas could be borrowed more rapidly than conceived, and logic and a native expression seemed unnecessary. England was the most obvious source of inspiration, although the eternal leadership of France could not be ignored. Designers also searched fields that were more distant in both time and place. The Victorian period witnessed a rapid succession of confused style revivals, all of which overlapped, were nonreflective of their times, and were impurely and inconsistently applied."[5]

To the modern eye, photographs of Victorian homes, rooms, and parlors suggest general confusion. In the most photographed of all rooms, the parlor, one generally finds an overly generous use of patterned surfaces along with marble-topped tables, bookcases, and overstuffed furniture including the ubiquitous chaise longue, Turkish divan, or *fauteuil*-style chair.[6] Sofas and chairs were "fringed, tufted, buttoned and ruched in a manner that can only be described as hysterical."[7] Bric-a-brac filled every whatnot, shelf, table, and other horizontal surface in the room; special cabinetry was created to harbor the surfeit of artwork, figurines, plants in vases, colored plates and cups, dried flowers, and heirlooms; walls were smothered with hanging baskets and pictorial arrangements of framed family photographs and favorite lithographic prints; and prominently placed wax crosses, biblical scenes rendered in needlepoint, pictures of saints, and the omnipresent family Bible acted to reinforce the ideology and moral piety of those who dwelt within.

American craftsmen, architects, and manufacturers, taking advantage of the unprecedented population and building boom beginning around 1840, put production into high gear. Revived Rococo and Gothic styles, in spite of (or because of) the extra expense involved, became a favorite style of the middle and upper classes in interior and exterior house design. Furniture designers and manufacturers used motifs from French sources as well as Italian, Greek, Egyptian, and neo-Gothic inspirations which remained fashionable through the Civil War period and strongly influenced Victorian domestic architecture and the decorative arts to the end of the century.[8] Not surprisingly, this stylistic trend also became increasingly apparent in reed organ cabinetry as middle-class aspirants hoped to display an increasingly higher level of aesthetic pretense through ownership of "positional," less utilitarian items. In response to the demand, "a few manufacturers concentrated their efforts on out-and-out cultural products such as pianos, melodeons, and seraphines for music in the home."[9]

Anyone who may have stumbled onto a Victorian reed organ in an antique shop knows that it is a formidable piece of furniture, especially those surmounted by a "high top." Unlike the piano, whose case has a largely protective and supportive function and retains the shape of the inner workings, the reed organ became much more of a display piece, its marginally-functional ornamentation extending far beyond the necessary minimum case size required by the mechanism.[10] Actually, the reed organ's vertical construction required much less floor space than a grand piano or even the more conventional square piano and, in this respect, was more practical for middle and working-class people who required economy of space, especially since small parlors were already hard put to accommodate the dense furnishing usual to that room. In addition to being a display piece itself, organ cabinetry usually doubled as a whatnot for the display of meaningful items.

The era's progressive-thinking, artistically-appreciative, secularly-minded middle and upper-class public[11] increasingly demanded more genteel material accoutrements and upscale home surroundings, each level of society imitating the one above.[12] The trouble, as argued by Victorian specialists, was that "the middle classes are generally not creative. They are ambitious and imitative, and for these reasons so many Victorian designs have a strong feeling of 'aping their betters.' Acquisition of possessions, concern with outward display, insistence on solid quality, are all middle-class characteristics, while the confusion between elaboration and worth, the insistence that cheap materials should imitate costly ones, the preference for reinterpreted, old-established forms rather than new ones, all express the dilemmas of a changing social structure, the uncertain participants of which require reassurance."[13]

Victorians, less satisfied with earlier utilitarian aesthetics,[14] valued items which, because they were over-embellished and glamorized beyond necessity, provided expansive associations and maximum emotional response.[15] In essence, American consumers began to demand that the useful also be attractive and fashionable.[16] As our story unfolds, we shall see that Jacob Estey, among the elite of music manufacturers of the nineteenth century, understood well this basic principle of American consumerism.

VICTORIAN DESIGN AND MASS PRODUCTION

As the transformation of machine technology continued throughout the second half of the nineteenth century, the dichotomy between fine art and industrial design, or form against function, became even more pronounced.[17] Designers and manufacturers responded more readily to popular demand for ostentation and display even in the most practical objects, often going to great expense to decorate strictly utility items with commonly-recognized symbols and motifs.

The demand for things that appeared expensive, but in fact were not, in turn fueled the development of technologies of reproduction. If a member of the emerging middle class "could not afford the unique treasures of the wealthy, he welcomed whatever semblance of the finer things of life that manufacturers could provide."[18] Bronze statuary, for example, could be cheaply reproduced in lead and cast iron, hand-wrought silver imitated in pressed tin and other cheap metals, hand-painted, marbleized patterns replicated on plaster of Paris, china simulated in papier-mâché, exotic wood grains painted on domestic species, and original paintings duplicated as chromolithographs.

And so styles continued to be borrowed and hybridized rather than created anew. Many American manufacturers sought solutions by sending designers to study the customs and protocols of Europe. Some manufacturers went so far as copying the name of the original designer. The Mason & Hamlin company sold an "Eastlake" style reed organ, for instance, after British tastemaker and designer, Charles Eastlake, who emphatically disavowed any connection whatsoever with American house and furniture builders who cloned his fashionable semi-Gothic designs.

Europeans not only disapproved of the manner in which Americans borrowed designs, but also of the way goods were mass-produced for low prices and a short life span. Could a nation that held such attitudes be capable of true art? It seemed that Americans were so intoxicated with new mechanized production devices and productivity quotas that they willingly accepted poor interpretations of what the experienced hand had done so successfully before.

It soon became obvious to manufacturers that it was the "ornamental arts," not the fine arts, which had become an indispensable ingredient in American homes.[19] Style books containing thousands of plans and patterns offering ready-made embellishment were circulated from coast to coast.[20] New machines were invented to facilitate the rapid production of exterior and interior adornment: mechanized circular saws, jig saws, bandsaws, and carving machines let customers indulge fully in ornate woodwork. The versatility and adaptability of wood as an architectural medium was thoroughly exploited; the millwright explored the absolute limits of his fancy. Today, Victorian homes in America, especially those of the rich and famous, have become an important symbol for the study of this nation's past.[21] Victorian domestic architecture will continue to attract and intrigue antiquarians, preservationists, antique collectors, history buffs, and local gentry for some time to come.[22]

Even strictly utilitarian tools and machines were not immune to the Victorian penchant for decoration as manufacturers often decorated the machinery itself with embellishment usually garnered from classical ornamentation and from raids into the animal and vegetable kingdoms.[23] Figures of vines, shrubbery, and lily-work often graced industrial machinery; stylized wheat sheaves, pineapples, and acanthus leaves dripped from huge hydraulic presses;[24] oil paintings, gilt and brass trimmings, and cast-iron figures decorated unlikely objects like railroad locomotives.[25] Perhaps this was not only an attempt to "beautify" mechanical devices, but also an unconscious desire to "tame" and "domesticate" them, which might also explain the additional application of zoomorphic motifs on machinery. Some scholars see this application of nature's imagery to mechanical devices as an attempt to mask a basic conflict between the nineteenth-century Romantic adulation of nature and the machine's "intrusion" into the landscape. Nature, after all, could not simultaneously be revered by man and dominated by the machine which man had erected.[26] Those not able to contend with the machine on its own terms could at least make it less of a threat by rendering a design supposedly harmonious to nature.[27]

Moreover, as engineering machinery became more complex and mechanisms more intricate, working parts were increasingly covered with decorated protective casing and ornate enclosure. This removed from view (and easy accessibility) the portion of the object one needed to inspect in order to assess its quality. Customers were thus prone to judge a machine more on outward appearance than inner attributes. Its "look" became at least as important as its actual function, which perhaps explains why so many of the Victorian era's machines look so unlike what they really were. Similar trends were to impact furniture and reed organ design.

Early types of reed organ cases—lap organs and folding melodeons used by circuit preachers, dance masters, music teachers, and singing societies—were relatively unadorned and, by necessity, sturdy and practical. Subsequently, melodeons with more substantial casework took on the appearance of a "square" style of pianoforte (figure 7). Since these were destined for rural and small-town homesteads and non-affluent churches, makers were initially not concerned with excessive fanciful adornment; though case designs are appealing, utility was still more important than cosmetic detail. Later, beginning in the 1870s, manufacturers began to produce parlor organs, as well as organs for churches, that epitomized "gingerbread" Victorian ornamentation. Now, the casing became as important, if not more important, than the inner mechanism (Appendix: Summary of Estey Reed Organ Casework and Tonal Design). Let us take a look at how reed organ design, especially in its later manifestations, factored as an important ingredient in Victorian social milieu.

As formulated by Thorstein Veblen in his classic book *The Theory of the Leisure Class* (1899), middle-class consumers who could not afford genuine affluent pretense could at least emulate upper-class behavior through "conspicuous consumption,"[28] by buying a piece of merchandise that was, if not better, at least somewhat larger, more elaborate, and more expensive than the average.[29] Early on, aspiring middle-class households gained social status by owning progressive, "upper-class" devices such as sewing machines, washing machines, and musical machines, including reed organs. The irony lies in the fact that upper-class households owned neither sewing machines nor reed organs; they hired others to do their sewing and washing and generally played grand pianos and pipe organs (later equipped with self-playing devices).

Because of the Gothic nature of late Victorian cabinetry, some reed organ styles seem in many ways more natural and appropriate in religious settings than in the parlor. And indeed, the more ornate instruments certainly found their most legitimate application as religious decor within the sanctuaries of American churches. This is attested, for example, by Estey catalogues advertising Church, Chancel, Chapel, and Cathedral organ models (figure 8). Regardless of the organ's destination, religious symbolism was an important element in manufacturers' advertising. "Victorian life was riddled with contradiction.

Figure 7.
Perfect Melodeon,
1867 Estey catalogue

The intense materialism and fervent revivalism of the [nineteenth] century, presumably antithetical, were both accommodated in the parlor organ."[30] In spite of the dichotomy between sacred and secular elements, much of what was natural to the church continued to find its way into the home. Some of the larger home-oriented organs, especially those with high tops or nonfunctional "dummy" facade pipe tops, exemplified by Estey's Parlor, Drawing Room, Grand Salon, and Boudoir organs, present a striking example of this crossover (figure 9).

Whether for church or home, organ manufacturers did their best to convince potential owners that virtue and prestige increased with the larger and more ornate instruments. As with the false facades on buildings of the day, elevation made for a bigger and more impressive look. Records indicate that in most instances the client needed little convincing. Loesser reports that a Kimball salesman[31] marketing reed organs in the West in 1880 said, "Three fourths of the buyers want a top that towers high above all the bedsteads in the country, and scarcely ever question the inside."[32] What was the public in search of—the "pleasantly appropriate ecclesiastical suggestion" of the high-backed reed organ or the secular stature provided by owning such a monumental structure? Probably

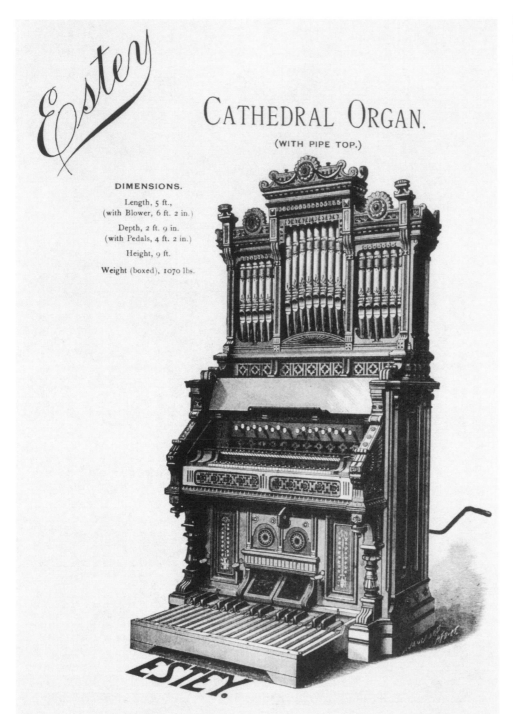

CATHEDRAL ORGAN.

(WITH PIPE TOP.)

DIMENSIONS.

Length, 5 ft.,
(with Blower, 6 ft. 2 in.)

Depth, 2 ft. 9 in.
(with Pedals, 4 ft. 2 in.)

Height, 9 ft.

Weight (boxed), 1070 lbs.

Figure 8.
Cathedral Organ with
pipe top, 1890 Estey
catalogue

Figure 9.
Boudoir Organ with
pipe top, 1890 Estey
catalogue

Boudoir Organ.—Pipe Organ Top.

LENGTH, 4 ft. 6 in.; DEPTH, 2 ft. 1 in.; HEIGHT, 7 ft. 7 in.

both. In fact, after the mid-1880s, nearly all parlor styles came with a high top, adorned with shelves, mirrors, a gallery, and fancy woodwork. In addition, built-in clocks, lamp holders, brackets for flowers and lamps, shelves and racks for music storage, and framing for sentimental pictures became part of the elaborate, ornamental high-top accommodation of bric-a-brac (figure 10).

Critics of the day complained, "The highest type of a thing beautiful is to have it at the same time useful. Can anyone imagine how such a monstrosity as

Figure 10.
Style A organ with
mirrored high top,
mid-1890s

a high top on a reed organ ever became fashionable? Is it a thing of beauty or can there be any excuse for its existence? We are glad to see a tendency of late to ignore such fungous growths. Organ manufacturers are probably like other manufacturers—they aim to produce what the people want, and as long as the country demands such things they will continue to put high tops on their organs, and among a certain class of dealers the organ that has [by] half an inch the highest top is the most valuable, without regard to tone or any other practical point. We believe that if more attention be paid to the case of the organ itself, high canopy tops would ere long be things of the past."[33] Regardless, high tops were obviously prized, as evidenced by their popularity. The rule of current fashion was simple: the taller and more elaborate, the better. "Such conspicuous instruments figure prominently as furniture, challenging designers of the stature of Duncan Phyfe to cloak their unwieldy innards in fashionable cases."[34] Manufacturers' designers lavished a great deal of consideration and effort on appearance; many, like Estey, even patented their best "gingerbread" designs.

Decoration of furniture, like that of machines and domestic architecture, began to far exceed practical necessity. Tables, armchairs, wardrobes, bookcases, and buffets sported spindles, wooden grilles, and dwarf columns in profusion; rosewood, walnut, oak, and mahogany were the cachet of respectability; carved fruit, flowers, foliage, animal heads, and replicas of medals and awards adorned every surface. And as in other arenas of changing fashion, organ designers also turned to natural shapes as inspiration for case decoration. Vines, leaves, buds, and blossoms filled borders and spaces alike, yet another example that representations of nature apparently helped ease the angst of an increasingly mechanized society.

Though these replications may have a delicate hand-carved appearance, most were machine-made with some small decorative medallions not even made of wood. From about 1860 through the 1890s, patterns of fragile-looking fretwork were cut with mechanized jigsaws and bandsaws, new tools that made much Victorian-style woodwork feasible. Beaded, fluted, and plain columns, mass produced on lathes, were mixed and matched in various combinations. Corinthian, Egyptian, and other more idiosyncratic column designs buttressed organ keyboards and high tops. In lieu of columns, machine-made newels stretched toward pendular swags to fill architectural spaces and voids. Eventually, after 1895, cases evolved to simpler designs with fewer rounded contours and less hand work (figure 11); instead of carving, machines now pressed patterns into damp wood under hundreds of pounds of hydraulic pressure.[35] Throughout this industrial design revolution, changing styles in organ cases were driven by prevalent tastes in furniture design and progress in manufacturing technology.

Advertisements of the day reveal that manufacturers of the famous "Murphy bed" occasionally hid the fold-up bunks in cabinetry made to resemble a reed

Figure 11.
Organ case design "17,"
1903 Estey catalogue

organ or sideboard.[36] Beds not only took up a great deal of space but, given its suggestive social implications to a developing middle-class mentality, were one of the less publicly talked about items of furniture. In extreme cases, a hideaway bed, storage cabinets, chest of drawers, and piano (strings, keyboard mechanisms, and all) might share space within the same enclosure.[37] Actually, it was not uncommon during this era for organs or pianos to be housed in the same cabinetry with sewing machines, writing tables, desks, and bookcases, a reminder of the American designer's concern with efficient functionality.[38] Some were unimpressed: "While it might be acceptable to disguise [a bed] when raised end-on against the wall as an elaborate wardrobe-cupboard, to make it look like an upright piano seems to our present-day thinking to be venturing into the realms of idiotic fantasy."[39]

ADVERTISING AND REED ORGAN IMAGERY

New technologies and ensuing psychologies were almost immediately exploited by advertising concerns: it became increasingly common for manufacturers to try the soft sell or hard sell to outsell competitors by making extraordinary claims for their products, offering phony enticements, and distributing irresistibly attractive advertising. Though artisans and merchants throughout history have always tried to make their goods as alluring as possible, it was during this period that advertising became a profession unto itself and a necessary part of the manufacturing and merchandising game.[40] Companies that did not do their own advertising hired agencies that, through publicity, campaign planning, and employment of the latest promotional techniques, promised that they could transform potential customers into devoted consumers.[41] The new dictum was "Make America Want."

To compete for ever-expanding markets, manufacturers launched large-scale advertising campaigns, offering prospective consumers various services that included mail-order delivery and payment by installment. New, attractive forms of promotion and publicity promised manufactured luxury, status, and wish fulfillment. "Publicity is never a celebration of a pleasure-in-itself. Publicity is always about the future buyer. It offers him an image of himself as he might be. . . . Publicity is about social relations, not objects. Its promise is not of pleasure but of happiness: happiness as judged by the outside by others."[42] Moreover, "increased sex appeal, a harmonious family life, a successful business career—these are the types of rewards projected by advertisers for those who would take advantage of their products."[43] Daniel Pope, in his seminal work *The Making of Modern Advertising*, makes the interesting observation that a majority of early advertising agents were preacher's sons, suggesting that whether marketing Jesus or Jell-O®, selling required religious fervor.[44]

In earlier days it was routine for customers to examine goods and pass judgment on site based on the object's quality and on its merit as a useful item. If it had to be bought sight unseen, one could also rely on the experience or advice of a friend or neighbor to give an honest appraisal of a product's worth. With intensifying urbanization and the advent of widespread popular printed media, this state of affairs underwent a radical transformation. The new strategy of news and advertising media—namely, mass-circulation magazines and newspapers —was not only to inform but to influence. Over time, space allocated to advertising went from small-print announcements of local goods to large-format spreads with attractive pictures and graphics proclaiming what consumers should buy before it was too late.

By the turn of the century, big business and its hired advertising agencies had developed scientific methods of marketing research: the compilation of data through personal interviews and sales statistics; market testing and analysis; demographic analysis of population densities, occupational peculiarities, income profiles, literacy counts, and regionalized consumer psychology; and keeping tabs on the competition. Emphasis was on market development, market segmentation, and targeted promotion.[45] Unfortunately, many manufacturers felt little social or moral responsibility for their promotional fabrications so long as they met their sales quotas; extravagant claims were made, ploys concocted, and superficialities touted.[46] To put it mildly, "unrestrained by government controls on false advertising, promoters sometimes used a curious mixture of fact and fiction."[47] Mention was made earlier of Daniel Beatty's unorthodox advertising practices. His extortionate claims and customer baiting were frowned on within the industry.[48] Prominent trade magazines celebrated his eventual demise with headlines such as "The End of Beatty . . . why not close him up and have done with it," and "Beatty's Bubble Bursts . . . a good day for legitimate trade."[49]

As we read early advertisements, the florid, effusive, quasi-poetic style of nineteenth-century writing, natural to the era, seems, from today's perspective, rather pretentious and overblown. It is interesting to note, however, that though writing styles have changed, expressions like "progressive," "unequaled," "superior," "highest grade," "the biggest," "the best," "new," "improved," and "perfect," ubiquitous in early ads, are still with us. Such words are persistently applied across the board, from breakfast cereals and exercise machines to automobiles and vacation destinations. And likewise, as overseas transport became more and more feasible, advertising horizons expanded as well: language such as "the oldest in the world," "the largest in the world," and "the best in the world" came into vogue.

Estey advertising was no exception (see figure 12). As with other advertising efforts of the day, most of the firm's publicity was done through catalogues, trade cards, posters, and ads in newspapers and journals. The company relentlessly claimed to "be the largest" and "lead the world" with its endless array of "valuable improvements" and ever-lengthening roster of patents. Following the suc-

Figure 12.
"Largest Organ Reed
Pipe in the World,"
c. 1915

cess of his early reed organ model, the Perfect Melodeon, the public was constantly assured that nothing less than "perfection" was the general Estey standard. In newspaper advertisements of this period, "The Most Perfect Reed Organ In the World" became a stock Estey headline.[50] Adding to this puffery, Estey accused other companies of winning customers by making outrageous assertions, claiming for himself the "admiration and confidence of the people" based on merit alone. Though Estey products were usually of a consistently high quality, his advertising was, in many respects, just as exploitive as any in the industry.

As for the soft sell, a more lighthearted ad in an 1890 issue of *Youth's Companion* contains a piece of corny but cleverly arranged poetry:

An *Estey*-Mate

*E*ven the savage is by music charmed,
*S*o says an ancient and romantic fable;
*T*he organ's strains repeatedly have calmed[51]
*E*nraged beasts by fright or pain alarmed;
*Y*ou see these strains were always Estey-mable.

*O*f all the organs made by mortal hands,
*R*ichest in tone the "Estey" takes its station;
*G*reat is its name and fame throughout all lands,
*A*nd not one instrument before it stands,
*N*or equals it in public Estey-mation.

A major goal for promotional departments and agencies was to enhance brand name and trademark recognition.[52] As manufacturers took control of their own marketing methods and distribution networks, they soon realized that the "name on the box" was a key factor in influencing habits of shoppers. Whether soap, soft drink, soup, or cigarettes, studies confirm that consumers generally prefer one product above any other as they recognize and become comfortable with the brand name that is most successfully promoted. A cycle of consumership is consequently set in motion: as customers request one particular brand over others, the product's desirability increases in the eyes of store owners and retailers, who then order more of that particular item from the manufacturer or wholesaler, thus making the advertising gambit pay off. A label, name, or trademark can itself become a status symbol; to own a product with a particular manufacturer's name prominently featured can give its owner social credibility. "Branding is a useful metaphor about a whole range of social relations."[53] And consumers will pay much more just to flaunt a special brand name. Advertising is designed to make the buying of particular products habitual through identification of the products with ideas, feelings, and status.[54] Whether the product is a Steinway piano, a Rolls Royce automobile, Nike sports gear, or a McDonald's hamburger, the name counts.[55]

Viewed in this way, sociocultural interpretations of a manufacturer's promotional materials reveal much information concerning fashion, cultural mores, class orientations, gender roles, and sacred and secular associations. Students of material culture must be reminded, however, that "there may be considerable difference between the public meanings of objects as evident in advertising imagery and the personal or private meanings that these objects had for their owners and users."[56] Collections of photographs offer a more accurate and realistic view of nineteenth-century culture than do promotional sales pitches; nevertheless, advertisements allow an opportunity to look at certain aspects of nineteenth-century aspiration and ethics.[57]

The growth of newspapers and periodicals throughout the nineteenth century was phenomenal and because these media's revenues depended largely on advertising, the news itself often seemed secondary to product promotion. Large-format lithographs, such as one of Estey's bustling factory, a favorite depiction, were often encountered in urban newspapers. *Frank Leslie's Illustrated Newspaper*,[58] for example, one of the earliest and most successful of the genre, printed an eight-by-twelve-inch ground view of the Estey factory that exaggerates the scale and expanse of the front rank of factory buildings (figure 13). The artistic perspective not only emphasizes the factory's size but features tremendous activity in the street: horse-drawn carriages and lumber wagons, parasoled strollers, cavorting children, and romping dogs. The only object higher than the American flag fluttering high above the factory shops is the manufactory's ever-smoking chimney, a manifestation of the constant industry within.[59] The idyllic forest set-

Figure 13.
Estey Birge St. manu-
factory, *Frank Leslie's
Illustrated Newspaper,*
December 27, 1873

ting assures us that industry and nature can coexist. On a subsequent page often appeared a smaller, standard Estey advertisement featuring a woodcut of a Cottage Organ, promised to be supremely suited for church or parlor use, and better "than any other Organ ever offered to the public."[60]

The great majority of Estey ads also included declarations regarding the innovative character of the company. Particular pride was taken in touting "The Beautiful Vox Humana and Wonderful Vox Jubilante . . . improvements peculiar to and original with these organs." One skeptical observer commented that "Vox Jubilante" and other stop descriptions were "Yankee Latin," a misjoining of Latin, French, and Italian—nevertheless acceptable, "because people who buy them don't know anything about it."[61] In fact, organ stops have for centuries been stamped with a uniquely curious hodgepodge of names with obscure linguistic origins. Each company had its originals and favorites, and a few of Estey's stop names (including the Vox Humana and Vox Jubilante) were used nowhere else.

Estey and other successful reed organ manufacturers formed potent marketing packages by setting up convincing metaphors in which particular terms were given symbolic equivalence through their semiotic linkage.[62] In other words, they combined the reed organ with various archetypal images reflective of American ideology. Cues gleaned from Estey's publicity reveal several favorite advertising portrayals, some of which have become iconographic for the period under investigation. These include the factory, the reed organ itself, the reed organ within a well-appointed parlor (usually with young ladies at or around the organ's keyboard), and church-related representations.

On one end of the advertising continuum, the images are provocative, whimsical, outlandish, sometimes zany, and often humorous; the more serious types generally revolve around ethnic or nationalistic subjects and sentimental or romantic themes. Later we will see that popular song falls into similar categories. Analysis of these images will help delineate various trends and attitudes in late-nineteenth-century culture and give us a greater appreciation of the reed organ's significant role within Victorian society.

Trade card advertisements appeared in many sizes, but most measured five to six inches by three to four inches; graphics were arranged both vertically and horizontally. Trade cards came into vogue in the 1870s as a result of technical advances in printing, especially the introduction of color. The number of printing enterprises, like that of newspapers, increased dramatically to meet the growing demand of advertisers. Posters, handbills, broadsides, circulars, post cards, business cards, and give-away calendars were designed and distributed by every trade imaginable—from sarsaparillas to stove blacking, rat poisons to pianos—even in series. The pictorial content, especially that found on posters and trade cards, often portrayed a glimpse of life in a ideal world. From there, one is left to create one's own story. Stereotypical images of lovely children, virtuous women, successful men, and charming anthropomorphized animals were couched symbolically within model social, domestic, and industrial contexts. Often an element in merchandisers' giveaway schemes, advertising materials were fun, easy to collect, and provided family entertainment: "What a bright relief it must have been to receive in the mail a set of six cards from the Armour Meat Company—a little color in a long, deep winter."[63]

The use of trade cards as an advertising medium dropped off at the turn of the century and by 1905 had almost ceased. The mass circulation of magazines and other developing media probably eclipsed interest in the trade card as an important advertising medium. Thanks to the invention of steam-powered printing presses and improved methods of lithography and photoengraving, new and spectacular styles of advertising and journalism began to catch on in the 1880s and 1890s, most of which took advantage of the halftone method of mechanically reproducing photographs in newspapers, periodicals, and books. As noted earlier, the amount of newspaper space given over to advertising expanded phenomenally during this period, with much of the space taken up by photographs, a widespread trend by the turn of the century.[64] With greatly increased circulation, the new media no doubt made the trade card seem outmoded.

Of the Estey poster and trade card advertisements I will analyze, the Estey "Parlor Musicale" trade card best exemplifies how Victorian manufacturers and advertising agencies manipulated certain images to evoke sensual and emotional reactions in prospective users.[65]

The advertisement shown in figure 14 declares that Estey organs are elegant and used by fashionable people. The instrument used in this picture is the Estey Grand Salon Organ, Style 900, obviously a favorite design, since we see it used in numerous other promotional ads.[66] Here the reed organ is portrayed as a nexus of social activity — a catalyst for the meeting of upwardly mobile young people. The luxuriant parlor interior represents wealth and affluence: the drapery, layered carpeting, stenciled and richly papered walls, classical bust, ceramics, and chromolithograph of Saint Cecilia (the patron saint of music) as keyboardist muse lend dignity to this stereotypical Victorian gathering. Participants are formally attired — notwithstanding the fact that it is still daytime — contributing a solemn, punctilious atmosphere to the occasion. The older woman seated in the chair on the left, presumably the chaperone, and the two children enjoying the view of the factory give the scene a familial aspect, suggesting that playing the reed organ was an opportunity for the gathering of the generations. The ratio of four women to one man illustrates the organ's sexually stereotyped orientation. The exaggerated anatomy of the standing woman reflects a public opinion that "firmly maintained that no female form could be regarded as divine without a plentiful supply of curves."[67] The chaperone, comfortably reclining in an upholstered gentrified chair and dressed in relatively demure attire in contrast to the bright dresses of the young ladies, holds her disengaged fan as if transfixed by the organ's tones.[68]

The atmosphere is formal but friendly; the stiffness of compulsory etiquette does not seem to lessen the spectators' enjoyment. Their enraptured, faraway looks tell of the power of music to transform experience — music selected, naturally, from Estey's *Organ Method*. No doubt the music prompts the little boy to put his arm tenderly around his sister's shoulder. Beethoven watches approvingly over the proceedings from within the organ's high canopy; the player and singer are positioned as if in private audience with the romantic master. Predictably, Estey slipped his own portrait in amongst the opulent furnishings and worked an idealized image of his organ factory into the window view.[69] A standard Victorian lithographic technique was to include someone pointing at

Figure 14.
Estey "Parlor Musicale"
trade card, c. 1885

something, and here the young girl directs the viewer's attention to the active Estey industrial complex.

Of all the icons representative of America during the last half of the nineteenth century, depictions of the expansive, ever-industrious factory stand as the most suitably capitalistic. Vast brick palaces with towering facades and militaristic exteriors stood for a complex of ideas by which America eventually gained immense global industrial power. With a few noteworthy exceptions, Victorian factories, often brutally utilitarian, usually boasted at least some external ornamentation.[70]

The industrial factory image (and other large edifices) stood for stability and reliability and was meant to inspire consumer confidence.[71] Factories became a shrine for middle-class Americans, who made the pursuit of luxury into a kind of secular religion.[72] Lithographs of monumental factory complexes were common in industrial advertising during the late 1800s and were usually depicted from a bird's-eye view (lest we see the miserable conditions within where the mill hands toiled). Naturally, the spectacular aerial view was no doubt more intriguing in the days before air travel. The structures' immense and imposing exteriors, dwarfing nearby pedestrians and vehicles, represented urbanity, prosperity, and American technological mastery. Unlike photographs of the day, graphic depiction of factories could be editorially adjusted in whatever way the owner felt necessary to show how his factory might appear in a more perfect world. Artists who drew them made free use of angular perspective techniques to create an effect of massiveness.[73]

Lithographers concocted clever ways to fit the factory image into promotional materials, and as we have just seen, a common device was to show the factory incidentally, most often from the window of an elegant parlor. In reality, it is unlikely that a mansion and a manufactory would have been in the same neighborhood, but the visual association underscored the ideological relation between the two. In other examples, Estey invariably places a framed picture of his factory (or himself as in the previous illustration) on a wall close to an Estey organ. In terms of advertising theory, the marriage of keyboard instruments and factory, both symbols of modernity and hard-earned social and economic success, was a publicity union made in heaven.[74]

As time went on, poster styles and factory buildings changed but the advertising intent remained the same. For instance, in figure 15, the obvious message is that the Estey Organ Company is a large, well-established organization. Here too the visual information of this often-used Estey "trademark" image emphasizes the unusual arrangement and expanse of the factory compound. Estey's front guard of matching buildings stands fortresslike—banners waving in the breeze—high on the Birge Street plateau. The street activity, perpetually smoking chimney, huge stockpile of lumber, and workers' village in the background attest to a thriving venture. We might wonder why, given the era's penchant for baroque ornament, Estey's stately but unimaginatively arranged buildings appear so severely regimental. In the final analysis, the production process was not concerned so much with elegance as efficiency. The explicit goals were to make a quality product quickly, get it to the marketplace, and entice the consumer to buy it.

In this example, the factory portrayal is a relatively close representation of fact, except that, as in most of Estey's factory lithographs, the width of Birge Street is wildly exaggerated. Though the factory wagons are understandable, one wonders why so many people are using this street for recreational strolls— a street that is in actuality rather short, narrow, especially muddy during spring thaw, and at least a half mile from the center of town. The intention, of course, was to show the plant as the nerve center of Brattleboro's social and industrial life. The small inserts of the three distinguished manufacturers and of a young woman moving into position for a session on her Estey reed organ help humanize and personalize the indifferent objectivity of the factory. The composite

images are contrived to project a sense of cosmopolitan progress, prosperity, and trustworthiness.

The advertisements reproduced as figures 16–21 indicate that the Estey Company supported community musical activity, especially for children. Estey, like other promoters, used a number of images of children in his trade cards (figure 16). Nationally, the trend of exploiting tykes, tots, and babies in advertising was at this time approaching cult proportions.[75] Advertising agents realized early that the enchanting innocence of young boys and girls is hard to resist; the symbolic import of youth still makes this a favorite theme in today's advertising. Ideally, children inhabit a word that is pristine, chaste, and unfettered by mundane concerns. Children symbolize a new beginning, another genesis of God's Eden peopled by little Adams and Eves before they shared the fruit of knowledge.[76]

Besides representing innocence, children symbolize continuity through time —a promise that the heritage will be carried to the future. In the two Estey trade card examples shown in figures 17 and 18, the fact that all the characters are

Figure 15.

Poster depiction of

Estey factory, c. 1880

"THE ESTEY" ORCHESTRA CLUB.

COPYRIGHTED 1897 BY TRAUTMANN BAILEY & ...

Figure 16.
"The Estey Orchestra
Club" trade card, c. 1897

female assumes that they will grow to womanhood having mastered the appropriate musical and social skills to fulfill their genteel female roles and eventual family obligation as the bearers of domestic culture.[77]

It is interesting to note that the majority of children on these trade cards play harps, horns, banjos, drums, and generic viols—almost everything but reed organs. The infrequent examples of young children playing organs is most likely due to the fact that children have difficulty reaching the keyboard and pedals at the same time, as is clearly seen in figure 16. In real life, children sat in their mother's lap or that of a female relative who pumped the pedals while showing them the notes.

Another form of trade card was the "fold-back, stand-up" figure. Estey offered, upon receipt of two 2-cent stamps, to deliver to the sender a set of five of these die-cut paper dolls. The implied symbolism of these appealing, orphic figures, though sometimes curious, is nonetheless instructive. Some more obvious examples of this genre relied on patriotic themes to attract customers (figure 19). There is no mistake that the cherubic female child represented here —wrapped in the American flag, eagle emblazoned across her breast, portraits of Washington and Lincoln cradled in each arm—symbolizes American liberty

THE ESTEY OVERTURE

PROSPECTIVE PURCHASERS OF ESTEY PIANOS.

and freedom, national attributes that every good industrialist supported. This card was likely printed for a special occasion.

Other examples of Estey's stand-up figures include nursery characters such as Little Boy Blue (figure 20), Tommy Tucker, Little Jack Horner, Little Bo-Peep, and Little Miss Muffet.[78] One rather unusual figure is of an Asian child swathed in the Japanese flag and holding a rifle in one hand and a samurai sword in the other (figure 21).[79] Each image features a stanza of third-rate doggerel on the back. Little Boy Blue's ditty proclaims:

Little Boy Blue come blow your horn,
'Til the air to tatters is trumpet-torn;
Telling the people the virtues grand
Of the Estey—sweetest in all the land!
Gently blow in a minor key,
Piping its wonderful melody—
Oh! Little Boy Blue its praises blow
And you only tell what the people know.

Figure 17.
"Estey Overture" trade card, c. 1895

Figure 18.
"Prospective Purchasers of Estey Pianos" trade card, c. 1895

Other trade cards depended on humorous or "exotic" imagery to catch customers' fancy. In the former category is a card depicting a dapper, well-dressed young man serenading, "à la Romeo and Juliet," his admiring cherub-cheeked sweetheart, who languishes, eyes dreamily closed, out the window of her home (figure 22). Bizarre, of course, is the fact that he is accompanying himself by strumming, not on a guitar or mandolin as one might expect, but on a tennis racquet—a sign, perhaps, of his participation in the recently fashionable game.

In the other category are cards such as the brightly colored, romanticized illustration—done in an Americanized Art Nouveau style—of a gorgeous Greek muse, casually draped in a loose-fitting tunic, adorned with plentiful jewelry, and posed with a provocative come-hither expression (figure 23). As is the case here, thematic portrayal often included one or more of the "nine sister goddesses of the arts." They were exploited in a variety of nineteenth-century advertising,

especially for musical products. What seems rather incongruous in this particular ad for a reed organ is that the instrument cradled in her arms is an Ethiopian lyre called a *krar*, definitely not one of the more fashionable instruments of the day in America. The illustration in figure 24 depicts a more contemporary style of "atmosphere advertising." It adopts an intensified psychoemotional approach by setting intriguing or mysterious subject matter within an artful layout.

Merchandise catalogues, usually sent free to interested customers, were yet another sales device developed by manufacturers. Fully as important as the broadside, trade card, newspaper, and magazine advertisement, they were highly effective in convincing people, especially country people, to spend their money. Catalogues contained such exciting descriptions of ordinary goods that they were often used for good fireside reading; some came fully illustrated and bound like books. Endorsements, guarantees, added incentives, and "send no money

Figure 21.
Fold-back, stand-up
"Japanese Boy"
trade card

Figure 22.
"Tennis Racquet
Serenader" trade card,
c. 1895

Figure 23.
"Exotic Harp (Karar)
Player" trade card,
c. 1902

until you see the goods" sales terms made ordering from catalogues by mail irresistible.

As an advertising medium, the sales catalogue has, in fact, become a necessary part of the American consumer landscape. One commentator compares the Sears, Roebuck catalogue to the Magna Carta as a key to American civilization, suggesting that the growth of democracy in Anerica was actually due to the widespread distribution of goods more than to any political or governmental initiative.[80]

The Sears, Roebuck catalogue, most likely the preeminent catalogue of all time, was a wish book for millions of Americans. It bears comparison with the almanac and the family album as an authentic piece of Americana. For years, the Sears catalogue has been a primary reference for the theater and motion picture industry and indispensable for the sociohistorical study of late-nineteenth-

Figure 24.
Art Nouveau trade card

and early-twentieth-century popular culture.[81] Richard Sears, however, viewed the catalogue as the trump card in a game of high-stakes salesmanship. Promising quality, cheapness, and variety, Sears played an important role in the transformation of shopping for mere procurement to acquiring things for the excitement of fulfilled ownership.[82] People who bought products through catalogues no longer saw themselves as mere users of goods but in a new role: that of consumer.[83]

In the Sears, Roebuck catalogue of 1897, the "Musical Goods Department" occupies nearly one hundred pages.[84] Even with this generous profusion of products, the company expresses regret that "the line of Musical merchandise is so enormous that even with the space allotted for same in this catalogue we cannot list everything." Even by today's standards, the availability of such an expansive array of instruments, accessories, and music (not to mention everything else Sears was selling) is truly impressive.

Though significantly different from Sears, Estey also used catalogues as an important means to distribute attractive propaganda about his products.[85] Judging by the number of copies that have survived, Gellerman notes that Estey probably distributed more catalogues than all the other makers together.[86] The ornate covers of most Estey catalogues featured a picture of one of their more elegant models with space allocated for the agent's name. The catalogue's introductory pages invariably proclaimed 1846 as the founding date of the Estey enterprise, followed by the name and place of the company and a self-aggrandizing section titled "A Brief Account of the Most Extensive Cottage Organ Establishment in the World."

Following the introduction, several pages of pictures and descriptions of various styles, with their "Peculiarities and Patented Improvements," were interspersed with testimonials from important and not-so-important users. A price list and picture or two of the Estey factory usually concluded the circular. The catalogue of 1871 took pleasure in touting over "one hundred and fifty medals, first premiums and diplomas [won] at Fairs and Exhibitions throughout the United States" and concluded with a sound admonition to manufacturers who, unlike Estey, "packed or bought" the awarding jury, claiming honors and distinctions they did not deserve.

Old catalogues are an especially important resource for present-day reed organ enthusiasts. The 1981 publication of *Estey Reed Organs On Parade*, by Robert B. Whiting, and Robert F. Gellerman's 1985 edition of *Gellerman's International Reed Organ Atlas* (as well as other books on reed organs listed in the bibliography) attest to a growing interest in promotional materials (especially primary source materials) as important analytical tools in reed organ documentation. Whiting's volume, basically a collection of Estey catalogues, is useful in helping collectors identify dates of organs and provides chronologies of changing styles of casework and evolving tonal developments.

The contrasting styles of the catalogues themselves make for an interesting study. The Estey company seemed not to publish catalogues on a regular basis, though updated versions were regularly distributed. They came in all shapes and sizes, some small enough to fit into a shirt pocket, others deluxe leather-bound affairs. Most generally, they were in a seven-by-eleven-inch format with thirty or so pages.

Product endorsements from famous, or at least reputable, people were (and are) a mainstay of the advertising business. Companies indulged fully in name dropping. The Bay State Organ Company, for instance, offered to send prospective customers a list of literally hundreds of testimonials from American and European musicians. Clever editing often made the testimonials seem more convincing than they probably were; it has even been suggested that some were entirely fictitious. It is unlikely that Estey stooped to such low tactics, for he enlisted some of the most prominent leading musicians of the day to comment on the high quality of his reed organs. He probably sent free instruments to certain celebrities in order to procure their endorsements, a standard practice in a variety of businesses, but especially in the piano and reed organ trade.

In the first known Estey catalogue of 1867, endorsements appeared from respected representatives of various segments of the local music community: L. O. Emerson (a Boston composer and professor), the Reverend Bishop Simpson (Methodist), William A. Johnson (a renowned Massachusetts pipe-organ builder), C. B. Seymour (music critic of the *New York Times*), and others affirmed the workmanship and quality of the Estey organ. Endorsements from authorities such as these were persuasive. After all, if Estey's organs could endure the scrutiny of the learned professor, the pious reverend, the expert builder, and the captious critic, then the public could expect complete satisfaction. Later, testimonials attesting to the internationality of the Estey organ included letters from as far afield as Liberia, South Africa, Persia, Norway, Russia, China, and India.

References from satisfied customers and famous people eventually filled several pages of catalogue content accounting for, in one example, approximately one-third of the catalogue's bulk.[87] The Estey "Testimonial Circular" of 1871 comprised no fewer than fifteen pages boasting 171 ebullient commendations. A reporter for the *New York Independent* wrote while visiting the Fair of the New York State Agricultural Society: "Floral Hall and Domestic Hall never before appeared so much like an Eden of delight as when every standing was occupied by enraptured listeners, drinking in the Heaven-born music of Estey's Cottage Organs, which received the Gold Medal. I never want to hear another piano, if I can hear such an Organ with the Vox Humana Tremolo Attachment. . . . There is no use in attempting to describe this prize instrument. Language fails in adequacy to convey a fair idea of its perfectly enchanting power. It must be heard to be appreciated. I saw old iron-sided Ajazes, at Saratoga, wiping unbidden tears, because the entrancing music not only charmed the ear, but sank into the very fountains of life."[88]

As Estey began to gain an international reputation, an article from the *Vermont Phoenix* reported in 1876 that "a fine Estey Organ was sent last week to Wagner, the musical composer of Baireuth *[sic]*, Prussia."[89] Wagner responded with an appropriate endorsing statement: "The tone of the Estey Organ is very beautiful and noble and gives me the greatest pleasure. My great friend, Franz Liszt, is also charmed and delighted."[90] In other entries, Ole Bull (the great Norwegian violinist), Madame Essipoff (the celebrated Russian pianist), Mme. Lucca (the world-renowned prima donna), Nikolai Rubenstein (the director of the Moscow Imperial Conservatory), Camille Saint-Saëns (the esteemed composer), Dwight L. Moody (the eminent evangelist), and Joseph Joachim (the director of the Imperial Conservatory of Music)—to name but a few—all commented favorably on the "full," "powerful," "noble," "round," "sweet," and "animating" tone of the Estey instrument. With advocates and luminaries such as these, sales rose dramatically. Estey was assured success.

Sing the Old Songs

Though there were plenty of professional reed organ players in the nineteenth century, the instrument's success in America and elsewhere was based in large part on the ease with which amateur musicians could master enough technique to provide music in the home.[1] As discussed, the reed organ's sustained sound lends itself most naturally to the playing of sacred music. Yet, the reed organ, like the piano, was also capable of producing lively arrangements of popular and sentimental songs. This dual sacred and secular nature was the second key factor in the reed organ's success. A closer examination of the role of the amateur musician and the music played on reed organs will help explain how and why the reed organ became an indispensable element of the American Victorian parlor.

CHURCH AND PARLOR:
SACRED SPACES AND SECULAR SPACES

Over the past century and a half, most pipe organ connoisseurs have asserted that the free-reed organ was not entitled to the name "organ"; they have frequently expressed disappointment that an etymological twist of fate categorized it as such. As we have seen, manufacturers of reed organs did try other labels, but the generic term remained in use. I will intentionally sidestep this organological quagmire and will examine instead areas in which their similarities caused the two instruments to share common musical ground, most predominantly in music for religious services.

Organs, for various sociohistorical reasons, found their most appropriate place in the cathedrals and churches of Europe, and an important body of music

We tend to put musical types into separate compartments with specific labels such as "parlor songs," "household music," "minstrel melodies," and so forth, as though they were utterly distinct and unrelated. We tend to emphasize categories rather than situations. This may do well enough for scholarly classification but not for the sociocultural context of actual experience.

  Gilbert Chase,
  America's Music

developed concomitantly with the instrument. As pipe organs gradually gained acceptance in early American churches, much of the sacred music played on them was transferred to reed keyboard instruments as the latter became more commonplace.

Though it is true that instrumental music was forbidden in the Puritan churches of early America,[2] recent insight suggests that the Puritans were not as closed-minded about music, especially vocal music, as the usual stereotype implies.[3] Musicologists explain that Puritans enjoyed a diversity of music within the home, and if musical activity suited Puritan decorum and decency, even the church leaders enjoyed making music.[4] In fact, as long as matters were kept within the bounds of propriety, ballads, homeland folk tunes, Elizabethan airs, topical songs, and the playing of instruments provided musical recreation in many Puritan households.

Hymn singing in parts and the use of musical instruments—being identified with the Catholic mass and, according to church leaders, having no biblical sanction—were not permitted in Puritan churches until well into the eighteenth century; psalm singing, on the other hand, was condoned.[5] Barbara Owen, in her work *The Organ in New England*, judged the amount of rhetoric expended on arguments for and against instrumental music in the church as monumental, and the issue remained a matter of contention in religious and academic circles far into the nineteenth century.[6] Such attitudes helped erode the general quality of group music-making. Documentation of the day noted that the level of congregations' musical literacy had deteriorated to an alarming degree, a condition that the musically educated clergy found intolerable and a cause for concern; the issue eventually estranged the urban learned and sophisticated from the less well educated and often superstitious country folk.[7] As a result, two levels of musical reform were implemented during the last half of the eighteenth century: the organization of shape note hymnody singing schools and, though opposition to pipe organs continued, the acceptance of selected instruments to accompany certain sacred pieces.

Church choirs became accustomed to the support of musical aids such as the tuning fork and bass viol because they were condoned in New England singing schools. Cautious use of the bass viol enabled rural churches to stay within their sacred and economic boundaries.[8] Its size and accessibility (New Hampshire being a center for the making of viols in the nineteenth century) made it particularly convenient for small congregations. Gradually flutes, oboes, clarinets, bassoons, cornets, ophicleides (keyed bugles), trombones, and other instruments were admitted. The pipe organ, however, since Puritans continued to view it as a symbol of popery (and were perhaps otherwise defensive because they had probably never even seen one), was still derided and, along with the violin (the "Devil's box"), remained forbidden.

Other church denominations were less prejudiced against organs. The first pipe organ brought to America, purchased by Thomas Brattle, was later given to King's Chapel, an Anglican church in Boston, in 1714. Even so, Cotton Mather and other church dignitaries bitterly denounced the instrument, and it remained unpacked on the porch of the church for seven months before being installed.[9] There are many fascinating and intriguing stories surrounding the early arrival of pipe organs into America.[10]

Religious misgivings, transportation difficulties, cost, and the problem of finding trained organists contributed to the fact that even as late as 1800, only twenty organs were to be found in New England. But from that time, as urban and rural churches continued liberal trends, newly immigrated instrument builders began to deduce the pipe organ's market potential. The Embargo Act of 1807 and the War of 1812 brought importation of foreign goods—including organs—to a halt. Though unpopular, these conditions allowed domestic manufacturers to fill the void, stimulating America's industrial economy. Westward expansion and an ever-growing population encouraged new methods of production to satisfy the increasing demand.

Progress in instrument manufacture was still slow, however, especially for the new seraphine and melodeon until, beginning in the 1840s, the reed organ industry began to experience a period of rapid growth. Because the pipe organ had by this time generally become an accepted church fixture, the inexpensive, easily maintained melodeon became a highly marketable item for many church sanctuaries and for smaller rooms in affluent churches. And as they began to sell equally well to schools and social organizations and for domestic use, the number of reed organ builders in the United States soon outstripped the number of builders of pipe organs.[11]

Though beginnings were tentative, the organ's reputation was naturally enhanced through associations with the church and organized religion. The first quarter of the nineteenth century witnessed the birth of a moral reform movement that resulted in profound changes in the social lives of the American people.[12] The revivals that swept the country grew to immense proportions. Social theorists suspect that religious revivals were part of an organizing process that helped people on the move find meaning and collective cause within the disorienting ferment preceding and following national liberation. Thousands of churches were built, which gave people a "sense of community, a common world of experience, a code of morality, and a sense of meaning and purpose in life."[13] And within these important social institutions were found a multitude of organs. From 1713 to 1890 a church's theological and cultural orientation and relationship to its contemporary coreligionists could be judged by the presence or absence of an organ.[14]

Manufacturers' advertising makes clear the fact that organs were considered equally appropriate for church, chapel, meeting hall, and parlor, usually in that order of importance.[15] The transfer of Christian virtue from church to home was

Figure 25.
"Woman at Estey
Phonorium" trade card,
c. 1897

available via the organ, so that the sound of the reed organ becomes iconographic —a sonic symbol of morality. With this degree of epistemologic accord, its promise of wholesome and uplifting reward was assured.

For the same reason, the reed organ was promoted as an instrument for women, a tool with which they might engender moral values in the home, a matter we will return to shortly (see figure 25).[16] As instruments slowly gained acceptance in churches and the reed organ began to replace the bass viol for hymn singing, small organs became more acceptable in homes as well. Reed organ manufacturers capitalized on the church-related character and virtue of the instrument, claiming that its use created a "distaste for foolish sports, and coarse, vapid, pernicious, time-wasting descriptions of low literature, and thus improve while they recreate and refine the young, and enhance their love of home."[17] As time went on, articles in popular taste-making books and periodicals of the day routinely recognized the soul-raising powers of music and often suggested the reed organ or piano as a necessity for every home.

Churches, however, remained a primary marketing arena for reed organ manufacturers. Preachers sometimes supplemented their incomes by selling organs to members of their congregations or by referring customers to manufacturers. It was not uncommon for the officers and managers of organ factories to be leaders in their churches. Manufacturers who made products for churches, schools, and respectable parlors were expected to display moral integrity and a visible profession of faith. These attributes had commercial import, since potential consumers assayed a manufacturer's personal reputation as much as any characteristic of his product.[18]

Jacob Estey, Riley Burdett, E. B. Carpenter, and Levi Fuller (to cite only those with whom we will soon be more intimately concerned) were all deeply involved in matters of the Baptist church.[19] A popular saying at the time was that "it has become the invariable practice on Sundays for Baptist ministers all over the land to preach upon the Crucifixion in the morning and Jacob Estey and his cottage organs in the afternoon."[20] There is little doubt that Deacon Estey benefited greatly from the reputation he gained as a staunch supporter of Brattleboro's First Baptist Church and contributor to regional churches in Montpelier, Randolph, Hinsdale, Putney, and West Brattleboro.[21] One historian at least has little equivocation about the matter: "Only when our approach to reed organ history becomes inter-disciplinary are we able to understand fully the phenomenon which we have before us. Our attitude has been perhaps to regard these machines as examples of 'art for art's sake.' We have failed to see, did not want to see, that they were conceived principally out of the philosophy of 'money for God's sake'."[22]

Later in the century, overseas missionary markets became increasingly important for Estey. Tens of thousands of small, portable reed organs, sometimes called "missionary organs," were sent into remote "heathen lands" as symbols of Christian salvation (and Western imperialism). In the case of Estey's organs, countless advertising testimonials from missionaries in far-off places told of the Estey organ's ability to withstand inclemency and the rigors of primitive living.[23]

Schools, singing societies, lodges, and other organizations, though not as important as the church and home markets, accounted for other appreciable areas for sales. In community gathering places, as in the church and home, the organ, especially one with a high top, provided a shrinelike focus. And like a shrine, it remained a symbol of continuity even though people's life situations changed. Social cohesiveness and bonding were strengthened through the sharing of music and song. Even today, reed organs provide connections to the past, especially for those who live in rural areas and retain fond memories of playing the old reed organ in grandma's house.

The sound, too, harbors meaning beyond itself. To the discerning ear, the timbre or tone quality of a instrument is the most significant element in determining its success or failure as a mechanism of music within a particular cultural context. The ethnomusicologist David Reck observes that "the 'sound' of sound . . . becomes singularly mysterious and elusive when we attempt to describe it in words. It is no wonder, then, that some of the most poetic and imaginative writing by the world's master musicians, theorists, and musician-philosophers has centered around timbre."[24]

From the beginning, the sound of the reed organ was considered one of its weakest features. A common complaint about the melodeon was that its sound was monotonous.[25] To remedy this shortcoming, great amounts of time and effort were spent experimenting with technical issues such as reed voicing, reed environment, chest configuration, reed cells, and other sound-modifying systems. By the last quarter of the century, manufacturers and inventors had devised swell mechanisms to vary the volume, thus creating sounds that were more dynamic and diverse. Manipulating the reeds in various ways expanded and enriched the overall palette of tonal colors. Now, with the volume and timbral capabilities of the reed organ fully developed, players and audience alike could envelop themselves in an extraordinary amount of sustained sound.[26]

Free-reed timbre blends well with voices. This, and its capability to sustain tone created by air, gives the reed organ a warm vocal quality that cannot be matched by the more percussive piano. One testimonial from Europe commented that "the warbling of the melodious instrument is dignified in its expression, and under the fingers of an artist accustomed to make tremble cathedral organs, it ravished the ears of the audience by its variety of voices, its amplitude of sound and sweetness of the higher registers and power of the lower."[27]

The piano may have afforded higher status, but the organ offered a variety of sounds, surely one of its most attractive features. Different manufacturers created their own sound enhancements, added stop knobs, and devised gimmicks that were sometimes suspect if not downright fake. The names of the stops (usually borrowed from the pipe organ) were designed not only to describe timbral qualities and pitch relationships but to stimulate players' imaginations as well.

The *Estey Organ Method* describes thirty-three different stops, to be used in various combinations (see Appendix C).[28] It is supposed that the Barytone, Bassoon, Clarionet, Cornettino, Gamba, Harp Æolienne, Hautboy, Viola, and Wald Flute stops took their names from instruments they strived to imitate; the Delicante, Dulciana, Dolce, and Melodia stop designations expressed mood and attitude; the Vox Jubilante and Grand Organ stops stimulated visions of pomp and ceremony; and the Vox Humana and Flute d'Amour stops related to the more empathic side of human sensibility. Manufacturers hoped that greater tonal variety would intensify enjoyment and that sonic ethos would increase as players' mental and emotional imaginations were stimulated by the sound and nomenclature of various stops and their combinations.[29]

Three full pages of suggestions in the *Method* describe stops and their use. Understanding stop terminology is a crucial element in achieving proper registration, since reed organ keyboards are normally divided into bass and treble sections. Stops activated by the player control each half rank independently. Competent musical arrangements avoided crossing this point of division in mid-melody, since an unexpected switch in timbre would occur when contrasting bass and treble stops were drawn. Moreover, the relative dynamic strengths of various bass and treble stops had to be "orchestrated" so softer reeds were not drowned out. The addition of octave couplers was also of some concern since the outer, coupled octaves of a rising melody or descending bass line might drop out as it reached the limit of a coupler's effectiveness.

Estey's method took into consideration these and other matters of musical concern, providing suggestions, for instance, on special "desirable effects" such as Echo (playing a loud stop above middle C followed by a soft stop below middle C), and advice to keyboardists on accompanying singers: "the instrument is but the background of the voices and not the leader." Sections titled "Directions for Blowing" and "The Care of the Estey Organ" ensured maximum enjoyment of the instrument. For most players, it did not matter that the actual mechanics of some of the stop mechanisms were rudimentary. Effects as simple as raising a swell shade or opening a mute halfway provided variety and something else to manipulate and control.

The "Vox Humana Tremolo . . . the *ne plus ultra* of all improvements on reed instruments,"[30] was an Estey innovation consisting of a cardboard fan attachment, or "tremulant," which created a tremolo effect "imparting to the tone a wondrously thrilling effect unknown in instrumental music before its introduction. . . . Its soft, wave-like melody is so vibrant and pure that it never fails to enchant the listener. It is undeniably the first and only mechanical reproduction of the human voice ever given to the world."[31] Not everyone, however, was impressed. The *Musical Opinion* of March 1905 had this to say: "A sane man can only once be caught with a cardboard fan, from which 'a perfect imitation of the vox humana of pipes' is promised; while a 'vacuum viola'. . . is also a trap which can only once be set."

Although some critics were disappointed to find such a simple mechanism behind the exaggerated advertising, the fan attachment was widely copied by other manufacturers because it was musically effective. The mechanical reproduction of vibrato-like effects is in fact one of the most significant but overlooked developments in instrument technology. Whether achieved by spinning fan, fluttering valve, carefully mistuned reeds, vacuum tubes, Leslie speakers, transistors, or computer chips, the undulating effects of tremolo, vibrato, reverberation, and delay continue to attract modern musicians and delight audiences.

Throughout the last half of the nineteenth century, Protestant America increasingly sanctified the home by cultivating an ideology that placed the domestic space, not the church, at the center of religious and patriotic concern.[32]

It is doubtful that most Victorian reed organs enjoyed surroundings as luxurious as those shown in Estey's advertisements, but the instrument's status as a fixture in the Victorian parlor begs closer examination.

Though the Victorian home, especially the parlor, embodied the essence of respectability of middle- and upper-middle-class taste, its purpose remained essentially the same regardless of class setting: christenings, weddings, and funerals took place as acceptably in the parlor as in a church. (Since funeral homes appeared only after 1918, a few parlors even had special casket doors.) Moreover, of all the rooms in a Victorian house, the parlor provided the greatest opportunity to exhibit and enjoy all that had been acquired and to demonstrate the fine taste of the owner as revealed by an impressive array of beautiful things, things that connected meaningfully to a person's history[33] and the larger world.[34] Sometimes called the "first parlor," "sitting room," or "front room," it became the best room, which, through furniture and appointments, set the tone and style of the residence. One Victorian enthusiast described it as a place "full of beauty and brightness, testifying at once to the large and generous hospitality, as well as to the taste and wise discrimination of the queen-mistress who reigns over the realm of which this is the state chamber."[35]

From about 1850 the fashion for parlors spread rapidly among middle-class consumers. Borrowing from the elites, they made the parlor not only a place for rites of passage, quiet reading, and Sunday devotions, but also a specialty room for social activities that included formal calls, family household celebrations, teas, theatricals, game playing, music making, and other domestic entertainments.[36] Later it also accommodated such lively activities as charades, blindman's buff, fox and geese, pin the tail on the donkey, and soap-bubble blowing.[37]

Since the reed organ was never taken seriously as a concert instrument in America, it achieved one of its greatest roles in the circle of the American home. Unlike its industrial cousin, the sewing machine, which could be situated in most any room, the reed organ was invariably installed in the parlor. Consequently, sharing music became one of the most important of parlor activities. Playing and singing went hand in hand, and when not done alone, most often involved the immediate family circle and friends. Much has been written about the low quality of musical performance that took place in Victorian parlors but it should be emphasized that the parlor musicale was not a concert performance. A concert is generally a formal, one-shot event; parlor performance was a continuing social institution.[38] Lessons were inexpensive enough to allow private instruction from hymnals, methods, and songbooks (which often came with the purchase of the organ) or more costly sheet music. Since songs were all well known—many were in print for fifty or sixty years—and in many households played time and time again every day of the year, there was ample opportunity for performers to improve their delivery. High musical attainment was not necessarily expected; rather, one hoped for a lively, energetic, feeling performance.

A high level of continuity and uniformity in the parlor repertoire guaranteed that players would not have to learn too many new tricks before old ones were mastered. Even if the standard of accomplishment was low, parlor performance was nevertheless valued as an important social and musical occasion. Almost any kind of music was acceptable fare, and performances were often filled with imagination and surprise. In spite of the fact that home performance was regarded as the domain primarily of young ladies, all family members enjoyed playing and singing; whoever could make music made it.

An oft-quoted passage regarding a house plan devised by Catherine Beecher and her more famous sister, Harriet Beecher Stowe, for an 1869 volume titled *The American Woman's Home*, describes a domestic design characterized as "a Christian house," carefully arranged so that house members could contribute "for the common good, and by modes at once healthful, economical, and tasteful." The floor plan suggests only two pieces of furniture, both situated in the parlor: a sofa and a piano. Likewise, the July 1867 edition of the *Atlantic Monthly* stated that "almost every couple that sets up housekeeping on a respectable scale considers a piano only less indispensable than a kitchen range." One may reasonably substitute the reed organ for the piano, taking into account certain class differences. Most commentary of this nature specified that young women of character were expected not only to excel in needlework and drawing, but also to be prepared to entertain family and friends with a musical performance on the piano or organ (figure 26).

Playing the piano or organ, in fact, became one very familiar way for ladies to display their aesthetic and cultural accomplishments. It was understood that musicianship increased a woman's sexual allure and marriageability; the notion of "music as mantrap" was ubiquitous and in vogue.[39] Given the stringent rules that governed relationships between men and women, rendezvous over the reed organ must have seemed attractive to both sexes.[40] Though not as strongly mandated, keyboard ability was a definite asset in genteel courtship for men as well as women (figure 27). Some duets (four hands on one keyboard) were composed so that the players' hands frequently crossed, for no apparent musical purpose. The intention, of course, was to create an opportunity for some euphonious fun and flirting.

It was hoped that after marriage a young woman's musical skill could help relieve her husband's vexation, the children's restlessness, and her own personal sorrow and hardship. She was to be musically competent but not aspire to excellence, since it was feared that excessive talent might undermine her domestic virtue.[41] Ultimately, she was expected to bring beauty and cultural connectedness into the home.

Accomplishment on the reed organ helped fulfill the Victorian requirement not only for genteel ladyship but for moral motherhood as well. A central theme in this discussion is how the organ, through its various semiotic linkages,

Figure 26.
"Women Friends" trade
card, c. 1888

simultaneously involved the mundane world of secular consumerism and the
Christian world of the spirit. Nineteenth-century women bore the greatest responsibility for the religious, educational, social, material, generational, and ethical orientation of her family. With such high expectations and moral burdens,
most of which were increasingly reinforced by stereotyped advertising, placed
on Victorian females, it is fortunate that the reed organ could accommodate both
secular and saintly roles simultaneously.[42]

Toward the later part of the century, labor-saving devices—especially the
sewing machine, washing machine, carpet sweeper, and, to a lesser extent, gadg-
ets such as the apple corer, sausage grinder, lemon squeezer, bean sheller, bat-
ter mixer, knife sharpener, ice maker, and numerous other items—helped to
"liberate" women from the household routine.[43] Puritan conceptions about hard
work and toil notwithstanding, even the slightest easing of home maintenance
operations such as sewing, laundering, carpet sweeping, furniture cleaning, meal
preparation, dishwashing, food preservation, and heating was an important step
in a then-fledgling feminist movement.[44] With their supposed free time, undoubtedly more available to upper-middle-class women than to others, women
attempted to improve their social standing and reach for the bourgeois ideal

Figure 27.
"A Social Gathering"
trade card, 1888

with the intention (conscious or subconscious) of setting themselves apart from the thousands of newly landed working-class immigrants. One way middle-class women mirrored elite culture was by joining all manner of social organizations, including art clubs, book clubs, dramatic clubs, sewing circles, philanthropic associations, and scientific, literary, religious, athletic, musical, and decorative arts societies.

Nineteenth-century sheet music covers and parlor-song texts clearly indicate the ideal persona and disposition of the proper Victorian young woman. Physically, she was "lovely" or, better yet, beautiful: blond hair, blue eyes, and fair skin were the best. Dark skin was evidently not welcome in the parlor.[45] Illustrations of the day generally featured unblemished ladies dressed in piquant, fashionable costumes. The tone in favorite songs like "Bird in a Gilded Cage" and "She's More to be Pitied Than Censured" is subtly condescending and patronizing, implying that female intelligence and initiative were not particularly admired (except among her peers); unassertive, submissive, mild behavior was the expectation. The ideal woman was chaste, nurturing, compassionate, and childlike, her demeanor, gay, cheerful, solicitous, and free from care.[46] This image, asexual and completely nonthreatening, represented social stability and enduring moral values in an increasingly secularized world. But beyond these enormous social expectations, the Victorian woman knew, unquestionably, that she was always assured haven in the parlor. Favorite images of Victorian domestic domain—

Figure 28.

"The Cleric" trade card,

c. 1900

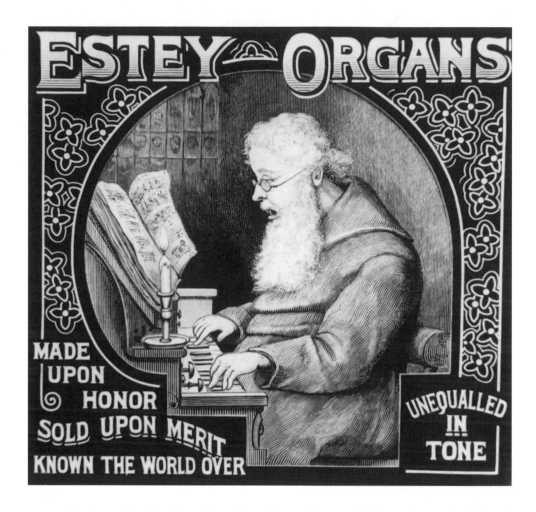

warm kitchen, glowing hearth, and active parlor tended by a devoted wife and mother—were central to a cluster of images that defined the norm in American life.[47]

It is important to note, however, that women's role regarding playing of the organ rarely passed beyond the boundaries of the home. In the outside world, keyboard players, particularly those affiliated with church and theater, were nearly all men. And conversely, though men were often depicted as standing beside the organ, absorbed in the sweet strains of some tune or other, there are relatively few examples of reed organ advertising that place a man at the keys. Men organists are generally placed either within formal circumstances, "at the club" with their cronies, or in religious situations (figure 28), another clear example of the sacred-secular duality of the reed organ. And though there were many excellent women songwriters, men were responsible for the bulk of the popular song repertoire.

By enriching the quality of life at home, women reinforced values and behaviors held in esteem by larger segments of American society. In this way, music provided an element of social cohesiveness within an elaborate system of associations that relied on the maintenance of conventionalized roles for its functional organization. Since the instrument and the music were of the "popular" genre and thus familiar to a large portion of the population, skills learned and exercised around the home reed organ reinforced social bonding not only within the immediate family, but also within one's social group and society at large.[48]

POPULAR MUSIC FOR THE REED ORGAN

The development of popular music in America follows a sequence of events similar to those of other areas of culture: literal importation from Europe, creation of similar styles in America, and finally, development of indigenous forms which combined various regional and ethnic styles.[49] Nicholas Tawa points out that before 1815 secular songs composed by Americans were rare.[50] By 1828 the amount of native material rose appreciably, and by the 1840s the floodgates had opened.

Prior to the nineteenth century, the "music of the people" came through various traditional ethnic folkways and tended to exist in somewhat isolated rural enclaves. Appalachia and the pioneering West are perhaps the areas most thoroughly researched in this regard.[51] As time went on, fiddle tunes (adaptable to other instruments), cowboy songs, mining songs, canal songs, and railroad songs materialized into an appreciable body of uniquely American music.[52] This native repertory of orally transmitted folk music shared certain traits with the newer, more stylish highbrow material coming from European urban centers. Both genres brimmed with tuneful, well-honed melodies and messages with a moral, easy to listen to and hard to forget. As cross-cultural exchange intensified, early formulations of American popular music were born, with the earliest types coalescing from various, though mostly English, musical sources.

Throughout the first part of the nineteenth century, an especially close relationship existed between the music being performed publicly in London, on the eastern urban concert stages of America, and by amateurs in the households of both nations. Songs by George Frederick Handel and other fashionable British composers were brought from overseas to provide elegant music for culture-conscious Americans.[53] Material from English ballad operas found its way to the American east coast as popular broadsides and eventually became part of the home repertoire. These included airs from ballad and British comic operas by Samuel Arnold, William Shield, William Reeve, and Charles Dibdin, along with the concert songs of Thomas Arne, James Hook, and Reginald Spofford.[54] In American theaters, assembly halls, and playhouses, rich and poor enjoyed the same fare; professional musicians from Europe, many of virtuoso stature, played to upper- and lower-class audiences together—though seating was arranged accordingly.[55]

Topical songs shared concert bills with the classical masterpieces, so that American music continued to absorb and hybridize musical mannerisms from European sources. During the latter part of the eighteenth and early portion of the nineteenth centuries, there was much less distinction between categories of musical type in America than at present and, as we shall soon see in the case of reed organ repertoires, seemingly disparate types of music were likely to be found cheek by jowl in the same music book. The "First Kiss Polka," "Home Sweet Home," and "Flick and Flock Galop," for instance, might share the page with a Felix Mendelssohn "Song without Words," Giuseppe Verdi's "Anvil Chorus," or a theme from Gaetano Donizetti's *Lucrezia Borgia*.[56]

The aforementioned body of traditional folk music helped augment the swelling stream of popular American music.[57] Generally, arrangements of folk material consisted of tunes and texts harmonized in a semiclassical manner for one to four voices and keyboard accompaniment. Thomas Moore and Robert Burns, for example, masterfully mated original texts to traditional folk tunes, creating music of a seemingly timeless quality. Moore's famous collection *Irish Melodies* became a long-lasting favorite of this type and provided a successful model for other songwriters in Britain and America.[58]

English tastes in music also predominated in the sacred repertoires of most American churches. In answer to the growing problem of congregational musical illiteracy, and therefore bad-sounding music, various systems of shape note notation, alluded to earlier, were devised.[59] Sung unaccompanied, shape note hymns became very popular in England and America in both rural and urban churches. Beginning early in the nineteenth century, American "tunesmiths," many with little or no formal music education, composed their own brand of shape note hymns. Popularly called Sacred Harp hymnody, it remains a living tradition still enjoyed by both sacred and secular groups.[60]

Instrumentally, until mid-century, ecclesiastical organ repertories consisted of works by English composers including John Stanley, William Boyce, William Felton, Thomas Arne, and Maurice Greene. Improvised voluntaries, transcriptions of Handel's choruses, and Scottish airs were also standard fare. Gradually, American composers, often recently arrived from England, began to write their own hymn tunes, voluntaries, fugues, and other forms of instrumental music appropriate for the church; among these were William Selby, George Jackson, Alexander Reinagle, and James Hewitt. Other composers working in America began to compose music specifically for the organ as well. Notable among these pioneers were Raynor Taylor, Benjamin Carr, and Lowell Mason. In the period before music was written especially for melodeons, reed organ literature was padded with pieces for piano and relied heavily on technically easy pipe organ material and transcriptions of choral music.

The eminent music historian Gilbert Chase said of American music at mid-century: "In the musical activity of the United States during the first half of the nineteenth century, it seems to me that two things stand out as most typical of the age. One is that the leading musical impresario of that period was also the creator of the American circus, the great master of ballyhoo, the exploiter of Tom Thumb and Joyce Heth—that incomparable and sensational showman, Phineas Taylor Barnum. The other symbolically significant phenomenon is that the leading musical figure of that mid-century period, Lowell Mason, was in his career and his character the prototype of the self-made, successful American business magnate."[61] Lowell Mason and Thomas Hastings wrote hundreds of sacred solos, anthems, and hymn tunes—with and without words. Most were uncomplicated melodically, harmonically, and rhythmically, acting primarily as a vehicle for the words, and were designed never to exceed the ability of the congregation. Many of these works eventually found their way into compilations for reed organs, which were enjoying an increasingly substantial market by the third quarter of the century.

In addition to specific British musical influences on American composers, broader philosophical changes were beginning to transform European culture and music.[62] As the century progressed, the romantic era was gaining momentum in both Europe and America. Immigrants from Germany, Scandinavia, Italy, and eastern Europe—some sixteen million between 1840 and 1900—brought European romantic philosophies to America, enriching the dominant Anglo-American culture stream.[63] Italian operas by Gioachino Rossini, Vincenzo Bellini, Gaetano Donizetti, and others were readily absorbed by an American public hungry for transatlantic culture. Many favorite arias and choruses from operas performed by touring professional European companies were arranged for domestic use as simple English strophic songs with keyboard accompaniment. These influences continued to provide momentum and musical substance for a developing American song style. Throughout the nineteenth century, diffusions from the cultured artways of Europe fed an intensifying appetite of the American bourgeoisie for this new, popular variety of music.

Composers, songwriters, arrangers, instrument makers, and performers on both sides of the Atlantic were quick to accommodate the growing market. Performers such as the Englishman Henry Russell—composer, singer, and promoter of popular Italian opera pieces and of his own material—achieved unprecedented fame and financial success touring American theaters. Russell's songs combined sentimental and nostalgic subject matter with a melodramatic performance style to profoundly affect his audiences.[64]

While overseas performers came and went, many musicians and composers came to America with the intention of staying. From this stock came important early songwriters in America: Francis Hopkinson (a signer of the Declaration of Independence), Benjamin Carr, James Hewitt, Alexander Reinagle, George K. Jackson, and Raynor Taylor, to name but a few.[65] All were immigrants with wide-ranging musical interests. Besides composing, they often performed, conducted, published, and managed others' musical affairs. Mention must also be made of other early figures such as the organist Oliver Shaw, credited with being the first successful native-born songwriter in America,[66] and John Hewitt (born and raised in America and the son of James Hewitt), who attained commercial success in 1825 with the song "The Minstrel's Return'd from the War."

Music as an expanding area of enterprise was helped along by a general increase in American musical literacy. It was during this period that the effort begun first by William Billings and his contemporaries in New England with singing schools began to pay off.[67] As we have seen, musical ability became desirable as a social skill, particularly for women.[68] Singing schools in turn acted as successful models for other educational institutions across the continent. Later in the nineteenth century, dedicated music educators such as the aforementioned Thomas Hastings and the ubiquitous Lowell Mason developed "scientific" (a word much exploited in this era) methods of teaching music that further expanded the market for all kinds of music, especially of the popular variety.

Mason is generally considered the founder of the music appreciation format in American music education. His vision was noble and his impact considerable. Tawa states that "Lowell Mason, certainly one of the most important music educators in American history, recognized the power of music to affect and influence people; he believed that values and common interests could be nationally shared through musical feeling. Prominent educators and social-minded leaders were confident that music could shore up humanity's ethical and emotional being, teach democratic principles, and encourage allegiance to an undivided national society."[69] Mason's pioneering efforts in the Boston public school system received encouraging support from a government committee assigned to evaluate his methods. Among various positive commendations and pronouncements, the committee declared that ultimately, to "feel rightly" was generally more educationally important than to think profoundly, and further, that singing—popular songs included—seemed best fitted for this purpose.[70] In other words, music had the power to shape moral character; a person might know a lot and still be no good, whereas a person who feels rightly can be only good.

Lowell Mason is additionally important to our story because it was he who encountered Emmons Hamlin in Oliver Ditson's Boston music store in 1854, the outcome being the formation of the Mason & Hamlin Company, a cooperative enterprise between Lowell's son, Henry, and Hamlin. Ditson and the elder Mason financed the pair to begin manufacturing reed organs. Their company went on to become a leader in the industry throughout the world.[71]

As mentioned earlier, the American band tradition became a major component of this country's musical heritage. After the Civil War, wind bands became a national institution and an influential part of America's nascent popular movement. Operas, symphonies, and chamber music were generally unknown outside urban centers. In the 1880s only New York, St. Louis, and Boston hosted major symphony orchestras. Church music and the town band were the only live music available for a great majority of rural Americans. Most heard their first classical masterpieces as brass band transcriptions.[72]

The minstrel show is also well documented as one of the more important movements in the history of American music and, in spite of initial English influence, is recognized as the first distinct performance genre for a uniquely American form of popular song.[73] The minstrel show's significance in the development and shaping of America's popular culture is appreciable.[74] As a group performance, minstrelsy began around 1840 and developed throughout the rest of the century. The shows consisted of loosely organized sequences of songs, dances, skits, dialogues in dialect, and ensemble numbers. Typically four in number, the blackface musicians generally played banjo and fiddle, with bones and tambourine endmen acting as rhythm section and the most active showmen. After the Civil War shows became more lavish in costume, stage direction, and decoration, were more varied in content, and began to deal with other ethnic groups as well as blacks. The minstrelsy repertoire was to have a huge impact on the future development of popular music in America. Burlesque and other theatrical variety shows developed from this genre, and Tin Pan Alley, musical comedies, and vaudeville eventually eclipsed it.

Cities and towns alike enjoyed the variety afforded by minstrel performances.[75] Brattleboro's newspapers evidence the minstrel show's importance to life in that community. A newspaper review described one such evening of entertainment in 1893: "The lovers of minstrelsy were delighted with the performance given by the Luciers company at the town hall Monday evening. The stage was very prettily arranged with plush background, and the minstrels were arrayed in plush costumes. The band is one of unusual merit and includes several good soloists, among them the blind Lucier. The clever things in a musical and farcial [sic] lines evoked applause, and approval was also earned by the frog man, whose contortions were more wonderful than those of any other similar performer; Billy Fries, the tambourine spinner, who is also the skillful baton wielder; the lamp balancer, and others."[76]

From this tradition came the trendsetters of American minstrelsy, George Washington Dixon: Thomas Darthmouth Rice, the Virginia Minstrels, Christy's Minstrels, and Henry Russell. Other prominent contributors to the nineteenth-century musical mainstream must include Stephen Foster, a giant among songwriters, and the Hutchinson family, social reformers as well as entertainers.[77] This all too brief listing of significant composers and performers of popular music was to influence what was being played on American stages and in people's parlors for decades to come. More composers, aided by performers, attempted to produce music that listeners would respond to favorably; rather than creating works of great artistic merit, they penned simple texts and crafted charming melodies designed to appeal to large audiences.

Though performers of the caliber of Ole Bull and Jenny Lind transcended developing class boundaries,[78] one begins to sense a disparity of preference in music emerging between those who aspired to cultivated European tastes and those who responded to more endemic elements.[79] As middle-class and upper-class partialities became increasingly distinct and markets more clearly defined, American popular music began to come of age as an unique entity.[80] In response, the output of publishers comprised an eclectic promulgation of vernacular and cultivated music, which though relatively unsophisticated and somewhat simple-hearted, was nonetheless sincere and accessible to aspiring amateur musicians.[81]

The thousands of music publications that have come to us confirm that nearly all types of sacred and popular music discussed above were arranged for keyboards: hymns and patriotic anthems, sentimental ballads and comic songs, jigs and reels, marches, polkas, and waltzes, as well as simplified arrangements and transcriptions of art songs, operatic arias, and ballet airs (see the accompanying compact disc). Early secular music collections and method books designed specifically for reed organ, though few in number, were available almost from the beginning of reed organ manufacture. John Green's *Airs Adapted for the Royal Seraphine*, published in London around 1833, contained songs already popular in the early 1800s as well as original tunes by Green himself. Though Loesser suggests that the "melodeon families were more given to singing than to dancing, that they suffered music more gladly to hum and to whine than to tinkle and to plunk," by the end of the century collections and methods especially for reed organ reveal a diversity of popular composition equal to that for the piano.[82] The piano itself contributed to the reed organ literature through transcriptions for organ of piano compositions by nineteenth-century European composers. Ultimately, most all music books and sheet music could be used on any keyboard instrument and were equally at home on either piano or organ music rack. Eventually a separate repertoire of popular music developed specifically for the reed organ, though in general it continued to share the repertory of the piano in the home and that of the pipe organ in the church.[83]

Music book compilers discovered early that combining established hits with their own works helped ensure the publication's success, and the practice developed into a standard strategy for hundreds of organ music books. For instance, James Cox Beckel, a Philadelphia music teacher with many apparent skills, wisely included in his 1855 *Amateur's School for the Melodeon* popular compositions, including the well-known hit, "What Is Home without a Mother," by "Alice Hawthorne." This was the pen name of Septimus Winner, who, not coincidentally, published Beckel's collection.[84] E. B. Phelps, co-compiler of the *Estey Organ Method*, interspersed a few of his own compositions and arrangements among those by famous European classical composers, another common tactic.

In spite of critics' opinions of the reed organ's limitations, and contrary to the reed organ's stodgy reputation, it was fun to play. Pumping one's way through a pastiche of polkas, quadrilles, schottisches, marches, mazurkas, and other dance forms provided relief from the more plodding sentimental fare. And timeless songs like Bishop's "Home, Sweet Home" (which appeared in virtually all reed organ collections[85]), "In the Gloaming," "Long, Long Ago," "Love's Old Sweet Song," and "Annie Laurie," and Stephen Foster favorites like "Old Folks at Home," "De Camptown Races," "My Old Kentucky Home," "Swanee River," and of course, "Oh! Susanna" (a particular favorite with the gold rushers) were widely circulated and never seemed to go out of vogue.[86]

Collections of parlor organ music, especially instructional method books, included with the sale of the organ or sold separately, were often commissioned by organ manufacturers or distributors themselves.[87] Constantly on the lookout for advertising opportunities, it was not unusual for manufacturers to use several pages in their own method books to extol the virtues of their product.

In addition to providing an explanation of music basics and a varied selection of tunes and songs, manufacturers' method books sometimes offered advice on the use and maintenance of the organ. This was a matter of practical as well as economic concern because manufacturing criteria, especially regarding the number, nomenclature, and arrangement of organ stops, was never standardized within the American reed organ industry, making nearly every manufacturer's stop designations and specifications somewhat different. Methods suitable for any organ were also published, often in sequential, graded form. Judging from the abundance of music "tutors" offered in one late-in-the-century Sears, Roebuck catalogue, there was decidedly no shortage of music books written especially for the reed organ.[88]

Publishers carefully chose arrangements of music that were technically simple enough for amateur performance but still packed an appropriate emotional punch. The general formula was strophic form, diatonic tune, major key with an occasional chromatic twist, and avoidance of extremes in meter, tempo, and dynamics. Songs and accompaniments tended to flow into clear, symmetrical shapes with little superfluousness. Accompaniments were pared to the essentials, avoided difficult keys and harmonies, and usually consisted of a three-chord progression (which sometimes modulated to a related key) arranged for easy rendering on a keyboard. Ordinarily melodies were free of chromaticism, large leaps, and wide ranges. The shape of the melody—which often contained predictable musical "sighs" as well as other descending motivic sequences and, more often than not, a dramatic climax (usually a high note held as long as the singer dared) —generally provided amateur vocalists easy emotional and technical access.

One might wonder how such a basic, simple, unenhanced song style reflects the Victorian ideal of elaboration and ornament. The baroqueness is evident not so much in a song's arrangement as in its conception, presentation, and effect. Songs, method books, and the instruments themselves were generally mass produced, like the high-Victorian houses and unrestrained scrollwork of the day.

To stretch the comparison, the images evoked in songs were like the decoration available for houses: endless variations on themes of innocence, love, and death were metaphorical musical equivalents of the hundreds of styles of Victorian bannisters, wallpaper, drapery, and doors. Just as rapid construction methods and inexpensive cookie-cutter architectural millwork provided access to fashion that appeared upper class, songs of formulaic construction imbued with predictable fervor gave musical aspirants the feeling of cultivated, genteel accomplishment.[89] Ultimately, the customary dramatic delivery and excessive bathetic response to the music is a kind of psychoemotional elaboration.

Collections of nineteenth-century American reed organ music may be judged from various vantage points: (1) the technical appropriateness of the arrangement, based on the mechanical capabilities of each style of organ; (2) whether the selections are idiomatically convincing when performed on the reed organ; (3) whether the compilations are balanced regarding representation of styles; (4) whether transcribers retained the value of the original composition; and (5) whether the amount of instructional advice regarding the registration and selection of stops is sufficient to make the instrument sound its best.

Russell Schulz, in his doctoral dissertation "The Reed Organ in Nineteenth Century America," surveys several reed organ method books to gain insight into their methodologies.[90] As a prime example, he examined one in some detail: *Kimball's New Method for the Reed Organ*, written in 1872 by Horace E. Kimball (not the Kimball of piano manufacturing fame). Schulz, a professional organist himself, offers particular insight into pedagogical aspects of Kimball's method by outlining and critiquing each section of the book in turn. The reader is referred to his paper for a full analysis. Essentially, the first sixteen pages of the Kimball method introduce students to the musical rudiments: the keyboard, staff notation, time and meter, and hand position are explained and diagrammed. The next forty pages explain scale and chord construction and offer exercises that, if practiced faithfully, assure mastery over the instrument; the student is encouraged to transpose the exercises and tunes into *all* keys. A short miscellaneous selection of music follows each scale and drill.

The third part, eighty-eight "Progressive Pieces," proposes to musically evangelize students who may, "with musical appreciation and culture at a low point," require systematic weaning from the "trashy literature" Kimball presumes they are accustomed to enjoying. So, "rather than to start from the outset with a grade of music above their appreciation," he proposes to cultivate the player's "brain and ear" through a "gradual crescendo in aesthetics" by way of the technically progressive pieces. Among these pieces—all judged to be superior music by Kimball himself—are, not surprisingly, several of Kimball's own compositions.

The final sections of Kimball's book deal with minor scales, modulation, and some church interludes and vocal selections. All told, the book contains well over two hundred pieces of music, including no fewer than twenty-four operatic transcriptions. This quantity of music seems to be characteristic of such books in general.

Other method books reviewed by Schulz include a later publication from John Green, *Concise Instructions for the Seraphine and Melodeon* (1847); George F. Root's *School for the Cabinet Organ* (1860) and *Model Organ Method* (1873); and *Lyon and Healy's Excelsior Method for the Parlor Organ* (1884). Like music method books today, every author makes particular (and sometimes peculiar) recommendations, each proclaiming a new and improved system by which anyone can readily master their instrument.

Generally, Schulz judges that the potential for success of most of the method books is uneven and that some are even largely unworkable. He concludes that the quality of content for understanding musical rudiments varies enormously, finds an imbalance between technical and compositional information, and declares nineteenth-century flowery phraseology "charming, engaging, naive, campy, and sometimes unforgivable." In the end, he submits that, regardless of their general tendency toward patchwork pedagogy, "some apparently were successful"—hardly a ringing endorsement.

Nevertheless, the literature for reed organ is generally representative of the music played and enjoyed by the majority of Americans during the nineteenth century. Judging from the tattered condition of the relatively few reed organ methods that have survived the years, there can be little doubt that they were well used. The reed organ gave the populace access to making music when none other may have been available. Even though the compositions were sometimes homely and arrangements less than expertly done, we should appreciate that it was this repertoire that provided Americans with a sense of increasing artistic status and a genuine aesthetic experience, and nurtured their national identity.

FROM THE *ESTEY ORGAN METHOD*

In 1879 Estey published the *Estey Organ Method*.[91] Because the collection features three pages of explanation and instruction on organ care and use of the various stops, it was considered better than many; in fact, aficionados proclaim the *Estey Organ Method* far superior to most. The book reportedly sold well and received the commendation of many reputable musicians of the day. An 1879 issue of Brattleboro's newspaper, the *Vermont Phoenix*, announced 4,000 copies on the market with 5,000 more coming off the press. The publication was revised at least once (in 1882) to reflect changes relating to technical improvements and musical tastes.[92] With a format similar to Kimball's, the Estey *Method* was designed to satisfy multipurpose requirements: equally useful in church, home, lodge, or school.

Though Estey himself knew little about music, he appreciated the value of designing a profit-making method book that would meet his high standards and maximize the special character of the Estey organ. He hired two competent Boston arranger-compilers, E. B. Phelps and George S. Cheney, to prepare the volume. The Estey *Method*, like all such books, was designed to be accessible to those with limited keyboard facility. "The Carnival of Venice," for example, a non-vocal piece comprising a single melody line with some arpeggiated harmony, is the stylistic norm.[93] In songs such as "Consider the Lilies," the left hand establishes a minimal bass line while the right simply outlines broken chords.[94] Hymns such as "Old Hundred"[95] (as this well-known tune was called in the *Method*) follow a standard SATB choral format with two parts per hand.[96] "The Star Spangled Banner" and other national anthems,[97] whose aggrandizing effect depends on full reed organ sonority, utilize strong bass lines, coupled octaves, full-fisted chords in the treble, and some interesting harmonic resolutions (see the accompanying compact disc).

Except for an occasional countermelody or inner-part movement, polyphonic textures are rare. Expression markings are not as abundant as one might expect from music with an effusive, emotional reputation. Stop registrations are also generally minimal; some pieces contain no stop or expressive recommendations whatsoever, presumably allowing players to determine their own dynamics and delivery. Forms are relatively short and symmetrical, usually AABA (a common scheme for popular musics), two to five stanzas, with marked and unmarked options for endless repetition. The overall rhythmic style tends toward cliché: "The Last Rose of Summer,"[98] for instance, uses the "Scottish snap," a favorite "short-long" rhythmic twist found in many popular nineteenth-century instrumental pieces (see the accompanying compact disc).

Most likely, one of the arranger's greatest perplexities was in condensing full operatic scores into conventional two-staff keyboard arrangements. Considering the number of these transcriptions in print, however, it is not surprising that the technique became formulized over time. Lush orchestral scores were pared down to short forms featuring a single trademark melody with metrically appropriate chording. Within these rather restrictive boundaries, compilers used every available gimmick to achieve variety. A brief comparison (see Appendix F, examples 1 and 2) between two nonvocal keyboard arrangements, one by Franz Liszt and the other by Phelps and Cheney, of Richard Wagner's popular "Pilgrims' Chorus" from *Tannhäuser*, will serve to heighten our appreciation of the arranger's procedures (see the accompanying compact disc).

Paraphrased versions of the "Pilgrim's Chorus" by Liszt[99] and by Phelps and Cheney[100] are not transcriptions of the famous chorus as sung in the third act of *Tannhäuser* (the key and form are different), but simplified versions of the opening section of the overture, which is built on the same melody. At a glance, even the untrained eye can see that the Liszt version (in the key of E major, which has four sharps), is far more complex than that in the Estey *Method* (in the key of F major, which has only one flat). The Liszt rendition suggests a common tendency of this era's concert keyboardists to embellish popular melodies by improvising onstage. After a fairly straightforward statement of the binary melody in the first part, Liszt develops a variation based on tumbling sixteenth notes to accompany the melody; later, a change of meter from 3/4 to 9/8 increases the rhythmic density. The fortissimo dynamic level, marcato melody, jam-packed chording, and pedal-heavy bass remind us that performers of this period had license to indulge in unrestrained bombast and emotion. Liszt even provides inserts for other variation ideas (including three possible endings). After exercising numerous variant potentials, a third and final portion of the arrangement brings the player back to the basic melody, which, toward the end, is quietly stated in the bass. This is a difficult piece of music.

Like Liszt's, the Phelps and Cheney version retains the same overall soft-loud-soft shape of Wagner's original composition but uses technically straightforward repetitive triplet chording in the climactic middle 9/8 part to provide the momentum and intensity required. In contrast to the Liszt model, the melody is maintained in the highest part throughout the piece with the accompaniment left relatively uncluttered. While Liszt utilizes the entire piano keyboard and dictates specific phrasing, dynamics, fingering, and special techniques such as rolled chords, the reed organ version uses only the middle range of the keyboard, and players are largely left to determine their own expression. Besides a simple "dim." and "cres." (respectively, diminuendo and crescendo), suggestions for interpretation are scarce throughout the organ reduction; in contrast, the piano rendition frequently uses such cryptic parlance as "il canto sempre un poco tenuto" and "ppp perdendo," for example. This modest analysis points up the fact that ultimately, distinct contrasts between concert music and parlor music, increasingly divided along boundaries of social class, became more pronounced. Yet, developing schisms seemed not to deter those wishing to partake of music; in a musically democratic society, the presentation of music, whatever the proficiency level, wherever the performance, was most always appreciated.

The *Estey Organ Method* is divided into five sections: Learning the Rudiments, Miscellaneous Selections, Songs, National Airs, and Selections of Sacred Music. Over two hundred musical pieces are represented (see Appendix C, table of contents of the *Estey Organ Method*). The first part, approximately fifty pages, contains a well-organized sequence of exercises and musical explanation interspersed with short compositions and "recreations" for applying and drilling newly learned techniques. Carl Maria von Weber, Ludwig van Beethoven, Wolfgang Amadeus Mozart, and Giuseppe Verdi are among the contributors, though their compositions are, like the Phelps and Cheney's Wagner transcription, simplified and abbreviated. Scattered amongst the masters' pieces are several short generic tunes, common to most beginning methods, designed to reinforce particular points of pedagogy. Included among the elementary selections are such favorites as "Barcarolle," "Blue Bells of Scotland," "Bohemian Waltz," and "Robin Adair."

The second part, Miscellaneous Selections, exhibits true Victorian eclecticism—analogies can be made between chock-full organ methods and overstuffed domestic parlors—and accounts for almost half of the volume's bulk. An ample selection of church "Interludes," "Prayers," "Responses," and "Preludes" are scattered willy-nilly among reductions of classical operatic standards from, for example, Weber's *Der Freischütz*, Charles Gounod's *Faust*, Verdi's *Il Trovatore*, Mozart's *Magic Flute*, and Wagner's *Tannhäuser*. Additionally, "Adeste Fideles," "Happy Farmer," "Home, Sweet Home," "The Last Rose of Summer," "*Poet and Peasant* Waltz," "O for the Wings of a Dove" and other ever-popular pieces find their places among less well known compositions from anonymous sources and among those penned by the compilers themselves. Several sentimental songs round out this section, the majority by popular English songwriters: "Annie o' the Banks o' Dee" by Stephen Glover, "Consider the Lilies" by R. Topliff, "Eve's Lamentation" by Matthew King, "I Love My Love" by Cino Pinsuti, "Battle Prayer" by Friedrich Himmel, "Call Me Thine Own" by Jacques Halévy, "Last Greeting" by Franz Schubert, and "Three Fishers" by John Hullah.

Let us pause and examine more closely a song from this section, composed by Charlotte Alington Barnard (1830–1869), an English songwriter who published under the pen name of Claribel. "I Cannot Sing the Old Songs" (see Appendix F, example 3) occupies about a page and a half, the average length of most songs in the method, and is generally reflective of the genre (see the accompanying compact disc).[101]

For the "round, full tone" required by this piece, the player is advised to pull the Diapason stop for the treble portion of the keyboard and the Melodia stop for the bass, both eight-foot stops that, we are informed, comprise the basic "foundation set of reeds by which all others are tuned." Only two expressive suggestions are offered: "slowly" and "mp" (mezzo-piano). The organ leads off with a short introduction, generally maintains a flowing eighth-note accompaniment pattern throughout, and ends with a generous coda. The piece's featured motivic contrivance tends toward a series of upward leaps followed by downward stepwise movement—the common musical "sigh" configuration mentioned earlier. The singing range is an octave and a third. The highest note, a C, predictably the final climax, is approached by a B-natural, the only accidental in the vocal part, adding a slight sentimental, sinuous stretching of the melody.

The text—"I cannot sing the old songs, they are too dear to me"—indulges in unabashed nostalgia. That songs from our past have the power to rekindle memory is one of the great fascinations of music. In this case, the nostalgia is ambivalent and bittersweet, and we are not told the exact cause of the singer's melancholia. Perhaps remembered songs from the old country, with their different language and contexts, are somehow disquieting and still cause

foolish tears to flow . . . their charm is sad and deep
their melodies would waken old sorrows from their sleep

and tho' all unforgotten still, and sadly sweet they be
I cannot sing the old songs . . . for visions come again
of golden dreams departed, and years of weary pain.

However, the song may relate to one of the many social inequities in American life during the nineteenth century: "the injustice done to Indians, the horrors of slavery, the subjugation of women, the suffering of the penniless, the abuse of alcohol, the addiction to gambling, and the indifferent treatment accorded the orphan, the insane and the blind."[102] Whether Barnard's song refers to one of these disorders or something more intimate and personal, such as lost family or remembered but irretrievable joys, we do not know. In fact, this song's appeal may lie in its lack of specificity; musical associations with love, family, places, and special occasions help us to mark the passage of time; singer and listener can supply their own meaningful past. Though many songs did detail specific common woes, this song's strategy of generalizing poignant feelings destined it for a larger audience. Its recurrent themes (both rhetorical and musical) beg the listener to recall memories (whether happy or sad) of home, childhood, and friends, or the difficulties of surviving in an imperfect democracy. Happily, by the end of the song, the final strain offers heavenly respite: "Perhaps when earthly fetters shall have set my spirit free / my voice may know the old songs, for all eternity."

We might be puzzled as to how, during a century with a reputation for social restraint, such open sentimentality was tolerated. The answer lies in the communal nature of the experience. To share a sorrowful moment as group catharsis within an appropriate context was sanctioned, whereas, under different circumstances, public display of emotion might be cause for embarrassment. Social analysts now feel that under the veneer of Victorian sentimentality and melancholia is a foundation of topical and social symbolism worthy of consideration and respect.[103] Popular song provided a "crossroads where Americans could meet, agree on essentials, and inwardly relive and integrate their most intense remembrances."[104]

The third part of the Estey *Method* is comprised of fourteen "National Airs," none with words (see the accompanying compact disc). Many home songbooks of the day were organized along nationalistic and ethnic lines and clearly reflected the immigrant nature of nineteenth-century American society. Anthems from Brazil, France, Italy, Ireland, Norway, Russia, Scotland, Sweden, Spain, Germany, Austria, and England make up a virtual roll call of America's multiethnic population.

"Selections of Sacred Music" complete the final section of the *Method* (see the accompanying compact disc). Church and brotherhood services used various musical preludes, interludes, and voluntaries to fill time while clergy and congregation moved from place to place during offertory, communion, and other segments of the ceremony. More-accomplished organists could use the written material as a point of departure and improvise to accommodate the exact length of time required by each activity. Religious hymns by such diverse composers as Martin Luther, Mason, Handel, Oliver, Beethoven, Phelps, and others again reflect the broad base on which American music developed. The *Estey Organ Method* had something for every occasion.

The emotionalism encountered in Barnard's "I Cannot Sing the Old Songs" is such a dominant feature of the repertoire that it is necessary to briefly highlight the music and text of two other songs from the Estey *Method*, "I Love My Love" (Appendix F, example 4),[105] and "Call Me Thine Own" (Appendix F, example 5).[106] Though both are love songs, they differ in interesting ways. The first was written for a popular audience after mid-century; the latter, originally written before mid-century, was adapted from a French opera.

The music of "I Love My Love" (see the accompanying compact disc) was composed by Ciro Pinsuti (1829–1888), a celebrated Italian singing master who divided his time between Italy and London and the writer of a few operas and some two hundred songs. The cantabile melody is paced in an easy 3/4 lilt marked allegretto moderato and is clearly reminiscent of Italian operatic style. "I Love My Love" contains more expression markings and changes in tempo than most songs, which presumably affords musicians room to swoon and heighten the drama at will. The echo effect, a loud motif followed by a soft imitation in another octave, is also used here as a dramatic device.[107]

The eight-measure organ introduction begins with the chorus melody, which is built on a four-note motif, ta-*dum*-ta-*dum* (short-long, short-long), with the first note anticipating the downbeat. The soloist then enters with two repetitions of an eight-note descending passage, each ending with a musical sigh. The third musical motif, a light staccato phrase with increasingly difficult intervals for the singer, eventually culminates—but only after an "e leggiero," "diminuendo," "rinforzando," "crescendo" to "forte," a sudden piano and ritenuto, and some brief echoing between voice and organ—on an extremely hazardous four-measure high F. Meanwhile, the organ repeats the primary theme to prepare the way for a final vocal chorus, which ultimately leads to yet another climax on high F, this time with a fermata, allowing the singer to show off his or her lung capacity. A short four-measure coda of ascending triplet patterns by the organ and a final landing on a chordless three-octave B-flat bring performers around to the next verse. The harmony harbors a few surprises in the form of chromatic passing chords, wrenching the ear just enough to make revelations of resolutions, and the organ part is nicely varied with imaginative fills at the end of phrases, allowing the singer a moment to breathe—which is doubtless needed after three verses of high F's. More complex than most, this is a challenging song, even for a practiced voice.

As in previous examples, the text, by Charles MacKay, tends toward cliché. The repeated chorus line, "I love my love, I love my love, because I know my love loves me" (totaling twelve rapid-fire repetitions of the word "love"), might remind one of some well-worn, generic folk lyric, the source of which is long forgotten. In the first verse, the object of the singer's affection, a lady, is compared with several songbirds: "Thou nightingale, . . . thou lark, . . . thou joyous thrush, up in the walnut tree." The "maiden fair and young" has her admirer bedazzled with the "pleasure in thine eyes, . . . music on thy tongue, . . . [and] glory on thy face." Captivated, he implores, "What says thy song? . . . What can the meaning be?" Then even to old age, "when the early summers pass, and care comes on with time, . . . still be it ours, in care's despite." Love helps one to endure.

The final song, "Call Me Thine Own" (see the accompanying compact disc), adapted from an 1835 opera, *LeClair*, was written by the French composer Jacques-François-Fromental-Élie Halévy (1799–1862). Though this song was written very early in the Victorian period, it was probably included in the 1882 revised edition of the Estey *Method* because of its popularity and appropriately gushy subject matter.

The song begins andantino espressivo, with a ten-measure organ introduction consisting of triplets in thirds in the treble part and, in the bass, a root note followed by a chord in an eighth note/eighth rest sequence. The slow, sparse "boom-chunk" accompaniment pattern (usually more useful in marches than in love songs) is evidently an attempt to approximate the pizzicato strings called for in the original score, or possibly to imitate a lute or a guitar plucked with a plectrum. This accompaniment then continues without the triplet motif, allowing the vocalist ample room to sink or swim. As with the previous selection, the vocal line is more difficult than most, requiring of the singer a range of an octave and a sixth, the ability to navigate a few accidentals, and the confidence to conquer the melody's several vocally challenging leaps. The austere accompaniment, wide range, tricky accidentals, and a modulation leave the listener hoping for a vocalist with some talent because toward the end the now-familiar climactic fermata places the soloist on a high G, sustaining the "-ing" of "endearing," a potentially precarious and unflattering syllable for any singer. The organ concludes the piece with a coda nearly identical to the introduction.

The text resembles that of most love songs in that the songwriter has filled it with archetypal images and commonplace symbolism that diffused from favorite song to favorite song.[108] Appropriately Victorian in spirit, love is depicted as a formal, virtuous, caring, idealized form of affectionate companionship, the answer to an age filled with confusion and contradiction. The song invites us to believe that to be loved (i.e., to be called "thine own"), whether at home, through family ties, or by a mate, imparts hope and cheer along life's pathways and enables one to endure life's difficulties. Love evokes "whispers of home," that most hallowed Victorian haven, the shelter against all woe. Love is sacred, "for only thro' faith are we secure," and though "all else may fail, with love in our hearts, heaven still remains." It matters not that "years may roll on, youth's dreams may leave us, hopes faint and die that lighted our way, trials may come, sorrows may grieve us, friends may depart, or falsely betray, [for] love shall prevail." The condition reflected in this last excerpt suggests the insecurities of aging, separation, and deception, and the concerns of a migrant population. "Call Me Thine Own" describes a genderless and sexless love; commitment and dedication replace physical passion and desire. No matter "what lies before us, sorrow or joy," to be called "thine own" gives "each bond . . . fresh vigor" and victory "o'er life's tempests." Love strengthens and redeems.

To summarize, there is much to appreciate about the reed organ: musically it engaged immense numbers of players, singers, and listeners; financially, the world of musical enterprise, including composers and arrangers who wrote fresh new pieces every year, profited enormously from the reed organ's popularity; and culturally, the instrument spawned one of the most vigorous periods of amateur music-making in American history.[109]

The three recurring images that permeated the Victorian era were the home, the church, and the factory; together they provided an important focus for the great majority of nineteenth-century Americans. The reed organ, embodying the essence of Victorian culture, carries associations with all three. Another institution, also important for sorting out emerging social and economic constructs, was the marketplace. It was here that the mold for today's immensely powerful and pervasive popular consumer culture was formed. Victorian symbols were conspicuous as merchandisers capitalized on archetypal images they ingeniously combined with their products.

In the symbolism connected with reed organs, the dichotomies are striking. Thus far in this study, we have seen how the reed organ accommodated both sacred and secular contexts, upper- and lower-class needs, and male and female conventions. Women carried the greatest burden of symbolism and were portrayed as materialistic consumers on one hand, saintly revivalists on the other. In Victorian sensibility, that unrestrained artistic emotionalism should become entangled with conservative social restraint seems unavoidable. Conflicts about ownership and wealth versus moralistic puritan dispositions are equally complicated.[110] I have suggested how the reed organ and its associated music repertoires provide a means to better understand these and other social and aesthetic confusions typical of the age. In our effort to better assess the situation, it becomes evident that in the annals of nineteenth-century American history, the reed organ, as an artifact of material culture, is of considerable importance.

II

The Estey Saga

ESTEY ORGAN
ESTABLISHED
1846

ESTEY ORGAN
ESTABLISHED
1846

ESTEY ORGANS

ESTEY · ORGAN · COMPANY

The Perfect Melodeon

PROLOGUE

The Estey ancestry is traceable to English origins. Early in the seventeenth century the Esteys arrived in America and took up residence in the Massachusetts colony. One Estey descendant, Mary Towne, even became a victim of the infamous Salem witch trials in 1692. Like many other settlers, the Estey clan gradually migrated to neighboring areas. Early in the nineteenth century, Isaac and Patty Forbes Estey moved from Royalston, Massachusetts, to Hinsdale, New Hampshire, into a house on the "east road," which led from Hinsdale village to Chesterfield. There Jacob Estey was born on September 30, 1814.

Since supporting a family of seven children on a road builder's salary was evidently beyond the means of Isaac Estey,[1] Jacob, at the age of four, was "farmed out" to Alvin Shattuck, a Hinsdale resident.[2] In spite of initially being the pet of the family, it was recorded that Jacob, when he was thirteen, ran away because of mistreatment. Later he was said to have been reluctant to speak of this period of his life, saying only, "I thought they whipped me too much when I didn't deserve it."[3]

On Monday, April 14, 1828, while Shattuck was away driving logs on the Connecticut River, a hired man, seeing the marks on Jacob's back and legs, a result of "the usual Sunday interview with Shattuck and his wife,"[4] assisted him in running away. In classic fashion, "With his bundle of clothes under his arm and two dollars in his pocket," Jacob took to the woods and joined one of his brothers in Worcester, Massachusetts.[5]

Jacob worked as a farmer in towns neighboring Worcester; his salary was six

Figure 29.
Estey "Industrial
Genealogy" catalogue
illustration, c. 1931

dollars a month, later increased to "twelve or fifteen dollars"—good wages at the time. He continued to be haunted by the possibility of being returned to the Shattucks. The hired man who aided in his escape generously covered for him, but not until the man told him, "Why, Jacob, I never would let them take you back in this world. I would spill my last drop of blood for you before they should do it!" were Jacob's apprehensions finally mitigated.[6] Those who later heard Estey recount this story commented that he had no lingering bitterness.

As Estey took control of his life, winter provided him with time to acquire some education by bartering odd jobs for board and instruction. After four years of farming, the seventeen-year-old Estey took up an apprenticeship as a maker of lead pipes and copper pumps for a Worcester plumber, Thomas Sutton.[7] While there, young Estey graduated from the Worcester Manual Labor Academy.

The death of Jacob's father on December 31, 1834, briefly brought the twenty-year-old back to Hinsdale, after which he decided to move to the neighboring town of Brattleboro, Vermont (see Appendix B, map of central New England). Brattleboro, of course, had no idea how enormously Estey's relocation would impact the village's future.

Historically, Brattleboro, now the largest town in southeastern Vermont,[8] in many ways typifies the quintessential New England village (figure 30). Perhaps best known for its fashionable "water cures," exactly why Brattleboro became an important center for reed organ manufacture is, on the surface, a bit of a mystery. Generally, industrial manufacturing concerns were better suited to urban environments. True, the town is on the Connecticut River,[9] a central feature in New England topography and one that was essential for early trade and migration throughout the region.[10] But as a valley town facing the river on the east (the boundary shared by Vermont and New Hampshire, with the latter "owning" the river) and abutting the expansive Green Mountain range on the west, we might wonder what defining element of Brattleboro caused it to blossom so bountifully as a center for the manufacture of reed organs.

One answer has to do with the extensive lineage of reed organ builders in the town, a tangled history I shall soon broach. Also, since the major source of energy for mills and factories throughout the 1700s and well into the 1800s was water power, Brattleboro, like numerous other New England towns, was well situated to take advantage of the free rushing water—in this case the Whetstone Brook, a middling tributary that wanders through the center of Brattleboro into the Connecticut River (see Appendix B, map of Brattleboro) and is historically renowned for an occasional seasonal flooding tantrum. A precipitous drop in elevation from the Green Mountains made the Whetstone most useful as an energy source. Streamside sites were especially desirable during the period when small shops and individual craftsmen formed the sum of early American production. So it comes as no surprise that until the advent of steam power, all of Brattleboro's early melodeon makers, including Jacob Estey, located their shops

Figure 30.
Brattleboro in 1849

along the Whetstone Brook. Gradually, as steam power took over, the need to situate next to running water ceased to be a concern. By that time, Brattleboro melodeon makers had a firm foothold in the area. But eventually Estey's organ company trumped them all.

Jacob Estey's amazing career officially began when he commenced working for Stephen Parker, the proprietor of a Brattleboro pipe and pump (i.e., plumbing) concern. Before long, Parker offered to sell Estey the business for $200, supposedly half of what it was worth. The budding young entrepreneur returned to Worcester, where he had been more recently employed, to raise the sum. Since he collected only the exact amount necessary for the transaction and was unwilling to borrow more, Estey reportedly walked the entire distance back to Brattleboro.[11] Meanwhile, Parker had changed his mind, saying that he would sell his business only if Jacob would also buy his house and tools. The price had risen appreciably to the sum of $1,275. Though this was a large amount, Estey's judgment told him that there was still a profit to be made in the deal, and at the Brattleboro law office of Keyes & Bradley, on a leap of faith, he signed a contract of intent with Parker.

With grave misgivings, feeling that he may have assumed an obligation that could not be fulfilled, Estey approached "Uncle" John Stearns, an old friend twelve years his senior, for advice.[12] Stearns's opinion was that Jacob had surely "got stuck like the devil" but upon reflection added, "If you have made a good trade, Jake, I'll help you, otherwise not a red."[13] Stearns and another friend, Oliver Adams, helped Jacob negotiate.

Meanwhile, Parker (who evidently was not as generous as some records might suggest) once again reneged, offering instead $50 to be released from the contract. The contract, however, set forth a binder of $500, to which Stearns held Parker. This brought matters to a focus, and Estey took possession of his newly acquired business and house in 1835, a few months before his twenty-first birthday. Stearns and Adams kindly loaned Jacob additional money for the down payment.

Two years later, Estey married Desdemona Wood and set up housekeeping in Parker's small cottage on the north corner of Canal Street and Homestead Place. They lived there until 1854, when a new house was built on the same site. This residence, standing today and little altered, was to be their lifetime home (figure 31).

Estey's new plumbing shop was in "the old tannery building," one of the first water mills constructed in Brattleboro and the site of many early industrial efforts (figure 32).[14] The best known of these were the Dunklee Sewing Silk & Twist Company, Buddington & Brother Grain Company, and the Valley Mills Company, the name when Estey bought it.[15] The building itself was originally a two-story Guilford church that had been dismantled and brought to Brattleboro; another story was added later.[16] Afterward, when the railroad was extended through a covered bridge over the Whetstone Brook, a corner of the building had to be removed to accommodate the railroad tracks. The building burned in December 1886, and today only a few foundation stones remain.

Information concerning Estey's initial business activity remains rather sketchy. The earliest newspaper entry I found in this regard, dated March 21, 1839, reported the first of many "connections in business," this one with William Briggs for the manufacture of pipes and pumps.[17] Estey's proclivity toward entrepreneurship was already becoming evident; he was to carry on a successful plumbing trade for more than fifteen years.

Among Brattleboro's growing list of businesses were some of New England's first melodeon makers, whose efforts helped lay the foundation for Jacob Estey's organ building empire. Many of these early craftsmen had distinguished and noteworthy careers in the music industry, some more successful than others.[18]

Figure 31.
Jacob and Desdemona
Estey's home

BRATTLEBORO'S EARLY MELODEON MAKERS

Facts concerning the origins and growth of the organ business in Brattleboro are reasonably well documented, though wishful thinking and romantic retrospect have on occasion clouded reality. Some responsibility for this situation falls to a group of professional chroniclers who traveled from town to town recording the lives and times of important personages.[19] These historians, whose livelihood depended on flattering reportage of the accomplishments of those who could pay, were understandably at the mercy of their employers. Another problem is that myth often makes for a more exciting story than does truth, and it was not unusual for the truth to expand in the heat of self-promotional aggrandizement. Pretentious advertising, if relentlessly and compellingly applied, will eventually take on the guise of fact.[20]

For instance, the Estey Organ Company always implied, if not claimed outright, 1846 as its date of origin, even though no Estey involvement was recorded until 1852. He was not even listed as a partner until 1853. Perhaps we can forgive these little liberties, for embellishing the truth was and still is an accepted practice in American commerce and merchandising. Fortunately, there are enough

Figure 32.
Site of Estey's first
plumbing shop in 1856

reliable records to document a line of descent from the earliest efforts at reed organ production in Vermont to Estey's involvement. Not all of Brattleboro's early organ pioneers, however, had Jacob Estey's business acumen. Fleeting partnerships and evaporating pools of capital caused many of them to abandon their cottage industries; relocation and the search for more successful markets characterized the age. The contributions of these early music merchants, businessmen, and instrument makers were nonetheless appreciable. Though continual reorganization and shuffling of ownership were the norm, these resourceful, inventive men provided enough momentum and continuity to transform a small industry into a major manufacturing enterprise that eventually paid off under the direction of Jacob Estey. The following chronology outlines the personalities and innovations of these irrepressible Brattleboro organ pioneers.

1839: Woodbury & Kibling

The first entry relevant to the development of music-related enterprise in Brattleboro appeared in the *Vermont Phoenix* exactly two months after Jacob Estey's announcement of his pipe and pump partnership with William Briggs. It put on record the opening of Brattleboro's new and probably first music store by John Woodbury and Joseph Kibling. The advertisement, dated May 21, 1839, announced a "new music and Umbrella store." Little is known of the history of John Woodbury except that he was born in Dummerston, Vermont, lived in Brattleboro for most of his life, and had established a reputation as an ingenious machinist. At this particular time he was also making bass and double-bass viols, instruments used extensively in churches for pitch orientation and for reinforcement of the vocal bass lines of hymns. Even less is known of Kibling, and their partnership was evidently short-lived. The firm probably made no reed instruments.

1841: Woodbury & Burditt

Riley Burditt was born on December 29, 1819, on West Hill, Putney, Vermont. Burditt was to become an enduring and significant figure in the development of reed organs in Brattleboro and later in the Midwest. As a youth he moved to Brookline and then to Newfane, where he remained with his family until he was nine years old. The young Burditt then worked on the farm of Warren Richmond in Westminster, Vermont, where he was given three months of schooling each year.[21] At sixteen he returned to Putney and worked as a clerk in Isaac Grout's store. During the winter months, "armed with a violin by which to test voices," he taught in schools as a singing master.

At eighteen Burditt began developing his mechanical ability by working with Jonathan Cutler, a local machinist. Two years later he further honed his skills working in Colt's gun factory in Paterson, New Jersey. As will be seen, Burditt's proficiencies in music, commercial business, and technology combined to make him an important catalyst in Brattleboro's melodeon business.

In his travels as an itinerant singing teacher, Burditt met John Woodbury, with whom he began making and selling violins, cellos, double basses, and viols. They soon shared ownership in Woodbury's Brattleboro music shop.[22]

1842: Foster & Thayer

All records credit the actual beginnings of Brattleboro's reed organ industry to Samuel H. Jones. One of ten children, Jones was born in Berlin, New Hampshire, on March 30, 1822. He was educated in the common schools and academies of Keene and Jaffrey, after which time he settled in Keene, where he learned the cabinetmaker's trade. Jones evidently showed mechanical ability as a youngster: he was said to have invented a clever device on the rotary engine. Mary Cabot, an important Brattleboro chronicler (see note 19), cites Jones as "the oldest reed organ maker in New England, and probably in the country."[23] This is questionable since, as mentioned earlier, A. M. Peaseley of Boston and others were issued U.S. patents for reed organs before Jones was born. It is likely Cabot meant the oldest *living* maker.

Jones finished his apprenticeship in December 1842. He then moved to Winchester, New Hampshire, and worked for Joseph Foster (1805–1875) and Albert Thayer, manufacturers of church and parlor pipe organs. Though Foster had reportedly constructed a reed instrument in 1831, the melodeon business was yet to be developed. Besides pipe organs, what Jones probably saw upon arrival at the Winchester shop were only a few patterns for melodeons and Foster's novel reed instrument. It was of the curious rocking variety mentioned earlier, playable on lap or table, small enough to carry, with bellows worked up and down by the player's left forearm (thus the nickname "elbow machine"). Foster's had a three-octave range, ivory-covered keys, and reeds cut from common sheet brass.[24]

Some rocking melodeons of this type were mounted on folding legs for stability and comfort. Records tell how Alonzo H. Hines (son of Isaac Hines, who will soon figure in this account), a local professional musician, earned his living traveling "thousands of miles on his trips through the country" playing "a quaint specimen of the folding organ of that period" for dances and festive occasions.[25]

1844: Jones, Woodbury, & Burditt

In 1844 Foster left the partnership by mutual consent to establish his own organ and melodeon business in Keene, New Hampshire. Samuel Jones stayed in Winchester, manufacturing a limited number of instruments on his own. (It is not known what happened to Thayer.) As with many craft endeavors in this preindustrial era, Jones's beginnings were modest: the concern initially owned only one machine, a foot-powered lathe. Soon he hired his youngest brother, Joseph L. Jones, and a Whitingham boy, Walter Jewell, to help build a working force.

Since the small factory had limited resources, they occasionally visited the now historically important Graves Brothers' brass instrument factory in Winchester, New Hampshire, then the largest brass instrument manufacturer in New England, "to do a little work by power," mostly cutting ivory key covers from African and Indian elephant tusks.[26]

As things progressed, Jones met Riley Burditt (later changed to Burdett), who stopped in Winchester every two weeks to teach singing. It seems Burditt and Woodbury's music store business in Brattleboro was going well enough to expand their line of instruments, for an 1845 advertisement announced that they were now acting as agents for a Boston piano manufacturing company headed by Stephen W. Marsh.[27] An agreement was reached in May 1846, and on June 15 "the Jones brothers loaded upon a hayrack all their factory and personal belongings, including two workbenches, and with two horses started for their [Brattleboro] destination."[28] Thus Sam Jones and Burditt began the manufacturing of melodeons in Brattleboro.

1846: S. H. Jones & Company

In Brattleboro, the Jones brothers rented three rooms on the upper floor of Smith & Woodcock's gristmill (later owned by Gaines & Crosby, Buddington, and Larkin; the roadway was eventually named Larkin Street) and began work as S. H. Jones & Company (figure 33). The flour mill, first used as a paper mill,

Figure 33.
Smith & Woodcock's
gristmill, site of the Jones
brothers' melodeon shop
in Centerville, Vermont,
1846

was situated in Centerville, an area between Brattleboro and West Brattleboro. Woodbury and Burditt bought in as half partners and in addition maintained a "sales department" in their music store in Steen's building at the corner of Main and High Streets. There they sold instruction books and musical merchandise as well as instruments.

Because reed organ production was in its infancy, it took Jones the summer and autumn of 1846 to design and mobilize machinery for manufacturing the instruments. A later report gave tribute to the ingenuity and efficiency of Jones's mechanical creations by noting that "during the seven years it has since been in use, no alterations in the general construction and arrangement have been found necessary."[29] This clearly marks the beginning of a transitional phase from what had previously been a small shop operated by one or two individuals to a larger, more production-oriented situation. (The reader should also remember that this is the year the Estey company claimed as its founding date.)

Several reports confirm[30] that the first melodeons were finished in November 1846, as a result of Jones & Company's taking orders earlier in the spring of the same year.[31] The pioneer period of the new enterprise was not without its troubles, however. An account in the *Brattleboro Eagle* remarked that "at that time the reed instrument was a comparatively new thing, but few having been made in this country, and a majority of those by very inexperienced workmen. Their music—if such it might be called—was better adapted to accompany the scraping hum of a wood sawyer, or to marshal together the web-footed bipeds of a farmer's barnyard. In consequence of these imperfections, very unfavorable impressions in regard to the quality and capacity of these instruments had so generally prevailed that our manufacturer had many difficulties to encounter, discouragement to bear, and violent prejudices to contend with."[32]

Undaunted, Jones & Company took their first instruments to Boston as samples and obtained a number of orders. They made connections with a prominent urban dealer, E. H. Wade, and arranged to have him sell their melodeons and seraphines through his Boston musical merchandising concern at 176 Washington Street. Boston was by far the most important center in the northeast for music marketing. It was a logical step for Jones to place instruments in an urban center for maximum exposure, since publicity and distribution from Brattleboro was as yet limited.

Meanwhile, Burditt learned to voice and tune reeds. Before mechanization brass tongues were cut out by hand, hammered and filed to a thickness that was thought to produce the best vibration, and riveted to an appropriately sized frame. Final tuning was done by hand. Burditt himself later commented in a court proceeding that organ reeds at this stage of development sounded "very coarse, and I might say repulsive."[33] Techniques for improving the tone and timbral variety of the reed organ were still relatively new, and some aspects of voicing, such as curving and twisting the tongue to reduce high harmonics and produce a smooth timbre, were not yet common knowledge. Other American organ makers were looking for solutions to the same problem,[34] though they worked independently and in relative isolation and did not identify themselves collectively as a trade.[35] Gellerman notes that "the number of reed organs built in the United States before 1846 was exceedingly small. Elias P. Needham and Emmons Hamlin, in a patent hearing in 1860, both estimated that the total number of reed organs of all kinds built in this country before 1846 was less than three hundred. The organs were hand-made in small shops by individual craftsmen who usually built a variety of different instruments."[36] Concentrated experimentation was just beginning to bring the reed organ to a satisfactory level of musical refinement and efficacy.

1847–1850: Jones & Burditt

In May 1847 Burditt shifted emphasis by trading his interest in Woodbury's music store for Woodbury's interest in S. H. Jones & Company. By the end of that year, Woodbury had begun to list his concern as a "Music & Fancy Goods Store" and his advertisements became longer and bolder in their claims. In 1849 he began selling watches and jewelry as well. Woodbury maintained his Brattleboro store and continued to manufacture violins until he eventually moved a few miles east to Keene, New Hampshire, where he took up engraving. In 1871, having fallen on hard times, Woodbury was found dead in a Keene shoe shop where he had been allowed to spend the night. He was sixty-five years old.

Meanwhile, the new arrangement for manufacturing melodeons was renamed Jones & Burditt. Up to this point about forty instruments had been made. By the fall of 1848 the firm was employing seven workmen — all the shop could handle. Jones and Burditt realized an appreciable margin of success in the three years they worked together and soon had to relocate to accommodate an expanding operation. First they rented an office at the corner of Main and Elliot Streets (the site later occupied by the Revere House, a landmark hotel), and in November 1848 they moved the factory itself from the flour mill to the "Typographic Building" on Canal Street. An ell of the building that adjoined the paper mill was vacated by Hollister's silk factory and provided enough space for a combined office, salesroom, and work area. Consolidation of this sort became a logical step for fledgling business ventures, and it gave owners greater control over what began to resemble a true manufacturing operation.

During this period, the business was in full swing. The local newspaper later reported that Jones and Burditt had increased the number of workmen to between twelve and fourteen.[37] This is somewhat of an increase over an 1850 census report, which documented a force of ten men who worked for an average wage of $33 per month. The census report goes on to estimate production of Jones & Burditt for 1850 at seventy-five instruments.[38] They had begun to diversify their line of organs, offering instruments with "any number" of reed sets and with assurances of "any quality and strength of tone required." An entry in the *Brattleboro Eagle* waxed poetic: "The reed instrument metamorphed [sic] from a contemptible 'squeaker' to a beautiful and desirable parlor ornament whose zephyr-like tones would bear no mean comparison to Apollo's Lyre."[39] In addition, the firm repaired and tuned pianos, seraphines, melodeons, and accordions.

It is also noteworthy that on February 20, 1849, with great ceremony, the last section of the Vermont & Massachusetts Railroad was formally opened. It effectively connected Brattleboro with many local stations and, most importantly, with Boston. On the dedication run a train carried fifteen hundred people, including many Boston and New England dignitaries, into Brattleboro. A crowd of four thousand to five thousand people welcomed them with cannon salutes, speeches, parades, banquets, dances, and other festivities.

Despite confrontations between railroad laborers and local authorities, the state had its first route established by 1848, and by 1851 four hundred miles of track connected most key interstate regions.[40] A line to Montreal also created economic opportunities, most of which were undermined by inexperienced management, tangled interests, and weak financial foundations. Nevertheless, the "railroad reoriented everything it touched, and it touched nearly everything."[41] The railroad became the lifeline of Estey's enterprise, for it opened commercial opportunities in urban centers across America and in Canada. The establishment of connections with Boston, New York, and Albany created a long-looked-for access to the world's markets.

1851: Burditt & Carpenter

In August 1851 Sam Jones evidently decided to pursue an alternative livelihood. A notice appeared in the *Semi-Weekly Eagle* officially announcing the dissolution of the seemingly successful Jones-Burditt partnership.[42] For the next two years, Jones and a Mr. Crossett of Bennington reportedly worked in Maryland and then Virginia, where they operated a patent machine for cutting barrel staves. Jones's younger brother, Joseph, continued to work with Burditt.

Two weeks after Jones's departure, Edwin B. Carpenter, a Guilford farmer (the grandson of Colonel Benjamin Carpenter, a Revolutionary War hero and lieutenant governor of Vermont) who had taken a fancy to reed organs through selling them as an avocation, expressed an interest in buying the share left by Jones. On August 22, 1851, the new firm of Burditt & Carpenter was formally announced, along with an invitation for the public to call, examine, and test their new line of double and single Aeolians of various sizes. Clearly, the days of harsh-toned seraphines and small melodeons were passing as refined models emerged. The new partners were especially proud of their new line of Aeolian Seraphines.[43] "[The Seraphine] has features that give it greater musical flexibility than lap organs have. Most important is the elevation of the case on legs, with swell and bellows pedals beneath. This frees the player's left arm and hand from pumping and operating the loud-soft shutter, and so allows a more agile technique and broader repertoire."[44]

The following month they advertised for "two young men from fifteen to twenty years of age to learn the finishing business," which testifies to their continuing growth. Soon thereafter, they moved into two stories of a newly completed building where Jacob Estey carried on his plumbing business. The workforce was increased to eighteen. This is also the first occasion (of which we are aware) on which Estey and the melodeon connect.

Burditt & Carpenter continued in business for a little over a year, manufacturing about 250 instruments with a total value of $12,000 to $15,000. Toward the end of this period newspaper advertisements listed double and single Aeolians, Aeolian Seraphines, reed organs, and pianos for sale on both retail and wholesale terms, as well as instruction books, tuning forks, pitch pipes, and other musical wares.

Estey and the Melodeon

Throughout the 1840s Estey continued expanding his business dealings, which included a brief sojourn in the nearby town of Townshend. There he formed a partnership with Deacon William A. Dutton, Dutton providing the capital. In 1847 Estey moved his plumbing concern back to Brattleboro. By this time he had not only developed a growing trade in water pipes and pumps, but had also formed the company of McDonald & Estey, dealers in slate and marble products, especially gravestones.[45] In 1850 Estey and Dutton cooperatively took over

Figure 34.

Estey's second plumbing

shop, c. 1860

the gravestone venture, and Dutton's brother-in-law, John H. Kathan, joined the partnership in 1854, forming the company of Estey & Kathan. Eventually Estey sold his share to Kathan.

In a newspaper ad, Estey announced that "lumber and most kinds of produce [were] taken in exchange" for his plumbing wares.[46] Understanding that customers had more raw materials than money, Estey's use of the old system of bartering for goods probably enabled him to establish a lumber business as well. In an 1847 newspaper ad he was selling appreciable quantities of "seasoned pine of the 1st and 2nd quality"[47]; a later advertisement mentioned "lumber, spruce clapboards, spruce shingles, and floor boards" for sale.[48] This experience in the wood trade would prove useful later.

There is little doubt that Estey's business acumen and entrepreneurial savvy matured over this period of ten to fifteen years. His clientele began to extend into New Hampshire, Massachusetts, and eastern New York. In time, he developed a keen sense of salesmanship; stories mention his disconcerting habit of whittling wood while "driving a sharp bargain."[49] In 1850 Estey built a two-story shop by the Whetstone brook just south of the Main Street bridge (figure 34), part of which was rented to the melodeon makers Riley Burditt and Edwin B. Carpenter.[50]

During this time old methods of making plumbing wares—pouring molten lead into a mold, cutting it into ten- or twelve-foot chunks, and then "drawing it out to any desired size over a steel rod"—were being replaced with newer techniques.[51] These and other developments probably motivated Estey to begin applying additional investment money outside of the pipe and pump trade. So, in addition to his other business interests, Estey further expanded his concern by buying Riley Burditt's portion of E. B. Carpenter & Company's melodeon business on February 1, 1852, for the sum of $2,700. This marked Estey's official entry into the manufacture of reed organs.

1852: E. B. Carpenter & Company

Carpenter may have been in some financial difficulty at this point, for if a story in an 1876 Estey Cottage Organ catalogue can be believed, Estey was said to have "reluctantly consented to accept an interest in the business as payment of rent due him." Whatever the reason, Jacob Estey bought up the share left by Burditt. On February 9, 1852, E. B. Carpenter & Company succeeded Burditt & Carpenter. Though Burditt gave up his share in the business, he continued to work in the factory as head tuner and superintendent. It appears Burditt's involvement in Brattleboro's civic scene increased during this period, as he was listed as a new member of the Vermont and New Hampshire Musical Association and elected foreman for the Fire Engine Company No. 3. By this time Carpenter's organ company reportedly had twenty-five men in its employ.

The facts surrounding Estey's entry into organ manufacture have become embellished over time. Local lore has it that Estey was the savior of a insignificant and sinking venture that had been run by seemingly irresponsible "originators" who "lost heart in the enterprise" and were "anxious to get out of the business" so they could rush to California to look for gold.[52] On the contrary, we have seen that Carpenter and Burditt were not particularly irresponsible and, as will be seen, most likely did not go to California.

It is probable, however, that some employees did leave at this juncture to get rich quick in the West. By 1850 eleven hundred Vermonters had actually reached California; many more had either turned back or died on the way. Most went by sea, some sailing around Cape Horn, while others crossed the isthmus by mule train through Panama, Nicaragua, or Vera Cruz. The euphoria was short lived, however, since when the mining boom ceased by the mid-1850s at least a third of the Vermont forty-niners had returned home or settled in the Midwest.[53]

Though Estey may have had enough insight to know "that the musical instinct was just awakening in the American people," he probably fell into the organ business simply because of the "originators'" search for venture capital, a prime motivation that often precipitated the continual shuffling of ownership and organization characteristic of the age.[54] Romantic embellishment notwithstanding, Jacob Estey did indeed make practical contributions to the developing enterprise: investment money, diversified interests, business sense, and factory space.

His immediate involvement in the firm was probably minimal because he knew little about melodeon manufacture and, in his own words, "didn't know a note of music and so I didn't waste any time playing on the melodeons."[55] Though Estey was no musician, he instinctively enjoyed the new enterprise and intuitively anticipated the potential of melodeon manufacture. His travels no doubt informed him of the fact that home music-making was fast becoming an American passion.

As mentioned earlier, Stephen Foster's "Old Folks at Home" and "My Old Kentucky Home," both issued in the early 1850s, were performed and enjoyed nationwide,[56] and by November 1854 publishers had sold 130,000 and 90,000 copies, respectively.[57] Lowell Mason's book of hymns, *Carmina Sacra*, and its supplement had sold half a million copies by 1858.[58] And "the Swedish Nightingale," Jenny Lind—only one of many singers and performers whom promoters such as P. T. Barnum brought before American audiences during this period—intensified the nation's interest in music with her beautiful renditions of operatic arias and sentimental songs such as "Home, Sweet Home." Surely Estey observed that keyboards and "instruments of general use" were increasingly finding their way into people's parlors and that singing was fast becoming an especially important part of the nation's expressive culture. There is little doubt that melodeons were coming to increasingly fascinate him.

Installing melodeons in people's parlors, however, required transportation and distribution. Since transportation by the freight boats that plied the Connecticut River between Hartford and Bellows Falls, Vermont, belonged generally to an earlier era, it seems improbable that organs made in Brattleboro utilized this form of distribution.[59] During Estey's early involvement with the reed organ business, when he traveled the northeastern territory in a wagon, it was reported that he enjoyed packing a few melodeons amongst the pipes, pumps, and other plumbing wares he sold as part of his initial enterprise. As his involvement with the nascent organ business rapidly increased, Estey "took on himself the duties of salesman, and for several years he personally sold the whole product of the modest factory."[60] Transport was by horse and wagon over a rather large mountainous territory that included New Hampshire, Massachusetts, Vermont, "York State," and eastern Canada. The territory would vary as trade prospects dictated. He was said to have never returned from a trip with his stock of melodeons unsold. From that time, the life of Jacob Estey was inextricably linked with the development of the reed organ.

Estey understood that one part of the business was good for the other: selling plumbing wares provided an introduction for his new musical product, and the instruments in turn provided a friendly medium with which to delight and mesmerize his customers. Since he was constantly on the lookout for new business possibilities, the idea of having a few extra goods to hawk interested him, and the melodeons undoubtedly enhanced his general sales pitch. This was not particularly innovative since, after all, itinerant Yankee peddlers had always carried a wide variety of items, including musical instruments. Yet, he was likely the only plumbing engineer in the region who peddled pipes, pumps, and melodeons at the same time. "Sometimes I took a boy along to play on them," he would say, "and sometimes I found someone in the vicinity to come into the farmers' houses and show them off. If I could get an instrument into a neighborhood there was pretty sure to be a call for others."[61]

He later learned a few chords so he could join in on a favorite hymn or demonstrate an organ on his own. Cabot reports that "the price of the instruments varied from $75 to $225; sales were rarely made for cash down; the terms were usually a note at twelve months. Often the trade was in barter—cheese, butter or other farm produce, horses from Canada, young cattle, anything that the shrewd Yankee knew could be readily turned into cash."[62] The keys to Estey's success were his willingness to negotiate time payments and to barter for anything he felt could be quickly converted into capital.[63]

Traveling by wagon was by necessity a seasonal activity: plumbing supplies were fabricated in the winter and marketed in the summer. Even in the summer, traversing the mountainous ranges of rural New England must have been an arduous task. We must also respect and admire Estey's ambition and determination if one appreciates the fact that topographical and economic difficulties generally inhibited manufacture and industry in Vermont. Overall, the state seemed unable to achieve the same level of industrial success that Connecticut and Massachusetts enjoyed. Except for those towns that produced specialty items—Rutland, Dorset, and Fair Haven in marble quarrying, Barre in granite products, St. Johnsbury in platform scales, and Bennington in carpenter's rules, pottery, and glass—industrialization in Vermont did not readily thrive.[64]

1853: I. Hines & Company

In February 1853, one year after Estey's first became involved with the melodeon business, Isaac Hines arrived on the scene with investment capital and bought up Carpenter's share. Carpenter probably felt a squeeze from the new ownership since, instead of staying with the new firm, he continued to manufacture organs in a new location over Clark's planning mill near the railroad depot. Perhaps he had hopes of reconstructing the profitable situation he shared earlier with Burditt during 1850 and 1851. Through the remainder of 1853, Carpenter maintained his company name and line of instruments but on a smaller scale.

In 1853 the new firm's name was changed to I. Hines & Company. Records show that the enterprise had in its employ such names as Foster, Rose, Gray, White, and the tenacious Burditt, who, with a few others, decided to remain with the new ownership.

H. P. Green, a local cabinetmaker by trade (who has a documented history of various partnerships in furniture manufacturing and had extensive knowledge of music), also developed a practical interest in the melodeon business. Green must have shown up soon after Carpenter moved out, because in May 1853 an announcement was made that Isaac Hines, Jacob Estey, and H. P. Green had purchased and at last taken full control of Carpenter's share. It is likely that Green not only became a musical force in the firm, but also applied his woodworking know-how to melodeon case design. This juncture also marked the first time Estey had officially and publicly announced his entry into the organ business.

All the while I. Hines & Company continued business on "a greatly enlarged scale." The major part of the factory operation was now probably carried out by Green and Burditt, since they were familiar with the actual manufacturing process (with Burditt probably being the most technically proficient and musically literate of them all). They added Carhart's Patent Melodeon to their inventory selection, manufactured the largest organ yet produced by the company, and maintained a high profile, for instance, by winning top honors for a melodeon exhibited at the Windham County fair.

The Brattleboro chronicler Mary Cabot states that during this time I. Hines & Company employed six to eight men and produced six or seven melodeons a month, which, if her record is accurate, is quite a retreat from previously stated tallies.[65] Possibly the instruments were becoming larger and more complex, so that fewer were produced. The discrepancy is compounded by a newspaper article of this period that reported a workforce of twenty.[66] Perhaps some of the workmen followed Carpenter, who, as noted, continued manufacturing elsewhere. To further confuse matters, the *Musical Courier* reported that "at the time he [Carpenter] and Burdette [sic] were together their books show that they had 35 men in their employ instead of six, as the Brattleboro 'History' states."[67] This points up the difficulty of accurately ascertaining data from conflicting historical records.

1854: Jones, Carpenter, & Woods

Meanwhile, Samuel H. Jones, who had sold out to Carpenter in the first place, returned from Maryland in the fall of 1853, rejoined forces with Carpenter's new enterprise, and once again began making melodeons. Soon after, George Woods, a young native of Keene, New Hampshire, who had worked in Boston, joined the partners, and in July 1854 they established the firm of Jones, Carpenter, & Woods. In addition to selling melodeons and pianos, they offered repair and tuning for these and a variety of other instruments. Newspaper advertisements confirm that Carpenter was in direct competition with the newly formed I. Hines & Company. The fact that the village of Brattleboro supported two organ factories suggests that the business of making melodeons must have been relatively profitable—at least for a while.

Figure 35.
E. P. Carpenter Organ
Company manufactory

The three partners eventually dissolved their business relationship in January 1856, with Woods moving to Boston and Jones following soon thereafter. Woods eventually became a very prominent organ and piano manufacturer in Boston, and many of his reed organs were shipped to England. He closed his business in the 1880s and died in 1913. Carpenter repeated history by holding his Brattleboro business together on his own until June 1857, when he sold out, for the last time, to Jacob Estey. Carpenter went on to develop a variety of lumbering pursuits and to connect with various other organ companies throughout the country including, in 1865, the formation of Tewksbury, Carpenter, & Comany in Mendota, Illinois. He was to try several other partnerships until, from 1876 to 1882, he once again manufactured organs on his own.[68] Carpenter eventually returned to Vermont, where he died in 1891, at the age of seventy-two.

Carpenter's son, E. P. Carpenter, showed a capacity and liking for the organ business, and after making instruments in Worcester, Massachusetts, returned to Brattleboro, where between 1882 and 1883, he "started in a flourishing business in the place where his father was a pioneer in the organ manufacture."[69] The *Vermont Phoenix*[70] reported a brisk local and foreign trade for the young Carpenter at their six-story Flat Street location (figure 35). A public relations booklet issued by the Brattleboro Board of Trade reported that in 1886, Carpenter employed over seventy skilled workmen who were producing about 250 organs per month.[71] Cabot later reported that E. P.'s son, W. E. Carpenter, became

Figure 36.

Estey wagon en route

to the railroad station,

c. 1915

manager of the company in 1894.[72] When the company closed its doors in 1917, three generations of Carpenters had built over 126,000 organs.

1855–63: Estey & Green

The initial pattern of upheaval that had characterized the organ business in Brattleboro continued. In February 1855 Estey and Green ousted Hines. Hines reported that he had been retired against his will and took the case to court, demanding his share of the profits. The judge spent one hundred days hearing the stubborn litigation and making his report. Four years later a settlement was reached and the amount due was paid. In the interim, the firm of Estey & Green was announced.[73]

For the next eight years the new partnership enjoyed steady growth. Orders by mail became an important aspect of the business and shipping networks could now forward orders to all parts of the country. With the opening up of western markets (but before the construction of the transcontinental railroad), Estey's organs were reported to have been packed over the Rocky Mountains by mule. It was often noted that as the new lands filled up, the first musical instrument to arrive was a melodeon.[74]

After the arrival of the railroad in Brattleboro in 1849, Estey's wagons made still more trips, but thankfully much shorter ones, mostly between the factory and Brattleboro's railroad station. Even into the next century, several personal accounts recollect Estey's horse-drawn wagons with their cargoes of boxed reed organs (figure 36) making several trips per day from the factory to the railroad

THE PERFECT MELODEON.

Portable Melodeon.

Nos. 1, 2, 3, 4, 5,

Piano Style.

Figure 37.
"The Perfect Melodeon"
portable and square piano
case styles

station, which was situated close to the junction of the Whetstone Brook and Connecticut River (see Appendix B, map of Brattleboro). A standard Estey advertising strategy, and a common practice among a variety of manufacturers, was to emblazon his shipping crates with stickers, posters, and stenciling: "Estey Organ, Established 1846." Without doubt, the railroad became a key asset for marketing operations in New England and later a principal means to tap national and international markets.

One of the most popular organ models to come out during this time was the Perfect Melodeon, Estey & Green's trade name for a one-manual reed organ enclosed in lyre-legged portable or "square piano" styles of cases (figure 37).[75] They invariably won first prize at the state fair (at that time held in White River Junction), though it must be pointed out that competition was usually limited. Customers were amazed by "the ease with which rapid and difficult passages of music may be performed on them"[76] and were assured that "in many instances they are entirely superseding the use of the Piano Forte."[77] Reed organ manufacturers were already trying to make the reed organ more acceptable to cultivated tastes by capitalizing on the status and popularity of the piano. The article guarantees customers that "this is no humbug."

Riley Burditt's contributions continued to be noteworthy. Sometimes in collaboration with fellow inventors, he regularly introduced improvements and refinements, many of them patented, that gave the organ more variety and responsiveness. Among the most important of this period were the "Base [sic] Damper," which subdued the volume of the bass reeds when the swell was opened, and a coupler that sounded the octave above. This latter attachment, which Estey & Green called the "Harmonic," made the instrument louder, and thus more practical for larger halls and churches.

During this stage of industrial development, one begins to note a growing disparity between the owner-manufacturers and the craftsmen-workers. Burditt and other craftsmen increasingly took the role of the unsung hero. While business entrepreneurs such as Estey were indeed taking risks, it was still the craftsman who, behind the scenes, improved and refined the product. Estey's name was on the outside of the instrument but Burditt's ingenuity and hard work were inside. In fact, Burditt, who fully grasped mechanics, merchandising, and music, was in some ways more inventive and versatile than Estey. Yet, as an employee, he could advance only so far; encroaching mechanization, administrative stratification, and workforce regimentation began to provide gains for some and losses for others.[78]

Though relatively little detail is known of the operations during the Estey & Green era, Nadworny's analysis of production and income figures shows that the business had passed through the stage of a small production shop and into a larger scale of manufacturing. Based on the Windham county census of 1850 and 1860, it contrasts economic activity reported in those periods: "figures represented an increase over 1850 of 800 per cent in estimated production, 250 per cent in employment, and 700 per cent in capital investment."[79]

This period also marked the beginning of a series of catastrophes that eventually drove Estey to build his factory on high ground and to organize his own fire department.[80] Strangely, the first setback, the flooding of Whetstone Brook on August 9, 1856, was not recorded in the usual historical accounts except for the *Vermont Phoenix*. It reported that water flooded the lower floor of Estey's building and undermined it, threatening to cause its collapse. Losses were estimated at $600 to $800.

Fire was also a constant threat to piano- and organ-building concerns everywhere. Fire and steam for machine power combined with large stores of warehoused instruments; dry wood stock, sawdust, and wood chips; the constant warmth necessary for proper gluing; and highly flammable finishes to create some of the most spectacular conflagrations of the century.[81]

And not only did early manufacturers have to contend with various natural hazards such as floods and fires, but they risked commercial and economic misfortune as well. The year 1857, in fact, witnessed one of the great financial panics of the nineteenth century.

The second Estey setback was a fire on September 4, 1857. The alarm was given at 1:30 A.M., and because half the volunteer fire department was away attending a muster in Worcester, Massachusetts, the fire raged unabated for over four hours. Although the remaining firemen did their best, the fire destroyed sixteen town structures, including the building that housed Estey's organ factory, plumbing business, and marble processing operation. Estey's losses reached over $20,000; insurance paid only $3,900 in damages. Though no lives were lost, Alfred Dolge, the piano manufacturer and historian, later observed that "Estey found himself almost a poor man once more, as all his money had finally been invested in the melodeon factory. With the grit of the Yankee, Estey did not give up."[82]

With the assistance of a stock company, Estey & Green was back in operation within six months at a new location and with almost back-to-normal production. While the new fifty-by-seventy-foot, five-story building (two of which were basement level) was being erected on the site of what is now the Plaza Park (figure 38), organ factory employees were temporarily placed in other shops to insure uninterrupted progress.[83]

Adjoining the new main building was a smaller structure that housed the steam engine and its boiler, which kept the shop warm day and night and helped expedite the finishing process. It is noteworthy that although hand and water power were the norm, Estey was now using steam power. Attached to the boiler was a whistle that could be heard throughout Brattleboro and even in neighboring towns. Its blast signaled the boundaries of the workday (6 A.M., 12 noon, 1 P.M., and 6 P.M.)—an indication of increasing regimentation of the workforce—and at 9:00 P.M. to indicate curfew for the town's children. The whistle was also a signal for workers to stand clear of the machinery and belting before they were set in motion by the engineer and additionally valued as the area fire alarm.

Estey continued to aggressively develop his economic interests by rebuilding rental space on the site of the original factory and renting the basement levels of the new building to related businesses. At this time he employed some twenty men and produced about ten instruments a week at prices ranging from $75 to $200 each.

By mid-1859 Estey had a workforce of thirty. Sales during one month of that year reached over $6,000. An 1861 issue of the *Vermont Phoenix* reported that "Estey & Green's Melodeon establishment is one of the 'institutions' of Brat-

Figure 38.
Estey buildings in
foreground, c. 1860

tleboro. It makes little difference if times are easy or hard, their instruments
sell so rapidly they find it difficult to fill their orders in any sort of season. During the past year they have made and sold instruments to the amount of over
$55,000."[84] Their sales continued unabated in spite of the approaching Civil War.

Perhaps the most significant development during this period of expansion
was the hiring of a nineteen-year-old youth by the name of Levi Knight Fuller,
future governor of Vermont. When Fuller first came to work for Estey & Green
in 1860, his ambition was obvious. During his early employment at the organ factory, he started a machine shop of his own, manufacturing wood-planing machinery. Early signs of civic-mindedness also became evident when in 1861 he was
enlisted to help organize a military drill team in case the Civil War forced local

Figure 39.
The Fuller Battery,
c. 1886

men into service. His effort which eventually evolved into the "Fuller Battery," an early forerunner of the Vermont National Guard (figure 39).

I shall speak more of this exceptional man later, but suffice it to say that within six years of entering the Estey operation, he became vice president of the corporation, a position he was to hold for thirty years. His alliance with Estey became truly a family matter when in 1865 he married Jacob's daughter, Abby Emily.

Abby Fuller was to become as politically active, in her own way, as her husband. In a 1928 compilation of her addresses, she speaks of the encroaching Civil War: "Brattleboro, at the beginning of the war, had business interests in the South. Ira Miller's carriages and wagons were sold to Southern planters on account of their thorough workmanship and durability. Our Water Cures were patronized largely by people of Southern wealth. They brought some of their slaves with them; gay-turbaned black nurses were a common sight on our streets in my childhood. The Zyragars, the Eustaces, the Buckners from Louisiana, the Stoddards from Savannah, and many from Charleston, South Carolina, summered here. They worshipped with us in our churches on the Sabbath; they loved our hills and streams; they helped to keep the beautiful gardener's path in order, and some stayed late in the autumn to see the reds and yellows of our maples that shaded our streets. But after the war came, the Water Cures felt the loss of Southern patronage."[85]

Brattleboro, like the rest of the country, was polarized by the war; those few citizens with Southern sympathies were viewed suspiciously and usually ended up moving out of town. Fuller's military drill team undoubtedly saw action, as Brattleboro men were well represented in various Union regiments, cavalries, sharpshooter companies, and artillery batteries. For a time a military mustering site was set up in Brattleboro, a point of departure and return for the combatants. Nearly every family had kin in the field of battle, and every homestead opened its doors to the returning wounded. The stalwart women of Brattleboro labored hard to feed the soldiers and repair their war-torn uniforms: Mrs. Fuller commented that "it was considered a disgrace to attend a concert or lecture without taking a soldier's sock for knitting work."[86] Because the local government hospital was overwhelmed with causalities, many a young man died in the spare rooms and parlors of Brattleboro homes.

According to Mrs. Fuller, Estey turned over a good portion of his factory for production of materials necessary to fit barracks for the troops summoned by Abraham Lincoln in 1862 yet continued to produce reed organs without a hitch. Of the 300,000 new troops, 4,000 were encamped in Brattleboro. Mrs. Fuller commented on hearing the Estey planes and saws humming even on Sunday.

In spite of the Civil War, Estey's enterprise continued to come together. But before Levi Fuller assumed an executive position, the company underwent yet another shift in ownership. It is not clear why Green withdrew from the enterprise; records indicate only that after leaving Brattleboro in 1871, he relocated to Jacksonville, Florida, where he developed a business in leather manufacture.

1863–66: Estey & Company

This latest reorganization, which took place in January 1863, marks the first time that Jacob Estey assumed full control of the operation, probably because it was the first time in the history of the enterprise that one person had enough capital and intellect to keep the business afloat. In spite of the war, his company hired twenty-five expert workmen, and the enterprise was in obvious good health. The organs themselves were beginning to take on more of a "Victorian" look. Besides the popular Perfect Melodeon, several styles of Cottage Organ were offered.[87] These one-manual instruments, now with bellows operated by two large treadles, took the form of fully enclosed units, the entire space beneath the keyboard encased with solid walnut cabinetry (figure 40). In addition, larger models with "double banks" (two manuals), "blow levers" (pump handles), and impressive upper casework incorporating optional imitation pipe tops (nonspeaking wooden dowels shaped, proportioned, and painted to resemble metal organ pipes), were for "Churches, Lecture and Society Rooms, &c." Organs with the pipe-top additions (figure 41) were for more elegant homes and were a natural substitute for "churches which are unable to bear the expense of a pipe organ."

While Estey was responsible for the finances, the actual manufacturing was handled now by the two very resourceful and inventive gentlemen: the newly arrived Levi Fuller and the old standby Riley Burditt. Factory improvements and additions were frequently ballyhooed in the local papers. A new one-half

Six Octave Cottage Organ.

Figure 40.
A small Cottage Organ,
1871 Estey catalogue

Length, 4 ft., 4 in.; Depth, 2 ft.; Height, 3 ft., 2 in.

story addition was made to the melodeon factory in June of 1863, and sales were consistently between $6,000 and $7,000 per month. Then disaster struck again.

On January 6, 1864, a second fire devastated Estey's organ factory. A report tells us that the combination of extreme cold and highly combustible materials soon left it a "mass of ruins."[88] The heroes included Elmore Briggs, who, while the engine company doused him with water, ventured into the fire with a rope tied around his waist to rescue the company safe before the floor burned and fell to the cellar. The safe and its contents of valuable papers were retrieved intact. Two less fortunate firemen were killed by falling timber. The financial losses reached $27,000; insurance covered only $2,500. Most of the other occupants lost everything. The thirty employees, despite offers from other establishments, remained loyal to the enterprise and helped Estey rebuild on the same site.

By mid-March of 1864, observers noted that "the new Melodeon shop of Estey & Co. is going up as if by magic," and the first shipment of organs made

Figure 41.
Double Bank Organ with
pipe top, 1871 Estey
catalogue

in the new shop was sent out in early May. By September of the same year, Estey was employing forty-five to fifty workmen who produced twenty-five to thirty finished instruments each week. He had at this point withdrawn completely from the water pipe and pump business, probably using the proceeds to rebuild the melodeon factory.

In December 1864 the now predictable pattern of reorganization occurred once again, this time including Silas M. Waite (1825–1895), a powerful Vermont banker and speculator who later funded the famous Supreme Court suit brought against the Estey company. Waite was a colorful and influential Brattleboro figure who had worked his way up from bank cashier to several positions of authority in Brattleboro and beyond. A retrospective newspaper article noted that when he was president of the First National Bank of Brattleboro, his "peculiar, magnetic composition enabled him to exercise almost unlimited power over those he permitted to be on his board of directors."[89] His extensive manufacturing enterprises, real estate holdings, railroad connections, and political prestige gained him a reputation "as a man of clear methodical mind, and a good debater. He excelled others in comprehensiveness and definiteness of his views in dealing with financial questions."[90] Without question, Waite contributed significantly to the welfare and prosperity of the town. Unfortunately, every story must have its villain, and as will be seen, Waite turned out to be rather corrupt. Riley Burditt was also among the new partners, and there was a minor contributor, Joel Bullard, a Brattleboro builder.

Estey evidently sought additional investment backing because of the company's desire to capitalize on a growing western market. It was apparent to anyone possessed of some degree of foresight that Chicago was fast becoming the manufacturing center of the Midwest and was the obvious location for a new Estey factory.[91] In January 1865 the new partnership purchased a large four-story brick building in Chicago at a cost of $22,500. Jacob's son, Julius J. Estey (1845–1902), who had recently graduated from Norwich Military Institute, went to Chicago to help manage the company's new concern.[92] This undoubtedly provided experience that was to later benefit the young Estey when he assumed his father's enterprise. Since 1865 promised to be the firm's biggest production year ever, Burditt was sent to Chicago in the winter of that year to take control; it is likely that Jacob needed a man with Burditt's experience to manage the increased demand.[93] Thanks to his foothold in Chicago, Estey's national reputation grew, as evidenced by his reed organs winning "first premiums" at various midwestern state fairs. By the end of 1865, the Brattleboro factory employed sixty men and made about one hundred instruments per month in thirty styles; the firm informed the newspaper that about the same volume of business was realized in Chicago.[94] By the beginning of 1866, a total of nine thousand instruments had been manufactured.

All accounts mention Josiah Davis Whitney (d. 1902) of Fitchburg, Massachusetts, as a significant figure at this point in the company's development. Whitney invented a highly specialized machine that could mass-produce organ reeds.[95] His extensive knowledge of organs (he was the eldest of four sons of an important early builder of pipe organs) not only prompted Estey to buy Whitney's invention but led him to hire Whitney to run it. In fact, all the Whitney sons were eventually associated with the Estey company as they turned their attention from pipe organs to reed organs.[96] Josiah Whitney remained with Estey until 1874.

On April 2, 1866, the final reorganization of the century took place when Julius J. Estey and Levi Fuller became sole associates with Jacob thereby forming J. Estey & Company. The previous partnership was dissolved, and Waite and

Figure 42.
Silas Waite's Brattleboro
Melodeon Company,
c. 1867

Burdett (who had changed the spelling of his name) obtained ownership of the Chicago firm and exclusive sales rights west of Ohio.[97] The firm became R. Burdett & Company. Most of their product, like Estey's, was sold through the Chicago merchandisers Lyon & Healy.[98]

The great Chicago fire of 1871 burned Burdett's plant, and in spite of animosities over pending litigation against Estey regarding patent rights, Estey helped raise over $800 to contribute to the fire's victims. The disaster caused Burdett to move the enterprise to Erie, Pennsylvania, and plans were laid to manufacture pianos in addition to organs. A successful business was continued there with Judge C. C. Converse from 1871 to 1885, after which time Burdett returned to the Chicago area and retired. Upon his retirement, company advertisements in the *Musical Courier* encouraged the public to purchase a Burdett organ: a "rare chance to secure an instrument which a few years hence will be as scarce and valuable as an Amati violin."[99] Burdett died in Chicago on January 26, 1890 (also the year of Jacob Estey's death). His contribution to the development of the reed

organ was enormous: well over forty important improvements for the instrument were credited to his name.[100] His business dealings were judged impeccable by the industry. After his death, Burdett's many patents and designs were sold to the (Hobart M.) Cable Piano Company of Freeport, Illinois. Eventually the Burdett rights were acquired by the Edna Organ Company of Monroeville, Ohio.[101]

Silas Waite, desiring to continue business in Brattleboro, moved into the building that had been used by E. B. Carpenter for organ manufacture and organized the Brattleboro Melodeon Company in 1867 (figure 42). Interestingly, records list Julius J. Estey as treasurer of Waite's new firm, so one assumes that Waite and Estey were still friendly at this juncture. Meanwhile, Estey continued to enlarge his Brattleboro factory. In March 1866 he purchased about two acres of the Frost Meadow, near the Whetstone Brook on Frost Street, an extension of Flat Street, for $1,000.[102] On it he built a four-story, 100-by-38-foot building with a three-story 50-by-30-foot wing (figure 43). The additional factory boasted

Figure 43.
Estey's third factory location on Flat Street, c. 1866

state-of-the-art machinery and efficient heating provided by steam conveyed throughout the building in iron pipes. The power plant, a 26-by-26-foot fire-proof brick building adjoining the main structure, housed a Chubbuck & Sons thirty-horsepower steam engine. An "Otis Brothers & Company power elevator" transported heavy items between floors. Completed before the winter season, the additional space allowed a total employment of 125 to 150 people. For a while, the Main Street and Flat Street factories ran simultaneously. Julius Estey and Levi Fuller were satisfactorily installed as the new partners. The stage was set for an era of continued expansion and growth.

The Estey Organ Company

The year 1866 was the beginning of a new era for J. Estey & Company. On May 8, 1865, Levi Fuller had married the boss's daughter, Abby Emily, doubly securing his place in the family enterprise. He was a man with extraordinary ability and wide-ranging interests (figure 44). With a heritage dating back to the voyage of the *Mayflower*, Fuller, like Estey, personified the American way of doing things. One biography even went so far as to compare him with Benjamin Franklin and Thomas Jefferson.[1]

Levi Knight Fuller was born on February 24, 1841, in Westmoreland, New Hampshire. He attended the local public school until the age of thirteen, when he left his parents, then living in Bellows Falls, and "with only twenty-five cents in his pocket, determined to make a place for himself in the world." From 1853 to 1857 he learned the telegraphy and printing trades and with his exceptional mechanical engineering skills began to garner awards for his inventions. After an apprenticeship with a mechanical engineering firm in Boston, Fuller moved to Brattleboro in 1860 and was hired as a machinist and mechanical engineer by Jacob Estey. Shortly thereafter, in 1863, he began manufacturing sewing machines, establishing a factory in the wake of one Charles Raymond, who had given it up and moved to Canada. The Fuller shop burned in the same fire that destroyed part of Estey's second melodeon factory. Fuller started a new factory, which he later sold. Subsequently, in 1883, Fuller and Estey developed yet another successful sewing machine enterprise in Centerville, for which Fuller designed "the Estey Sewing Machine . . . a new model machine, which should take the lead of all the machines before the public."[2] Over one hundred patents are credited to Fuller, many of which relate to the railroad: the invention of railway recorders for registering the condition of the roadbed, important improvements

In America . . . success was not simply being rich or famous. It meant attaining riches or achieving fame. You had to know where a man began and where he ended in order to determine how far he had become.

John Huber, "When Success Turns Sour"

Figure 44.
Colonel Levi K. Fuller

in ventilators and dust arresters in railroad cars, and innovations in hydraulic engines in car couplings.[3] He also designed processes for the artificial drying of lumber.

During the early 1890s Fuller, an authority on acoustics, spearheaded the consolidation of an international pitch standard for piano manufacturers. His involvement began as a result of the Estey piano manufacturing concern in New

York. Fuller was asked by the Piano Manufacturers Association of New York City to study and recommend measures for the adoption of a uniform pitch standard for musical instruments in this country. As with everything he took on, Fuller made it a labor of love and applied his considerable energy and expertise to purge the existing vexatious practice of instrument builders and orchestras to cling to various local or regional pitch standards. A committee was formed to address the issue, with William Steinway as chairman and Fuller as committee secretary. Fuller immediately tackled the problem by sending out questionnaires to instrument manufacturers, artists, orchestra leaders, and teachers, soliciting their pitch preference and suggestions. According to the *Music Trades* for January 30, 1892, "Col. Fuller is conceded to be the best authority on the subject of pitch in the country, and his services to the committee and through the association to music as an art, are beyond conception. He worked month in and month out, made several trips to Europe in connection with his investigations, and by his conclusions made it possible for the Association to clearly understand the matter and finally reach an end for which the members had long been hoping."

Everywhere he traveled Fuller sought out and collected all types of tuning forks, and he eventually compiled a history of information, dating from 1711, regarding musical pitch.[4] He owned tuning forks used by Handel (A = 422.5), Mozart (A = 421.6), Wagner, and many other notables. One of his tuning forks was purported to be the oldest in the world; it had been made by John Shore, a trumpeter for Queen Anne.[5] At the 1893 World Columbian Exposition in Chicago, Fuller's exhibit comprised a collection of hundreds of tuning forks, a display of "acoustic apparatus," and a demonstration of the new "artificial" welding of tuning forks. It received commendation as one of the most interesting exhibits in the music section and was honored with a special award by the judges.[6]

Based on information he had gathered, Fuller recommended a standard musical pitch: "that A which gives 435 double vibrations in a second of time at 68 degrees Fahrenheit." From July 1, 1892, all instruments sent out by association members conformed to Fuller's recommendation, and soon his standard was adopted internationally.[7] Though there was naturally some resistance to the new conformity, most concert organizations and instrument manufacturers recognized the benefits of standardization. The Buffalo Orchestra, in fact, upon using the new pitch, reported that "the change for the better was very marked, especially among the brass instruments." Not surprisingly, as a consequence of all this activity, Fuller began to manufacture his own patented style of tuning fork, as well as a new process for its manufacture.

Considering that his work on pitch was only one of Fuller's innumerable accomplishments, of which more will be said later, it is a wonder that he had the time to work so energetically and fruitfully with the Estey enterprise. In fact, "ambitious and conscientious to an exalted degree, Fuller would often over-work himself in a manner which finally caused his untimely demise . . . at the age of 55."[8]

Figure 45.
Julius J. Estey in Estey
Guard uniform

Jacob Estey's son, Julius J. Estey, also contributed considerably to the Brattleboro community and became especially prominent in the state's military establishment (figure 45). He served as captain of the Vermont militia during the
Civil War and eventually became brigadier-general of the Vermont National
Guard. He was a Vermont legislator and served in the state senate in 1882. Like
his father, he was a staunch Baptist and involved in many of the state's Baptist
associations. In 1867 Julius married Florence Gray, a woman who was loved
and admired by everybody in Brattleboro.

1867–69: THE FROST STREET FACTORY

These years were the peak of Jacob Estey's career. One reason for the
significant increase in organ production was the hiring of Josiah D. Whitney,
inventor of a highly specialized reed-making machine. Also, after rebuilding
and quickly outgrowing the factory that burned down in 1864, Estey built the
aforementioned larger facility at the corner of Frost and Elm Streets. The combined factories accommodated 110 to 120 workmen whose salaries amounted to
$6,000 to $7,000 monthly. Each month, 50,000 to 60,000 board feet of lumber
were used, with 300,000 to 500,000 feet drying naturally in the yard, on hand
at all times. Monthly sales at this time averaged 160 instruments, with a monthly
revenue return of $19,000 to $20,000. Organs were being sent to markets in
California, the British Isles, the Mediterranean, and the East Indies. The Estey
organ won over fifty first prizes at various fairs, consistently affirming its high

Figure 46.
Damage done by the
Whetstone flood
of 1869

quality. In spite of the fact that Estey had to temporarily discharge four work-men during the first month of 1868 because of market fluctuation, production continued to grow to an average sales of 200 instruments per month. By the spring of 1869 his 170 employees were making and selling 310 organs every month. He laid plans to further enlarge the Frost Street factory to accommo-date 15 or 20 more men. With such stiff competition from the Estey factory, it is not surprising that Silas Waite disposed of his Brattleboro Melodeon Com-pany. Waite's assets probably went into Burdett's prospering Chicago enterprise.

In October 1869 the Whetstone Brook swelled to unprecedented propor-tions as a result of thirty-six hours of uninterrupted rain, causing a flood that swept away both the Connecticut River and Main Street bridges and under-mined buildings on both sides of the brook (figure 46). As it obliterated a good part of the foundation under Estey's Frost Street factory, "employees . . . were taken from the second story windows with ropes." In spite of the tragic loss of one Estey employee, who went down along with thousands of dollars worth of lumber and stock, the factory was repaired in a matter of days, and business continued. Estey decided to build a dike to protect the shop from future floods.

At this juncture, after two fires and two floods, Estey was understandably determined to increase his protection against such natural hazards. He began by buying sixty acres in the southwest part of town just above the recently flooded factory high on a prominent terrace above the Whetstone Brook. He also made plans to organize his own private fire department.

1870: THE BIRGE STREET FACTORY

On the new property, J. Estey & Company built four 3-story buildings, lined up along Birge Street, each measuring one hundred feet long and thirty to thirty-eight feet wide, with forty feet between them. These made up the central set (later numbered 3 through 6 by the company) of the eventual eight front-rank buildings (figure 47) that became so emblematic in Estey advertising. Behind them was a large lumber-drying facility, a blacksmith's shop, a fireproof building that housed the factory's central steam engine, and a garage for the company fire engine. Two houses, shared by the expressmen, firemen, and watchmen, were also nearby.

Estey recognized that housing his factory in separate buildings would be advantageous in the event of another conflagration. Each building was protected all around with slate shingles and tin-covered corners and cornices, presumably to prevent fire in one building from consuming adjoining structures. All the buildings had slate roofs as well. Most of the buildings had elevators for vertical transport, and for horizontal movement and the shuttling of materials between buildings, "the buildings are all connected at the second story by a bridge, containing a track, on which is run a car conveying material from one shop to another."[9] Windows galore provided each workman with optimum lighting conditions. Gas provided illumination in the evening, and steam pipes, laced throughout the factory, furnished heat.[10] In departments where glue was used, workmen had a personal source of steam heat to warm their bench area, which insured proper glue adhesion and shortened drying time.

As is attested by the thoughtful design of the factory, Estey spared no effort in protecting the new plant from the hazards that had plagued him in the past. He even formed his own fire company and trained employees to operate the steam pumpers (figure 48). The *Vermont Phoenix* reported that "the steam fire engine (an 'Amoskeag') recently purchased by J. Estey & Co. was taken out for trial. Although not of the latest pattern, it proved itself very serviceable."[11] The average steamer weighed approximately four thousand pounds, burned coal, and

was pulled by horses. The better ones could pump, on average, 350 gallons per minute. Later, as the company gradually upgraded the fire equipment, they took pride in showing off a new thousand-foot-long rubber hose that could throw a stream of water two hundred feet high. One account tells of the pump's capability to shoot water "some 20 feet above the eagle which surmounts the flag staff on the Brooks House, . . . proving the great superiority of steam engines over hand-pumped engines."[12] Friendly competition developed between local fire companies, and annual "play outs" provided a topic for conversation months afterward. A large water reservoir was also built uphill from the factory (under the gazebo in Esteyville park) to provide an ample supply of pressurized water to hydrants, which were spaced at intervals behind the shops. In addition, an emergency heated water pool, kept from freezing in the winter months in case of wintertime fires, was installed between two of the buildings. The inside of the factory was equally well equipped to combat fire, and each floor of every building had a row of filled water pails and Babcock fire extinguishers.

Figure 47.
The Birge Street
buildings, 1875

The Estey Organ Company ⌊ 117

Figure 48.
An Estey steam pumper
and employee firemen,
c. 1880

Estey also installed a clever machine that instantly gave the location of a fire anywhere in the village: fire boxes were situated in every part of town and when one was activated, a signal was transferred to a mechanism in the factory, which deciphered its whereabouts and automatically blew the factory whistle in a sequence of blasts and pauses that notified the townspeople and fire department of the location of the blaze. The constant threat of fire prompted Estey to be very thorough. Indeed, on August 5, 1870, fire consumed the roof of a company building on the south side of the Whetstone Brook, not part of the new operation, and at the time occupied by a number of small businesses. By the end of 1870 the company had mostly moved into its new Birge Street headquarters.

The new complex enabled Estey to enlarge and refine the assembly line process, indicative of a common growth pattern that developed in many industries during this period (though Estey was ahead of most). His factory employed the best continuous-flow production equipment available: conveyer belts, traveling platforms, small-gauge railways, elevators, and interbuilding networks.

The first phase of manufacturing began by moving wood stock from an ex-

Figure 49.
Estey workers in the
lumber yard

tensive lumber yard (figure 49), where it had dried naturally for two years, to a sawmill housed on the first floor of the first building (probably the building later designated Number 3). From there the wood was taken to the "dry house," held to a constant 120 to 150 degrees Fahrenheit, to season for two to six months, after which time it was run through a "gauntlet of kilns" designed to accelerate the final curing process.[13] The organ cases were then fashioned on the second and third stories above the mill (figure 50).

The second building (later called Number 4) contained the reed works and machine shop and was also where the action and bellows were made (figure 51).[14] The reed room became the most carefully guarded department of the entire works, and as Estey's reeds became the envy of the industry, visitors were required to obtain a special pass in order to enter the area. In this room "about a dozen costly and delicate automatic machines," most of them invented and built on the premises, molded and processed sheet brass into musical metal (see Appendix E for an explanation of Estey's reed-making process).[15]

Behind this same building were located the engine house and boiler rooms (figure 52), which supplied power for all the machinery. Even though the harmful nature of wood dust (which can cause respiratory ailments and flash fires) was not as well understood then as it is now, Estey's concern for cost efficiency and for the health of his workforce was evidenced by the installment of a large exhaust fan that moved wood dust and shavings from the workrooms through underground pipes to the boiler room, where they were utilized as fuel.

Figure 50.
The casework
department, c. 1875

Instrument actions were assembled and cases finished in the third building (figure 53), and the last building was reserved for "set up," tuning, crating (figure 54), and office space.[16] Thirty-four people were employed especially for tuning, for "until manipulated by a tuner, the instrument is simply a machine but now it becomes endowed with life."[17] A network of speaking tubes connected various parts of the factory for "instantaneous communication," yet another trapping of progress toward increased production.

By the fall of 1870 the workforce had increased to 225, with a monthly production of 250 organs priced between $50.00 and $750.00.[18] At the beginning
of 1872, 350 workmen were employed, with an output of 500 to 600 organs per
month. By the end of that year monthly production had increased to 700 organs, totaling 8,000 instruments for 1872. It was estimated that one organ was
coming off the line every twenty-five minutes. The workday was ten hours long
but still the company could scarcely keep up with the demand. The firm's success must be credited to the high quality of the product, convincing advertising, and efficient distribution. Estey, a seasoned businessman by this time, responded to the increased ability of Americans to afford keyboard instruments
and satisfied their growing passion for things both mechanical and cultural,
scientific and artistic, combinations epitomized by the reed organ. The available
documentation regarding the markets indicates, as expected, that churches, sing-

Figure 51.
The keyboard
department, c. 1875

Figure 52.
The boiler room

ing societies, lecture and social organizations, lodges, schools, and private house-holds, many of which were in New England, counted for nearly all of the orders.[19]

But from the very beginning, Boston and New York City were the most significant major distribution centers for trade in the Northeast, and access to these markets was definitely expedited by the railroad. As transport systems became more efficient, shipping by rail and waterway expanded marketing areas to the West, especially after the opening of the transcontinental railroad in 1869. Further, Estey sales representatives (often Julius Estey) traveled more frequently to foreign lands, enhancing the company's international reputation. By 1876 forty organs were being shipped to Europe every week.

In 1871 the company erected two more buildings (eventually designated Number 2 and Number 7), increasing the front rank of nearly identical sentinel-like structures to six.[20] Yet another visible sign of growth was a one-hundred-foot-high chimney erected to accommodate two new boilers required for additional power. "The black smoke from the Estey chimney dirtied the wash on every line in that part of town. Complain, and be damned."[21] All the while Estey continued to maintain a sawmill on the Whetstone Brook, which was at this time turning out one million board feet of lumber per year.

To meet his increasing need for power, Estey installed a new Corliss steam engine on February 3, 1871. Practically and symbolically, the steam engine was probably the greatest innovation of the nineteenth century. No longer was progress held to nature's rhythms. Oliver Evans's first steam contraption created a

new, faster beat, the rhythm of the piston and wheel. The transition from power by muscle, water, and wind to power by fire and steam forever changed the nature of production and commerce. The history of American industry in general was most vividly played out in response to the never-ending, ever-increasing need for unstinting power. For a while, steam engines filled that need splendidly.

When the gigantic Double Walking-Beam Corliss Steam Engine was shown at Machinery Hall in Philadelphia during the United States Centennial Exposition of 1876, it was considered a contemporary masterpiece of technology in the

Figure 53.
Typical assembling room
(Estey attribution
doubtful), c. 1875

Figure 54.
Crating organs for
shipment, c. 1900

industrial design tradition. It was a primary attraction of the exposition, and nearly ten million visitors came that summer to marvel at the colossal machine. Historians of nineteenth-century industrial culture all agree that the exposition's Corliss steam engine was one of the greatest symbols of an age filled with symbols (figure 55).[22]

"The largest and most powerful engine that had ever been built up to that time, [the Corliss] was installed at the exhibition to provide power for all the lathes, grinders, drills, weaving machines, printing presses, and other machinery displayed by the various exhibitors. It weighed altogether 1,700,000 pounds, yet so perfectly was it made that it worked almost as quietly and with as little vibration as a watch."[23] Compared to other engines of the day, which were often designed with arches and columns in the industrial-Victorian manner, the Corliss was unquestionably severe.[24] Nevertheless, commentators spoke of the Corliss in aesthetic, not mechanical, terms: its appearance, they said, equaled any masterpiece of art. It seemed part animal, part machine, part god. At a cost of $200,000 dollars, the automaton was a fantastic success.

The sheer physical facts of the Corliss steam engine remain awesome: the heart of the Exposition Corliss had a 40-foot-high framework that supported a 56-ton, 30-foot-diameter gear flywheel that turned 36 revolutions per minute; its gunmetal crankshafts were 12 feet long and 19 inches in diameter and attached to two cylinders 40 inches in diameter; the crank assemblage had a stroke of 10 feet. This enormous monument of mechanical motion transfixed all who beheld it. With a network of belting amounting to miles of connections over acres of

display area, the Corliss, capable of generating 2,500 horsepower, animated over 8,000 assorted machines exhibited in Machinery Hall.[25]

Activating the Corliss engine signaled the opening of the exposition. President Ulysses S. Grant, Emperor Dom Pedro of Brazil, and scores of American dignitaries were in attendance. After a thousand-voice chorus sang Handel's famous "Hallelujah Chorus," a 150-piece band played the "Centennial March" commissioned from Richard Wagner, a 100-gun salute, and blasts on steam whistles, Dom Pedro turned the engine's emerald-studded throttles. At that moment America literally and symbolically proved her industrial clout.

Though Estey's Corliss steam engine was of earlier vintage and not nearly as large as the exposition's—Estey's generated 100 horsepower, the exposition's twenty-five times that—it remains noteworthy that he installed only the highest-quality state-of-the-art technology to bolster production. Newspaper reports stated that when the steam engine was installed and set running, everybody was "very pleased." The Estey factory, in fact, went through several steam

Figure 55.
The Corliss engine at the 1876 Philadelphia Centennial Exposition

The Estey Organ Company 〔 125

Figure 56.
Estey's Corliss steam
engine, c. 1898

engines during its history, starting with a couple of the Corliss design (figure 56). Most were replaced because of the need for more power.

In 1892 a Brattleboro newspaper printed this perspective concerning the growth of the Estey factory: "Methods of work have changed. Most approved machinery used in every department, many having been invented and built in Brattleboro especially for the Estey works. Forty years ago lumber was sawn by hand, ivory for keys was brought in tooth, brass for reeds in sheets and reeds cut with tinmen's shears, holes drilled with the old-fashioned bow drills and so on. Today every workman's time and productive ability's [sic] are multiplied several times over by improved machinery and improved methods."[26] It is worth noting that during Estey's life, the transition from small shop to industrial complex spanned four different eras of power utilization: small organs were first built entirely by hand, the second phase utilized water power, then came steam mechanization, and finally, steam power making electricity.[27]

As technology advanced, systems for the maintenance, repair, and improvement of the factory's machinery became more refined and economical.[28] It is no coincidence that in addition to his mechanical genius, Levi Fuller had great ability in science (though the term was more loosely interpreted then than now). From the 1870s on, scientific calculation was increasingly applied to the daily arrangements and affairs of factory life.[29] This progression signaled new opportunity for professional engineers and provided a basis for the formulation of the turn-of-the-century scientific research laboratory.

Estey's catalogue of 1871 allocated a number of pages for boasting of his new, up-to-date, and "most complete and extensive Reed Organ Factory in the world" and for furnishing details of the company's many new patents.[30] In addition to the extremely successful line of cottage organs, an expanded selection of newer, more ornate case designs and pipe top attachments was described. And several styles of pedal organ (which had a pedalboard, or a keyboard for the feet like those found on pipe organs) were made and advertised as early as 1867. Finally, it was increasingly apparent that more numerous and varied sets of reeds and a greater selection of stops, a result of the patent improvements, strengthened the organ's market appeal by offering customers greater tonal variety and a few more things to manipulate and control.[31]

Two more factory buildings were added (Number 1 and Number 8) during the next two years. But the structural growth of the factory was not the only concern of a booming business, for the workmen and their families required housing as well. Estey sold the extensive acreage behind the factory buildings in part for the dwellings of the workers, who took timber from the land while Estey took the mortgages on the houses. The attractive neighborhood (still called Esteyville), in which living conditions contrasted sharply with those in urban centers, is located just southwest of town on a series of terraces overlooking the village (figure 57).

Very little information about life in Estey's workers' village exists. Except for "Esteyville Etchings," a tiny weekly column in the *Vermont Phoenix* (which generally related real estate developments rather than social activity), the personal affairs of workers were left out of the media. One unusually long entry from the *Phoenix* gives this account of Esteyville's development:

Esteyville lies in a south-westerly direction of town hall and embraces all sections west of Birge St. formerly known as Dickinson pasture and part of the Rufus Clark farm. It was bought by Estey in 1869. A wooden house which stood where Number 8 now stands was torn down by J. Estey and Co. and moved to the place south of Fuller Park. The two brick houses were moved just north of L. E. Yeaw's and are still owned by the Co. All buildings in the rear and around the large brick house, formerly the Dickinson Farm house, have been built except the two little houses in the lane where Thomas Cain

Figure 57.
Esteyville overlooking the
factory buildings, c. 1900

now lives. The iron bridge and roads leading to it have all been built. The bridge crossing the brook just north of Flitcher's saw mill was destroyed by flood. A woolen factory stood where the saw mill now stands. The farm was soon surveyed into streets and building lots. The first streets were named Estey, Chestnut, Cottage and Organ; newer streets were Locust, Vine, Pleasant, Cherry, Southern Ave. and also extensions to Organ, Cherry and Advent. By spring 1870 many workmen from the organ shops were building themselves homes. D. A. Fay was first on Chestnut St. The large maple trees on Chestnut St. were set in 1871. Esteyville was settled by honest and industrious, law-abiding citizens who kept neat homes and tidy streets. It now has 78 houses 106 families—424 people—and a primary school with a basement for holding meetings, socials, etc. The artillery band meets there. Fuller Park was a gift of ex-governor Fuller. Advents are soon to build church. The town has beautiful surroundings.[32]

Within this exceptionally supportive physical and social environment, workers were able to retain a sense of continuity between factory and community, a trait sorely lacking in urban industry.

Swedeville, not as much an Estey enclave, was another area of Brattleboro where new immigrants of Scandinavian heritage grouped. Though a small number of Swedeville residents worked at the Estey factory and were highly regarded for their woodworking skills on the organ cases, most were house painters. A newspaper entry regarding the building and consecration of the Lutheran church —a prominent symbol of Swedish solidarity—counted 170 Swedes, including children. Native townspeople welcomed the newcomers and seemed to enjoy the ethnic variety. Swedish singing, crafts, and Viking heritage were highlighted at Brattleboro pageants, fairs, and other social gatherings (figure 58).

French Canadians and Irish filled out the bulk of Brattleboro's ethnic minority population. Besides the English, the earliest immigrants were probably the "French Canucks." Legends of their skill as woodsmen spread during the many log drives down the Connecticut River. Passing through Brattleboro, loggers camped on the island between Vermont and New Hampshire. When too many dams terminated the logging business, some of the laborers returned to Brattleboro to live. To this day small pockets of traditional folk music reflect this French Canadian heritage.

As railroad construction intensified in Vermont, many Irish workers also decided to settle in the area. Correspondence between the Estey office and company employees indicate that highly skilled German craftsmen were on the payroll as well.[33] The relative representation of ethnic minorities in Estey's factory is, however, difficult to surmise. Judging from company ledgers, it appears that people with other than English backgrounds did not generally work for Estey until after the turn of the century.

The municipality of Brattleboro was understandably very proud of Jacob Estey, who afforded the town worldwide fame and enhanced the general economic well-being of the community. In addition to building and later enlarging the First Baptist Church, he cofounded the Vermont Peoples Bank.[34] He was elected to the Vermont house of representatives for the 1869–70 term and later, from 1872 to 1874, represented Windham County in the state senate. In 1876 he was one of the presidential electors who cast Vermont's vote for Rutherford B. Hayes.

Figure 58.

Swedes in Brattleboro:

the Pageant of 1912

Throughout this period of continuous expansion and political activity, the elder Estey remarkably still found time to form various partnerships in businesses unrelated to reed organ manufacture. And joyously, on August 2, 1871, Jacob Estey became a grandfather. Florence Estey, the wife of Julius J., gave birth to a son, Jacob Gray Estey.

THE ESTEY ORGAN COMPANY

In 1872 the state legislature approved the incorporation of the Estey Organ Company.[35] On November 26, 1872, Jacob Estey officially became president, Levi K. Fuller, vice president, and Julius J. Estey, secretary and treasurer (figure 59). The move to corporate status was significant and reflective of business activity nationally. The familiar forms of managing capital—proprietorship, family businesses, and partnerships—were diminishing in importance. The advantage of incorporation was that it permitted a number of people to pool their capital resources as a single entity under one name. Essentially, the corporate association was strictly contractual, a legally sanctioned fiction that enabled its membership to discipline large sums of money and ensure its existence beyond individual circumstance.[36] Shareholders voluntarily gave up control in return for limited liability. Estey combined the best of all worlds, for though his company was now a corporate organization, it still retained aspects of the old-style partnership and family enterprise.

By the spring of 1873 Estey had hired 100 additional workers and he hoped

to reach a goal of one thousand instruments a month by fall. At the same time, the firm was finishing the eighth and final building, now Number 1, facing Birge Street. (Other buildings were built later behind the eight on the street.) However, the expected production projection was soon postponed, as the business panic of 1873 forced Estey to discharge 50 of the 512 workmen employed at the time. The workday was reduced to eight hours and salaries cut by 25 to 50 cents a day.

The plight of the late-nineteenth-century urban factory worker in America is complicated but reasonably well-documented, though the causes of the gulf that developed between labor and capital after the Civil War are still debated among historians. Workers continue to struggle with the problems of rampant industrialized (now globally computerized) capitalism, unequalized wealth in a demo-

Figure 59.
The owners of the Estey Organ Company—Julius J. Estey, Levi Fuller, and Jacob Estey—with a Grand Salon Organ, c. 1881

Figure 60.
Manager and a youthful
employee in the planing
room, c. 1880

cratic society, bogus political promises in the face of destitution, and increasing dependence instead of independence.

In essence, after mid-century, shifting relations between worker, craftsman, and managerial entrepreneur caused an appreciable change in the lifestyles and values of Americans from earlier times. Though industrialism supposedly encouraged upward mobility, replacing the apprentice-journeyman-master arrangement with a workman-craftsman-proprietor hierarchy actually increased class consciousness, thus generally inhibiting workers' potential for self-betterment. By refining production and merchandising processes, businesses became more complex, and organizational "pecking orders" gradually evolved as a consequence of task specialization (figure 60).

Such profound changes prompted major political shifts in towns and cities across America. The artisan class could not have foreseen that their success in improving production techniques and developing new markets was to eventually be their undoing.[37] A schism developed between employer and employee, resulting in a more marked economic disequilibrium, and personal self-sufficiency was sacrificed. In the process, artisans forfeited not only freedom but also social status. Economic development caused a drastic shifting of roles, creating a critical change in society's basis for determining status. An employee's position within the factory could determine "the food he ate, the neighborhood he lived in, his rank in the militia unit or fire company, and even the cemetery in which he was buried."[38]

Working-class wage earners often attempted to protect themselves from exploitation by banding together. Indeed, few industrialists were free of worker unrest and organized labor unions, as exemplified by the Baltimore & Ohio and Pennsylvania Railroad strikes of 1877, the 1886 Chicago Haymarket Riot, the violent management/labor confrontations at Homestead, Pennsylvania, in 1892 and Pullman, Illinois, in 1894, and the assassination of President McKinley by a self-proclaimed anarchist in 1901.[39] The reed organ industry was no exception. Ord-Hume reports that from 1877 to 1878 workers in Worcester and Chicago began to rally for more pay. After a series of bitter strikes, a settlement for higher wages was eventually reached. The combination of a higher payroll and a coincidental rise in the cost of materials caused an increase of 5 to 10 percent for both pianos and organs. The recession of the late 1870s further discouraged investment, resulting in depressed sales, price cutting, and low profit margins.[40]

Considering that such Vermont towns as Rutland and Barre had histories of labor unrest, it is noteworthy that Jacob Estey appears to have avoided any major labor confrontation during his lifetime. This achievement must have been attributable, in part, to Estey's concern with the well-being of the workers. In his classic history of pianos and their makers, Alfred Dolge deduced that "Jacob Estey was a man of firm character, molded in the school of adversity from his earliest childhood, but, perhaps because of his own sufferings, he became a very sympathetic employer and enjoyed the respect and love of his employees."[41]

Early in the Industrial Revolution, most mill owners treated their employees with paternal solicitude, but as the industrial tempo quickened, most, unlike Estey, forgot the gentler times and often neglected niceties. One wonders if the Estey Organ Company workers appreciated the fact that theirs was one of the few industrial efforts in Vermont to attain such a high degree of cooperation, achievement, and relative prosperity.[42] The impression is that they did value the opportunity to work in a situation that was, for the day, enlightened. On August 17, 1892, during the proceedings celebrating the completion of the 250,000th Estey organ, a little-noted speech was given by the company spokesman, George Hines, recounting "the resolutions passed by the Estey workmen, appreciating the wisdom and energy of the management and expressing confidence in the Estey Organ Company, while keenly aware of the delicate relations between labor and capital."[43]

One senses a mutual regard between Estey workers and management; indeed, Estey valued their suggestions and contributions. From the earliest times, the Estey factory always encouraged innovation and invention from his employees. Joseph F. White,[44] for instance, had been working on an idea he heard about in Baltimore, manufacturing music sheets that bore notes in relief—the beginning

Figure 61.
Departmental photograph
of some Estey employees,
c. 1890

of the player piano.[45] When the operator turned a crank, the imprinted sheet music was fed into an aperture so that each projection, upon reaching a certain point, activated a lever, which struck a key. Lest real keyboardists take offense, it was quickly stipulated that the invention was not meant to take the place of skilled musicians but only to "render the use of and enjoyment of a cabinet organ available to all members of a family possessing one." White sold the idea to interested companies in New York City.

Besides such tidbits, there is amazingly little actual information concerning the attitudes and lives of Estey's workforce (figure 61). In the past, labor historians generally emphasized economic and political changes and incidents of conflict with management rather than expressing concern over social relations of workers beyond the workplace.[46] Gathering information pertaining to Estey workers' everyday activities is also made difficult because, as was the general rule elsewhere, Brattleboro newspaper reporters normally discussed upper management (i.e., the Estey family and Levi Fuller) or the general progress of the organ factory instead of workers' lives. Very few personal documents have been archived. The few records that do exist regarding working conditions and family life suggest a progressive factory atmosphere and a healthy community environment in comparison to situations in many American manufacturing centers, especially those located in large cities.

In a speech presented at a factory commemorative event in 1892, J. L. Martin summed up the company's idealistic attitude toward its workers:

> The performance of a single operation by the toiling hand does not tend to expand the intellect. In such labor the skill required is partial and the tendency is to sacrifice the intelligence of the operative to his work and thus to lower his destiny. The members of this firm were fully aware of this principle of political economy and of metaphysics. They clearly foresaw that the remedy of this evil tendency must rest in the higher degree of workmanship required, and in the social development of the workman, his education and that of his family. Labor is not the whole of life. If the operative lives the other parts of his life well, he will wholly escape the threatened evils of a single or even a narrow employment. I say, without flattery, that the workers of this firm are possessed of that social wealth which, among the men, embraces enterprise, industry, art, science, religion and philosophy; and among the women those social attractions which develop prestige, rivalry, grace and personal merit.[47]

One sign of progressive management in the Estey company was the organization of a benefit association on January 20, 1892, to help mitigate problems resulting from injury.[48] Records indicate that in 1893, 309 members paid $1.00 apiece in insurance membership fees. Fifty-three accidents to workmen were recorded and twenty-nine claims paid; twenty-six of the accidents occurred outside the premises of the company.[49] It is curious to read some of the claims reports: an employee's thumb, cut off by a surface planer, was valued at $24.00; sprained backs generally brought compensation of $5.00 or $6.00; minor cuts were usually appraised under $5.00.[50]

During a period when conditions within large, noisy, unsanitary, and often dangerous urban factory systems were creating deep class schisms and crises of impersonality, Estey's workers were able to retain their identity and sense of self-worth more easily because of the intimate village atmosphere within the Brattleboro community. Generally, company employees not only worked together in the factory, worshiped together in church, and lived in close proximity in

Figure 62.

Estey exhibit at a Valley
Fair, early 1900s

adjoining neighborhoods, but joined for other community and recreational activities as well: "A very interesting season of matched games of old-fashioned round ball has opened among the Estey workmen during the past week. The first game was played last Saturday between the second floor of shop Number 8 and the third floor of the same building. . . . The stakes, we understand, were a half-bushel of Gorborino's best peanuts."[51] Sporting games were also organized between in-town businesses and with neighboring towns.

Esteyville children attended Esteyville School, a two-room grade school conveniently located at the top of Estey Street. Other neighborhoods had their own district schools as well.

Reports on Brattleboro's many civic clubs and community events, especially the annual Valley Fair (1886–1930), give us a general indication of the high level of participation in local affairs and a sense of community spirit. "The Valley Fair had everything that a fair could have: horse races, agricultural exhibits, rides and souvenirs. It had something more besides—the enthusiasm that the whole town put into the preparations. It was everybody's party."[52] Beyond the fact that the Estey company always had a prominent exhibit for the display of its latest organs and pianos, it is not known exactly how Estey employees contributed to the fair's organization. Photographs confirm large turnouts, exhilarating activity, and sizable representation of local merchants (figure 62).

By encouraging a general climate of civic cohesiveness, Jacob Estey engen-

Figure 63.
"Fifty years each for
Estey": Joseph Jones, Asa
Field, and Dan Bemont

dered strong feelings of loyalty among his employees, as evidenced in a *Vermont Phoenix* article: "Jonas Putnam, born in Guilford in 1814, came to Brattleboro in 1835 and began to work for Jacob Estey in his pipe and pump business, staying with him until Estey entered the Organ business then joined him in that. They never had any differences and [Jonas] takes as much interest in the success of the establishment as does the owner. He has remained a workman at the bench [and] one of his sons is a foreman in the organ works. There are other men who have been there 10, 20, 30 or more years."[53] Several expert craftsmen, among them Asa Field and Patrick White (see figure 63), spent their entire working lives in Estey's service.

Stories tell of Estey's regular jaunts through the factory, where his informal and personable manner captured the favor of the workers. When in the mood, he showed a ready sense of humor and spontaneity that was undoubtedly charming and endearing. It was said that some of the brightest spots in the round of drudgery were those when, at some unexpected moment, Estey entered in his peculiar, half-hesitating way, dropped into a chair, reminisced for ten minutes about the past, and then left as unexpectedly as he came in, begging his audience's pardon for the intrusion.

As attested by the well-documented labor histories of Waltham and Lowell, Massachusetts, women and children were the most grievously exploited labor forces during the early years of industrial growth. But Jacob Estey's views on the importance of women in the workforce were quite enlightened, as seen in a newspaper article:

> He has always been an advocate of woman's right to do any work for which she is fitted and receive the same pay as a man would. While the shop was still on Frost St., he began to employ women to file reeds. The men objected and complained they couldn't do the work properly. The Deacon knew this was only "a notion" and repeatedly changed the reeds when the men were at dinner so they unwittingly used the reeds filed by women supposing them to have been filed by men and vice versa. He was therefore fully prepared, as he related with glee, when a delegation of men waited on him one day and told him it was impossible to do good work with the reeds filed by women. He told them he had switched the reeds and "when I want your advice about running my business, I will send for you!" From that day on, women have filed reeds for the same pay as men.[54]

What few newspaper reports there were tended to emphasize the light side of the worker's routine: "William Hudson, one of Estey's workmen was offered by a brother workman a 75 lb. bag of meal if he would carry it four times up and down the 64-step stairway in front of the shop without stopping. After work he did it in his stocking feet in about seven minutes. Besides the meal he received a nice contribution from those who enjoyed watching the sport."[55]

Unlike many larger "big business" manufacturing ventures, the majority of Estey's workforce was composed of skilled craftsmen, among them master wood-carvers, designers, engineers, and inventors.[56] Some came from Europe with letters of reference addressed specifically to Estey, indicating they had probably communicated with him and made arrangements prior to their arrival. Much of the woodworking detail, for example, was done by expert carvers:

> New designs in shape, size and general style are constantly being made. The fittings and endless minutiae of ornamentation call for something more than mere mechanical dexterity. A score of carvers ply chisels, gouges, and other delicate tools, that are directed by subtle ingenuity and refined taste, rather than physical force. The polishers and varnishers, too have an important part to perform in smoothing the walnut with sand paper and pumice-stone, and then applying shellac, oil or varnish. Every part of the Estey Organ, it will be seen, is made with equal fidelity.[57]

Though working conditions in teeming metropolitan centers may not have been as genial and supportive as in Brattleboro, the lure of the city doubtless enticed at least some of Estey's workers to investigate opportunities in more urbanized environments. Skills gained in Estey's service were salable elsewhere. Many of the craftsmen who "graduated" from the Estey factory went on to make names for themselves in the organ world. Alfred Dolge's history mentions several: "Joseph Warren, of Clough & Warren; the four Whites, father and sons, of Wilcox & White fame; Stevens, of the Stevens Organ Company; Putnam, of the Putnam Organ Company, Wright, of Mason & Hamlin, and last, but not least, Votey, of the Aeolian Company."[58]

With the business in good health—and to ensure that it stay that way—Estey pursued various other interests, the most important among these being religion. Though it is naive to suggest that Estey's churchly interests could be divorced from any business benefit, his involvement with the church seemed to reflect a genuine concern for his neighbors, regardless of their social status. He was a faithful member of the First Baptist Church in Brattleboro from 1840 to the day of his death. For decades, Deacon Estey and his son supported the denomination throughout the state and elsewhere with influence and generous donations. Stories tell how, in the spring of 1872, Estey and Levi Fuller, by then Estey's son-in-law and vice president of the organ company, were riding through West Brattleboro and noticed a "For Sale" sign on the door of the Brick Meeting House previously used by the Universalists.[59] By midsummer of the same year, the partners had purchased, repaired, and reopened the house for religious services. During the inaugural ceremonies, speeches were given by Estey, Fuller, the Reverend L. J. Matteson (pastor of the West Brattleboro Baptist Church of Brattleboro), and other important local figures. With no furnace, the church used kerosene lamps and two wood stoves for light and heat. The brethren banded together, formed a Sunday school of sixty-one members with Levi Fuller as superintendent, scheduled a Wednesday evening prayer meeting, and, with continued support from the mother church in Brattleboro, hired a permanent pastor from upstate New York. Today the enduring and active congregation still uses the edifice Estey purchased.

In 1873 the *Vermont Record and Farmer* reported that the proceeds from a northern concert tour by the "Jubilee Troupe of Singers" would go toward building a seminary at Shaw University in Raleigh, North Carolina.[60] Completed in 1874, the four-story Italianate structure, the second building on campus, was named Estey Hall after its largest benefactor, who contributed $8,000 to the cause (figure 64). Constructed from bricks made on site by students, Estey's building is said to be the first in the United States dedicated solely to the education of African Americans. According to a North Carolina Archives and History Survey report, "Estey Hall is a major landmark of south Raleigh; . . . as the oldest surviving building of Shaw University, it is one of the most important monuments of North Carolina's black history and is of particular significance in the history of the education of black women." Though most students were from the southeastern United States, the 1893–94 "Catalogue of the Officers and Stu-

Figure 64.
Estey Hall at Shaw
University, Raleigh,
North Carolina

dents of Shaw University" records a first-year missionary training school student from Palabala, Congo Free State, West Africa, named Estey Carolina Fleming, likely among the enrollees who benefited from Estey's generosity (figure 65).

Vermont Academy at Saxtons River, a preparatory school, also received financial support from Estey's firm. With the blessing of the Baptist State Convention, thirty acres were bought and school buildings erected. Though under Baptist patronage, it is nonsectarian and remains open to all.

By all accounts, Jacob Estey was genuinely charitable and often openhandedly generous.[61] According to an 1876 story in the *Rutland Globe*, he championed individuals as well as institutions. Estey reputedly came to the aid of an old acquaintance who had fallen on hard times "because of the failure of others —not by any fault of his own. Deacon Estey went to him and handed him his check for $10,000 and said, 'Use this; make no account of it. If ever you get so as to repay it, do so.'"[62]

Another example of Estey's unfailing commitment to civic betterment was his laying of a pipe from the "gas house" near the Birge Street factory (where the company manufactured its own gas) to the First Baptist Church on Main Street. While he was at it, he allowed property owners along the way who needed a gas supply to tap into the pipeline. His involvement in town utilities

Figure 65.
Shaw University
students, c. 1885

expanded in 1875, when he and a partner purchased a controlling interest in the Brattleboro Water Company. This comes as no surprise when one remembers that Estey began his business career in the plumbing trade.

An additional display of Estey's beneficence was the outfitting of two town military organizations, "The Estey Guard" (figure 66), led by Julius J. Estey, and "The Fuller Battery," headed by Levi Fuller. Ubiquitous in towns throughout New England, these kinds of groups styled themselves as a category of national guard and were in great demand for exhibition drilling and parading.[63] Both were good for public relations and increased Estey's fame. Much of the equipment was furnished by the leaders, and uniforms were fashioned along the lines of Civil War styles. Evidently there were friendly competitions and makeshift war games between the two partners' regiments and with neighboring military companies. Fuller, a far finer mechanic than poet, wrote some doggerel about one such confrontation, from which the following excerpt is taken:

The Battle of Keyes' Farm

They came from the North,
The soldiers brave and steady;
They came from the West
With muskets bright and ready.

On tented fields they camped—
Historic fields of other days;
On the plains of Brattleboro
They ate and drank in many ways.

On yonder hillside
Estey with his brawny brags,
Supported Fuller, his cannon,
And his fancy nags.

The skirmish was very hot,
The flank was fairly done;
The boys moved not an inch;
They knew 'twas far from home.

When the roll had
Been called, it was found
That only one darling mother's boy
Was suffering from a wound.

Had been wounded awful bad,
Had been smashed all in jelly,
Had fallen upon a stone
And punched his little belly.

In sorrow, to the soldiers
This awful tale was told,
But with a wink they said,
Too bad, brave boy and bold.

And thus was fought
The battle of Keyes' farm.
In verse I tell the story
Of a battle without harm.[64]

In addition to participating in the Fourth of July celebration during the 1876 Centennial Exhibition in Philadelphia, the Estey Guard attended the 1889 centennial of Washington's inauguration in New York and President William McKinley's 1897 inauguration in Washington, D.C. The Estey Guard Dramatic

Figure 66.
The Estey Guard at
muster, c. 1890

Club (figure 67) and Estey Guard Glee Club also actively contributed to Brattleboro's cultural and social life. The military companies were not solely for parade and entertainment, however. They were mustered into service the summer of 1898, after enlisting for the Spanish-American War. Throughout his life Julius J. Estey gave wholehearted dedication to these military organizations, eventually retiring with an honorary commission as a general.

Meanwhile, Levi Fuller's light artillery battery had expanded to seventy-five men, half as many horses, four "twelve-pounder" cannons, and a drum corps. Fuller supported the company for two years before turning it over to the state; it continued until 1899. According to one contemporary source, "Both organizations represented splendid types of young manhood, reflecting the ideals of their honorable commanders, who spared neither means, expense, time nor personal effort in perfecting their patriotic spirit and military efficiency."[65] Music was also an indispensable accoutrement in the military arsenal, as important as guns and artillery; every respectable town militia had an attached military band.[66]

Brattleboro's martial organizations sponsored great annual festive balls. An 1874 newspaper report tells of one Guard and Battery event where "banners and paintings of a military nature decorated the hall. The Guards wore their uniforms and demonstrated in silent drill and bayonet exercises showing the results of good training. A beautiful fernery was raffled. Music was furnished by the Brattleboro Cornet Band."[67] The band, directed by F. C. Leitsinger, had been organized by "a few of the boys who could drum" and eventually grew to a playing membership of about fifteen musicians and a small honorary paying

Figure 67.
The Estey Guard
Dramatic Club,
c. 1900

membership of civic-minded supporters. The ensemble was ranked as one of the leading bands in New England, and for decades "discoursed sweet music" for town functions.[68] At the 1892 and 1893 Military and Civic Concert and Balls, sponsored by the Estey Guard and Fuller Battery, Lietsinger's First Regiment Orchestra offered an eclectic program followed by a dance. Reportage tells of "an exceedingly good program" of concert band repertoire, including a patriotic march, classical overture, cornet solo (played by the leader), and a galop. Immediately after the brief program, ninety couples formed the grand march and "from that time the hall was a brilliant scene of color, light and motion . . . gold lace, braid and epaulets vied with bright-hued silks and dainty laces and ribbons for brilliancy." Quadrilles, waltzes, polkas, reels, lanciers, and a schottische filled the dance cards. After twenty-one dance figures, a "choice supper" was served (at 11:30 P.M.) and then "the gayeties [*sic*] at the hall were resumed with fresh enthusiasm."[69]

In the mid-1870s organ production began to pick up again, and for a time the proprietors changed the winter eight-hour workday to ten. It was reported that a thousand pounds of brass was prepared for reed manufacture and some ten thousand dollars worth of ivory was used up each month.[70] Local reportage commented that the shops, well lit during the evening hours, made a splendid sight from below. Within a year and a half, Estey was temporarily forced to re-

The Station.
Brattleboro, Vt.

duce workmen's pay by 10 percent; but less than a year later business was reported to be unusually brisk, evidence of a fluctuating market. During an upswing, Estey finally reached a goal he had dreamed of for years: shipping a thousand organs in one month. Organs were now being dispatched to ports worldwide. Estey's European shipments reportedly accounted for half of all organs exported from the United States in 1876.

In her recollections Amy Jones Rice, then a girl of eight, remembers horse-drawn wagons, each with three or four well-boxed organs, shuttling all day long between the factory and the railroad station (figure 68). She was sometimes in-

Figure 68.
Brattleboro's Victorian
railroad station, c. 1900

The Estey Organ Company ⸤ 145

vited to ride on the wagons as they returned to the factory and heard tales of the "old country" from immigrant drivers. She especially remembered riding in Estey's phaeton carriage, drawn by a single black horse, and being awed by the tall man with snow-white hair and a long white beard, who she felt looked just like God.

1877–79: BURDETT VERSUS ESTEY

Much to the dismay of the Brattleboro townspeople, two of the village's most notable citizens, Jacob Estey and Silas M. Waite, were often in conflict. From the beginning the two powers seemed to vie for the same political office, property, or business opportunity. This rivalry was to play itself out in one of the most bitterly fought patent cases of the industrial age.[71] Sensational accusations made against the Estey partnership forced a battle that dragged on for fourteen years and was finally settled in the United States Supreme Court. A summary is included here because the litigation gained wide public attention in the late 1870s.

The story begins with a patent filed by Riley Burdett, who claimed that he "was the first inventor and discoverer of a certain new and useful invention, to wit, a new and useful improvement in reed organs."[72] The first application to the Commission of Patents, dated October 12, 1867, was primarily concerned with the arrangement of sets of reed in a reed board. The original patent application made four claims; because these are worded for the specialist and require patent drawings to be fully understood, the principal facts are summarized here. Basically, Burdett claimed to be the first to arrange a half set of reeds obliquely, and therefore most efficiently, between two full sets of reeds, which resulted in a clever economy of space. Because this arrangement placed all three reed sets above just one pallet with its one pallet spring, manufacturing resources and playing effort were conserved, rather than spent on an additional pallet and spring for each key. The half set was tuned slightly flat or sharp to the other sets, creating a "celeste" effect, in Burdett's own words, "a most wonderfully pleasing and captivating effect . . . which cannot be realized without being heard."

Burdett's first patent application was rejected on November 4 of the year it was submitted. The patent office reported that he was not the first to claim said innovations. An experienced inventor, Burdett amended his claims and resubmitted them later the same month. The application was returned in December 1867, again rejected. Finally an appealed version gained acceptance, and a patent was granted on February 23, 1869.

Two years later Silas Waite filed suit against the Estey firm for infringement on Burdett's patent claims. It was later revealed that Burdett, who at this time was living in Chicago, never actually signed or swore to the bill of complaint. One is led to assume that Waite may have instigated the litigation against Burdett's wishes. This assumption becomes more tenable if Cabot's character reference of Burdett is credible: "Mr. Burdett was known in every town in the United States by his musical instruments, and yet there was scarcely to be found a man so modest and unassuming. A man whose word was never questioned, gentle and guileless; one who never wronged a fellow being—and so retiring that only the few who knew him intimately appreciated that he was one of Nature's noblemen."[73]

The *Musical Courier* had few reservations about the situation: "Mr. Burdett himself was a quiet, modest man, devoted to his business, a good tuner, a good mechanic, and in many respects a genius in his particular field. In the great litigation that was carried on it has never been believed that he had much heart or even interest, but that it was a scheme of Waite to replenish his wasted treasury, and he took this opportunity to accomplish his end, taking advantage of Burdett's confidence."[74] Nonetheless, the allegation accused Estey of ignoring the rights afforded Burdett by the patent and required compensation for damages to be assessed by the court.

Estey responded that Burdett was definitely not the inventor and, moreover, that the innovations were owned jointly by Burdett, Waite, and Estey from the time they were partners in Brattleboro. Estey claimed he was given verbal license to make use of the improvements. He went on to state that Burdett had furthermore "knowingly, surreptitiously, fraudulently, and unjustly" obtained the patent. Finally, the defense cited several other organ makers that used the inventions before Burdett ever applied for the legal rights.

Estey then brought in several organs that were made by a Connecticut builder, Arvid Dayton, as evidence that the inventions were in common use long before Burdett's patent application. During examination by Waite's party, it became evident that the instruments had been tampered with to make them appear to be of a more recent fabrication and were therefore inadmissible. Estey responded by filing a countersuit accusing Waite of attempted destruction of evidence. To make matters worse, the U.S. Circuit Court judges assigned to the case kept expiring before a verdict could be reached. The case came before Judge Smalley, Judge Woodruff, and Judge Johnson, all of whom passed away before giving a decision. As a last resort, because of the serious character and large stakes involved, Circuit Judge Samuel Blatchford and District Judge Hoyt H. Wheeler heard the case together.

Finally, on December 20, 1878, after much maneuvering and scheming by Waite, it was decided that Estey had infringed upon Burdett's patent and rights. An accountant appointed by the court later determined that damages to Burdett amounted to $161,011.79. Estey continued to deny patent infringement and soon afterward appealed the decision to the United States Supreme Court. The outcome of this lengthy and important case will be discussed later.

The three most important breakthrough technologies that allowed mechanized production processes and workforce regimentation, both essential for widespread industrialism, were the steam engine, the timepiece, and the telegraph. They became symbols of nineteenth-century culture and, by extension, modern civilization. Successful entrepreneurs grasped early that the secrets of progress lay largely in the understanding and control of these devices. As with the aforementioned steam engine, the timepiece and telegraph altered the pulse of daily and seasonal life forever.

In early societies, different vocations required people to work varying hours of the day or months of the year depending on the occupational work rhythms imposed by nature.[75] Before the widespread use of clocks, people were generally given a wider margin of time for attending appointments and meeting deadlines, with the angle of the sun providing enough of an indication for general punctuality. To help coordinate activity, towns and villages rang a large bell or blew a whistle when the sun reached its zenith. During these days, the hopes of a lifetime were seldom destroyed by tardiness. The historian Susan Hirsch paints an attractive scenario: "the artisan valued leisure as well as work. While artisans rejected indolence, they freely mixed work and play. A constant pace of unceasing labor was the ideal not of the mechanic but of the machine. The artisan was bound to neither the machine nor the clock, and could set his own pace. Many masters and journeymen would stop to drink whiskey or other alcoholic beverages several times a day, and the apprentices were sent to fetch the refreshments from the tavern."[76]

With the advent of accurate timekeeping devices, moments became crucial, and one might lose pay, upset the balance of a day's production, or miss a coach or train if one was tardy.[77] In fact, it was the railroad that eventually necessitated national cooperation for the regulation and standardization of time. After the transcontinental hookup in 1869, it became increasingly obvious that different railroad companies could not adjust to different local time patterns without confusion, danger, and economic loss. Finally, after some consternation (and without waiting for legislative support), railroad corporations agreed to organize four standard time zones to which most communities across the country, some more reluctantly than others, eventually adjusted. The zones remain in effect today.

In Estey's case, time consciousness was evidenced by the addition of a highly audible steam whistle, time clocks for employees and watchmen, the placement of a grand clock on the front of building Number 5 on Birge Street (figure 69), and a telegraph line direct from the railroad station to the factory office.[78] The ever-intensifying number of wagonloads of organs rumbling to the railroad station attested to the cumulative importance of time as the pace of business quick-

Figure 69.
Estey clock on
building Number 5

ened. Internally, workmen were increasingly organized as teams, each group with a particular responsibility. The large gilded clock on Estey's building still exists today as a testament to the days when economy of time became a critical industrial consideration. The effort to coordinate local and national time was greatly facilitated by the development of item number three on our list: the telegraph. Its impact was similar to that of the timepiece.

Merchants were far less worried about market fluctuations when communication was by horseback or sailing vessel. Competition intensified dramatically with the arrival of the telegraph. Instantaneous communication forced commercial concerns to accelerate decision making, boost production, and streamline marketing techniques. An American commentator, George M. Beard, in an 1881 article titled "Causes of American Nervousness," reported: "Within but thirty years the telegraphs of the world have grown to half a million miles of line, and over a million miles of wire—or more than forty times the circuit of the globe. In the United States there were, in 1880, 170,103 miles of line, and in that year 33,155,991 messages were sent over them."[79] The ability to follow constantly shifting market values, he observed, was the scourge of businessmen everywhere.

The telegraph had reached Brattleboro in the spring of 1851, two years after the Vermont and Massachusetts railroad line was established there. People knew little of the telegraph then, and some were afraid of the mysterious phenomenon. James H. Capen was the first telegraph operator. According to a newspaper report:

> Finally, everything was ready, the wire having been quietly run into the business block on the corner of High and Main streets, when the lessee, Joseph Steen, "caught on," and ordered the infernal thing removed forthwith. He declared it would attract the lightning and absolutely kill his insurance, so Capen moved across the street into a back room, where he rather timidly began business. So strong was the local prejudice against the new invention and so general the fear, that some of the oldest citizens refused to receive a message till it had first been opened and read by the operator himself.[80]

Beard goes on to observe that the telegraph, in spite of causing nervousness in the marketplace, had become an absolute necessity for manufacturers to carry on effective national and later international commerce.[81]

Locally, the time it took to traverse the half mile or so from the Estey factory to send a message from the Brattleboro railroad station telegraph terminal meant time wasted and possible opportunities lost. Local newspapers made special note of the day Estey installed a telegraph line directly to his office, putting him in immediate contact with Boston, New York, Montreal, and nearly thirty local stations.[82] In addition to the obvious business benefits, it is significant that with this link an accurate standard time could be established for the town. Across the country, towns and villages arranged activity in relation to the most influential community timepiece, which in Brattleboro's case was the one at Estey's factory. Every day at 12:00 noon the telegraph station operator touched the key, which in turn rang a bell in the boiler room of the Estey factory. The fireman promptly gave a blast on the factory whistle that, on a calm day, was audible six miles away. The subsequent invention of the long-distance telephone,[83] installed in the Estey factory in 1898 (figure 70), and other business machines such as the adding machine, typewriter, and the mimeograph machine, revolutionized the business world of the nineteenth century, much as advances in photocopy reproduction, digital technology, and computer communication have today.[84]

By the last quarter of the nineteenth century, no place was so remote as to be unreachable by the telegraph and railroad, and therefore by the long arm of manufacturers' merchandising and advertising agents.[85] Estey, like most of his more forward-thinking contemporaries, came to view production and sales as connected, with factory output paced to consumer demand.[86] Efficient sales distribution networks expanded, first nationally, then internationally, with urban centers acting as hubs linked by communication and transportation systems. But perhaps the most important element in reaching rural areas or foreign re-

Figure 70.
Estey's switchboard,
c. 1920

witch-board
tey Organ

gions was the corps of manufacturers' representatives, agents, and dealers who maintained company offices in out-of-the-way places. These regional sales forces were the foot soldiers of the producer's industrial army (figure 71).

The worldwide success and prominence of the Estey organ was largely attributable to the integrity of Estey's agents. A few maintained well-stocked stores and were extremely successful, and according to the *Vermont Phoenix*, "the Company has always stood by their agents and given them generous treatment in return for faithful service."[87] Faithful service was in some cases imposed through contractual agreements with the Brattleboro office specifying that the agent could not sell organs made by other manufacturers.[88] With a few exceptions, records of the lives of these essential salespeople remain little researched.

It seems likely that Estey's system of agents grew naturally from the earlier tradition of salesmen who sold musical instruments door to door. One story

tells of the father of an informant who sold Estey organs around Lampasas, Texas, from the back of a horse-drawn wagon: "He would drive all over the country selling organs and may be gone several weeks at a time."[89] This particular salesman was so devoted to the company that he even named his son after Estey.

Overall, as distribution became more organized, many agents and salesmen affiliated with particular manufacturers, while others elected to represent more than one company or product. According to Dolge, agents were responsible for a restricted territory and, despite the fact that most manufacturers published retail price lists, generally had control over the terms of sales and pricing. In addition to full-time professional salesmen who maintained offices in particular territories, it is apparent that teachers, performers, and others in organ-related vocations functioned as agents of a sort by selling organs to supplement their incomes. One wonders whether there was any conflict in the minds of the hundreds of preachers who represented God on one hand and an organ manufacturer on the other. At least from a business point of view, it made good sense to maximize one's return on mutually related enterprises.

Records tell of one of Estey's most prominent early agents, George Saxe, an important figure in establishing the reputation of Estey products outside New England. Originally a minister by profession, Saxe's failing voice forced him into adjunct ventures. Beginning in 1862 with a single organ, he soon found himself managing a flourishing business of furnishing organs for use in churches. For twenty-five years Saxe sold organs throughout New York, Connecticut, New Jersey, and parts of Pennsylvania. In 1866 he became associated with James A. Robertson, a musician with whom he formed Saxe & Robertson of New York. In good years they sold an average of 1,500 to 2,000 organs of various makes and models. Accounts mention that Saxe also contributed to changing the style of organ cases from plain, rectangular flat tops to more-elaborate parlor organs with elevated ornamental high tops, which, as we know, caught the fancy of many thousands of customers late in the century.

Estey enjoyed telling the story of an unimpressive pocket watch he had acquired early in his organ-making career. One of his agents had evidently bartered the watch in exchange for an instrument and given it to Estey as part of the payment. "I scolded him well for doing it," Estey said, but he confessed that he valued the watch more than any other timepiece he could buy. Watches, in fact, were mentioned as barter items more than once. Early in his career, E. M. Bruce, who had started as an Estey agent in Philadelphia in 1859, sold organs in the West. During the days of the memorable Lincoln-Douglas debate, Bruce accepted a gold watch of English make in Galesburg, Illinois, in exchange for an Estey melodeon. A native of Wilmington, Vermont, Bruce resided in New York and Illinois where, as a schoolteacher, he peddled a few Estey melodeons on the side. On one of his trips between Illinois and Vermont, Estey arranged for Bruce to make a short detour to New Jersey to look after some special business. With Estey's support Bruce soon moved to Philadelphia and became a prominent figure in the music trade of that city for more than forty years. Bruce's obituary in the February 4, 1898, issue of the *Vermont Phoenix*, made note of his enduring relationship with the Estey company and his philanthropic work with prisoners in Pennsylvania.

Clearly, the network of company branches and manufacturer's agents was a critical and essential part of the Estey distribution system.[90] In addition to branches in New York City and Philadelphia, the most important outlets included offices in Boston, under the management of Alexander M. Davis (who with a large corps of assistants did an immense trade throughout New England

Figure 72.
Estey & Camp, Chicago,
Illinois, c. 1885

and the maritime provinces); Estey & Camp in Chicago (figure 72) and St. Louis;
Nathan Ford in St. Paul; Sanders & Staymen in Baltimore and Washington; and
Hodge & Essex in London, England. Agent representation expanded to global
proportions as the century progressed.

In spite of late nineteenth-century periods of economic ebb and flow and
protracted legal distractions caused by the Silas Waite litigation, Estey continued to expand his markets overseas.[91] Even as early as 1885, Estey had agencies
throughout Europe, Asia, and Australia. Ocean transport was not without its
hazards, however. Ord-Hume notes that between 1864 and 1869, Lloyd's Registers recorded a world shipping loss of 100,000 ships. He recounts hair-raising
tales of particular ships, loaded with cargoes of reed organs, that wrecked plying

the waters between Britain and America. Hazards notwithstanding, the Estey company sent a special selection of organs to the Vienna Exposition in March 1873, and on the following May 17, Levi Fuller sailed for the first time to Europe on the *Nova Scotia*, hoping to expand operations of the Estey agencies on the continent. (He toured Europe and visited a number of musical instrument manufacturers again in 1878 and 1884.) For his visit to the exposition, he received a special appointment as commissioner from Vermont from President Ulysses S. Grant, a title and responsibility he politely "declined because of the press of business." A private letter from Vienna to the local newspaper declared the Estey organ the best instrument in the exhibition.

As time went on, many foreign awards further supplemented the over 150 "Medals, First Premiums and Diplomas" the company amassed at fairs and exhibitions throughout the United States. Estey continued to court overseas business by sending eight different organs to the Paris Exposition of 1878. Included was a special Occidental or "acclimatized" model designed for use in Asian and tropical countries.[92] Along these same lines was the introduction of a sturdy and practical Estey portable folding organ for missionaries and military chaplains that, in various incarnations, became a mainstay in Estey's inventory (figure 73).

From the mid-1880s and into the final decade of the century, one begins to notice an increase in number of organ models and a gradual change of stylistic emphasis. The term "Cottage Organ," for instance, was eliminated from Estey catalogues beginning in the late 1870s. Becoming more apparent were Chapel, Chancel, and Cathedral styles for church use; Boudoir, Drawing Room, and Grand Salon models for the home; and Gothic, Philharmonic, or Triumph (figure 74) organs for large homes and community halls. Though relatively austere models for libraries and schools were available at one end of the spectrum, current design trends still encouraged vertical enhancement (though slightly more conservative than before) as evidenced by various decorative high top options that began to supplement tops with dummy pipes on the more ornate styles (see Appendix D). Most feel that Estey showed somewhat more restraint in decoration than some manufacturers. Estey's designs, for organs large and small, displayed a grace and refinement that fit in everywhere and, unlike the overly ornate cases, did not soon go out of fashion.

1880–85: WAITE'S DEMISE

Jacob Estey, approaching three-quarters of a century in age, was beginning to attain "grand old man" status. Newspapers as far away as Augusta, Georgia, wrote: "It is something worthy of attention that more than one half of the population of Brattleboro obtain their support from the business enterprises of a man who came to the town at the age of twenty-six, poor, friendless,

Figure 73.

Portable Organ, 1890

Estey catalogue

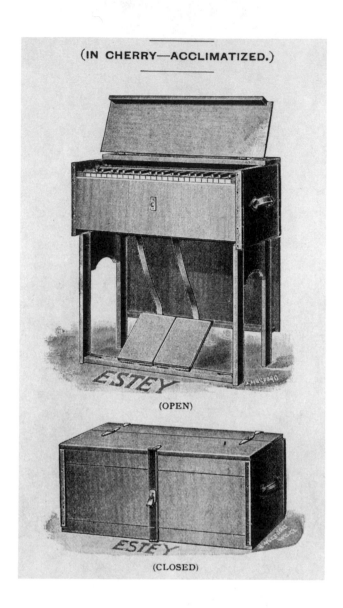

(IN CHERRY—ACCLIMATIZED.)

ESTEY

(OPEN)

ESTEY

(CLOSED)

and unknown. Jacob Estey is one of those strong-brained, iron-willed men more current a century ago, when, on an anvil of pioneering hardship, the hammer of necessary self-reliance shaped them into solid form."[93]

The now-familiar pattern of expansion continued in the new decade, with Estey hiring more men and leasing an empty building in town to alleviate over-crowding at the Birge Street facility. A catalogue of the 1880s boasted two million board feet of stored lumber ready for transfer into enlarged "new brick dry houses" (designed and patented by Fuller) where 100,000 board feet of lumber could be artificially seasoned at one time; raw material was shuttled from yard to dry house by means of a miniature railway (figure 75).[94] The factory's annual consumption of Vermont lumber, including the stock used for packing boxes,

Figure 74.
New Triumph Organ,
1890 Estey catalogue

Figure 75.
Conveying lumber by rail
for milling, c. 1900

was reportedly over three million board feet. The most commonly used species for organ cases were red oak and black walnut.

Separate buildings were constructed to house the factory's fire engines. A company of Estey employees, with discipline equal to the municipal firefighters', were ready to protect both factory and village property when necessary. Another sign of increased efficiency in safety and supervision was an internal system of telephones and electric bells that supplemented the old network of speaking tubes connected to the main office. In addition, two watchmen were constantly on duty day and night, and their rounds were recorded on a time clock they carried throughout the plant. "Woe to the man whose love of gossip leads him to tarry anywhere for a friendly chat with anyone, for the constant ticking of the clock, although unheard by him, tells the tale of the delay on the following morning when inspected by the Superintendent." A facility with 15,000 square feet of flooring was required for the storage and crating of increasingly large numbers of organs; it was an area larger, Estey enjoyed pointing out, than the entire organ factories of many self-styled "largest manufacturers on the globe."

Development in Esteyville continued concomitantly with the enlargement of factory facilities. Estey continued to sell building lots and encouraged the construction of houses, which were sold to workmen at low prices, payment being taken from their salaries in installments. He was said to have given generous financial assistance during difficult times to help workers meet their mortgage obligations as payments came due. Early in the 1880s Esteyville contained about fifty-four dwellings, which housed eighty families—about 250 people in all. Another 125 people, most connected with the factory, lived just below Esteyville.

The factory now employed over five hundred people. That employee relations were excellent and the workforce productive is confirmed by production numbers of fifty organs coming off the line daily. By the end of 1881 sales topped 1,500 instruments per month, and annual receipts for 1882 amounted to over one million dollars. Though not directly involved in day-to-day activity, Estey had two large manufacturing firms in New York City building pianos as well.[95] Julius Estey was making regular trips to Europe, and organs were being shipped as far away as Africa and Australia. One of Estey's Australian agents wrote that he had saved all the organ shipping boxes over the years and had collected so many that he "sawed them into pickets and fenced his whole farm."

Meanwhile, new facts relating to the ongoing litigation with Silas Waite began to surface. Due to the economic, interpersonal, and managerial difficulties of running a business in late-nineteenth-century America, it was not unusual for leading businessmen to apply the "hammer of self-reliance" to themselves. In this case, however, Estey was forced to "hammer" his old competitor and adversary.[96] New information had been uncovered concerning Waite's credibility. In 1880 an extensive article in the *Vermont Phoenix* declared the ruin of the First National Bank of Brattleboro, of which Waite was president.[97] Suspicions were initially aroused during a routine audit by a state bank examiner. Though the bank appeared sound, the examiner's attention was drawn to one entry relating to a line of credit with a well-known firm of private bankers in New York City. Finding no verification of credit at the New York bank, the examiner confronted Waite with the discrepancy. Waite coolly responded that there was a mistake and that he would produce affidavits substantiating his claim. The examiner gave him a week to do so and left with the understanding that Waite was to remain in the vicinity. Soon thereafter, on Thursday morning, June 10, Waite left town on the 4:20 express.

His nephew was the first to receive a letter, "incoherent in expression, and in a hand scarcely to be recognized as Mr. Waite's." In it he admitted that he was in trouble and announced that he planned to sail away and that his family would never hear from him again. Closer examination of the bank's books turned up evidence of forgery and defalcation eventually amounting to half a million dollars. Detectives were sent from the comptroller in Washington, and a $5,000 reward was offered for Waite's arrest.

Those who knew Waite respected his grasp of business affairs and great public spirit. Some were also quick to comment on a occasionally harsh and autocratic side of his personality or, in the extreme, his "supreme audacity and villainous cunning." Evidently, through force of character, he had held the bank's management strictly in his own hands, the board of directors having been shown falsified documents during routine bank meetings. It seems that Waite's trouble had started fifteen years earlier, when he fraudulently loaned his brother a large sum of money to establish a coal yard in Chicago. The great Chicago fire not only wiped out this venture but Riley Burdett's Chicago organ factory as well, also largely financed by Waite. Added to this was the expenditure over the aforementioned patent infringement, all of which Waite expected to get back, based on the court's decision in his favor.

Waite's family and friends were naturally stunned; one of his sisters, Lizzie, entered an insane asylum and died soon thereafter. Here was a man who, in addition to heading the bank, held several other positions of responsibility: chairman of the board of trustees of the Congregational Society, chairman of the board of the village bailiffs, twice chief engineer of the fire department, longtime member of the school committee, director of the Connecticut River Railroad Company, active contributor in building many of the town's bridges, and developer of the town's utilities — a man who served Brattleboro well. The shock was enormous.

Waite was finally apprehended at the home of his brother-in-law in Omaha, Nebraska, by federal agents on September 24, 1880. He was returned to Brattleboro and was forced to disembark from the train a mile outside of town to avoid a large, and probably very angry, crowd of townspeople. After a brief visit with his family, he was taken to the county courthouse in Newfane and held for trial.

His poor health, resulting from this stressful ordeal, delayed the trial until June 17, 1881. In his own defense, Waite maintained that he never used the stolen money for his own benefit and could have survived were it not for the Chicago fire. He did not think of himself as an unmitigated villain and hoped to collect enough from the organ suit to reimburse those who suffered on his account. He was sentenced to six years in the Rutland prison. There he recovered his health — unlike many of the inmates, he did not have to work — and spent time reading and writing. His quarters were reportedly cozy and comfortable, with a large window, white plastered walls, three or four armchairs, several wall decorations, and shelves stocked with choice reading material, and he was well away from the other inmates' cells. Later he was allowed to visit Brattleboro in the company of a marshal and was reported by the *Vermont Phoenix* to have regained "his old-time air of enjoyment and careless indifference, showing no remorse or compunction for past sins and crimes. . . . He is as confident and aggressive as ever." The jail superintendent was reprimanded for his leniency. Waite, attempting to take the offensive, said that he was ready to demonstrate that instead of his owing the bank $367,000 as alleged by the government, he could prove that actually, the bank owed him $130,000. He was, however, never to live down the reputation of bank embezzler.

Needless to say, these developments cast a new light on the Burdett versus

Estey patent case. Upon further investigation into this affair, it was found that a Moses Nichols had been hired by Waite to blackmail Estey. When Estey refused to pay, Waite bribed Nichols with additional incentives to help plot Estey's ruin. It was also confirmed that the Dayton organs, used as evidence for the defense, were premeditatedly "mutilated and prepared for Burdett's fiendish scheme" by Waite and his cronies.

Up to this point Estey had yet to pay any money in regard to the initial court decision. The case was reopened on November 21, 1883, before the United States Supreme Court. A full bench of nine judges gave each side five hours instead of the usual two. The case was finally settled on January 7, 1884, in favor of Estey.

The appellant's argument rested on the facts as succinctly stated in Whiting's volume *Estey Reed Organs on Parade:*

> that Arvid Dayton since 1855 had made organs with two and one-half sets of reeds with the half set tuned to form a celeste; that Henry K. White, an Estey employee, discovered for himself celeste tuning of reed organs in 1865; that Burdett's patent application, after being rejected twice, was issued after a third examination because of political letters of recommendation, presumably obtained by Waite; that Silas M. Waite schemed to damage the Arvid Dayton organ; that many efforts were made to damage the character and credibility of Jacob Estey and Levi Fuller; and that several of Burdett's patent claims were false.[98]

The lower court's decision was reversed, the case being remanded to that court with instructions to dismiss the bill. "When the news of the victory reached Brattleboro the populace was greatly rejoiced. Flags and banners were thrown to the breeze and hundreds of people turned out to congratulate the members of the firm. Telegrams and letters were received by the house from all over the country. Thus ended the most remarkable lawsuit in the music trade."[99]

It was rumored that Waite, now sixty years old, would receive a pardon on the grounds of failing health. A petition against a pardon was quickly circulated in Brattleboro. The rumor proved false; after serving his prison term, Waite was released and in 1888 settled in Omaha, Nebraska.

Estimates put the cost of the litigation at hundreds of thousands of dollars. A good portion of the blame was eventually laid on the patent office for their inconsistency in the issuing of Burdett's patents. The *Musical Courier* asserted on February 5, 1890, that such "mistakes and blunders cost inventors and capitalists great expense, and sometimes ruin as well as misfortune."

The notoriety the case generated did not seem to affect the organ business; if anything, Estey's vindication reaffirmed his integrity, and integrity was everything in an enterprise that did so much business with churches. One small example of Estey's integrity was the special pride he took in numbering all his organs consecutively. He often spoke disparagingly of manufacturers who were less honest and was critical of "the custom quite prevalent now-a-days among some Organ houses, of taking an arbitrary number (say 50,000) as a basis, and then rapidly increasing their numbers."[100] By 1886 the Estey factory was running six days of the week, with the production milestone of 200,000 organs close at hand.

1886–1900: APOGEE

Generally the elder Estey stayed in Brattleboro while Julius J. and Levi Fuller developed foreign markets. During this time Julius—at this point known generally as Colonel Estey—began to take primary responsibility in the business and a greater role in local and state politics.[101] Newspaper items give the impression that he participated in almost every society and organization in town. In the year 1885 alone, he was elected president of the YMCA, superintendent of the Baptist Sunday School, a trustee of the new Brooks Library, treasurer of the Valley Fair Association, and president of the Peoples National Bank.

To increase the firm's involvement with piano production, in 1885 it acquired the Arion Piano Company and formed the Estey Piano Company in New York City, yet another project Colonel Estey helped develop during this productive time period.[102] The new five-story plant on Southern Boulevard near the Harlem Bridge (figure 76) was reputedly "one of the most complete of its kind in the country." The main product was stated by the *Musical Courier* to be the "coming piano" (figure 77) having "all the qualities of a 'grand' with the convenience of an 'upright'." The *Courier's* assessment continued in a later article that called the Estey upright "a most beautiful specimen of piano manufacturing" and a "revelation" which the Estey company "will find no difficulty in disposing . . . in the best musical circles of the land."[103] (Present-day evaluation of these instruments is not so magnanimous.) For an additional ten cents, the company included a self-published booklet of pieces arranged specifically for piano titled simply *Old-Time Songs.* The twenty-six songs within make up a can't-miss list of nineteenth-century favorites, now among the classics of American music.[104] Within a year and a half of moving into their New York factory, plans were under way for plant expansion.

As observed earlier, Levi Fuller maintained a nonstop pace as well, evidenced by a list of a few of his responsibilities. In Vermont politics, he served as senator (1880–82) and lieutenant governor (1886), and was eventually elected governor (1892–94). He erected several state institutions, including the Waterbury Asylum and the Rutland House of Correction. He also became nationally renowned for upgrading the roads and highways of Vermont. A Boston paper reported, "He has given of his time and attention far beyond what could reasonably be demanded, sparing nothing that the state might be well-served, her interests guarded, the comfort and happiness of her people assured, and her laws

Figure 76.
Estey piano factory in
New York City, c. 1890

executed." Probably no other person associated with organ building ever reached the political heights achieved by Levi Fuller.

Fuller lobbied for a simplification of election ballots for easier use, the right of women to vote in municipal elections, the provision of free textbooks for schoolchildren, and more uniformity of law between states. Other forward thinking included standardization of village charters, construction of fish hatcheries, and banking reform. Additionally, Fuller was opposed to unnecessary increases in the defense budget and encouraged citizens to organize their own town regiments, as he had done.

Fuller was also active in civic and philanthropic activity. He helped the cause of black people in the South by serving on the board of trustees of Shaw University as well as that of the Baptist Society. He was president of Vermont Acad-

Figure 77.
Estey parlor piano,
c. 1900

emy, a member of the Sons of the American Revolution, vice president of the Poultry and Pet Stock Association and of the New England Trout and Salmon Club, a member of the Professional Club and the Village Improvement Society, and president of the Philharmonic Society.[105]

In science, Fuller was a member of the American Society of Mechanical Engineers, the American Society for the Advancement of Science, the American Society of Electrical Engineers, the Natural History Society, the American Society of Associated Science, and the Astronomical Society of the Pacific. Fuller was also an accomplished astronomer. His private observatory housed one of the finest equatorial telescopes and libraries on astronomy in the eastern United States.

In business, Fuller was vice president of the Estey Organ Company, owner and president of the thriving Brattleboro Sewing Machine Company, and holder of over one hundred patents. In military affairs, he organized the Fuller Battery and the first Vermont National Guard.

A renaissance personality, Fuller applied his great energy and talent on several fronts: in the service of music, art, science, statecraft, social reform, and economics. Indeed, it was unusual to find a club, society, or organization in Brattleboro in the last decades of the nineteenth century that did not include his name.

By the end of his term as governor, great waves of immigrants, along with widespread urban labor trouble, seemed to provoke in Fuller a tendency toward isolationism, a persuasion felt by many of the old guard. In a less than flattering biographical sketch, David Fox characterizes Fuller's political and ethical proclivities as an "unlikely combination of progressive reform and reactionary xenophobia."[106] At one point Fuller went so far as to ask the Vermont General Assembly for the power to close the borders of the state if necessary to keep out the "disturbers of society."[107] These opinions were shared by a majority of the American old stock, as well as the rising bourgeois class. "Economic fear bred ethnic intolerance. Immigrants came to be regarded, not as a source of strength, but as a drain on American resources. This was especially true of the East, where most immigrants arrived and where the social system was already hard and fast."[108] Fuller also became increasingly suspicious of citizens' paramilitarism, which he felt was getting out of hand. During the 1880s it had become all too common for "concerned community leaders" to amass stockpiles of munitions and organize vigilante leagues to discourage domestic insurrection.

May 2, 1887, marked Jacob and Desdemona Estey's fiftieth wedding anniversary, and two to three thousand invitations were sent out to agents and friends around the world. Letters and wedding poems poured in from near and far. The Estey saga was reviewed time and time again, and always he was portrayed as a man of simple tastes, born with an aversion to show or pretense, up early in the morning and early to bed, always watchful and concerned over every detail of the business.

> In the long years of middle life, when the hard struggle was on him, and what the end would be was not always assured, the community as a whole knew him best as the shrewd, far seeing businessman who compelled events to work towards his own ends, but in these later years, with the victory won and his faculties less put to strain, his real self—his kindness of heart, his playfulness of speech, his feeling of neighborliness and genial companionship —have been the qualities most often felt, and have met a quick and warm response.[109]

The golden wedding celebration was one of the happiest events of his life; after the event employees noticed a new warmth, friendliness, and sentiment in his demeanor.

During the fall of 1888 the 200,000th Estey organ was sent from the factory. By the end of 1889, the output for the year was 13,000 organs. The factory was making a large number of piano cases for the New York concern, as well. It is also interesting to note that Fuller had begun to apply his inventive genius to the proposition of using electricity to wind the organ bellows. A few organs, using "a small Edison dynamo," had already been sent to the company's salesrooms.

Jacob Estey continued to work every day. On Monday, April 14, 1890, he worked until 11:00 A.M., at which time he suffered chest pain. He had had a mild attack the previous fall but recovered and assumed his normal active routine until this episode. At 3:00 A.M. on Tuesday, April 15, Jacob Estey died, aged seventy-six, of a heart attack.

Estey was a man of his time. His life fit the Victorian paradigm: irreproachable conduct involving home, church, and family in harmony with God. "His home was the embodiment of the Christian ideal," eulogized the pastor of the First Baptist Church, of which Estey had been a member for fifty years. Few towns owed as much for their growth and material prosperity as Brattleboro owed to Jacob Estey. On the day of Estey's funeral and interment, the town stopped business to pay their respects, and two thousand people joined the funeral procession (figure 78).

Decades later, sentiment for Estey remained strong:

Young Estey heard the Whetstone's song
As sad as death the winter long;
He heard it laugh, when summer came,
Like children's voices, bright and gay,
And as he made his pipes, an aim
Was born to make those sweet notes stay.

His instruments made our town known
In many a strange and distant zone—
When services are held abroad,
From war's great strain, an interlude,
And men sing hymns of faith in God,
An Estey organ sets the mood.[110]

Jacob Estey's business stratagem—micromanaged organization, efficient mechanization, aggressive consumer marketing, and international distribution—was destined for the new era. He embraced capitalistic industrialism with extraordinary zeal and against the odds built a thriving business. Estey's enterprise developed during an era of industrial benevolence; for a time, industrialists were seen by many as father figures—willing, through their own success, to help those less fortunate. Unlike some industrialist manufacturers, Estey seems to fit this mold.

A less generous interpretation might be that people revered Estey simply because he had money, helped the town, and paid honest wages. It might be ar-

gued that with Estey, the statements upon which we make judgments of temperament and disposition are of varying reliability: company spokespersons, company catalogues, and countless testimonials from company celebrants provide marginally credible character references. The local newspaper, for obvious reasons, never dared quibble with community leaders of Estey's stature lest the benefactor's largesse be withdrawn. Since such reportage was invariably biased to the positive, it is difficult to objectively assess the man. Though it is easy to portray Estey as an enlightened employer during a period of increasing labor unrest, we have little insight into his darker side, if indeed there was one. There can be little question, however, that Estey was sharp, wily, and hard-nosed when the occasion called for it. Shrewdness was a trait frequently cited to characterize

Figure 78.
Jacob Estey's funeral procession, Main Street, Brattleboro, Vermont, April 15, 1890

The Estey Organ Company [167

the more autocratic side of Estey's business persona. He could doubtless be a tough boss—justifiably so, since such attributes were most likely requisite for success in selling a rather exclusive, genteel item in a highly competitive, cut-throat market.[111]

And with wealth came social and political prestige, especially for those in the upper echelons of the business. The reality was that Estey craftsmen, though well cared for, reached no such promontory. Riley Burdett, a genius in his own right, and others like him, achieved a certain level of success but, because they were employees instead of employers, enjoyed little status within the upper social ranks. Successful entrepreneurs gained advantage over the artisan class because of their ability to muster capital and command labor.[112] Eventually industrial workers became typecast, self-determination was constricted, class stratification became more distinct, and popular taste became more prescribed. Collective difficulties arose as new forms of social organization were sorted out. These issues remain quandaries in the arena of mass production and consumer enterprise.

Nonetheless, there is little doubt that Jacob Estey, nonmusician though he was, had a tremendous impact on the nineteenth-century American music scene. The standardization of reed organ manufacture strongly affected a standardization of musical taste, a development that brought music within most anyone's province. Since the reed organ was cheap, portable, reliable, and in fashion, it offered more advantages than any other instrument of the day. As one of the most noteworthy and largest manufacturers of reed organs in the world, Estey made available hundreds of thousands of instruments on which Americans and others throughout the world could make music. The organs were designed to make simple arrangements of popular sacred and secular music sound complex yet emotionally satisfying. In terms of popular culture, by helping create a mass market for "home entertainment" (with its attendant accessories), Estey's generation was the first to ascertain the potential and derive commercial gain from the do-it-yourself phenomenon: allowing the customer some control, "success guaranteed," over the outcome of product application. With the eventual development of products such as the Victrola and the radio, the idea of no-fail implementation and instant gratification through "push-button music" was soon to follow.

In the final analysis, we know that as a person, Jacob Estey was modest and unassuming, had a somewhat reserved personality, maintained a low social profile except when called upon, and lived in a humble house. He was also a very good businessman. Those who knew him well commented on his "wide reading and large intelligence" and his "ready wit and bright play of fancy." Estey summed up his own secrets of success in an 1887 publication titled *One Hundred Lessons in Business*, by Seymour Eaton: "Economy, avoid the use of tobacco and all stimulants, and bad company." Add to this his dedication to the church and a happy home, and Estey's life personifies the quintessential Victorian success story.

1890—1900: APEX

Jacob Estey's affairs were left in such perfect condition that he did not bother to leave a will. After his passing, business continued without a hitch, thanks to his meticulous organizational foresight. The business was "so strongly and securely established that others could take it from his hands without shock or jar, and carry it forward to still greater success."[1] By the beginning of the final decade of the nineteenth century, the Estey factory occupied almost four acres of floor space and employed over five hundred workers who were paid a total of $25,000 monthly to produce more than 1,500 organs per month.[2] Jacob Estey had doubtless provided inspiration and insight for the formation of the Estey Piano Company in New York as well.[3] And since Estey was always looking for opportunities beyond keyboard instruments to increase profitability, it was his money and counsel that laid the foundation for the Estey Manufacturing Company of Owosso, Michigan, a leading furniture manufacturing concern in the West.

At this juncture, Julius J. Estey assumed the presidency of the company (figure 79). Born in January 1845, the second child and only son of Jacob and Desdemona Estey, Julius J. Estey was forever to live in the shadow of his father. Even in Julius's obituary at his death in 1902, the well-worn story of his father's life preceded the recounting of his own. Nonetheless, Julius further strengthened the initiatives devised by his father and carried the Estey legacy into the twentieth century.

Admitted at the age of twenty-one into the Estey firm, Julius was promoted to treasurer upon the incorporation of the Estey Organ Company in 1872. A man with a bent for the military, he organized the Estey Guard in 1874 and was

Americans make immense progress in productive industry, because they all devote themselves to it at once; and for the same reason, they are exposed to unexpected and formidable embarrassments. As they are all engaged in commerce, their commercial affairs are affected by such various and complex causes, that it is impossible to foresee what difficulties may arise. As they are all more or less engaged in productive industry, at the least shock given to business, all private fortunes are put in jeopardy at the same time, and the state is shaken.

Alexis de Tocqueville,
Democracy in America

Figure 79.
Julius J. Estey in
military attire

elected its captain, a position he held until his elevation to lieutenant colonel of the First Regiment, Vermont National Guard, in 1881. He became colonel of the regiment in 1886 and in 1892 was promoted to the command of the brigade with the title of general. Truth be told, it was said that Julius would perhaps rather made his name as a military man, winning his laurels in the field instead of the factory.[4]

Julius J. Estey's reputation for handling finance was universally regarded. One rather unflattering anecdote in the *Vermont Phoenix* reported on Estey's task as official ticket-taker at the annual Valley Fair: "and to this day, while Colonel Hooker guarantees the weather, General Estey sells the tickets, counts the money and signs the checks with all the enthusiasm of a horny-handed Vermont farmer."[5]

In addition to shepherding the Estey Organ Company in Brattleboro, the Estey Piano Company of New York, and the Estey Manufacturing Company of Owosso, Michigan, Julius became president of Brattleboro's Peoples National Bank, treasurer of the Vermont Academy at Saxtons River and of the Northfield Seminary, president of the Brattleboro Young Men's Christian Association, and a member of the Columbian Lodge of Masons and of the Beauseant Commandery of Knights Templar. He was a devoted and philanthropic Baptist and close friends with the renowned evangelist Dwight L. Moody and his famous music director Ira D. Sankey. It seems probable that Sankey's instrument of choice was the Estey reed organ. A newspaper account of Julius's life noted that "General Estey is one of the men to whom Mr. Moody looked as a friend of his heart, to whom he confided his plans, and on whom he leaned as on a good right hand."[6] Julius was also active in Vermont politics. An active Republican, he represented Brattleboro in the legislature of 1876 and served as state senator for the biennial term beginning in 1882.

By all accounts, the son of Jacob Estey appears to have been just as even-handed and able as his father. He was characterized in the *Vermont Phoenix* as a man who had "a large grasp of affairs, and acquaintance with men, broadened by much travel, such as few enjoy, and a natural tact in mingling with all sorts and conditions of men, while strictly maintaining his own individuality."[7]

Julius's two eldest sons, Jacob Gray Estey (1871–1930) and Julius Harry Estey (1874–1920), worked their way through the various factory departments, both mechanical and administrative. His third son, Guy Carpenter Estey (1881–1897), did not have the good fortune of his older brothers. At nine, he lost a hand when a cannon prematurely exploded during a political celebration; later, a leg became crippled owing to a "diseased knee." In spite of these handicaps, Guy asked no odds and considered himself a boy among boys. He became an accomplished long-distance bicyclist, and it was evidently not unusual for him to cover over 2,000 miles in a season. By transcending adversity, Guy endeared himself to all who knew him. He died of meningitis at the age of sixteen.

After serving their apprenticeships, J. Gray and J. Harry Estey advanced to assistant superintendent and general office clerk and eventually became vice president and treasurer, respectively. Both assisted in running the Estey Piano Company of New York, with J. Harry again as treasurer. In addition to his bookkeeping expertise, J. Harry was probably the first of the Estey family to have appreciable artistic inclinations, including theatrical talent and a working knowledge of music, a gift that obviously made his association with reed organs more enjoyable. And like their father, both sons were involved in state and national military matters. One late winter's day, J. Gray and Mattie H. (Poor) Estey, had a son, Jacob Poor Estey (1895–1952), thus ensuring another generation of family legacy.

During the fall of 1897 the factory was running ten hours a day, six days a week. Orders were declared flowing in from agencies in the midwestern states of Wisconsin, Iowa, Minnesota, Nebraska, and the Dakotas. The Estey Organ Company had a paid-up capital of over $1 million and was renowned worldwide. Special catalogues were printed for Estey's Canadian representatives, Gourlay, Winter, & Lemming, and for England with prices in guineas, and in Spanish for South American distribution.[8] An affiliation with the DeRees-Bush Company of New York expedited the Estey company's representation in Buenos Aires, Rio de Janeiro, Santiago, Valparaiso, Caracas, and Bahia.

As testament to its global involvement, the company received a letter from Ira D. Sankey, who wrote that he was able, on short notice, to find an Estey organ for his meetings in Jerusalem and Cairo. Other reports mention forty organs being sent to Africa and Tasmania. One tale recounts the travails of an organ ordered from deep in the interior of the African continent: "A special case lined with zinc was built, then two more cases built around this. There was no landing place to unload, so goods had to be thrown bodily overboard and towed ashore by natives in canoes."[9] A missionary in Shanghai, China, reported that as a result of a shipwreck, two Estey organs had sunk to the bottom of a river. "Your two were warped and suffered severely with the soaking while under the river but we were able to use them as if nothing had happened."[10]

The demand for organs seemed limitless. The shops ran even on Christmas day, 1890, an extremely unusual occurrence. Over the next decade, three new boilers and several new molding machines were added to the factory; a 300-horsepower Greene engine with a 16-foot drive wheel was installed; new sheds and lumber storage barns were built, along with many new homes in Esteyville; employees began negotiating an insurance plan with the new management (figure 80); and Saxe and Robertson, the agents for Estey's New York City piano concern (which was producing 250 pianos per month), became Estey and Saxe. The Esteys owned and controlled retail businesses in Boston, New York City, Philadelphia, Chicago, St. Louis, Des Moines, Atlanta, Rutland (Vermont), and London. They were well represented internationally by a corps of 2,500 agents spread throughout the world.

Just as important as global expansionism, especially to those back home in Brattleboro, was that the Estey Organ Company spawned a "great body of intelligent, useful, and self-respecting" citizens (figure 81), many of whom grew old in the company's service, a fact the company enjoyed publicizing: "There are many gray-haired men at work today in the Estey factory who have been working there for fifty years, and in all that time they have never been hurried or told

Figure 80.
Some of the Estey
management staff,
c. 1906

to 'let it go at that,' or pushed beyond the limit of the best and most careful work." [11]

The probable apex of reed organ manufacture by the Estey Company was signaled by the commemoration of its 250,000th organ, "an event," according to the *Presbyterian Journal*, "which stands by itself in the history of the musical and industrial world, . . . having no parallel, in this country or abroad." [12] Julius Estey and the Brattleboro community threw a grand party to which thousands of guests were invited. On a sunny August 17, 1892, the gaily-decorated town welcomed Governor Page and his staff (Fuller was governor-elect at this time), other distinguished Vermont citizens, the press, members of leading houses in the music trade, and all those involved with the organ factory, including the company's five hundred workers (who were granted a paid holiday) and their families. Congratulatory telegrams poured in from as far away as London, Hamburg, Berlin, Vienna, Leipzig, Budapest, Bern, Odessa, and Alexandria.

The celebration was occasion for reviewing the numbers: Brattleboro had progressed from a town with a population of 2,624 and a valuation of $1,177,404 in 1850 to one with a population of 7,000 and a valuation of $4,830,334; the factory had grown to occupy over 150,000 square feet on more than three acres of land; since 1873, the disbursement for wages alone amounted to over $5 million, in addition to the "thousands and thousands of dollars" apportioned for materials. The raw statistics verified the importance of the Estey concern to the economic and social welfare of the town and to the reputation of the state.

Figure 81.
The Estey employees,
c. 1900

Florence Terrace (figure 82), Julius Estey's home on School Street, was elegantly lit with Japanese lanterns, and the event was lavishly catered with long tables of food, including various sculptures of ice cream—one, of course, shaped like an Estey organ.[13] From 5:00 P.M. on the crowd toured the grounds and buildings of the factory. The band played, and speeches and congratulations were offered, resolutions presented, and Brattleboro history reviewed. At 7:00 P.M. formal commemorative exercises were held in the Baptist Church. The main floor and first gallery were reserved for Estey workmen and their families, and for out-of-town guests. The second gallery and the chapel in the rear of the main room were at the disposal of other citizens. The church was packed to standing room only.

Like a guest of honor, in the front of the sanctuary on one side of the pulpit platform stood the 250,000th organ, handsome and solid, its oaken case beautifully carved. Opposite the organ was an upright Estey piano, also of quartered oak. Not to be forgotten, nestled amongst the potted palms surrounding the platform were two early lap organs, a reminder of how far the company had come. Overhead was a life-sized portrait of Jacob Estey, "reproducing in a remarkably realistic way the strong lines of his head and face."[14] The newspaper chronicled

that at the end of the ceremony, Julius Estey expressed how deeply the words of the fine speeches and heart-felt testimonials touched him, "and there was a break in his voice when he said in closing, 'and may God bless you all,' which found a quick response in the heart of every listener."[15]

Afterward, fireworks lit the sky for more than an hour; a final, climactic, custom-made, incendiary display showed the number 250,000 with the dates 1846 and 1892 on either side. We can only imagine the beautiful scene presented, as night enveloped the festive event, by the hundreds of Japanese lanterns adorning the grounds surrounding the proud Promethean factory, fully illuminated from within. For the citizens of Brattleboro and reed organ users around the world, the celebration symbolized a true "triumph of industry." Ironically, as we shall soon see, it also marked the high point of the reed organ's popularity in the United States.

By the end of the 1890s the *Vermont Phoenix* reported that business was thriving: "Looks like old times to see three wagons in constant procession to the station with organs." More than one hundred different styles of organs were being manufactured. The 300,000th organ was finished before the end of the century.

A remarkable decade was marred only by Levi Fuller's death at the age of fifty-five, on October 10, 1896.

Figure 82.
Florence Terrace,
residence of Julius J.
Estey, c. 1906

From the very outset to the turn of the century, the Esteys produced only melodeons, reed organs, and pianos (the latter being made only in New York City). But around the beginning of the twentieth century, new social trends—which did not escape the notice of the company—began to appear, especially in growing urban environments. By the turn of the century, mobility changed the social patterns of American families. The bicycle, popular in the 1890s, augured the preeminence of the automobile. Now youngsters could escape their elders and journey to the soda fountain, the beach, the country club, and, later, the movies. Parlor singing, chatty soirées, and romancing on the porch were doomed.[16]

The bicycle (in its current configuration by 1884) and motorcycle (for the more daring) afforded new sport and some freedom of mobility. But with the advent of the automobile age, families could journey farther to and from mechanized amusement parks and trolley parks, nickelodeons and movie theaters, playhouses and musical reviews, dance halls and cabarets, and spectator-sport arenas.[17] The auto expedited an evening of listening to Wagner at the concert hall, a night dancing to the latest ragtime music at a community center, or attendance at a variety show at one of the more cleaned-up vaudeville houses.[18]

There was, naturally, still much to do at home if one so desired, though the nature of the domestic habitat and the activity within it were also changing.[19] The older ritual-specific parlor gradually gave up its Victorian grip to a more efficient multipurpose space: the living room.[20] To the delight of manufacturers of home furnishings, the contemporary living room required a set of decorating accoutrements much different from those of the parlor. Increasing numbers of department stores, chain stores, and mail-order houses unsparingly supplied the modern necessities for the thriving middle-class household. As personified by the Sears, Roebuck catalogue, the tantalizing, bountiful choices were enough to make a conscientious consumer giddy. What becomes apparent throughout this era is that America's special form of capitalistic commerce—with its unique industrialized, commercialized, popularized, and democratic approach to consumerism—was beginning to fully blossom.

The hoped-for result of industrialism was to make machines do more of the work humans had done in the past. Indeed, for some Americans, the notion of prosperity and leisure was increasingly becoming a reality. Leisure did not mean inactivity, however. As is the case today, affluence and an easing of life's imperatives seem to stimulate consumer restlessness and induce material desire. To satisfy the craving, well-to-do shoppers with disposable money responded by searching out and purchasing goods and commodities—things with which to fill their discretionary time. As socially conservative Victorian attitudes relaxed, women as well as men enjoyed pastime activities such as bicycling, lawn tennis, archery, croquet, and other exercise sports that, as time went on, became more accept-able as an outlet for personal expression and fulfillment.[21]

In fashion and notions of beauty, the Gibson Girl offered a model for the "new woman," supplanting earlier feminine ideals. Dressed simply and practically in skirt and stylish shirtwaist, hair arranged á la pompadour, marcelled, or, later, in a bob, her slender, athletic figure contrasted with the frilly, overblown femi-nine fashions of the Victorian age.[22] Her flirtatious posture and direct gaze added to an attractive allure that exuded self-confidence, perhaps even defiance. Con-comitant with this feminine transformation, the beauty parlor and the cosmet-ics industry had, by the advent of the twentieth century, already set the pattern for their modern form.

Like all marketers, music merchandisers survived and prospered so long as they responded to changing fashion. In the modern home, new popular enter-tainments such as jigsaw puzzles, home-grown magic shows, table tennis, view-ing slides through a stereoscope (the Kodak camera appeared on the market in 1888), board games, card games, and other recreational table games seriously undermined traditional parlor music-making. As a result of changing social and domestic patterns, the old sentimental standards were less frequently taken out of music cabinets and given voice.

Nevertheless, music continued as an important middle-class pursuit. Heed-ful music consumers, in order to maintain pace with up-to-date novelty and pop-ular culture, were exhorted through progressively slicker advertising and pro-motional ploys to stay abreast of the most recent fashion trends. As production techniques were further refined, pianos in particular became less expensive and thus more attractive to families aspiring to the upper class. Retailers offered many new styles of piano to choose from; the upright model, spatially and financially economical, became particularly popular as a preeminent emblem of modernity in domestic furniture. Arthur Loesser in his entertaining book *Men, Women, and Pianos*, put the situation in perspective: in 1870, one American in 1,540 bought a piano; in 1890, one in 874; and by 1910, one person in every 242.[23] The burgeon-ing piano trade began to undermine reed organ sales. The Esteys had foreseen this eventuality by entering the piano business in 1885 and by conducting player-piano experiments.[24] Their intuitions were justified: beginning in the 1890s, the allure of the automated self-playing piano made this instrument one of the most successful musical media of all time (figure 83).

Still, Estey and a few other diehard reed organ manufacturers encased reed organs in piano cabinetry well into the second decade of the 1900s so that, for appearance's sake, the owner created the illusion of being in vogue by owning the fashionable upright piano, thus "enhancing the prestige of their home."[25] Estey's reed organ "pianos" were good instruments and featured eighty-eight keys, two and a half or more sets of reeds, an improved, more efficient foot

Figure 83.
Estey player piano,
Style 8

pumping mechanism, and enlarged chests and cases that generated an excellent sound.

But with the eventual introduction of the phonograph in the 1900s[26] and radio broadcasting during the 1920s,[27] the reed organ did not stand a chance. As each new musical medium became the current status symbol of home entertainment, domestic organ-playing became more old-fashioned.

One attractive characteristic of at least some of the new musical machines was that innovative technology made access to music a far less demanding pursuit than before. Playing the piano and reed organ requires practice; playing the Victrola and radio does not (so much for the Victorian work ethic). But perhaps most importantly, the new musical media offered wider exposure to novel and meaningful aural encounters. The latest opera, band, and orchestral music, as well as musical vogues such as ragtime[28]—an engaging style that did not easily translate to the reed organ — were becoming more available through mass-manufactured musical replicators.

The self-playing reed organ, developed to keep pace with the growing demand for automated music, could not keep up with the craze for stylishly fast, complex music that was being manufactured for the Pianola and its imitators. The player piano itself eventually came under attack: "When all is said and done," reasoned an Edison phonograph ad, "[the player piano] gives you nothing but piano music." The outcome was that instead of singing around the organ or piano, by 1915 Americans preferred dancing around the Victrola.[29]

In spite of a brisk trade in used and second-hand instruments, the popularity of the reed organ declined appreciably at the onset of the twentieth century. As one indication of a dwindling market, a 1912 government publication, *Foreign Trade in Musical Instruments*, reported that between 1899 and 1909 production of piano and player attachments had increased twofold and phonograph and recording sales had multiplied five times, while reed organ production barely maintained an even keel.[30] New entertaining diversions coupled with market saturation and the penchant for pianos and "push-button" music would ultimately lead to the demise of the reed organ.[31]

THE ESTEY COMPANY IN ITS FINAL THROES

As the years passed the century mark, a pronounced change could be detected in national and international architectural style and creative sensibility. In this country, the Progressive era was filled with aesthetic ferment: various artistic movements, such as Beaux Arts, Arts and Crafts, and Art Nouveau, began to overshadow high Victorian fashion. Some of this shift in taste was reflected in organ case design.

A comparison of the Estey organs of the 1880s and those of the 1890s reveals a gradual trend toward less elaborate cabinetry. Whiting notes "that the newer case designs are 'lighter' and much less 'massive' in their details."[32] Though there are still a number of extremely ornate Victorian styles in evidence, organs in the 1895 catalogue show a decided retreat from the heavy and overabundant scrollwork, fretwork, and lathework so characteristic of earlier models (see Appendix D). As the new century arrived, instruments looked less like caricatures of a cathedral organ and began to take on features of the popular upright piano. Granted, high-top options for organs continued well into the 1900s, but they appear more like fireplace mantels and bank counters than altarpieces: more enclosure, less verticality. The gothic aspect, though still apparent, seems to reach out to the player instead of up toward the heavens. Within the canopied recesses of new high-top styles were all manner of beveled mirrors from fine plate glass; every high-top model in Estey's 1903 catalogue featured one or more. Also, the

pretentious names of Estey's various models and case styles had generally been reduced to simple identification letters and numbers.

One sure sign of the reed organ's popular decline was reflected in the decision by the Estey management in 1901 to begin pipe organ manufacture.[33] Julius J. Estey organized the new department, placing William E. Haskell (1865–1927) of Philadelphia, "one of the most gifted inventors in modern organ building,"[34] in charge of running the pipe organ division. Haskell's reputation alone sold the first hundred pipe organs (albeit mostly in the Philadelphia area). Small tubular-pneumatic-action pipe organs, predominately two-manual and pedal instruments, began to come off the assembly line. The first Estey pipe organ, a seven-stop, two-manual instrument known locally as Estey Number One, was installed in 1902 in the sanctuary of Brattleboro's First Methodist Episcopal Church. It was later moved to a new church location and is still in use today.

As the company gathered momentum, buildings Number 7 and Number 8 were renovated and joined (figure 84) to facilitate the assembly and testing of the sizable new pipe organ line (figure 85). Further plant modification was not necessary for a time. This final configuration of the company's main buildings

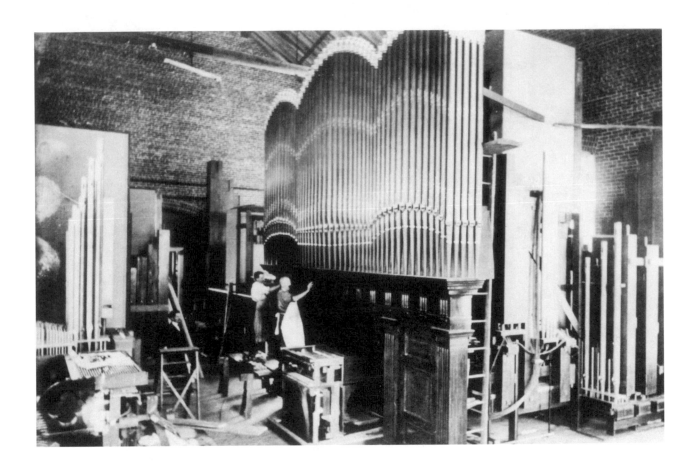

exists today as a noteworthy example of nineteenth-century industrial architecture, unrivaled in the state for its scale and mass.

The Estey company continued its time-honored commitment to stay abreast of changing times by implementing scores of Haskell's pipe organ inventions and refinements.[35] They also redesigned their two-manual reed organs to the pipe organ standards set by the American Guild of Organists, which included reconfiguring flat and straight pedal keyboards to a concave and radiating design. In fact, for several years an overabundance of Estey contracts made it necessary for them to order pipes from other manufacturers. We know that Estey purchased many ranks from at least one supplier, Anton Gottfried in Erie, Pennsylvania.

Between 1901 and 1960 Estey sold 3,261 pipe organs, the greatest lot shipped to customers in South Africa and England. All were beautifully made using first-class materials. However, like most American organs (including mechanical-action instruments), their interior compactness made them difficult to work on. The firm tried various forms of stop mechanisms but used only stop tablets (tilting tablets and stop keys) and draw knobs after 1930.[36] The workmanship was exceptional, but as the years passed, constantly changing tastes in tone quality and

Figure 85.
Erecting a tubular-
pneumatic pipe organ
for testing and
adjustment, c. 1906

Figure 86.
J. Gray Estey

the need to periodically releather pneumatic components led to the replacement of many Estey organs. Early Estey pipe organs have a charming sound, but most of the later ones are generally judged ordinary. It is certain that in the first years of pipe organ manufacture, the Estey company's volume of production was built on its fame with the reed organ, which remained their best-known product. Nonetheless, particularly because of the influence of the highly esteemed Haskell and the improvements he designed, pipe organ sales continued to multiply.

On March 7, 1902, Julius J. Estey died of a diagnosed "fatty degeneration of the heart." The factory was shut down for the day, and the community lamented his passing. His eulogy affirmed that this Estey, like his father, was everybody's friend and an honest, conscientious, sincere man. The presidency of the business was left to his son Jacob Gray Estey (figure 86), who, with his brother, Julius Harry (figure 87), kept the wheels of production running.

J. Gray Estey continued to expand the business by erecting additional buildings, including a spacious brick hall—the "setting-up room"—to accommodate the growing demand for pipe organs (figure 88). Twenty-three pipe organs were built in 1902 and seventy-one in 1903; production was phenomenal until the Great Depression. One successful product developed during this period was the Estey Residence Organ (figure 89), a roll-playing instrument (also playable from the keyboards) that was installed principally in the more elegant homes and funeral parlors. While the perforated roll played, "operators" could electrically select their own registrations and control the expression devices independently of the instrument's note-playing functions. An extensive catalogue of compositions transcribed for the Estey Residence Organ, mostly from the classical tradition with a smattering of popular fare (see the accompanying compact disc), fills two bound volumes. Owners were encouraged to suggest new compositions, which the company promised would be expeditiously arranged for the roll format and placed in the catalogue. Among the copious selection of orchestral and operatic transcriptions was even some legitimate organ music.

Brattleboro would not soon forget September 24, 1915, the day Henry Ford, an industrial maestro himself, arrived in town to view the grand Estey Residence Pipe Organ he had ordered for his new mansion near Detroit. Estey craftsmen had worked on it for over a year. Ford had planned a "whistle stop" in Brattleboro on his way to New York but became so engrossed with the factory and the process by which organs were made that he missed the appointed train and stayed overnight, talking with workers and enjoying his new organ. The organ weighed several tons and boasted fifty stops, a concert harp, cathedral chimes, and the latest automatic self-playing mechanism. The cost was reportedly $25,000.[37] The firm was duly proud of the millionaire's organ, especially since Ford had visited other organ companies around the country before entrusting Estey craftsmen with the task.

After Ford left town, the factory opened their setting-up facility so the public

Figure 87.
J. Harry Estey

Figure 88.
Building for setting up
pipe organs

Figure 89.
Estey Residence Organ,
c. 1910

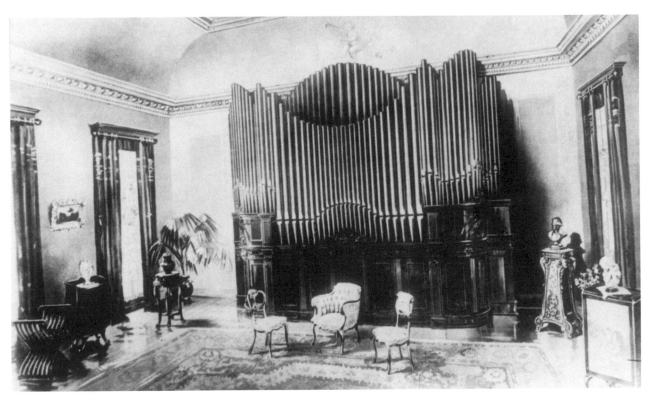

Figure 90.
Estey managers with Jacob Gray Estey (top row, 3rd from left), Luther P. Hawley (top row, 5th from left), Jacob Poor Estey (top row, 3rd from right), William E. Haskell (top row, 2nd from right), Joseph Gray Estey (top row, far right), c. 1925.

could view the elegant instrument and hear a Boston musician perform before it was dismantled, crated, and sent to Michigan. Ford was so taken by the final installation that he requested a list of all the Estey employees who had worked on the organ, to each of whom he sent a letter of appreciation and a monetary bonus, mostly checks in the amount of five to twelve dollars (some larger), a sizable sum during a time when the usual day's wage for many workers was one dollar. The employees responded with a letter of gratitude and a rousing three cheers for Ford and for those who had superintended the organ's construction.

By 1916 the company's fiscal business was divided about equally between reed and pipe organs. Reportedly, prior to the disruption caused by the World War I, over half of the reed organ output was exported, with most of it going to Europe (especially England) and Australia.[38]

After the death of Julius Harry Estey in 1920, the fourth generation of Esteys became involved in the business. Jacob Poor Estey and Joseph Gray Estey, the two sons of Jacob Gray Estey (who was still president of the company at that time) (figure 90), and Paul Chase Estey, son of the deceased J. Harry Estey, joined the company's ranks. Reed organ production continued, but pipe organ manufacture predominated.

By 1921 the Estey company reportedly had tallied its 2,000th pipe organ.[39] With minor exceptions, Estey's claim that it was the only company in the country that made every component in its organs was true. The factory space had expanded to 250,000 square feet. By 1923 the company maintained sales offices in Cleveland, Atlanta, Memphis, Richmond, St. Louis, Seattle, Sioux City, Dallas,

Pittsburgh, Syracuse, San Francisco, and Springfield (Massachusetts), and had studios in New York, Philadelphia, Boston, Chicago, Los Angeles, and London.[40] The core Estey sales staff had logged an average of eleven years for each man and, totaled as a group, had spent 241 years in Estey service.

The beginning of the Great Depression in 1929 devastated financial institutions nationally, stunned the country's populace, caused the demise of a vast number of businesses, and hurt the organ market considerably. The public simply stopped buying organs for home use. One year after the market crash, the Estey Organ Company was dealt another critical blow: Jacob Gray Estey contracted pneumonia while vacationing in Bermuda and soon after, on May 20, 1930, died at the age of fifty-eight from complications involving an "acute dilation of the heart."

True to his family's tradition, J. Gray had devoted his life to the global commitments of the corporation and concern with numerous local enterprises and philanthropies. His list of affiliations and accomplishments closely follows the pattern of his father and grandfather: president of the Vermont-Peoples National Bank, a trustee of the Vermont Savings Bank, president of the Memorial Hospital Corporation, director of a life insurance company, and, though not as involved as his father, a participant in state politics. His obituary stated:

> Colonel [J. Gray] Estey was a man who could probably have achieved almost any position he sought in state politics, for he was gifted as a leader and organizer, but outside of being a staunch Republican at heart, he had no desire whatever to enter public life. The nearest he came to it was accepting a place on the Republican delegation from Vermont to the national convention at Chicago in 1912, when occurred the famous rift between Taft and Roosevelt. In that convention, Col. Estey cast his vote, as did the other Vermont delegates, for the regular and successful nominee, Mr. Taft.[41]

Other of his involvements ran the gamut from holding the presidency of the Brattleboro Council of Boy Scouts to being a prime mover in organizing the Brattleboro Country Club, of which he also became president.

And as we may have guessed from his patrilineage, his preeminent interest was military: twenty-three years in the Vermont National Guard (which he joined at the age of 16), eleven of them as colonel of the First Regiment.[42] Reports in the *Brattleboro Daily Reformer* concerning J. Gray's military record confirm his extensive efforts to organize and "prepare nearly 800 young Vermonters to take the field at a moment's notice if the country should ever need them." Upon Jacob Gray Estey's death, his sons, Jacob Poor Estey and Joseph Gray Estey, along with Julius Harry Estey's son, Paul Chase, took over the concern.

During the early 1930s, as the nation struggled to regain some semblance of economic equilibrium, Estey sales dropped from $600,000 to $200,000 per year, enough to force the company into bankruptcy.[43] For the first time in the history of the enterprise, Estey assets were sold to nonfamily parties. In 1933 the business was reorganized into the Estey Organ Corporation with Jacob Poor Estey as president, his brother, Joseph, as vice president, and Alphonse Brungardt as manager. After Brungardt's death in 1942, Premo Ratti took over managerial responsibilities. We know little concerning these two managers' dispositions. Departments within the factory were consolidated into a few buildings, and a mere sixty employees returned to run the shops.

From the Gay Nineties through the Roaring Twenties and on to the post-depression 1940s, the pace of cultural productivity, innovation, and modernization intensified. As a case in point, the musical eclecticism that materialized throughout this period is formidable: John Philip Sousa and Edwin Franko Goldman in band music; George M. Cohan, Irving Berlin, Jerome Kern, Florenz Ziegfeld, George Gershwin, Victor Herbert, and Richard Rodgers in musical theater; Scott Joplin, Eubie Blake, W. C. Handy, Jelly Roll Morton, Louis Armstrong, the Original Dixieland Jazz Band, Duke Ellington, and Count Basie in ragtime and jazz; Uncle Dave Macon, the Carter Family, Jimmie Rodgers, Ernest Tubb, Bob Wills, Roy Acuff, Bill Monroe, Hank Williams, and Woody Guthrie in folk and country music; and Charles Ives, Roger Sessions, William Grant Still, Ruth Crawford Seeger, Walter Piston, Aaron Copland, Virgil Thomson, Henry Cowell, and Samuel Barber in art music. This sampling, each with its own interesting story, suggests that Americans were not only becoming accustomed to a wide variety of musical choice but demanding it.

The ascension of market-oriented publishing through these years, with Tin Pan Alley as the alpha model, proved that manufacturing the musical artifacts of popular culture was a very lucrative business indeed.[44] Intrinsic to this sociomusical ferment was the fact that finally Americans were proud of what they had become. Though yet to be fully forged, American expressive culture, especially of the popular sort, was reflective of a unique, distinctive national character. Though still hesitant to admit it at the time, Americans began to realize that jazz in particular, with its "counter rhythms and new tricks of orchestral coloring . . . made [American] popular music ingenious and musically something to be reckoned with."[45] This nation's music and art could now stand up to any in the world. Unfortunately, few of the new music types included the playing of organs, which continued to lose commercial cachet throughout this time period.

Augmenting Estey's conventional pipe organ design, perhaps out of desperation, was the organ-with-gimmicks category.[46] One such instrument, the New Estey Visual Instruction Organ, a player pipe organ designed and built at the beginning of the depression for school and church use, featured a "luminous console" consisting of lights (actually flashlight bulbs) that displayed the performer's current choice of stop registrations. Seven such self-playing organs were purchased and installed in selected New York City public schools. George Gartlan, director of music for the schools, waxed poetic over the Estey product: "If this instrument brings cheer to the weary, inspiration to the ambitious, solace to the unhappy—if it brings to the heart of a little child a new faith in himself—if it brings joy, and I know it will, the director of music in the city of greater New York will be happy."[47]

Attempting to keep up with changing times, throughout the 1930s and 1940s Estey updated the lines of Chapel, Church, and Gothic Organs, the old reed organ standbys. Even the venerable square piano-style melodeon of the 1860s was revamped in 1934 with "mechanical and tonal improvements," including electrically operated bellows. Additional options were available on some models, including a clever "transposing keyboard," which allowed players to mechanically shift the tonal center chromatically by one full step either above or below the written key to avoid having to adjust their fingering. In addition, new models of Student Organ, Practice Organ, Artist's Organ, and Virtuoso Organ began to appear along with the stylish Art Deco Modernistic Organ, "especially designed to meet the demand for organ music outside the church . . . ideally suitable for residences, lodges, broadcasting studios, and orchestras." Clearly, promotion through radio airplay and from the concert stage was desirable and offered fresh opportunity to bring new Estey products to public notice.

As we saw in earlier advertising, Estey had long exploited the connection between organs and children, and now developed a line of pint-sized, foot-pumped, miniature "children's organs" for small players (figure 91).[48] Marketed through large department stores as toy organs, the Little Esteys were verifiably genuine musical instruments, some even with electric blowers. Smaller than the folding organ type and not collapsible, these instruments, with their three-octave keyboards, were advertised as promising hours of self-absorbed entertainment for children ages five to twelve, who would be begging each other for turns to play. Weighing only thirty-one pounds, it was, according to an undated Estey catalogue, easily "movable from child's room to living or game room." The somewhat larger four-octave Junior Organ presumably attracted a slightly more mature youngster. Late in the 1930s, the electrically blown Estey Spinet featured 8' reeds, standard key size, matching bench, "double guarantee," and "a gay collection of 10 Top Tunes" written especially for beginners (figure 92). Instruments were available in four different "Spectolite" colors: speckled ivory, speckled black-and-gold, mahogany-colored, and self-blending pearl gray. Another reed organ with electric blower, the modest, single-manual Estey Chorus, was described in an undated Estey catalogue as having a four-octave range with two full sets of reeds housed in an "attractive seasoned hardwood case, finished in limed oak, walnut or mahogany." Since there was no need to pump treadles, thus freeing the feet for other tasks, players were encouraged to employ the single swell pedal for "unique effects . . . exciting volume or intriguing shades of expression. It's as easy as accelerating a car!"

Figure 91.
Estey Miniature Organ

Figure 92.
Estey electric Spinet
organ advertisement,
c. 1957

Innovation and accommodation remained an important aspect of the company's design and production. Marketed as the Estey Orgoblo, electric suction units became a common option on many new reed organ models.[49] The company also experimented with Minshall amplifiers which, it was claimed, could produce pipe-organ effects from reed organs.[50] In the late 1930s they developed a two-manual-with-pedal electropneumatic reed organ, the EPRO, to compete with the Hammond electric organ, which had just come on the market.[51]

But cosmetic alteration, niche marketing, and more gimmickry did not turn the tide of the reed organ's decreasing appeal. In the waning years of the 1930s, reed organ manufacture in the United States almost ceased as more and more keyboard instrument makers concentrated on pianos and electronic organs. A few companies were forced to diversify their product base by manufacturing items that were altogether unrelated to keyboard instruments. Some pinpointed new markets in foreign lands, India being the most receptive at that time. Others simply went out of business.

Also during the 1930s, Estey intensified manufacture of its enduring best-selling folding reed organ. Popular since the 1880s, they remained in great demand through World War I and with the onset of World War II continued the promise of a strong return. Though organs that collapsed into their own casing were deployed everywhere from midwestern logger's camps to foreign missions, the most lucrative contract for portable organs came from the United States government. Called field, chaplain's, or missionary organs, these small, lightweight, compact, easily transportable instruments were increasingly coveted by religious crusaders who relied on organ music to elevate their proselytizing and boost troop morale.

Later models, such as the Estey Missionary Folding Organ, had hardwood cases usually covered with brown, olive drab, or navy blue cloth, weighed sixty-five pounds, and when opened measured approximately thirty inches long, thirty inches high, and sixteen inches deep (figure 93). Featuring 8' and 4' reeds, this practical, no-nonsense instrument became an extremely important bread-and-butter item for the company.

Robert Gellerman has compiled interesting correspondence between three of the major manufacturers of folding portable reed organs during this time—Estey, A. L. White, and Bilhorn—that documents each company's struggle to gain the upper hand for the profitable U.S. Army portable organ concession.[52] The army's corps of chaplains evidently took their musical responsibilities seriously and mandated that the little organs be tough, reliable, and able to withstand the vagaries of extreme climate and conditions. Gellerman reports that during World War II, Estey produced the majority of folding organs.[53] The organ deal was supplemented with required but gainful military contracts for bomb and ammunition boxes, skis for the troops, and pontoon bridges.

Figure 93.
Estey Folding Organ,
c. 1952

Predictably, most manufacturers' response to a decreasing market were economic: prices of reed organs were cut as competition for consumer dollars increased, and as noted, many factories discontinued building reed organs altogether in favor of pianos. By the fourth decade of the twentieth century, only three out of several hundred recognized reed organ manufacturers had endured; predictably, one was the Estey Organ Corporation (figure 94).[54]

Several noteworthy changes occurred in the 1950s. Control of the company returned to the Estey family with Jacob Poor Estey still at the helm, and with the entry of Wilson Estey, the son of Joseph Gray, a fifth generation of Esteys were in the business. Nearly 500,000 reed organs had been manufactured, with over 3,000 pipe organs augmenting the grand total. Though hard times caused the company to occasionally diversify their output (for instance, by making silverware chests and phonograph cases), the essential and fundamental product remained the organ. Early in 1952 the company filled its single most expensive pipe organ order, a $52,000 instrument installed in Florida A & M College in Tallahassee.

Shortly after attending a Red Sox–Yankees game at Fenway Park in Boston on August 15, 1952, Jacob Poor Estey died, aged fifty-seven, of a heart attack.

Figure 94.
Reed organ Number
400,000. Note the "ST"
logo, 1915

Like his predecessors, he had spent his life actively involved in several community organizations, including executive positions with the town's hospital, the country club, a local church, the Elks and Odd Fellows Lodges, the Masonic Order, and the American Legion. His wife, Edith M. (Tyler) Estey, and daughter, Susan, survived him. His son Jacob, named after his great-great-grandfather, was lost in a 1945 accident at sea while serving with the army in Italy during World War II. Jacob Poor's brother, Joseph Gray, died the following year.

In the early 1950s, three years after the Estey family had regained ownership, Henry Hancock, of Rieger Organs of New Jersey, a subsidiary of a notable Austrian pipe organ firm, bought the company. The stratagem seemed plausible, since in the past Estey had sold many Rieger tracker-action pipe organs to American customers. Soon, however, the truth of the matter was revealed in an incident involving master organ technician John Wessel. Brought from Holland under Estey sponsorship in 1954 and hired ostensibly as a voicer, Wessel was confronted with several Rieger organs that had split and fallen apart. The instruments, imported from Austria and made with European woods, had quickly degenerated because of the seasonal wintertime lack of humidity, made worse by New England's heating requirements. The dismayed Wessel soon found himself assigned to a variety of other tasks both in the factory and on the road.[55] Wessel was quick to note, however, that "[Hancock] always came up with the payroll; and wherever he got it, we didn't know or didn't care."

The collaboration with the Minshall Organ Company had introduced a new product line: electronically amplified reed organs to compete with the Everett Orgatron and similar ones made by Wurlitzer.[56] Minshall maintained a building on Estey property, and employees filled in at Estey when quotas required additional labor. Minshall made the electronic components, and Estey built the organ and combined the parts. Minshall also produced their own particular line of very basic electronic organs. Most agree that the Minshall-Estey product, though clever and timely, was inferior, and that the collaboration was a bad idea.

In 1954 Estey set up its own electronic division in building Number 1 and, with Leslie Nicholas in charge of operations, produced an organ designed by Harald Bode.[57] An additional plant for production of electronic organs was established for a few years in Torrance, California. With new management, product, and another location, the company workforce increased to the highest level in decades.

Another sign of economic respite was reported by the *Brattleboro Daily Reformer* in May 1955 when a new Estey Organ Corporation "salon" opened on West Fifty-seventh Street in New York City. Organs were only sold, not manufactured, in the New York studios. Pipe organ recitals were broadcast on radio from the new showrooms every Sunday between 4 and 5 P.M., immediately after the New York Philharmonic Orchestra concert. In stark contrast to the old Victorian parlor, organ studios and showrooms now flaunted highly fashionable, modern, chic settings, as one may infer from the description in the *Reformer* article of the Estey salon:

> Flooring is of black marble and is covered with beige nylon rugs. The ceiling is dark charcoal and the walls beige with imported murals. The couch is raspberry red and the settee, green to provide color accent. Draperies are of beige and are shot with gold. Claire Coci, official organist of the New York Philharmonic Orchestra, played the Rieger organ that is manufactured here by Estey. It is expected that Miss Coci will appear in one of a series of 'erecting room' recitals to be presented in the Estey factory on some of the large instruments due to be shipped to churches during the summer.

The report is wrong, however, on two counts: Rieger organs were never manufactured in New York, and the anticipated factory recitals by the flamboyant Miss Coci never happened.

Desirous of keeping up with other pipe organ manufacturers that looked to Europe for tonal ideals, Estey placed Georg Steinmeyer, member of a famous German firm, in charge of the pipe organ division. Steinmeyer was likely hired for his salesmanship abilities and for his well-known name. But it was almost too late for a rally; financial manipulations and a "too hastily prepared" product left the company vulnerable.[58] A certified public accountant was hired to analyze operations covering a fourteen-month period ending in April 1956. The audit revealed that the Estey corporation was dangerously close to insolvency. Faced with bankruptcy action, the board elected Frederick L. Chapman as president pro tempore. A new group of investors infused $600,000 into a new corporation, Estey Organ Corporation (Del.), which in October 1956 merged the Vermont organization into itself. Nevertheless, according to the president's report dated February 28, 1957, "it was obvious that the company could not continue." At this juncture, Arnold Bernhard took over as president and is said to have been the real owner, having bought Estey as a tax write-off. He proceeded to reorganize the company's financial situation through redistribution of debt load against projected capital income.[59] A reassessment of the product itself, the seemingly endlessly adaptable organ, was also forthcoming.

The newly incorporated Estey (Del.) was aware of increased competition in the electronic organ industry and consequently completely redesigned its line of electronic keyboards. Production schedules called for electronic organs in mahogany, walnut, ebony, oak, cherry, maple and fruitwood.[60] The new company also decided to have another go at updating the trusty old reed organ, for which there was now virtually no competition. As from the very beginning, Estey's aim was to produce a trouble-proof, low-priced instrument of pure tonal quality.[61] However, the problem of reactivating market interest in reed organs posed a daunting challenge for the promotion and sales staff. The pipe organ division also continued to founder; though not profitable, it was still maintained by a skeleton crew of about fifteen personnel (one-third of whom were administrators and draftsmen) because of the status and distinction it afforded and because "it keeps alive in America an art that honors the company's old name."[62] Unfortunately, Estey (Del.) went bankrupt in 1958.

Yet another reorganization led to a brief reprieve for the corporation. Though organs still remained its mainstay, the owners continued to make ancillary items such as downhill skis and "Klepper fold-boats," ventures that reaped a poor return.

Electric chord organs were now popular. One Estey model had thirty-seven keys, forty chord buttons, tone control, volume control, a three-button orchestra section, an eight-button instrument section, and a "vibrator"—a far cry from the old handcrafted melodeons and parlor organs, and in the opinion of many, a degradation of the Estey name. This cheaply made model, more like an accordion than an organ, was manufactured in Italy and only assembled in Brattleboro.[63]

With the last run of chord organs, a name change to Estey Electronics, Incorporated, and a corporate move to California, where the firm was taken over by Magna Electronics in 1959, came the termination of reed organ manufacture

in Brattleboro. When the pipe organ department closed in 1960, Brattleboro citizens and businesses contributed to meet the final payroll. Local folklore has it that Estey employees wept while hearing a recital on the last pipe organ to leave the erecting room.[64]

Thereafter, the stretch between Canal and Estey Streets became disturbingly quiet and lifeless (figure 95). The *Brattleboro Daily Reformer* observed: "Stark, unused factory buildings stand as uncomfortable reminders of a proud craftsmanship no longer in Brattleboro."[65]

Finally, the 115-year-old firm was sold to the Organ Corporation of America,[66] and on November 2, 1961, the Birge Street factory was purchased from the bank by George Mason, a wealthy Brattleboro citizen. Much of the contents of the office and shops was hauled to the Brattleboro dump. With the sale of the venerable old factory, the reed organ industry in the United States had ended.

Figure 95.

The factory in 1987

The fact was that times had changed to such a degree that for non-church use, older styles of organ had almost completely gone out of vogue. Barely surviving the jazz age,[67] the domestic organ was not to endure the onslaught of new musics[68] and their contiguous technologies, especially rhythm and blues and its offspring, rock 'n' roll. Only the Hammond B3 electronic organ found a niche in the popular textures of jazz, blues, gospel, and rock;[69] otherwise, the piano was generally the keyboard of choice.[70] Nevertheless, electropneumatic organs such as the Estey Virtuoso, as well as various types of so-called chord organs, did appear in many American living rooms and family rooms after World War II and throughout the 1950s and 1960s. They were all electrically blown with options regarding amplification, and they offered special features, such as chimes on electropneumatic models and a "rhythm section" (march, waltz, beguine, and such—nothing too outlandish) on the chord organs.

The mid-to-late 1960s and early 1970s was a rite of passage for America with the Vietnam War and the civil rights movement furnishing the most challenging issues. In the world of commerce and entertainment, the gradual evolution of popular culture to a mass pop culture culminated during this period and affected every aspect of American life.[71] Musically, the emphasis on amplified guitars, a heavy beat, exotic sounds (especially from India), politicized lyrics, nonconformist behavior, and intense drug experimentation was indeed a long way from Victorian provenance. The coming of the Beatles, the Rolling Stones, Motown, Woodstock, disco, psychedelic music, folk rock, and rockabilly signaled the arrival of a major social metamorphosis. With media hyperbole inflaming people's materialistic cravings (especially those of the postwar baby-boom generation), national consumption of music and other commodified goods reached levels never before imagined.

All the while, besides an occasional appearance in rock and soul music, electric organs were fading more and more into the background. Though the commercial future appeared bleak for organs of all types, it was during this period that a variety of small, portable electronic keyboards began to show up in retail department stores alongside other domestic entertainments. With built-in synthesized sounds and rhythms and novel ways to manipulate them, fledgling keyboardists could sound "symphonic" at the touch of a key. Sound familiar?

Except for some rather eccentric experimentalism in art music,[72] electronically synthesized sound ceased to be a novelty when, in the mid-1960s, Robert Moog invented a true keyboard synthesizer capable of producing an unlimited number of sounds and effects.[73] Further, he demonstrated how to marshal electronically processed "space-age" noise into intelligible music.[74] Subsequent innovation, including refinement of the microchip, the ascension of digital technology and microprocessing, and the development of MIDI (Musical Instrument Digital Interface) standards, opened many new sonic potentials. Soon the keyboard "synthesizer workstation" or "synth"—a digital instrument that can theoretically produce and manage an infinite number of sounds and rhythms (including those of reed organs, pianos, and instruments yet to be imagined)—essentially took over the keyboard market and soon came into conflict with other sectors of the music industry.[75] At this juncture, any possibility of a reed organ renaissance seemed remote.

Back in Brattleboro, in 1962 Mason sold the Estey buildings to Hyacinth Renaud, a former Estey employee, cabinetmaker, restorer of antiques, and father of sixteen, for about $35,000. Renaud sold most of the structures, retained three, and set up a woodworking shop in building Number 5. He dreamed of accumulating a collection of Estey reed organs for a museum he hoped to open in another of his buildings. It was a shame, Renaud lamented, that not many people knew much about Brattleboro's industrial past. Regrettably, Renaud's plans never materialized, and much of his property was sold to other interests, with the remainder passing to his wife, Louise Renaud, and his family.

Through the 1960s and into the 1970s at least five owners used buildings in the Estey complex for storage space, a trucking garage, a discount shoe store, a furniture warehouse, and other low-budget enterprises. Most of the space was left unheated, and a few buildings in the rear were removed. Some townspeople felt the buildings should be razed, since they had become a fire hazard and an invitation to vandalism. But in 1971 the factory complex was inventoried by the state in a Vermont Historic Sites and Structures Survey, and in 1979 Louise Renaud took the initiative to have the buildings listed in the National Register of Historic Places, an effort that successfully culminated in January 1980. Meanwhile, the various owners struggled to keep the buildings usable by repairing deteriorating roofs and foundations. Also in 1980, Mrs. Renaud sold building Number 5 to her sons, who in turn sold all the contents concerning organs to Ned Phoenix, a local musician and reed organ specialist then of Jamaica, Vermont.[76]

By the late 1980s and early 1990s new owners were beginning to renovate and invigorate the buildings for new uses such as offices and apartments. The Brattleboro town government identified the Estey complex as a potential area for development in its town plan.[77] But not all was to progress smoothly. Estey building Number 5 caught fire on a blustery Saturday afternoon, November 16, 1991 (figure 96). Called in at 4:17 P.M., the fire blazed for three and a half hours and required one hundred firefighters from eight departments in three states to bring it under control. At 500 gallons of water per minute, an estimated 607,000 gallons were pumped onto the burning building. The probable cause of the fire was speculated to have been hot coals from an untended wood stove, fueled by years of accumulated wood shavings.

Various interests nonetheless continued to work to upgrade the Estey build-

Figure 96.
Aftermath of Estey
building Number 5 fire,
November 16, 1991

ings and revitalize Birge Street. There was, in fact, much new activity. Some of the old buildings housed small businesses, offices, workshops, a church congregation, and a day-care center. Renovations began to reveal a raw but historic beauty beneath the insults of time, a patina that was enhanced through repair and restoration. Between 1993 and 1994 Brattleboro received grant money to carry out a feasibility study and develop a master plan for the entire complex. Town revolving-loan funds and some federal loans helped rehabilitation efforts, and gradually the buildings once again began to be used productively.

Though much valuable historical documentation was lost over the years, especially during the haphazard evacuation of the buildings, Estey ephemera have increasingly become objets d'art. Trade cards, posters, photographs, journals, correspondence, and other Estey-related materials have over time become collectible. A visit to a private New York antique dealer late in the 1980s enlightened me as to the escalating value of particular items. Parts of Levi Fuller's tuning fork collection, for instance, were being put on the auction block, along with some Estey correspondence and advertising materials for appreciable sums. Today such items are being bartered and sold through commercial and personal computer networks over the World Wide Web. And a color Estey company poster (showing a blue-hued, cherubic young woman offhandedly stroking a harp; see figure 97), hugely enlarged from the original, is mounted in an open promenade area on an exterior wall of a three-story building in the MGM Theme Park in Las Vegas, Nevada. Interest in Estey memorabilia promises to intensify in the future. The Brattleboro Historical Society is working diligently to keep

Figure 97.
Reproduction of 1890s
Estey trade card, MGM
Theme Park, Las Vegas,
Nevada

up with an expanding collection of materials and organs donated from around the country.

Even after a century and a half, organ producers continue to covet and exploit the Estey brand name. A 1992 article by Brent Bowers, staff reporter of the *Wall Street Journal*, revealed that one Bob Fletcher, "a displaced Yankee entrepreneur," had purchased the name of the Estey Organ Company and, much to the surprise and chagrin of everyone in Brattleboro, was successfully peddling "Estey" electronic organs in Port Richey, Florida, shopping malls to senior citizens. *Music Trades Magazine* confirmed that Fletcher Music was the real thing and, in fact, one of the largest sellers of home organs in the United States. Since home organ sales had slid to an all-time low by the mid-1970s, Fletcher's marketing dilemma must have been how to sell a big-ticket item that hardly anyone wanted.

According to the article, the perceptive Fletcher identified at least a couple of problems with contemporary "organs," especially the new synthesizer keyboards, which were arriving on the market in increasing numbers. They were aesthetically unappealing and so altogether complicated—too many tiny buttons, cryptic labels, incomprehensible instruction manuals, and digital "bugs"— that older adult amateur keyboardists became either intimidated or frustrated. In response, Fletcher signed up Italy's Orla company to manufacture models of electronic organs that emphasized simplicity and accessibility: large buttons friendly to arthritic hands, oversized lettering and straightforward labeling, and classic simulated-wood cabinetry.

Fletcher's strategy was to attract affluent seniors who participated in organized walking tours through urban shopping malls, the malls providing a place where elderly citizens feel safe and can socialize. With each purchase buyers would receive a lifetime of free group lessons and a potluck buffet after every lesson; sessions doubtless provided camaraderie for the lonely and stimulation for the bored. Fletcher reported selling 3,800 units in 1991 and planned to expand to other malls. Would Jacob Estey approve? I believe so.

Epilogue

As a tool for social adhesion and communication, the reed organ had few rivals. To own a reed organ meant that one was progressing in good form through the swiftly moving current of American life; to play the songs of the day provided not only personal catharsis but a sense of belonging. With the reed organ those on the frontier could enjoy "civilization," the middle class could feel "cultured," the religious could exercise their faith, young ladies could practice a feminine accomplishment, and community groups could strengthen and enrich their social bonds. The music played on the reed organ set the standard for much popular music in late-nineteenth-century America and remains an essential part of this country's expressive cultural heritage.

Today reed instrument manufacture has continued to proliferate through the making of concertinas, harmonicas, and many varieties of accordions. Small portable harmoniums are still played for both sacred and secular occasions in India,[1] Pakistan,[2] and other Asian countries.[3] Around 1930 limited numbers of reed organs were reportedly being manufactured in Japan.[4] The Chinese sheng, which, the reader will remember, is where true free-reed technology probably began, has been modernized with the addition of keys and a diversification of size.[5] In addition, enthusiasts around the world are restoring old reed organs and reviving interest in them as collectible antiques and as practical alternatives to electronic organs for churches and for organists' home practice.[6] Organ restorers report no shortage of business. Several significant private collections of reed organs now compliment those found in European, Australian, and American museums.

Furthermore, efforts in reconstructing historical music and performance practices of bygone eras have recently enjoyed a vogue here and in Europe. In 1997, for instance, classical small-ensemble pieces requiring a reed organ were resurrected and showcased at Lincoln Center by the New York Chamber Ensemble. Though the music was written for the European harmonium, a 1936 Estey one-manual, seventeen-stop Modernistic Organ was procured and featured in compositions by César Franck and Gustav Mahler.[7] Endeavors such as these help to make Estey's legacy a living heritage.

Though reed organ manufacture has generally been discontinued, one measure of the instrument's success is perhaps seen in the continued development and popularity of modern electronic keyboards. As on the reed organ, with minimal technical orientation one can create sounds and textures of "philharmonic" proportions on these instruments. Today computerized keyboards are capable of fabricating a vast spectrum of sound (musical and otherwise) and come in a wide variety of styles and setups. The most prevalent of these machines—synthesizers, MIDI controllers, digital samplers, and sequencers, with plug-in modules, software, and features galore—are used in many styles of popular music for creating new soundscapes in an ever-changing kaleidoscope of trend-setting musical genres. The sounds of the synthesizer are ubiquitous in contemporary jazz, Afro-Caribbean popular dance music, world music, and youth-oriented, urban-inspired rock stylings.[8] Though the piano (or at least the sound of the piano) remains preeminent, keyboard synthesizers have become a primary tool for composers of television and film music and de rigueur for all audio recording studios.[9] In the religious sector, as venerable churches begin to modify and replace old pipe organs, many are being enhanced with supplementary digitally synthesized organ sounds.[10]

But perhaps most importantly, as with the reed organ in its day, the availability of modern keyboard synthesizers has democratized the making and distribution of music to a radical degree; meaningful musical activity is accessible to everyone. With products to fit any price range, consumers can now place at their personal disposal an immense amount of sound-manipulating technology. And just as in the nineteenth century, twenty-first-century promises of manufactured musical and social accomplishment through owning the latest technology remain these instruments' greatest allure.

Finally, reed organs are still very much with us.[11] Many thousands of churches, community centers, living rooms, and other American institutions still house working reed organs. Ultimately, they connect us with our past and will doubtless continue to fulfill many of the social and musical functions they have performed so durably for the past one and a half centuries.

APPENDIX A   *Timelines*

Selected Historical Points of Reference

1726   Association of Benjamin Franklin and the printing press.

1753   First steam engine is assembled in the United States.

1776   Declaration of Independence.

1783   Treaty of Paris between Britain and the United States ends American Revolution; Ludwig von Beethoven's first compositions are published; U.S. population is 2.4 million.

1790   Samuel Slater builds first U.S. cotton mill, marking the beginning of the Industrial Revolution in America; earliest American circuses appear; U.S. population is 4 million.

1793   Eli Whitney invents the cotton gin.

1801   Oliver Evans develops a high-pressure steam engine.

1803   Louisiana Purchase; Meriwether Lewis and William Clark begin exploration west of the Mississippi River.

1806   Noah Webster's English-language dictionary is published.

1807   Robert Fulton builds steamboat *Clermont.*

1820   U.S. population is 9.6 million.

1825   Opening of the Erie Canal.

1826   John Stevens runs first American steam locomotive.

1830   First U.S. passenger trains.

1832   Samuel F. B. Morse designs an improved telegraph, patented in 1837; Cyrus McCormick successfully demonstrates a reaper.

1835   Alexis de Tocqueville's *Democracy in America* is published.

1837   Modern U.S. patent system is established; Victoria becomes queen of Great Britain and Ireland.

1838   Samuel F. B. Morse introduces the Morse code.

1840   U.S. population is 17 million.

1842   P. T. Barnum opens American Museum in New York City.

1843   Dan Emmett performs first minstrel show in New York, to great acclaim.

1845   Elias Howe develops his sewing machine; Wagner composes the opera *Tannhäuser.*

1846   Mexican War begins; Iowa becomes twenty-ninth state; pneumatic tire receives patent; planet Neptune is discovered.

1848   Zachary Taylor is elected twelfth president; California gold rush begins; Napoleon III becomes president of Second French Republic.

1850   U.S. population is 31.5 million; California becomes thirty-first state; P. T. Barnum brings Jenny Lind from Sweden for a national tour; U.S. railroads total 9,000 miles, three times the European mileage.

1851   London's Crystal Palace showcases U.S. goods; Isaac Singer patents a continuous-stitch sewing machine.

1852   Napoleon declares himself emperor; horse-drawn steam pumpers are invented; Elisha Otis invents the passenger elevator.

1853   Congress authorizes a survey for a transcontinental railroad route to the Pacific Ocean.

1854   Henry David Thoreau's *Walden* is published.

1856   Western Union is founded.

1858   Stagecoach service and mail delivery begin between San Francisco and St. Louis.

1859   Charles Darwin's *The Origin of Species* is published.

1860   Abraham Lincoln is elected president of the United States; Pony Express is organized.

1861   Civil War begins; telegraph wires are strung between New York and San Francisco.

1862   Passage of Homestead Act.

1863   Emancipation Proclamation.

1865   Civil War ends.

1867   Purchase of Alaska.

1868   Christopher L. Sholes patents his typewriter.

1869   Completion of transcontinental railroad; Black Friday on Wall Street starts panic; Suez Canal is opened.

1870   U.S. population is 40 million.

1871   Great Chicago fire; Fisk Jubilee Singers make their pioneering tour.

1872   Montgomery Ward issues the first mail-order catalogue.

1873   Jesse James's first train robbery; penny postcards introduced; Mark Twain and Charles Dudley Warner collaborate on *The Gilded Age*.

1876   Alexander Graham Bell patents the telephone; the beginning of National League professional baseball; Battle of Little Big Horn.

1877   Thomas Edison patents the phonograph.

1878   Edison Electric Light Co. is founded.

1880   U.S. population is 50 million.

1881   Barnum and Bailey create their circus, the "Greatest Show on Earth."

1882   Nikola Tesla discovers the basis of alternating electric current; first mass production of music records.

1883   Brooklyn Bridge opens; "Buffalo Bill" Cody takes Wild West Show east; beginnings of vaudeville in Boston; Metropolitan Opera opens in New York City.

1884   First modern bicycle.

1885   Louis Pasteur successfully vaccinates against rabies; sheet music begins to be produced for home use.

1886   Haymarket Square riots; Statue of Liberty unveiled; F. W. Woolworth creates first five-and-ten-cent store.

1887   Arrival of internal-combustion automobile.

1888   Kodak camera appears on market; John Philip Sousa writes "Semper Fidelis" for the Marines

1889   North and South Dakota, Montana, and Washington become states thirty-nine through forty-two; Oklahoma Territory opens; Eiffel Tower is built for the Paris Exposition.

1890   U.S. population is 63 million.

1891   Thomas Edison patents his kinetoscopic camera.

1892   The Duryea brothers, J. Frank and Charles, construct the first gasoline automobile; Ellis Island opens.

1893   World's Columbian Exposition held in Chicago's White City; Henry Ford builds his first successful gasoline engine; Czech composer Antonín Dvořák visits the United States and composes his Ninth Symphony, subtitled "From the New World" and based on American folk themes.

1894   Pullman Strike

1895   First amusement park opens at Coney Island, Brooklyn, N.Y.

1897   Klondike gold rush; first Stanley Steamer automobile.

1898   Spanish-American War.

1900   First vacuum tube developed; General Electric, Du Pont, AT&T, and Eastman-Kodak develop independent company research labs.

1901   Queen Victoria of Great Britain dies; Guglielmo Marconi sends wireless messages across the Atlantic.

1903   The Wright brothers, Wilbur and Orville, fly at Kitty Hawk, N.C.; Henry Ford launches the Ford Motor Co.

1905   Penny arcades appear; beginning of the nickelodeon's rise to popularity.

1906   San Francisco earthquake; Victrolas first appear on market.

1908   Model T Ford; Singer Building in New York City is the first skyscraper.

1911   First transcontinental flight.

1912   The *Titanic* sinks.

1914   Transcontinental telephone service; Panama Canal finished; World War I begins.

1916   Albert Einstein announces theory of relativity.

1918   World War I ends.

1919   Wax recordings are introduced.

1920   Regularly scheduled radio as a public enterprise begins in Pittsburgh, Pa.

1925   Bell Telephone labs record sound electrically.

1927   *The Jazz Singer*, with Al Jolson, is the first widely distributed film with sound.

1929   U.S. stock market crashes on Black Friday.

1931   Empire State Building is completed.

1941   First commercial television broadcast; U.S. enters World War II.

1944   Marki, the first true computer, is built.

1945   Dropping of atomic bombs on Japan ends World War II; first radio broadcast of the Grand Ole Opry from the Ryman Auditorium in Nashville, Tenn.

1948   Bell Telephone Laboratories announce invention of the transistor; 33⅓ r.p.m. long-playing records are marketed.

1956   Elvis Presley's first television appearance on *The Ed Sullivan Show*.

1957   USSR launches Sputnik I.

1958   Boeing begins transatlantic service; stereo records are marketed.

1960   John F. Kennedy is elected president; William L. Shirer's *Rise and Fall of the Third Reich* is published; Chubby Checker popularizes the twist; Alfred Hitchcock's *Psycho* is released.

1961	United States enters the Vietnam War.
Nov. 22, 1963	John F. Kennedy is assassinated.
1964	The Beatles appear on *The Ed Sullivan Show*.
1969	First manned lunar landing; Woodstock Music Festival.

Chronology of the Estey Enterprise

17th century	Esteys arrive in America.
Sept. 30, 1814	Jacob Estey born in Hinsdale, N.H.
1818	Jacob orphaned to Shattuck.
Apr. 14, 1828	Jacob runs away to Massachusetts.
1831	Plumbing apprenticeship, Worcester, Mass.
1834	Death of Jacob's father. Move to Brattleboro, Vt.
1835	Acquires business and house from Parker.
1837	Marries Desdemona Wood. Jacob Estey Co., plumbing and lumber ventures.
1839	Estey partnership with William Briggs in plumbing trade.
1841	Riley Burditt joins John Woodbury in Brattleboro music store.
1846	(Samuel) Jones & Co. make first melodeons in Brattleboro. Estey's claimed founding date for melodeon business.
1847	General expansion: Estey and Dutton partnership in plumbing and lumber; McDonald & Estey in slate and marble. Jones & Burditt expand melodeon enterprise.
1849	Railroad comes to Brattleboro.
1850	Estey and Dutton expand gravestone business. Estey builds two-story shop. Burditt and E. B. Carpenter rent space for melodeon shop.
1852	Estey buys Burditt's portion of E. B. Carpenter & Co.'s melodeon concern.
1853	I. Hines buys out Carpenter, forming I. Hines & Co.; H. P. Green also buys in. Estey announces entry into organ business.
1854	Estey joins John Kathan to make more gravestones. Jones, Carpenter, & Woods form new melodeon company competing with I. Hines & Co.
1855	Estey and Green oust Hines and form partnership of Estey & Green.
1856	Estey buys out Carpenter. Fire burns factory. Five-story organ factory built at Plaza Park.
1860	Levi Fuller hired by Estey & Green.
1863	Green leaves. Estey assumes full control of Estey & Co. melodeon business with Burditt and Fuller.
1864	Fire destroys factory. Rebuilt same location. Silas Waite and Joel Bullard enter Estey partnership on Dec. 30.
1865	Burditt and Julius J. Estey manage Estey's first Chicago factory. J. D. Whitney and his reed-making machines come to Estey.
1866	Waite and Burditt leave partnership and take over Chicago factory. J. Estey & Co. formed with Julius J. Estey and Levi Fuller.

1869	Estey factory flooded.
1870	Birge St. factory built.
1872	Estey Organ Co. incorporated.
1872–86	Estey ascendancy (see text for details).
1888	200,000th reed organ built.
1890	Jacob Estey dies.
1892	250,000 reed organ celebration.
1896	Levi Fuller dies.
1901	Estey management begins pipe organ manufacture.
1902	Julius J. Estey dies; J. Gray and Julius Harry take over.
1920	J. Harry dies.
1930	J. Gray dies; Jacob Poor, Joseph Gray, and Paul Chase take over.
1933	Receivership and bankruptcy. Estey assets sold to nonfamily parties. Estey Organ Corp. organized.
1950s	Organizational reshuffling and diversification: Minshall-Estey; Estey Electronics. Estey Organ Corp. (Del.) organized.
1960	Company demise.
1961	Estey shops sold.
1980–2000	Historical conservation.

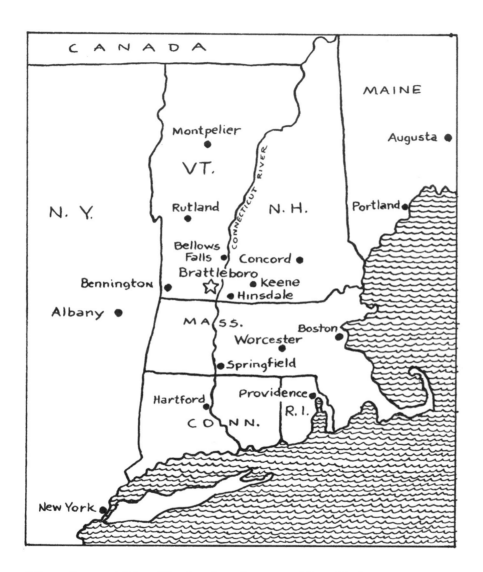

Map of central New England and eastern New York state

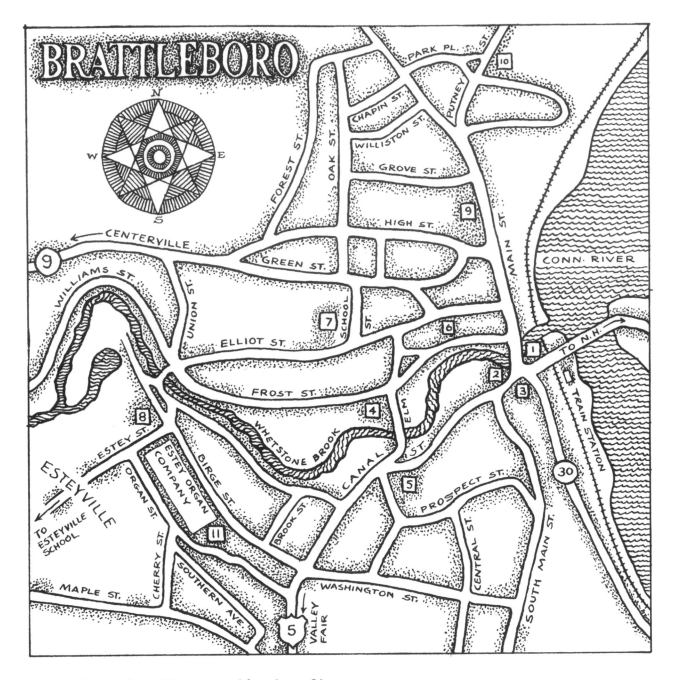

Map of Brattleboro, Vermont, with points of interest

(1) Buddington Brothers Grain Company and Estey's first plumbing shop; (2) Estey's two-story plumbing shop and first Estey & Green factory; (3) Estey's second location: Estey & Green and Estey & Company; (4) Estey's third location: J. Estey & Company; (5) Jacob Estey's house; (6) the Brattleboro Melodeon Company and the E. P. Carpenter Organ Company; (7) Julius J. Estey's home; (8) Gas and lumber house; (9) First Baptist Church; (10) J. Harry Estey's house; (11) Birge Street factory: Estey Organ Company

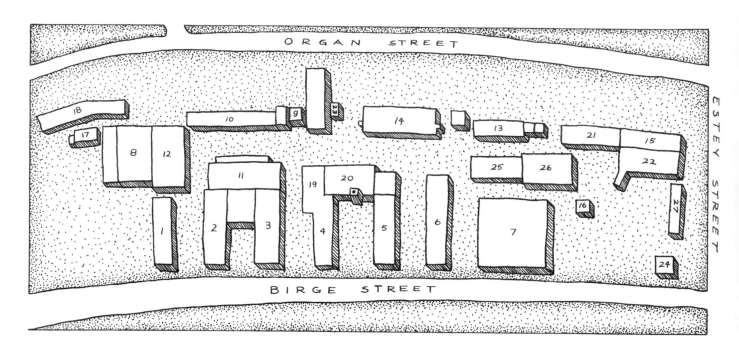

1. Plan of Estey Factory, c. 1930

(1) key making, cabinet and case work; (2) cabinet work, box shop; (3) mill, planers, molders, gluing, veneering; (4) reed organ parts and assembly; (5) reed organ bellows making and assembly; (6) office, drafting room, production room; (7) chest, wood pipe, console, pneumatic and electric action making; (8) veneer and dried lumber storage; (9) electric transformers; (10) lumber storage sheds; (11) sanding room, saw filing, belt room; (12) dry kilns; (13) pipe voicing; (14) machine shop, metal pipe making, bronzing; (15) packing and shipping supplies; (16) varnish and oil storage; (17) fire protection; (18) special lumber storage; (19) engine room; (20) boiler room; (21) packing and shipping; (22) packing and shipping; (23) metal casting; (24) garage; (25) erection shop; (26) erection shop; (27) horse stalls

2. Cross-section of an Estey reed organ

(1) pedals; (2) blocks connecting straps to pedals; (3) bellows straps; (4) bar holding strap rollers; (5) strap rollers; (6) springs on exhausters; (7) holes in exhausters; (8) valves over holes in exhausters; (9) valves over holes in center board; (10) exhausters; (11) bellows straps; (12) springs on reservoir; (13) screw to open safety valve; (14) holes in center board; (15) center board; (16) hole under safety valve; (17) safety valve, open; (18) safety valve, closed; (19) back board of bellows; (20) slot leading to action chest; (21) bellows top and bottom of action chest; (22) rims of action chest; (23) front swell over reeds; (24) hinged stops over reeds; (25) springs on valves on reed board; (26) sticker pins; (27) valves on reed board; (28) reeds; (29) post connecting stops [24] to stop rod; (30) bar connecting stops [24] to stop knobs [41]; (31) back swell over reeds; (32) hole in tremolo leading to chest; (33) tremolo head; (34) hub inside tremolo head; (35) valve on tremolo head; (36) binder holding keys at back; (37) pins in keys at back; (38) guide wires in stop rods; (39) pawls for operating stops [24]; (40) stop rods; (41) wire connecting pawl to [30]; (42) stop knobs; (43) stop board; (44) sharp keys; (45) natural keys; (46) oval guide pins under keys; (47) spring on safety valve; (48) block connecting strap to exhauster; (49) socket board for reeds; (50) outline of case

source: *Tuning, Care and Repair of Reed and Pipe Organs* (Battle Creek, Mich.: Niles Bryant School of Piano Tuning, 1906), 9–10.

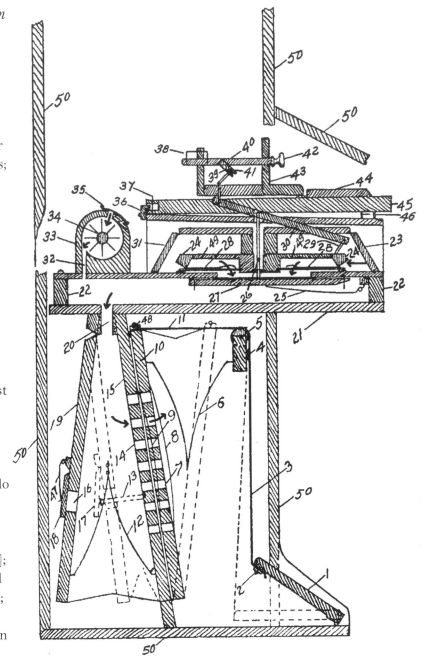

3. *Description of stops used in the Estey organ*

By referring to the following descriptions of Stops, it will be noticed that they are designated as being eight feet pitch, four feet pitch, &c. For the information of those persons who are not familiar with the technical phrases used by Organists and Organ builders, a slight explanation is necessary.

A given tone requires a pipe of a certain length to produce it; hence it is customary to say that a certain tone is of four feet pitch or eight feet pitch, as the case may be, by which is meant that a pipe must be four or eight feet long to produce this tone. The same terms are used when referring to the Stops of an Organ. When a key is depressed with an eight feet Stop drawn, and a corresponding key depressed on the Piano forte, the two sounds will be in unison, provided the two instruments are tuned to the same standard pitch.

A four feet Stop produces sounds which are really an octave *higher* than the keys depressed.

A two feet Stop produces sounds *two* octaves higher than the notes depressed.

A sixteen feet Stop produces sounds which are an octave *lower* than the notes depressed.

A thirty-two feet Stop produces sounds which are *two* octaves lower than the notes depressed.

For instance: if the Middle C be the key depressed, the sounds produced by the different Stops, drawn separately, will be the following:

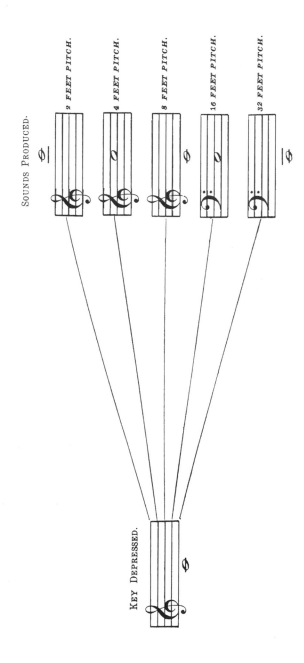

In speaking of a stop as a Treble Stop or a Bass Stop, we mean a set of reeds situated in the *upper*, or *treble* part of the organ, or in the *lower* or *bass* part. With this explanation, the following enumeration of stops will be readily understood.

Name.	Pitch.	Characteristics.
BARYTONE.	32 ft.	*Treble.* Full in tone, but slightly reedy; generally used in combination with other stops, but can be made very effective as a solo stop.
BASSET.	16 ft.	*Bass.* Rich, pervading tone.
BASSOON.	16 ft.	*Bass.* Very powerful.
BOURDON.	16 ft.	*Bass.* Full and round.
CLARIONET.	16 ft.	*Treble.* Resembles the Clarionet in quality.
CREMONA.	8 ft.	*Bass.* Soft and rich. Very fine for accompaniment.
CORNET ECHO.	2 ft.	*Bass.* Very soft echo effect.
CORNETTINO.	2 ft.	*Bass.* String tone, beautiful for solo or accompaniment.
DELICANTE.	8 ft.	*Treble.* Brilliant, piquant. Chiefly for solo, but valuable in combination.
DIAPASON.	8 ft.	*Treble.* Foundation set of reeds by which all others are tuned. Round, full tone. Used more generally than any other stop, except Melodia.

Name.	Pitch.	Characteristics.
DULCIANA.	8 ft.	*Treble.* Very similar in quality to Diapason, but softer.
DOLCE.	8 ft.	*Bass.* Similar to Melodia, but softer in tone.
FLUTE.	4 ft.	*Treble.* Brilliant, but not reedy. Generally used in combination.
GAMBA.	8 ft.	*Bass.* Smooth and pipe-like in tone.
HARP AEOLIENNE.	2 ft.	*Bass.* Closely resembles the tones produced by the vibrations of the strings of an Æolian Harp. Very fine for accompaniment.
HAUTBOY.	8 ft.	*Treble.* Reedy in character, and very effective as a solo stop.
MELODIA.	8 ft.	*Bass.* Same quality as the Diapason, of which it is the continuation.
PEDAL BASS.	16 ft.	A pedal stop, deep, round and full.
PRINCIPAL.	4 ft.	*Treble.* Very bright and clear.
ROYAL JUBILANTE.	16 ft.	*Treble.* Very fine solo stop. Large, round tone.
SUB-BASS.	16 ft.	*Bass.* Very deep and powerful.
SUB-BOURDON.	32 ft.	*Treble.* Beautiful solo stop, Full, rich tone.

Name.	Pitch.	Characteristics.
VIOLA.	4 ft.	*Bass.* Same character as Flute set, of which it is the continuation. Used much for accompaniment.
VIOLETTA.	4 ft.	*Bass.* Very soft, smooth tone; for accompaniment and echo effects.
VOX JUBILANTE.	8 ft.	*Treble.* Its name well indicates its character; very effective as a solo, and when used in combination with other stops, imparts a peculiar brilliancy to all.
WALD FLUTE.	2 ft.	*Treble.* Very clear and penetrating. Used almost entirely with full organ.

MECHANICAL STOPS.

Name.	Characteristics.
FORTE.	Opens, swells, and augments the tone.
GRAND ORGAN (Knee)	Brings into use all the reeds in the organ without the necessity of drawing a stop.
HARMONIQUE.	So constructed that when any key is depressed, its octave above is also depressed, thereby causing both to sound simultaneously.
KNEE SWELL.	Gives same effect as Forte, only more gradual if desired.
MANUAL COUPLER.	Used in organs with two manuals, and so connecting them that, when a key on the lower manual is depressed, it also depresses the corresponding key of the upper manual.
PEDAL COUPLER.	Used in organs having Pedal Keys, and so connecting the manual, that when the Pedal is depressed its corresponding key in the manual is depressed and responds also.
VOX HUMANA.	A revolving fan, placed just back of the reeds, which, when set in motion imparts to the tone a thrilling wave-like effect. It changes the reed tone completely, giving it the sympathetic sweetness of the human voice.

SPECIFICATION OF TWO-MANUAL ORGAN.

BELOW are given the Specifications of a very fine Organ, made to order for **Richard Wagner,** for use during his great Musical Festival at BAIREUTH. in Bavaria, August 13, 1876.

From the great number of Reeds and their compass, varying from a tone corresponding to that of a two-feet pipe to that produced by a thirty-two-feet pipe, it will be readily seen to what state of perfection the Reed-Organ has been brought by Messrs. ESTEY & Co. The Violin, Violoncello, Clarionet, Flute, Piccolo, French Horn, and other instruments are very finely imitated.

GREAT ORGAN.—NINE STOPS.

1.	DIAPASON,	8 feet tone.	clear and strong,	32 Reeds.
2.	MELODIA,	8 " "	" "	29 "
3.	TUBA-MIRABILIS,	8 " "	very full, bold, horn-like,	32 "
4.	OPHICLEIDE,	8 " "	" " "	29 "
5.	CREMONA,	8 " "	very mellow and soft,	29 "
6.	CLARIONET,	16 " "	fine imitation,	32 "
7.	BOURDON,	16 " "	deep, rich and round,	29 "
8.	PRINCIPAL,	4 " "	brilliant, penetrating,	32 "
9.	WALD-FLUTE,	2 " "	very brilliant,	32 "
				276 "

SWELL ORGAN.—SIX STOPS.

10.	DULCIANA,	8 feet tone,	very sweet and clear,	32 Reeds.
11.	GAMBA,	8 " "		29 "
12.	DELICANTE,	8 " "	imitative Violin—plaintive,	32 "
13.	FLUTE,	4 " "	imitative, clear, brilliant,	32 "
14.	VIOLA,	4 " "		29 "
15.	VIOLETTA,	4 " "	softest Stop in Organ, and a very fine and beautiful accompaniment,	29 "
				183

PEDAL ORGAN.—TWO STOPS.

16.	BOURDON PEDALS,	16 feet tone,	powerful, grand,	29 Reeds.
17.	SUB-BOURDON PEDALS,	32 " "	deep, pervading,	29 "
				58 "

ACCESSORY STOPS, MOVEMENTS, ETC.

18. VOX HUMANA.	20. MANUAL COUPLER, (Swell to Great.)	23. FOOT SWELL.
19. FORTE.	21. PEDAL COUPLER, (Pedal to Great.)	24. KNEE SWELL.
	22. GRAND ORGAN, (Draws Full Organ.)	

5. Stastical Analysis of the Estey Enterprise

Employee and Production Numbers

The figures in Table 1 were gleaned mostly from Brattleboro's newspapers. The lack of a standard time span for the production numbers makes the figures rather vague and inconsistent (with different sources reporting somewhat conflicting information, especially in the early years). Though the data are sketchy, general growth patterns can be surmised. Striking is the number of additional workmen hired in 1865, soon after Estey took over sole control of the factory. Also, production numbers increased appreciably after the Birge Street complex opened and incorporation of the Estey Organ Company occurred. As the turn of the century approached, a leveling off of employee and production numbers becomes apparent. Table 2 reveals a reversal in growth from 1900 on.

Table 1. Growth of Brattleboro's organ enterprises

Date	Company name	No. of employees	Production
1846–48	Jones, Woodbury, & Burditt	7	40 to date
1850	Jones & Burditt	10–14	800? to date
1851	Burditt & Carpenter	18	250/year
1852	Carpenter & Co.	25	1,500 to date
1853	Hines & Co.	20	
1858	Estey & Green	20	10/week
1859	Estey & Green	20	30
1864	Estey & Co.	45–50	25–30/week
1865	Estey & Co.	125–150	1,105/year
1867–68	J. Estey & Co.	110–120	160/month
1869	J. Estey & Co.	170	310/month
1870	(Birge St.)	225	250/month
1872	Estey Organ Co.	350	500–700/month
1873	Estey Organ Co.	512	
1876	Estey Organ Co.		1,000/month
1882	Estey Organ Co.	500+	1,500/month
1888	Estey Organ Co.		13,000/year
1889	Estey Organ Co.		1,700/month
1890	Estey Organ Co.	700–800	1,500/month

Table 2. Production numbers

Dates	Output
up to 1850	400
1850 to 1855	2,000
1855 to 1860	3,200
1860 to 1865	3,900

```
1865 to 1867 . . . . . . . . . . . 4,500
1867 to 1870 . . . . . . . . . . 10,000
1870 to 1872 . . . . . . . . . . 11,000
1872 to 1874 . . . . . . . . . . 13,000
1874 to 1876 . . . . . . . . . . 14,000
1876 to 1878 . . . . . . . . . . 17,000
1878 to 1880 . . . . . . . . . . 21,000
1880 to 1882 . . . . . . . . . . 22,000
1882 to 1884 . . . . . . . . . . 24,000
1884 to 1886 . . . . . . . . . . 24,000
1886 to 1888 . . . . . . . . . . 24,000
1888 to 1890 . . . . . . . . . . 27,000
1890 to 1892 . . . . . . . . . . 29,000
1892 to 1894 . . . . . . . . . . 34,000
1894 to 1896 . . . . . . . . . . 14,000
1896 to 1898 . . . . . . . . . . 12,000
1898 to 1900 . . . . . . . . . . 12,000
1900 to 1902 . . . . . . . . . . 12,000
1902 to 1904 . . . . . . . . . . 11,000
1904 to 1906 . . . . . . . . . . 10,000
1906 to 1908 . . . . . . . . . . 10,000
1908 to 1910 . . . . . . . . . . 10,000
1910 to 1912 . . . . . . . . . . 10,000
1912 to 1915 . . . . . . . . . . 15,000
1915 to 1920 . . . . . . . . . . 25,000
1920 to 1925 . . . . . . . . . . 24,000
1925 to 1930 . . . . . . . . . . 20,000
1930 to 1935 . . . . . . . . . . 14,000
1935 to 1940 . . . . . . . . . . 10,000
1940 to 1945 . . . . . . . . . . . 5,000
1945 to 1950 . . . . . . . . . . . 5,000
1950 to 1955 . . . . . . . . . . . 5,000
```

Note: These cumulative production tallies are based on serial numbers (Whiting 1981, 148). Readers should notice that the time increments are not consistent. Whiting admits complications because there does not seem to be an extant Estey serial number list, and some unusual styles of organs were given special serial numbers. Because Estey was more conscientious than most manufacturers in maintaining accurate tallies, the figures give a reasonably good indication of the factory's pattern of growth. From 1894 to 1896 (the time period during which the 300,000th organ was made), a drastic drop in production began. From that point, numbers diminished until the company closed.

Table 3. Table of Contents of Phelps and Cheny, Estey Organ Method *(1879)*

APPENDIX D
Estey Reed Organ Casework and Tonal Design
E. A. BOADWAY

Chronology of Estey Casework

Estey casework ran the gamut of Victorian and early-twentieth-century furniture styles, and the firm occasionally established a briefly popular design copied in part by other organ manufacturers. From the late 1860s through the early 1880s, Estey patented even minute details of visible woodwork. Many of the handsome documents and attached photographs exist.

The earliest melodeons were invariably clothed in rosewood veneer on pine, much like mahogany-veneered furniture of the late Empire period, though the lyre legs and stretcher of these instruments were often of pine or poplar fake-grained as rosewood. Early in the 1860s, black walnut became the preferred wood for cases, and only the end grains were veneered. Harder woods, such as chestnut, sometimes appeared beneath veneers. The flat-topped melodeons came in two styles: those with sometime bulbous and heavy legs, imitating "square grand" pianos (figure 98), and the more graceful type with folding legs of a modified lyre pattern, held open with a somewhat rococo stretcher that held the pumping and swell pedals (figure 99). In addition to elegant but simple moldings, there was nearly always a fretted and somewhat elaborate music rack and a pair of velvet-covered lamp or candle holders. The maker's name always appeared, stenciled above the keys. Around 1860, and likely upon special order, Estey & Green would build a large melodeon with a case

Figure 98. Perfect Melodeon, portable style

Figure 99. Perfect Melodeon, piano style

Figure 100. Five-Octave Cottage Organ

Figure 101. Double Bank Harmonic Organ, with pipe organ top

extending to the floor and which covered the wind system and 16' reed mechanism. Such an organ was generally for church use and the base also discreetly covered pumping done by a lady organist.

The Perfect Melodeon rapidly declined in popularity in the late 1860s, for in that decade, the completely enclosed base and increased volume of sound and tonal variety of Estey's Cottage Organ became the best seller. Retaining the flat top for most models, the fretworked music rack, and a few other melodeonesque remnants, these early reed organs had stop knobs, two pumping pedals, the new fan Tremolo, and a knee lever for operating the swell shades. For a brief time in the 1860s, a three-pedal system was sold, and one foot moved from pumping to operating the Tremolo (figure 100). Thus, the player had far more to manipulate than on the more humble melodeon, and Estey's well-made product rivaled that of Mason & Hamlin of Boston, the inventors of the American reed organ and the chief competitor of every American firm for decades.

By the early 1870s, the use of rosewood was almost completely discontinued in favor of black walnut (one extant cherry case of the 1870s was a

special request), and melodeons were no longer made by Estey. The Cottage Organ was part of a well-established line of Boudoir and Harmonic organs. The latter was available in sizes containing two manuals and pedals, with an optional top displaying dummy pipes resembling those of a pipe organ. Such an impressive case made an Estey suitable for church use. The 8'2" model in the 1867 catalogue cost $700 and came with a bellows handle for the organist's assistant (figure 101). Estey made a long-lived specialty of two-manual reed organs, selling many thousands of them well into the 1940s, an era of compact and inexpensive

Figure 102. Two-Manual Organ

Figure 103. The New Salon Organ

"unit" pipe organs. During the 1870s, the restrained and only moderately high decorative tops on some of the Cottage Organs became larger and more profusely decorated, as was the rest of the casework (figure 102). Occasionally, a little paper-thin French walnut veneer was used. Applied "carvings" and an obvious heaviness of external woodwork increased throughout the decade. But it was essentially a pleasing period for "gingerbread," with more than a nod by Estey's designers to the influences of the Classical, Gothic Revival, Eastlake, and "French" styles (figure 103). Nearly all gave way to the somewhat cumbersome and far less elegant styles of the 1880s, and with the advent of lengthier catalogues picturing every style, descriptions of the appearances of reed organs were shortened. Here are two paragraphs from Estey catalogues, the first issued in 1871 and the second in 1878:

CASES.

The American public demand in all those things which are manufactured for their convenience and comfort, that there should be a proper display of useful and beautiful ornamentation. In fact, no more annoying problem is presented to artisans and manufacturers than how to gratify this demand. The days of plain and severe style of cabinet work have passed. Modern skill and machinery have enabled us to thoroughly satisfy the refined taste of the people, and at a moderate cost. We have the gratification of presenting to the public new styles of Organ Cases, which for chasteness of design, elaborate embellishment and beauty of finish, have never been excelled or equaled—styles which will prove an appropriate addition to the architecture of any church, or the furnishing of the most elegant parlor. (Estey catalogue, 1871)

IMPROVED CASES.

The Cases of the ESTEY ORGAN are the result of a happy union of artistic handiwork and adapted machinery, and are calculated to satisfy the most cultivated taste without enhancing the cost of the instrument disproportionately. Tawdry tinsel and mere outside show are persistently avoided, while real beauty and fitness are everywhere encouraged. The aim is to meet every demand with something exactly suited to it, in character and execution, which shall combine utility and attractiveness. Styles in the furniture of public buildings and private residences are constantly changing; and musical instruments, such as organs and pianos at least, are naturally expected to conform to them in some degree. The resources and artisans of the Estey Manufactory are such that the vagaries of fashion in this respect are at once perceptible in the CASES of the ESTEY ORGAN. NEW CASES are all the time being brought out, which, for chasteness of design, rich ornamentation, quaint and elaborate embellishment, excellence of finish and general adaptability, have never been equaled. Special demands, whatever intricacy of art-work they may involve, are promptly met. Many of the styles illustrated on succeeding pages are entirely fresh, and must at once commend themselves as fitted alike to add to the attraction of the public auditorium, or grace the private parlor and boudoir, and every home shrine or fireside, however humble, has new attraction from their presence. (Estey catalogue, 1878)

Figure 104. Style S Parlor Organ

In the last decades of the nineteenth century, casework became less heavy, but not without hand or machine-carved and applied decoration, a few finials and spindles, and an occasional mirror. Designers gave a little attention to Queen Anne and later, Art Nouveau details (figure 104), but in general, organ case architects went their own way. By 1890, a small and plain Portable Organ (figure 105) in a compact cherry wood case was added to the line that included the Drawing Room, Parlor, Triumph, School, Chancel, Cathedral and Students' Organ (figure 106). Black walnut was still in vogue, but as the century ended, oak became quite popular. With the demise of elaborate walnut cases, Estey's gilt stenciling disappeared, and ebonized cases were a rarity. By 1900, the more refined high tops included galleries, mirrors, small shelves (figure 107), and a hinged music rack that revealed a cupboard behind. This innovation

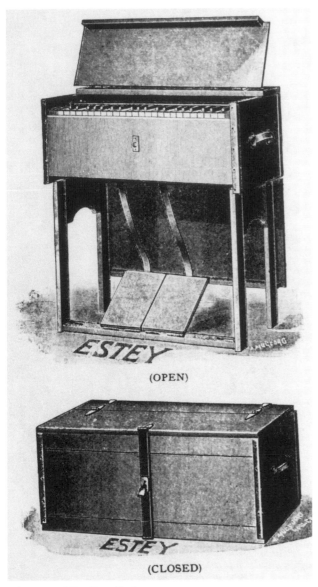

(OPEN)

(CLOSED)

Figure 105. New Portable Organ

Figure 106. New Students' Pedal Organ

Figure 107. Style Z Parlor Organ

replaced the "music pocket" of the high tops during the 1880s.

As World War I approached, there was an increasing simplification of designs, as evidenced by the elimination of handles and attached lamp stands, the reduction of fretwork, and the occasional use of veneers. Estey's finishing staff

Figure 108. Case Design 6

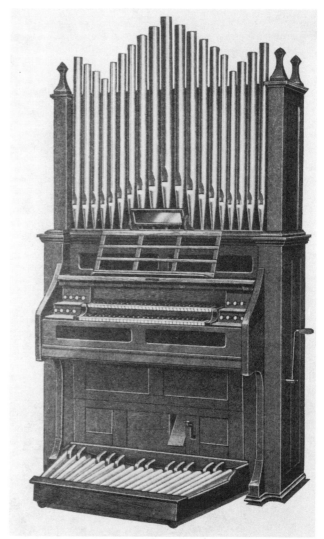

Figure 109. Style T

developed remarkably handsome and durable finishes by staining birch to resemble black walnut or mahogany, and it continued to use them almost to the closing of the business. The use of now-scarce real walnut declined in favor of the stained imitation, and golden and dark oak were preferred. In the larger models, screening replaced fretwork for the tone openings, the knee levers were no longer labeled, and electric blowers were available. By 1920, the old high tops were just vestiges large enough to keep books and bric-a-brac from falling off the case (figure 108). Pipe tops were obtainable for one-manual organs, but rarely ordered. Two-manual organs were available with a choice of pipe tops, and could be pumped by a crank operating four reciprocating exhausters (figure 109), a "Rimmer" motor in an oak box next to the case, or an electric blower in the cellar or another room. The dummy wood pipes, gold-leafed before the 1870s, then most often highly stenciled, returned to a plain gold paint not long before 1914.

Most reed organ manufacturers went out of business before 1925, but Estey continued to make an elegant and very durable instrument in a great variety of sizes and styles. Console measurements improved for the two-manual organs, which by 1915 had concave and radiating pedal keyboards. Electro-pneumatic action, by no means as durable as the former mechanical systems, was used in two-manual organs beginning in the late 1930s, and simple Modernistic cases were in keeping with the Art Deco style of that time (figure 110). For a few years after 1934, Estey produced a spinet-

Figure 110. Modernistic Organ

Figure 111. Folding Organ, Style 2

piano style of reed organ called a Melodeon, but the similarities to one made in the 1850s are hard to detect. The popular "folding organs," built especially for use in World War II, had oak or cloth-covered cases of very plain and practical design, and the mechanism was folded down into the pedal area to form what resembled a thick suitcase (figure 111). Older portable organs were lowered onto legs that folded up. The last reed organs for home use were in simple cases of the short-lived 1950s household style.

The high-topped organs of the 1880–1910 years are now popular among antique dealers and decorators, whether or not they can be played! The tops, often sold separately as "mantlepieces," have been removed from the majority of extant organs. While most Esteys have an undeniable visual charm and great musical merit, the rugged and plainly cased instruments of the 1910–1930 era are a special joy for many musicians (figure 112).

Estey seems never to have produced adjustable organ stools, which were often upholstered in horsehair and available from music dealers well into the twentieth century for about $2.50 to $10.00. Organ benches were made by the firm, especially for instruments with pedal keyboards, and by the turn of the century, an Estey bench was a sturdy affair with a music shelf and a "modesty" panel that screened the player's legs from listeners. Benches with sloping tops were made on the premise that the angle of the seated player permitted easier pumping of one-manual organs. Estey refinements included easily removable knee and back panels for maintenance access; nicely finished backs on low-topped organs when a player might face the congregation; tops that could be easily unscrewed or unlatched; the use of very few nails but many well-placed screws for taking apart an organ with ease; and after 1884, the use of a very fine grade of celluloid in favor of key ivory, which was the standard until the firm closed.

Appendix D: Estey Reed Organ Casework and Tonal Design ⌊ 227

Figure 112. Style O Case

Internal improvements are of less interest to the general reader but do indicate that as Estey kept up with the times in a reed organ's outward appearance, the mechanism was receiving every worthwhile refinement. By the early 1880s, the stop actions contained more metal, and the coupler assemblies, which formerly had intricate wooden backfalls, became sets of metal levers. Stop knobs controlled additional "dolce" mechanisms that softened sets of reeds also available at full volume, and swell shutters appeared in some casework rather than just over the sets of reeds. Wind systems that were built of leather and heavy cardboard became entirely made of "rubber cloth" in the 1880s, though the older materials have survived very well into the twenty-first century.

The Estey factory was so well managed and the patterns so carefully regulated and used that one can take any case part from an organ, put it on an organ of similar style but ten years younger, and the screw holes match exactly! It is even possible to take the entire contents of a very old Estey in a battered case and easily fit the assembly to a

case fifty years younger. So perfect had an Estey reed organ become that for years after beginning pipe organ production in 1901, the reed organ technology is very evident in those much larger instruments.

Estey Organ Keyboard Compass and Tonal Design

Estey melodeons and the majority of later reed organs had the standard American key compass of FFF to f³, 61 notes. Thus, the lowest octave of the basic 8' rank (unison pitch) extended well down into the 16' octave. Later in the nineteenth century, Estey's 16' stops began on CC, though a few extended into the 32' octave. But most 16' stops had no reeds for the lowest seven notes, or the reeds would sound notes an octave higher. The longer bass compass of a reed instrument permitted the playing of much piano music or music arranged for the piano, provided more notes for accompanying solos in the treble, and gave some hint of a "Pedal Bass," though the left hand played it. European harmoniums generally had a compass of CC to c⁴, 61 notes.

Most of the smallest organs, beginning with a four-octave model in the mid-1870s, had a 49-note C-compass, with two octaves both below and above Middle C. The Portable, Folding, School, and Junior models all had that compass, but the Miniature, with one set of reeds, designed for children early in the 1930s, had Estey's shortest compass, three octaves from Tenor C or Tenor F, 37 notes.

All two-manual instruments, beginning with the Double Bank Harmonic Organ of the mid-1860s to the last of the Electro-Pneumatic Reed Organs of the early 1950s, had manual compasses of CC to c⁴, 61 notes. The older C-compass flat pedal keyboards, very rare before the Civil War, had at least 12 notes, 18 notes by 1867, 27 notes by 1876 (the remarkable organ built for Richard

Wagner had pedals from CCC to E, 29 notes), 30 notes by 1886, and the standard American Guild of Organists compass of 32 notes, CCC to G, by the late 1930s. The number of pedal keys had grown in three generations with the increasing demands of organists who wished to play real organ music on an Estey reed organ. For a few years around 1920, the firm manufactured one-manual organs with a transposing lever, and the pitch of the instrument could be raised or lowered by two semitones.

Thinking that even a large reed organ is tonally limited, many players just pull all the stop knobs and play. But simple brass tongues riveted to frames can produce great tonal variety, if they are of proper scale, thickness, and curvature. So that solo effects were available, Estey divided the stops into bass and treble halves on all one-manual instruments except those with one set of reeds. Until the mid-1880s, and occasionally after that time, the break was between Tenor E and F, with the couplers dividing at the same point. Some older organs did break between the later and more common Tenor B and Middle C, while for a few years, the couplers still divided at Tenor E/F. The Bass and Treble Couplers, which "doubled" the power of the instrument, were very useful mechanical accessories, and Estey made many six-octave, 73-note organs that, with an extra treble octave, greatly increased the usefulness of the Treble Coupler. The most important of couplers (all of which sound a note an octave above or below what is played) was the Harmonic, the oddly-named 4' coupler that played the note an octave above, throughout the compass of the keyboard. First placed in Estey melodeons in 1857, the patented device was renamed the Octave Coupler by 1890, and in some organs, it was divided so that if the player struck very low notes, the gap in the tenor range would be filled in by the bass coupler. The coupler was more elegantly named "Harmonique" by 1878.

Estey melodeons had a single set of 8' reeds, permanently on and without a name. Larger models had the Harmonic coupler and a second set of reeds at 4' pitch, usually divided. Few melodeons were given more than two sets, and as the Cottage Organ grew in popularity after 1865 and the voicing staff learned the art of varying reed tone, even the larger melodeons passed out of favor. By the late 1860s, the 8' Melodia/Diapason set was augmented with a 4' Viola/Flute rank. The next additions were an 8' Vox Jubilante in the treble and a one-octave 16' Sub Bass. The much-touted Vox Jubilante was a strong celeste rank that appeared in nearly every Estey organ after the mid-1860s, and it was tuned flat to produce an undulating sound with the basic 8' treble reeds. The Vox Jubilante, which appeared in the late 1870s at 16' pitch, and around 1920 at 4' pitch as well, was so popular that some one-rank Cottage Organs had just one stop knob for an added Vox Jubilante commencing on Tenor F. The 16' Bourdon, softer than the Sub Bass, appeared on larger organs in the late 1860s.

Jacob Estey was a good friend of the renowned Westfield, Massachusetts, organ builder William A. Johnson (1816–1901), who placed a large two-manual pipe organ in the First Baptist Church of Brattleboro in 1871. That organ was replaced by a larger Estey pipe organ in 1906. Estey surely was aware of the tonal variety in a pipe organ and rapidly increased the number of stops available by the time of the 1871 catalogue. Making their debut at Estey were the 8' Trumpet, the 8' Delicante (a soft "string"), and the 4' Principal. By 1878, the firm had added to its roster of tonal offerings the 4' Violetta (a soft "breathing" bass set with shortened reed tongues), and the 2' Wald Flute, a Tenor F rank that added brilliance and was later to receive an appropriate bass. Two new soft stops were the Dulciana and Gamba at 8' pitch, and in the 1870s, the Clarionet at 16' and 8' pitches were exceedingly well-voiced imitations of the instrument. Single Pedal stops were simply "Pedal Bass" at 16' pitch, but the stoplist of the 1876 instrument built for Richard Wagner (see Appendix C) reveals three new Estey names for imitations of three instruments; the divided 8' Tuba Mirabilis/Ophicleide and the 8' Cremona. Wagner's Pedal division had two named sets, one of 32' pitch! Added to the available tonal range of the 1870s were Forte knobs that raised swell shades or halves of shades independently, though the "Knee Swell" could bring them on together. To subdue its brightness, a separate Forte knob operated the 2' Wald Flute shutter. Many of the stops listed for the Wagner instrument appeared for the rest of the nineteenth century in the Grand Salon and Cathedral models. During the tonal expansion of the 1870s, the old fan Vox Humana Tremolo was renamed simply Vox Humana.

An Estey of the 1870s usually has the very best and most abundant sound of any reed organ built by an American firm. The volume and brightness rivaled that of a good, small pipe organ, and in fact, an Estey's basic 8' and 4' stops were *not* soft. During the 1880s, a sweeter and more mellifluous tone seems to have been preferred, but the sheer strength of volume was always available in the two-manual organs of the early twentieth century.

During the 1880s, mechanical "dolce" mutes were added to the Melodia/Diapason reeds to soften the tone, and the knobs were labeled Dolce and Dulciana. For a few years around 1880, the Vox Humana was optional on many models, but it could be added for an extra $10.00. Among the speaking stops described in *The Estey Revised Organ Method* (1882) were a few new arrivals [see Appendix C]. The 16' Basset and 16' Bassoon were bass stops; the 2' Cornettino and its softer version, the Cornet Echo, completed the range of the Wald Flute and were the separated ranks of the new 2' Harp Æolienne, a soft two-rank Celeste in the bass that became immensely popular. The 8' Hautboy, a treble rank, later became a common full-compass Oboe. While the treatment of the reed itself was of prime importance, the placement of the sets and the size of the reed cells varied the quality

of tone [see Appendix E]. As early as 1874, Estey was placing reeds on two chests (one being above the level of the keyboard), and "solo" stops were often near fretwork at the rear of the chest. The 16' Sub Bass, usually at the rear, was rarely affected by the swell mechanism.

The 1890 catalogue names Pedal stops, and the 16' Double Open Diapason, Double Dulciana, Double Stop'd Diapason and Bourdon were nomenclature applied to large reeds and their softer counterparts. The basic 4' Viola/Flute rank now had softening mutes and knobs labeled Viola Dolce (later called Viol d'Amour) and Flute d'Amour. The splendid, large-scale Philharmonic Organ contained two new 8' treble solo stops: Choral and Regal. A decade later, three "string" stop names appeared: the 8' Salicional, the 8' Vox Celeste (a softer narrow-tongued rendering of the Vox Jubilante), and the 2' Violina, a bass set. Though tonal variety was available, most of the small Esteys had just two 8' stops in the treble half of the keyboard. The two-manual organs had from five to ten sets of reeds and four couplers, and by 1915, they no longer had any divided stops. The 16' Corno appeared by 1914, and it was a strong rank that often replaced the former Bourdon/Clarionet. The expensive and remarkable Phonoriums (figure 113), patented in 1892 and made for ten years or so, had the reeds well above the keyboard level and sported elaborate pipe tops. The usual names for an Estey two-manual appeared on the stop knobs, but the one-manual Phonoriums had an 8' Saxophone beginning on Middle C. Later, the Artist's Organ was Estey's deluxe one-manual instrument.

By 1920, the bass and treble stops of the same set had received the same names, and in 1925, the pitch was raised to the standard A-440. The larger "folding" organs had 8' and 4' sets divided at Middle C, and some included couplers even when the compass was four octaves. The electro-pneumatic reed organs produced from 1938 had eleven speaking stops (three from the 44-reed Pedal set), nine

couplers, and a Crescendo pedal. These heavy instruments contained many magnets, a motor for
the pneumatic pump, and a generator to provide
action current. To accommodate the 4' couplers,
the chests contained 61 or 68 notes in the Virtuoso
and 73 notes in the EPRO models [see Appendix
E]. The stop names, long familiar on Esteys, were
engraved on tilting tablets, and thus the centuries-
old stop knob passed out of fashion on the larger
models. Foot-pumped reed organs were made into
the early 1950s, but nearly every style larger than
the "folding" models usually had an electric blower.
However, foot-pumping, always a much quieter
method of creating the necessary vacuum in the
wind system, gives the player much greater control over the volume of sound produced. Free reeds
will never "fly off speech" when subjected to forceful or erratic pumping.

The Estey factory test was to empty the reservoir by pumping, hold Middle C on the 8' set, and
ascertain if a minimum of fifteen seconds elapsed
before the sound faded away. A restorer's test for
a recovered bellows is thirty to ninety seconds
with no reeds sounding. Estey wind systems were
so tight that the vacuum would draw open treble
valves slightly. So when necessary, small reeds
were "bled" to prevent ciphering by drilling small
holes in the reed frames. Typically, Estey reeds
stay in tune and only need cleaning and perhaps
minor tuning every couple of decades.

Figure 113. Phonorium

APPENDIX E
Sound Production with Free Reeds
NED PHOENIX

1. General Comparison of Reed Organ Types

BASIC CHARACTERISTICS OF DESIGNS AND
THEIR MUSICAL POSSIBILITIES

All types of reed organs are enjoyed worldwide today in the same venues and capacities as in their heyday. Many are a church's original instrument, in use for a century or more, while others are being discovered and restored by enthusiasts joining the reed organ revival. And, currently, reed organs have become desirable for pop bands and recording studios, venues undreamed of by their makers.[1]

Each maker produced varying qualities of instruments. Through restoration and playing I have experienced all extremes: poorly made instruments that sound wonderful, excellently built instruments that sound awful, large organs that can hardly be heard, and tiny organs with incredible volume. I have favorites of all types of reed organs; I do not take sides. As with other instruments, most reed organs can produce musical sounds when played with skill, some should be avoided, and the best can be played for hours without tiring body or ear.

Builders of free-reed instruments make the choice of pressure or vacuum wind; around each winding concept, design possibilities in reed organ construction are numerous. The legal and fiscal necessities of having unique designs (witness the typewriter during the same period) prompted great ideas and inventions. Interesting and musical examples of reed organs are extant in churches, collections, museums, attics, and the patent offices of many countries. Brilliant ideas have been successfully applied, but not all that is possible has been done. Many worthwhile designs have yet to be realized, and the majority of the good designs that were produced (especially in America) were prevented from achieving their greatest potential by industry conventions in design, adaptation of reed organ construction to factory processes, designing and making only the mechanical and musical minimum necessary to satisfy customers, and strong resistance to change. The few innovative improvements in reed organ actions and sounds usually were more involved to create, more difficult to adjust and repair, and more expensive in all respects. And in most cases these changes did not effect enough difference in performance to make the organs desirable enough for many people to pay their higher price.

Because of resistance to modernizing its design, production, and sound, the worldwide reed organ industry was left behind during the twentieth century as manufacturing and music rapidly evolved. Antiquated, wasteful production and dated sounds could not compete with electronics factories and contemporary electronic organs, pianos, and pipe organs. Amplified reed organs were a noble attempt to keep up, but they were too little, too late. Experimentation may yet produce a new reed organ appropriate to the age, with maximum musical results.[2]

The two most commonly manufactured types of free reed organs were harmoniums (made in Europe) and American organs (mostly made in the United States and Canada).[3] Harmoniums and American reed organs were created with different mechanical designs and for different musical uses. A comparison of these considerations will reveal the reasons that, although there is a substantial body of literature for harmonium, art music was not composed specifically for the American organ.[4]

MECHANICAL CONSIDERATIONS

Harmoniums	*American Organs*
Pressure wind	Suction wind
Reeds and chests better technology	Reeds and chests good, but minimal technology
Costlier, more time to build	Cheaper, quicker to build
Wood and leather bellows	Rubber-cloth bellows
Handmade, tuned chambers create timbres	Small, machine-bored reed cells modulate timbres
Reeds inside pan	Reeds accessible from outside chest
Valves outside pan	Valves inside chest
Ready access to inside of pan	Tedious access to inside of chest
Expression stop bypasses reservoir	No such arrangement; reservoir always active

It appears that suction-wind reed organs were produced by Americans because their manufacture was cheaper, quicker, and easier (in that order). If pressure-wind organs had these attributes, American organs would operate on pressure wind. There is no inherent difference in the sound wave of a reed moved by pressure wind or by suction wind.[5] It is true that instruments of each winding system are typically designed and voiced to produce the characteristic sound for that type; therefore there is, theoretically and practically, a difference between the sound of a harmonium and that of an American organ.[6] However, despite their streamlined design and manufacture, American organs can work well and sound very musical. Listening to a select group of instruments of these and other types will change a preconception of inherent differences in sound, and raise awareness of the musical possibilities of free-reed instruments. A good reed organ is a good musical instrument.

MUSICAL CONSIDERATIONS

Harmoniums	*American Organs: melodeon, flat top, parlor, chapel and piano-cased organs*[7]
Standard configuration	Various nonstandard configurations
1 or 2 manuals; 5 octaves; C compass	1 manual; 4, 5, 6, or 7 octaves; F compass (except piano-cased)
Keyboards divided at middle E/F	Most keyboards divided at middle B/C, some divided at middle or tenor E/F

Appendix E: Sound Production with Free Reeds ⌈ 233

Harmoniums	American Organs: melodeon, flat top, parlor, chapel and piano-cased organs[7]
Typical specification: bass and treble 16', 8', 8', 4'[8]	Typical specification: bass 8', 4', (Sub-Bass); treble 8', 8' (celeste)
Cheap specification: bass and treble 8'	Cheap specification: 8'
Expensive specifications: bass and treble 16', 16', 8', 8', 4'; celestes 16', 8'; some Mustels have treble 32'	Expensive specifications: bass 8', 4', Sub-Bass; treble 8', 8', 8', 4'; some chapel organs have 16' and 2' sets
Intermanual couplers only; no octave	Couplers: octave higher (Estey Harmonique); divided bass and treble couplers
Wider expressive range with treadling and devices: Forte, expression, double expression, Grande Orgue	Narrower expressive range with treadling, augmented by devices: Forte, swell shades, Full Organ (Estey: Grand Organ)
Greater skills required to treadle and play	Minimal skills necessary to treadle and play
Poor results with unskilled playing	Passable results with unskilled playing

Attributes of each type of instrument determine the music best played on it. Harmoniums were built to play European art (classical) music; their portability, expressiveness, and wide dynamic range are perfect for church and chamber music venues. From the venerable European pipe organ tradition harmonium builders borrowed the C-compass manual (some pipe organ manuals have fewer keys) and the concept of four families of tone —diapason (organ tone), flute, string, and reed— at various pitch levels (see section 3). The innovation of standard specifications for manuals and stops and their division means that the composer, organist, and audience hear the same relative sounds for each piece played on various harmoniums.

In Europe, the tradition of patronage of the arts reserved art music mostly for the elite; the notable exception was pipe organ and other ecclesiastical music, heard publicly in churches and cathedrals. The American organ is a folk instrument, designed and built by common folk, to look, play, and sound appropriate for music made in common places by other common folk. In the United States there were few patrons of the arts; like the government, music and the arts were by the people, of the people, and for the people. Compositions for American organ are in the popular, not the art traditions of the day, written by "folk," not "serious" composers. The democratization of music, in which the reed organ played a large part, meant that anyone could make music, and anyone could compose it.

In the same do-it-yourself spirit that crafted American shape note music to other than European classical rules, American organs were not held to organ building or organ music traditions. Thus the "standard" specifications of typical American (melodeon, flat top, parlor, basic chapel, and piano-cased) organs are not designed for rendering European classical music.

A five-octave organ keyboard with F compass has more economic than musical value (see figure 115, "Estey Range Chart"; note that although

Estey reeds are stamped with letter names, Estey charts number reeds with FFFF as 1. Some Mason & Hamlin reeds are stamped with letter names, but most are numbered 1 [= F] to 12 [= E]). The American organ F-compass keyboard has precedent in eighteenth-century pipe organs, harpsichords, clavichords, and pianofortes.[9] Five octaves, F compass, was the typical range for pianofortes in the 1780s; before 1800 the English had already expanded the treble by a few notes. "All of Mozart's and practically all of Haydn's pianoforte works are contained within this limited [61-note] compass, as well as Beethoven's until his third piano concerto published in 1804."[10] Many of these compositions were published in methods and compilations for American organ.

It is true that low reeds are mellower, their effect "grander," and thus they sound "better" (especially on initial hearing) than soft, "squeaky" top-note reeds, so they ostensibly provide the owner more sound for the money. And it is true that much of the pre-1800 pipe organ repertoire does not require notes higher than F^3, the top note of an F-compass manual. However, innovative specifications of pipe organs and harmoniums built during the nineteenth century expanded possibilities for composers. A body of literature was composed during the reed organ's first two hundred years that was and is largely unavailable to the player of American organs because the "new" pipe organs and harmoniums have C-compass manuals to which this music was shaped. Much of this music was composed at the same time that American factories were turning out reed organs with F-compass manuals. Even cheap harmoniums are configured correctly for pipe organ and harmonium music. To play this literature on an American organ requires more than a typical organ: a minimum of two full sets of reeds (8', 4'), and an F-compass manual of six octaves (to include the notes up to C^4). Although such instruments were

produced, they cost more, and comprised a small percentage of the general output. Apparently, these musical considerations were not important in choosing the F-compass manual.

Lower, larger reeds were cheaper, quicker, and easier to manufacture; to make and tune reeds in the highest octaves required more money, time, and trouble (see section 2). And small, high reeds are more easily broken or stopped with dirt when in use, so omitting them improved reed organs' reliability and longevity. The seven lowest notes of typical manuals beginning on FFF provide half of the 16' octave, which allows simulation of a pedal bass for hymns and pipe organ pieces. These practical considerations warranted a lower compass. Aesthetic considerations probably dictated five octaves as the most that were musically needed, but also the fewest that made a keyboard and its surrounding casework look impressive, thus achieving organs of a perfect size for the parlors of Victorian America. It seems that F compass was chosen because it is low enough to avoid the topmost reeds, it provides desired sounds (mellow and low), and (with precedent in harpsichords and pianofortes) it looks decorous, with its regular array of five times three-and-two black keys.

An essential element of pipe organ sound is ranks at various pitches that reinforce the overtones of the fundamental rank. Ranks are played alone, or in combination to synthesize timbres. Harmonium makers recognized the musicality of this design and built specifications accordingly, varying timbres and pitches relative to pipe organ ranks (though the harmonium is a distinct instrument, not necessarily a substitute for a pipe organ). Straight ranks (full sets) have one pipe (reed) for each key, whether or not the keyboard is divided. The minimum specification required to be useful for organ literature (i.e., to reinforce harmonics and to retain the integrity of contrapuntal voices) is 8', 4'–8', 4' (two full sets, an octave apart) which completes both sounds throughout the manual compass. In Estey terms, stops would read: Melodia 8', Viola 4'–Diapason 8', Flute 4', rather than the Melodia 8', Viola 4'–Diapason 8', Vox Jubilante 8' (Celeste) provided in typical American organs.

American organs include unmatched half sets (e.g., Viola/Vox Jubilante) of different pitches and timbres. American organ manuals are mostly divided at middle B/C, some at tenor E/F, and a few at middle E/F, the harmonium standard. When bass and treble stops are discontinuous half sets, crossing the break will sound disconcerting. Skill must be used to get around the break, or the discontinuity must be ignored. Large chapel organs with four to five sets may have full sets of reeds at 16', 8', 4' and 2' pitches, as well as half sets (thus providing proper voices for pipe organ and harmonium music), but usually the manuals have F compass and are divided other than at the harmonium standard.

Octave couplers are provided in American organs to offset the lack of treble 4' reeds or bass 16' stops. Couplers for melodeons (Estey's Harmonic Attachment) and flat tops (Estey's Harmonique) couple up an octave throughout the compass; these are generally more musically useful than the divided bass and treble couplers in later styles (parlor, chapel, piano-cased). Bass and treble couplers are usually divided differently than the stops (reed mutes), thus occasionally causing mechanically muddled music. At the top of the keyboard, treble couplers run out of reeds to couple to, except on the relatively rare six-octave manuals and seven-octave, piano-cased reed organs. A bass coupler can muddy a texture unless the organist rearranges the music, or it may disappear suddenly when most needed. This disappearance and reappearance is plainly heard in my recording of the hymn "Estey" (track 10 on the companion CD), in the second verse, during which the bass coupler, which operates up to tenor E, drops out when the bass note is higher than tenor E. When pipe

organ or harmonium music is played on a typical one-manual American organ, some discrepancies must be ignored if the music is to be played exactly as printed. For this recording, I played these measures of "Estey" as printed; however, in typical circumstances, I would play other bass notes (such as my last two in this rendition) in these measures to keep the coupler in operation and the sound continuously full.

For this hymn and the other selections from the *Estey Organ Method*, I tried to limit myself to the notated music. Usually, the reed organist adapts, revises, and arranges all music on sight to fit the instrument and the situation.[11] Success and enchantment with playing reed organs (especially in public) is directly proportionate to this ability.

Therefore, though not designed to render the classical organ literature, the typical American organ is perfectly suited to folk music, which generously allows for arranging, improvising, and mistakes. American organ configurations accommodate exactly what is provided in numerous reed organ methods and compilations: folk and popular musics, the easier classics originally for harpsichord or piano, and hymns. (These same genres of repertoire, updated, fill books for one of the reed organ's reincarnations: today's split-keyboard home electronic organs, which are set up to play popular, not organ, music.) Fortunately for folk players and their audiences, American organs and the music played on them are much more forgiving of unskilled playing than are harmoniums or harmonium music.

Certainly Estey and other American reed organs were built that could successfully play the reed and pipe organ literature, but these were larger inside and out, and more expensive (see the two-manual-with-pedal instruments in Appendix D, and Whiting's *Estey Organs On Parade*). Typical organs are those that were most prevalent, owned by typical people. Thus the societal and cultural partition was perpetuated between those who could afford, and desired, an instrument capable of art music, and those who could afford, and wanted, a basic folk music instrument. (The piano offered both musical options. One of the reasons for the piano's rise and the reed organ's decline is that, in addition to rendering the classics, the piano was more appropriate for the new trends of popular music: the blues, boogie-woogie, ragtime, and jazz.)

Irrespective of the direction of air through an instrument or its actual sound, these are the reasons that no art ("serious") music was written for American organ, whereas there is a wealth of literature for harmonium. However, four manufacturers in particular built reed organs that incorporated traditional and standardized elements of harmoniums and pipe organs for the express purpose of playing the "serious" organ literature.

Mason & Hamlin, of Boston ("the Hub of the Universe," through which European information and goods entered and were disseminated throughout the United States), was the reed organ maker most connected with European trends and the one who built the bridge between harmoniums and American organs. In addition to the typical American organ configuration, Mason & Hamlin produced Cabinet, chapel, and two-manual (some with pedalboard) organs with full 8' and 4' ranks (also 16', 8', 8', 4' with stops numbered according to harmonium specifications), C compass, manual division at middle E/F, and automatic bellows swell. In 1856 Mason & Hamlin advertised an Organ-Harmonium, also on suction wind.[12] These were (and are) musically successful, but did not become the norm in America. In 1904 the company announced a collaboration with Alphonse Mustel (the son of Victor Mustel, who built "Harmoniums d'Art" in Paris) that seems to have borne fruit in the production of a very few Style 1400 "Orchestral Organs," which combine Mason & Hamlin cases and imported Mustel harmonium actions with Estève reeds from Paris on pressure wind.[13] Though they may have worked well, these instruments would have been both very expensive and generally undesirable in America at that time.[14]

The Vocalion, with the Wright Patent chest, was originally built in Worcester, Massachusetts, by James Baillie-Hamilton in 1886, after which it was manufactured by various companies until 1903.[15] Its final incarnation was as the Aeolian Orchestrelle, a roll-playing reed organ, produced from 1889 to 1910. The Wright Patent is a hybrid pipe organ/American organ/harmonium consisting of a tracker (mechanical action) pipe organ chassis, action, chest, and pallets, with pressure-wind bellows, speaking through reeds of American organ construction, with timbres modulated by harmonium-inspired tuned resonating chambers. One-manual Vocalions are almost appropriate for organ literature: CC–A^3 compass, divided at middle B/C, four sets of reeds: 16', 8', 8', 8'. In my experience, the sixteen- and seventeen-rank two-manual-with-pedal Vocalions come closest to pipe organ operation and sound than any other reed organs, and are very successful musical instruments. In addition to common and midscale reeds, Vocalions include very wide manual reeds (.81 inches, 20.57 millimeters) with unusual, effective tongue scales, and very large pedal reeds (which also speak through large, tuned boxes). Such an instrument is an involved production to manufacture or restore, but well worth the trouble.

One-manual reed organs invented in the twentieth century by theater organist Sylvan K. Ketterman—including his first in 1930, the Gulbransen Magnatone (from 1935), and the Ketterman Organs (1945 to 1950)—have C compass divided at middle E/F, with full sets of reeds at 16', 8', and 4' pitch.

The Hallman Organ Company of Ontario, Canada, built unified amplified electrostatic reed organs with two or three manuals and pedals that incorporate their improvement of the Wurlitzer design and specifications usually found only in pipe organs.[16]

2. Reed Making at Estey

For the recollections and Estey materials that inform section 2 of this appendix we are indebted to the following people, some of whom were Estey employees.

Charles Henry Thomas "Tommy" Brockington (1897–1980), of Brattleboro, began working at Estey in 1934. He was foreman of Estey's machine shop and reed room from 1940 to 1960, after which, from 1961 until he retired in 1978, he worked for the machinist David Dunklee. (Dunklee bought some of Estey's remainder reed brass, which was used up by the early 1980s when I began visiting his shop to discuss reed making. He was happy to share with me what he knew.)

Christopher W. Brown, born in 1930, lived in Concord, Massachusetts, and graduated from Marlboro College. In 1955 his first job at Estey was in the electronic organ development lab. He was later detailed to the machine shop, then worked in the reed room from mid-1956 through May 1957, supervised by Tommy Brockington. Brown is now retired from a career in investment management, and is an active mentor with SCORE (the Service Corps of Retired Executives).

Charles "Charlie" Gunzinger was born in 1900 in Switzerland and immigrated to the United States at age ten. His father, Joseph Gunzinger, and uncles worked at Estey, most all as pipe voicers. Charlie Gunzinger was principally a pipe voicer, although he helped out in the reed organ division when the pipe side was slow. After Estey closed, he took early retirement, and repaired and tuned reed organs at his home in Williamsville, Vermont, until his death in 1974.

Merrill "Mel" Harris was born in Brattleboro, Vermont, in 1916. His father, Leon Harris (1889–1962), worked at Estey as head tuner from 1910 to 1960, when he received a fifty-year gold watch. In 1910, he worked ten hours per day at ten cents per

hour. During the Great Depression in 1933, Leon Harris worked part time as the only reed tuner. His wife, Elfreda Harris, was a reed filer (her name is inside the Estey voicing jack that Toelken got from Gunzinger). During the 1933–34 school year, Mel Harris worked afternoons and Saturday mornings as a reed filer, and from 1935 to 1941 he was a tuner. Every organ he ever tuned is listed in his tuner's book, including his first EPRO in February 1938, and his sixtieth and last. In 1941, the tuners went on strike over the EPRO, after which all returned except Mel Harris, who worked at American Optical in Brattleboro for thirty-seven years until he retired in 1979. From November 1956 through May 1957 he worked a partial shift at night as a tuner during a rush on three- and four-octave reed organs.

Ernest C. Kendrick, an all-around organ man, was born in 1901. Beginning about 1940, he worked at Estey at a variety of different things, as much on the pipe side as the reed side. About 1950 he moved to California, where he primarily rebuilt and maintained pipe organs and amplified reed organs until his death in 1990.

Sylvan K. Ketterman (S.K.K.) (1912–1993), of Muncie, Indiana, diverse inventor and self-proclaimed "Pioneer of the Electronic Organ," was the son of the inventor of the automatic transmission. He built his first electric-action reed organs while in high school. One of these instruments drew the attention of the famed theater organist Jesse Crawford and the Gulbransen Company in 1935. As assistant to the president and chief designer and engineer from 1935 to 1945, Ketterman designed and demonstrated the Gulbransen Electric Column Organ and the Magnatone amplified reed organs, as well as Gulbransen pianos. During World War II, he simplified and improved the Link Trainer (for aircraft pilot training), which was a tubular-pneumatic machine built by the Link Player Piano Company, technology very important to the war effort. During his tenure with Gulbransen, "the Estey boys [Jacob and Joseph] invited me to the Birge Street factory in hopes of wooing me to the Estey Company. After we talked awhile, they asked me how much I was making. I was making more than both of them put together, so I went back to Muncie." From 1945 to 1950, the Ketterman Organ Company of Muncie produced the Ketterman Organ (one manual, unamplified), one of his patented designs. Ketterman was a talented theater organist heard nationally. In his later years, he sold electronic organs and taught members of the Muncie Organ Club, which he founded.[17]

George Maurer was born in 1929 in Romania and immigrated to Canada when he was six. He worked at the Hallman Organ Company in Kitchener, Ontario, from 1948 to 1965, where, as one of two men in the reed department, he was the voicer and finish tuner for all of Hallman's amplified "electronic" reed organs during their years of production. He also was head voicer for Hallman's pipe organ department. After Hallman closed its reed organ department in 1965, Maurer continued with The Hallman Company until 1980 as purchaser for their other lines, primarily mechanical jacks, electric sensors, and wood splitters (which he helped redesign). He then worked at the Keates Pipe Organ Company (now the Keates-Geissler Pipe Organ Company) until he retired in 1992.

Leslie J. Nicholas was born in Brattleboro, Vermont, in 1932. In 1955, he began work on the production line in the Estey electronics division. He was quickly promoted through "emergency service" and "final test" to the small engineering department, where he designed and made all jigs, fixtures, test equipment, and prototypes for Estey's electronic organs. "For engineering, those were the best five years of my life." He spent his breaks at work questioning employees in the reed and pipe departments. "During late summer 1960, I was 'clean-up': I hand-manufactured more than twenty organs out of junk—incomplete organs, returns, and all available parts—which were sold

to employees. These were the last Estey organs made." After working for a few years in television sales and service, he became a certified Lowry technician and began a career servicing electronic organs, which he still does part time from his home in Spofford, New Hampshire.

K. Thomas Schaettle made two pilgrimages to Brattleboro, in 1977 and 1978, during which he spoke briefly with Achille "Premo" Ratti, C. H. T. Brockington, and Zylphia Eckberg, a reed filer. Brockington gave Schaettle a stack of papers pertinent to Estey's reed-making operations, which have been very important to this investigation.

Paul Toelken received his initial instruction in reed organ overhauling and pipe organ maintenance from his father, after which he serviced reed organs and pianos for many years until he semi-retired in 1996. Kendrick, a pianist friend of the musical Toelken family, imparted to Paul much about reed organs and reed work. From Gunzinger, Toelken received some information, reeds, and an Estey voicing jack.[18]

Johannes "John" Wessel was born in 1922 near Leiden in the west of Holland, and in 1936 he began working for the pipe organ maker G. van Leeuwen & Zonen. In 1954 he immigrated to the United States through Estey sponsorship and worked at Estey in the pipe organ division, voicing pipes and setting up new organs; he also had a short assignment in the reed organ department. His last day working for Estey was April 25, 1960, when he finished Estey's last pipe organ, Number 3261. He then built and maintained pipe organs until he retired in 1997.

HISTORIC OVERVIEW

Reeds for reed organs are of tempered brass. Since the inception of free-reed instruments, many materials have been tried, but brass has proven to be the best material for free reeds in reed and pipe organs. Accordions and concertinas originally had

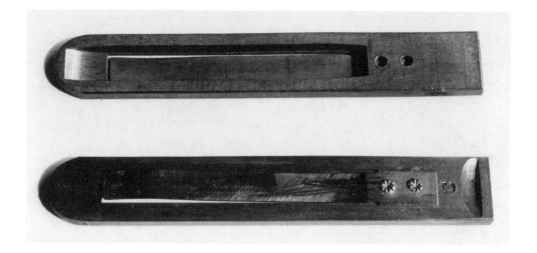

Figure 114.
Estey Tenor C reed
(actual block length $2^{3}/_{4}$
inches)

brass reeds; their reeds now have steel tongues on aluminum plates. Most harmonica reeds are still brass. Plastic reeds are incorporated into toys. Just before closing, the Estey Organ Company experimented with combinations of phosphor bronze or brass blocks, and phosphor bronze, brass, or steel tongues.

Free reeds have two parts (figure 114): the block (also called the frame, plate, or matrix), which has an open slot, and the tongue (also called "the reed"), which is attached to one end of the block and is just small enough to pass through the slot. When both stop action and pallet are open, the differential in air pressure caused by the pressure or vacuum reservoir moves air through the slot. The moving air bends the free end of the tongue through the slot until the spring of the tempered brass returns the tongue above the slot. This action is repeated many times per second as long as the air channels are open. A tongue's temper, dimensions, and shape and the wind pressure determine how frequently it oscillates and thus its pitch (also called frequency, number of oscillations, cycles per second [cps], beats per second [bps], and Hertz [Hz]).[19] Although American organ reeds and harmonium reeds have these two parts and

these attributes in common, they are dissimilar in all other respects.

That several companies made American organ reeds, if only for a short while, is attested by the various types of extant reeds. Gellerman lists seven companies who sold American organ reeds: Carhart & Needham,[20] J. Estey & Company (Estey Organ Company), A. H. Hammond (Hammond Reed Company), G. W. Ingalls & Company, Munroe Organ-Reed Company, Augustus Newell & Company, and J. D. Whitney (J. D. Whitney and Son).[21] Reed scales (the dimensions of each part of each reed for each set) from different makers are very similar; the differences and innovations are primarily in how the tongue is fixed to the block and the shape of the tongue when voiced. Many of the exceptional scales were made by Estey.

At Estey, reed blocks and tongues were created, assembled, and inspected in the reed room, which was originally on the ground floor of the machine shop, building Number 14, and later (at least during 1955–57) was set up on the ground floor in the front of building Number 2 (see Appendix C). Along with fabricating metal organ parts, the machine shop made and sharpened tools, such as reed scrapers, for the factory. (The machine shop was also called "the iron foundry," although no iron casting was done there in living memory.[22]) The reed room was off limits to visitors, and only one or two people at a time knew about the manufacture of reeds.

Block and tongue dimensions for each set of reeds were discovered empirically and a scale drawn, from which were taken exact dimensions for each part of each block and tongue in that set. "Scale" denotes a proportionate graduation of dimensions. In reed making, tongues, block slots, and undercuts are to scale, whereas block width and thickness, rivet(s), and nick are one size throughout each set. A block size can be termed a "scale," thus "common scale" reeds can have "narrow scale" tongues. See the Estey Range Chart (figure 115) showing scales in 1940 and the photographs of reeds in the figures. I have a board from the Estey reed room entitled "Scale for Philharmonic Reeds 3-10-1885" in ink (quill pen), shellacked, which gives some dimensions and the numbers of the appropriate plate punches and tongue punches. Unfortunately, it cannot be legibly reproduced here. This scale spans all octaves, from reed number one—FFFF in "0" octave—to C^5, number 92 (the top note of a 4' set of C-compass organ reeds or pipes, which is the eighty-eighth note on a piano.) To date, the highest Estey reed I have seen or heard is F^5, number 97, which is in the top octave of a 2' set. Large Vocalions include A^5, the highest reed of their 2' set.

Until 1865, when Jacob Estey brought J. D. Whitney and his riveter into the factory, J. Estey & Company (and its various preceding partnerships) purchased reeds. Estey began reed making with the common melodeon reeds in the tradition at that time, and developed scales as necessary for particular sounds (mostly larger, louder, or lower in pitch). Estey's unique scales for their Philharmonic (long and short tongues), Symphonic, Sub-Bass, pedal scales, and wide, narrow, long, and short tongue common reeds were developed at Estey. However, to date there is no record of experimentation with reeds at Estey, except for examples of late experiments with phosphor bronze and steel (which substituted materials, but did not create new scales). John Wessel reflects, "The experimenting room was part of the machine shop. Arthur Lonquil, an old guy, worked there, but I don't know what he did." Apparently, at least during Estey's last years, he experimented with phosphor bronze for reeds. Chris Brown recalls that although dimensions of reeds were not altered, "reed-making operations were in a process of constant change. Tommy [Brockington] was always interested in how to make it *better*, and he took suggestions. There was a constant evolution, a continuous upgrading of reed making, so that it was better, more efficient, cheaper."

It seems that all important reed development at Estey was completed by the mid-1880s, after which the only variation was a shorter scale of Sub-Bass-size pedal reeds for the EPRO in the late 1930s. (Estey's Electro-Pneumatic Reed Organ is a unit organ with two manuals and pedalboard, not amplified, which, reduced in capability, became the Virtuoso of the 1950s.) After the Great Depression, few large reeds, wide reeds, or standard reeds of different scales were in production (some scales were already in great supply in stock.) The Estey EPRO (Virtuoso) and the Cathedral (and similar one-manual chapel organs with electric blowers) used Sub-Bass reeds and various scales of manual reeds.[23] Chris Brown told me that when he worked in the reed room during its last years, Estey produced only common manual reeds and some Sub-Bass reeds, and that larger reeds came from an extensive supply Estey had manufactured earlier. Leslie Nicholas learned that in its last years Estey experimented in secret with pedal reeds in organ pipes, but apparently no instrument was manufactured.[24] Each successive generation of reed makers

Figure 115.

Estey Range Chart

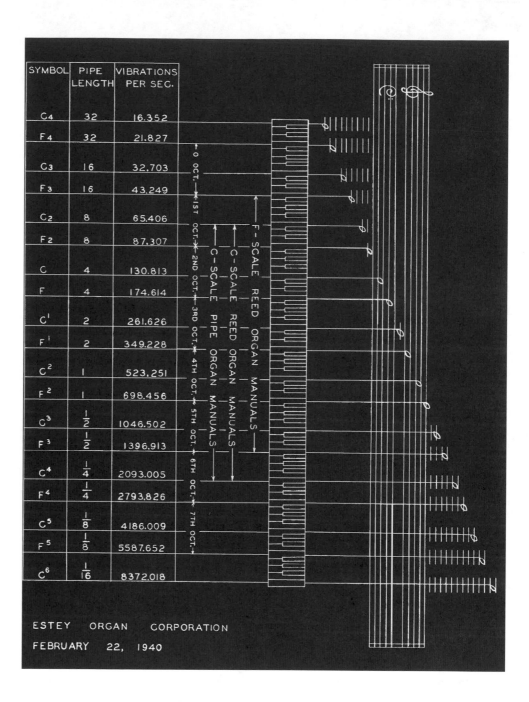

knew less because they did not need to know the theories and reasons why; they simply set up operations by the books and charts, doing what had been done.

The Estey Organ Company bought brass in large quantities from several mills in Connecticut —Scoville, Century, Bridgeport Brass, Revere Brass, and others—wherever it was cheapest at the time. Sheet brass was received in various thicknesses suitable for the various scales of blocks and tongues. In the reed room brass storage and machines were arranged along the walls. Punch-and-die sets and pertinent tools were stored at each station. In reed making, as all other aspects of Estey's manufacturing, as much as possible was created with machines. Although machines were essential for some operations, and quicker and easier for others, reed work and reed organ manufacture require much more hand work and attention than can be imagined by anyone without experience in the craft.

All steps in the production of Estey organs were trade secrets, especially reed making. No employee ever wrote anything down or gave a straight answer to probing questions for fear of losing their job—not because they might disclose a company secret to an outsider, but because the inquirer might be another Estey employee who could take the job if he or she knew as much as the informant. Leslie Nicholas bluntly stated: "You knew the secret of your job. It died with you, and others could figure it out for themselves." Contrary to this unofficial policy, in its last years Estey reed-making procedures were officially listed and time sheets instituted. This was probably prompted by the accountant hired in 1956 to help management better understand the company's production processes and costs. The following is a condensation of a list of reed-making operations and incomplete descriptions made on September 18, 1957, by Tommy Brockington, head of the reed room, and recent recollections of Chris Brown, who was Brockington's assistant from 1956 to 1957.

REED-MAKING OPERATIONS: COMMON REEDS

Blocks

B1. Get out stock and weigh	Brass is received in six-foot- (also three-foot- and four-foot-) long sheets, $3\frac{1}{4}$" to $6\frac{1}{2}$" wide. In order to keep an accurate inventory for the ensuing year, daily cards must be made out. (Brass was purchased by weight.)
B2. Clean	Use benzine or naphtha to remove grit. (Chris Brown wiped brass with a dry cloth only.)
B3. Strip	Each sheet is cut in half (lengthwise) on a stripper. On the first octave common reeds, the strip is $6\frac{1}{2}$" wide. F and F-sharp are stripped with D-sharp and E. G and G-sharp are stripped with C-sharp and D. A and A-sharp are stripped with B and C. That follows through on all the octaves.[25] One edge of each strip is filed by hand; this will be the back end, or heel end of the reed. (Chris Brown did no hand filing.)
B4. Chop and plane	A punch press chops the reeds to length, and at the same time, puts a round edge on the toe of the reeds, and automatically packs the reeds on a board. Speed of machine: 72 strokes per minute. Blocks are inspected on both sides. The planer planes the reeds on the top side and both edges. It also chamfers all four corners.
B5. Hollow out	[The undercut is milled out.][26] Reeds fall out automatically and are inspected to see that they are properly hollowed out.
B6. 1st pack	After inspection they are immediately placed on boards.

Figure 116. Reed parts before assembly. (1, 2) Pedal tongue blanks; (3, 4) Sub-Bass tongues, milled out; (5) Sub-Bass or Symphonic tongue strip; (6) Symphonic tongue with rivet holes; (7) Philharmonic tongue with rivet holes; (8) tongue blank; (9) block blank; (10) block blank used for unknown purpose; (11) block complete except for reed puller slot (nick), discarded because of skewed bevel at base (heel) of slot; (12) discarded because of short slot; (13) block brass; (14−18) tongues chopped out before assembly; (19) factory identification tags for organs;[27] (20) phosphor bronze stock milled out for tongues.

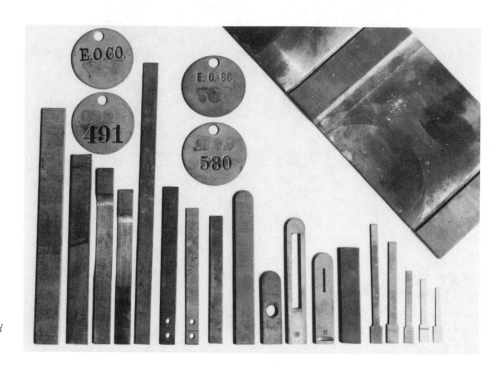

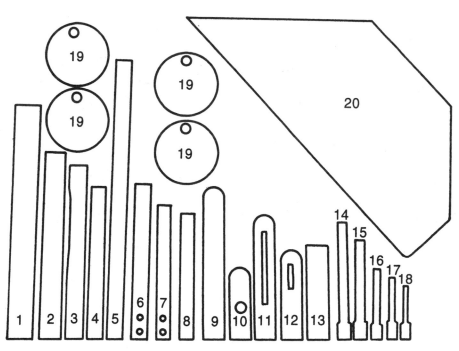

B7. Punch	The punch performs five operations: 1. Slots are punched, and blocks drop into a small hopper. 2. Heeling of the punched hole. The purpose of heeling is to give the tongue freer play so that it does not hit a sharp corner. 3. Lettering. 4. After lettering, the reed drops into a small hopper and is finish-planed to .095" thickness. 5. The reed is pushed down a small chute and is nicked.[28]
B8. 2nd pack	The blocks are then reinspected and packed for the riveting operation.

Tongues

T1. Get out stock and weigh	As above.
T2. Clean	As above.
T3. Strip	As above.
T4. Mark and roll	[The rolling machine probably flattened stripper marks.]
T5. Mill nos. 1, 2, 3, 4, 5, 6, and 7	[This operation is not understood. Though some tongues were milled before riveting, milling the tongue tops is specifically mentioned directly after riveting in the Blocks and Tongues section of this list (not included here.)]
T6. Chop and inspect	Punch out tongues. (Some thin tongues were chopped out five at once.)

ESTEY'S REED-MAKING MACHINERY

The earliest documented automatic reed-making machinery in the United States was built (and presumably designed) by Josiah Davis Whitney, who made reeds in Massachusetts from 1853 to 1865. It seems that Whitney made two sets of machinery during that time: one set (which he presumably invented and created) for his short-lived reed-making partnership with Rice and Robinson, and a second set that he made after he left that partnership.[29]

The invention of automatic reed-making machinery provided mass-produced reeds, which made the reed organ industry possible. Before punches and riveters (invented and built by Whitney and others) came into use, in small workshops and factories blocks and tongues were created individually, and tongues were riveted to blocks with brass or steel rivets, aligned in a jig, and hammered by hand (e.g., lap organ reeds and early Sub-Bass sets.) There must have been small bench jigs and hand-operated riveters with which to assemble reeds individually, though no such items are known to be extant. When set up well and operating precisely, Whitney's reed-making machinery created blocks and assembled hundreds of reeds per hour, at about two seconds per reed.

In the *Annals of Brattleboro*, Cabot states: "In 1865 J. Estey & Company purchased the machinery and hired Mr. Whitney to run it. He remained with them until 1874. About 1876 J. D. Whitney commenced a set of reed machinery, with which he began to make organ reeds in 1878, in the Harmony Block. July 1, 1879 he took his son, Edwin D. Whitney, into partnership, under the firm name of J. D. Whitney and Son."[30] Whitney sold his business to the Estey Organ Company in 1893; he died in 1902.[31]

Of the several machines in the reed room, the punch and the assembler were the only machines too specialized to have been built by Estey. These, one assumes, constituted "a set of reed machinery." The punch was "the magic machine" (Tommy Brockington, personal communication to Thomas Schaettle) that performed five operations on reed blocks, finishing them in preparation for the assembler, where blocks and tongues were riveted together. (See the table above, "Blocks," item B[7], and "Tongues.")

The innovation that made automation possible was punching the rivet up from underneath, which pushed a shaft of block brass up through the tongue to be headed over on top. This not only saved time and money in assembly, but also made it unnecessary to purchase and handle separate rivets, ensuring further cost savings.

Tongues with one round rivet may swivel and touch the frame, which is why Whitney's rivets were square (turned forty-five degrees; hereafter called a diamond). Other makers prevented swiveling by using one oval rivet, some used two small round rivets, and at least one maker patented and produced rivetless reeds (see figure 117). Whitney's diamond rivet seemed to be a good idea, but his design left little tongue metal at the corners of the rivets, resulting in an occasional split that forced the tongue against the block.

It appears that when Whitney left Estey to build his last set of reed-making machinery, he took the opportunity to improve the assembler and its resultant reeds by designing it to punch two small rivets instead of the problematic single diamond rivet, a worthwhile improvement, since these tongues never break at the rivets. Whitney's

reeds in organs of Wilcox & White and the Carpenter Organ Company have two rivets and a square reed puller slot. There is no doubt that in 1893 the Estey Organ Company bought J. D. Whitney and Son as much to acquire this improved set of reed machinery as for the reed business it would supply. Chris Brown believes that the punch and riveter machines he worked with (and on) in 1957 had been built "about seventy-five years before." This would date their construction to about 1880, which is close to Cabot's date of "[a]bout 1876."

It seems that, from 1894, Estey supplied only reeds with two rivets to other manufacturers. However, double-rivet reeds were not used exclusively in Estey organs after their inception. Reeds with one diamond rivet were used from stock before the up-to-date new reeds were phased in (as was done with Estey's labels, nameboards, and designs), until reeds with two rivets became the norm in 1895 or 1896.[32] Reeds with one diamond rivet, especially with wide tongues, were used in Virtuosos and other models until Estey closed, both for their quality of timbre and to use up valuable stock.

Leslie Nicholas noted that "Estey had two sets of identical reed making machinery"—that is, two punch-and-assembler combinations. During his conversations with employees from the reed side Leslie Nicholas heard that during the twentieth century the "spare reed machine" was leased to Wurlitzer on the condition that it return to Estey, which it did when Wurlitzer closed its reed operation. This may have been misinformation, because Wurlitzer sold organs with reeds during the 1960s, after Estey's close. Paul Toelken, reed voicer and tuner, is aware of two sets of machinery, but was informed by Ernest Kendrick that Estey bought its second set of reed-making machinery from A. H. Hammond & Company of Worcester, Massachusetts.[33]

Cabot records that "[J. D. Whitney] removed

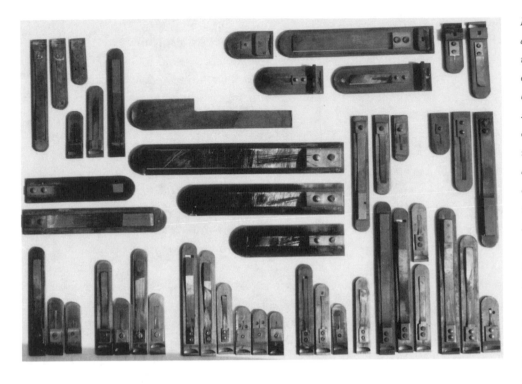

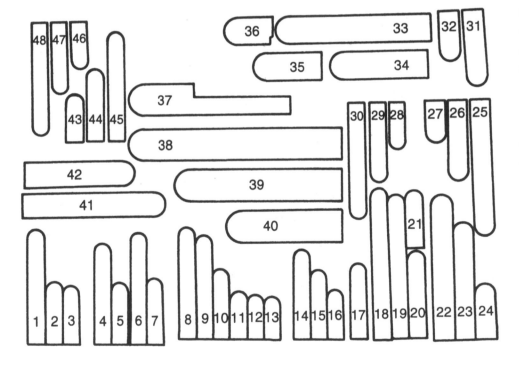

Figure 117. Estey reed chronology. (1–3) Estey melodeon reeds, common scale, one diamond rivet, reed puller bump; (4, 5) Estey common scale, common width tongues, one diamond rivet, quarter-moon nick; (6, 7) Estey common scale, wide tongues, one diamond rivet, quarter-moon nick; (8–10) Estey common scale, two rivets; (11–13) Estey common scale, single rivet, top notes; (14–16) Estey common scale, narrow tongues; (17) Estey common scale, wide tongue; (18–21) Estey Philharmonic scale; (22–24) Estey Symphonic scale [note weight riveted to longest tongue]; (25–27) Mason & Hamlin wide reeds; (28–30) Mason & Hamlin common scale; (31–32) Vocalion mid scale; (33–36) Vocalion manual wide scale; (37) pedal block blank cut for another purpose; (38–40) Estey Pedal Bourdon reeds; (41–42) Estey Sub-Bass reeds; (43–45) Munroe rivetless reeds, U.S. Patent No. 73,114, Jan. 7, 1868; (46–48) reeds from an E. P. Carpenter & Company organ, made by J. D. Whitney or Estey.

to Worcester, Massachusetts, in 1853, where he formed a partnership with Mssrs. Rice and Robinson for the manufacture of organ reeds. He remained there only one year, then went back to Fitchburg, and soon after got up a set of reed machinery and commenced making reeds."[34] It is probable that the reed-making machinery (assumed to be the first set he created) that Whitney left with Rice and Robinson in 1854 was acquired by Redding & Harrington, who made reeds in Worcester until they were bought out by A. H. Hammond & Company in 1885.[35] In 1909 the Hinners Organ Company of Pekin, Illinois, bought the Hammond Reed Company (as it was then called) to gain reed-making capability. The renamed Hinners Reed Organ Company continued until 1940 and was formally dissolved in 1942.[36] About this time ("during the war," my informants said) Estey acquired the "Hammond" reed machinery (presumably from Hinners).

The Estey Organ Company did not keep this valuable equipment for long. Ernest Kendrick wrote to Paul Toelken that Estey "needed the cash so bad" that around 1945 it sold "the reed making machinery by Hammond" to Wurlitzer for $86,000; Thomas Schaettle heard from Tommy Brockington that the price was $125,000. If this was actually Whitney's original set, the riveter had been retooled to the reliable double-rivet standard, because reeds that Wurlitzer made with these machines and installed in their amplified reed organs from about 1944 into the 1960s[37] are identical to Estey double-rivet reeds, with the same star design stamped into their two rivet heads and Estey's distinctive quarter-moon reed puller slot.[38]

Therefore, during its years of operation, Estey had three sets of reed-making machinery: its original 1865 purchase from J. D. Whitney (his second set), which punched one diamond rivet; Whitney's third set (improved to punch two rivets), acquired with J. D. Whitney and Son in 1893; and the "Ham-mond" set (possibly Whitney's first set, retooled to punch two rivets), presumably purchased from Hinners and soon after sold to Wurlitzer.

The fate of these three sets of reed-making machinery is currently unknown. It is unlikely that, after Estey installed Whitney's improved set of reed-making machinery in 1893, the Estey Organ Company would have discarded their unique and valuable original machines, purchased in 1865; however, there is no lore or record of their sale. Chris Brown never saw or heard of this old machinery while he worked in the reed room, and suggested that one set may have been made out of Estey's first two sets.

It is a shame that so much was indiscriminately discarded from the Estey buildings in 1960. Leslie Nicholas was one of a group of concerned citizens who, in the nick of time, saved Estey's Corliss 2 steam engine from the cutting torch. Some machinery was set outside in the yard and possibly sold for scrap. When Edwin Battison, former curator of mechanical engineering at the Smithsonian Institution and founder of the American Precision Museum in Windsor, Vermont, went to the Estey buildings in the early 1970s to salvage what he could, Hyacinth Renaud said that he had "buried many machines in the fire pond." Edwin Battison was allowed to save a large jigsaw.[39] Thomas Schaettle heard from Premo Ratti that "the reed-making equipment" was offered to the Smithsonian Institution, which refused it, so it was unceremoniously dumped into the Connecticut River. However, Leslie Nicholas heard that one set of reed-making machinery was stored in a warehouse in Delaware, where the Estey Organ Corporation (Del.) was incorporated. No information has been found regarding what became of the "Hammond" set of reed-making machinery that Estey sold to Wurlitzer.

The one riveter in use at Estey during living memory accommodated only blocks of the standard, "common" width. Estey parlor organs typi-

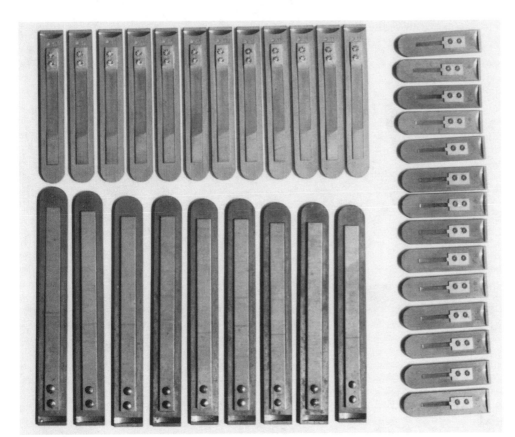

Figure 118.
New Estey reeds. Bottom
row: Symphonic reeds,
tongues not milled out;
top row: common reeds,
tongues milled out;
side row: top note reeds.

cally include only common scale (size) reed blocks; chapel organs include two or three scales; and two-manual-with-pedal organs may have three to five different scales of reeds. Each size (scale) of block may have various scales (dimensions) of tongues (see figure 117).

The assembler was a long, narrow box with two vertical magazines on top. Reeds were made in runs of hundreds or thousands: one size, one letter name. The blocks, completed to exact specifications, were stacked in one magazine; the chopped-out tongues were stacked in the other. The assembler that Chris Brown ran punched two rivets and operated from right to left: blocks were in the magazine on the right; tongues were in the magazine on the left. A lever on the far right (automated, though perhaps originally hand operated), swung back and forth to advance blocks from the

first magazine directly under the second magazine, where they were matched with a tongue. The block and tongue were then advanced to where the rivets were punched up through both thicknesses of brass, and advanced again to where the rivets were headed over. Assembled reeds fell off the end of the track out the left side of the machine.

More may be discovered regarding Estey's reed-making machines and their chronology. A photograph from the mid-1940s shows Tommy Brockington at an assembler that operates from left to right. This is not the machine Chris Brown ran, although both machines punched two rivets.[40] The photograph was probably taken in the machine shop before the reed room was moved to building Number 2. The machine may be any of Estey's three assemblers: is it Estey's 1865 purchase, its 1893 purchase, or part of the Hammond set? Perhaps Estey kept the Hammond assembler (or Hammond's set of reed-making machinery) and sold Wurlitzer their old one.

Chris Brown relates: "During the six to eight months I was running the reed machines, I was in the reed room all by myself. Tommy would come over [from the machine shop, where he was foreman] if I had a problem, or he'd come over to check on me. But he didn't bother me too much; he just left me alone there and I ran the reed machine."

The machinery was old and in constant use when operating, so parts became worn and functioned incorrectly. The original patterns for parts of the machines were hung on the wall. When a part that could not be made on site wore out or broke, its pattern was sent out to have a replacement made. Chris Brown told me that the assembler was almost daily in need of adjustment and repair, with plenty of down time:

> I spent half my time on repair and setting up of the punch and the assembler. The width of the blocks was constant, but of course I had to adjust the assembler for the length of the blocks. The tongues of the larger reeds were bigger and you could operate that a little, but when you got into those little ones, they were . . . I mean, they would come out sideways! The machine was very old, and it was shimmed up here and shimmed up there. It was a dreadful thing to run! I remember that I would work all day getting the thing going—that was the trickiest part—and then it would be time to go home. I would come in the next morning and it would be kerflooey again. You know, it had been working perfectly. I should have stayed there [to run the machine through the night], but they didn't cotton to that.

Estey time sheets from August 1957 (soon after Chris Brown's time in the reed room) record that on four consecutive work days no reeds were assembled because one or two employees were continuously engaged in repair and set-up of, or making parts for, both the punch and the riveter. Even after meticulous repair and set-up there were problems. Chris Brown remembers: "In a batch of five thousand reeds, about three thousand tongues were not lined up with the slot. On a good day I got three thousand good ones." Off-center reeds were sold with the scrap brass, not thrown out. Weekly totals varied widely with the number of hours that the machines actually operated.

Extensive repair and set-up of the machinery—and, when the machines worked, the fact that fatal riveting errors occurred so late in the reed-making process—contributed greatly to the fatal drain of company resources. In its last decades, the Estey Organ Corporation was an antique, a living museum. Its nineteenth-century machinery, manufacturing processes, and personnel requirements, the most modern and efficient when they were initiated, had become great liabilities.

There is no living memory of assembling Estey reeds of other than common and Sub-Bass scales, and no memory of the riveting operation for Sub-Bass reeds. Our informants agree that reeds wider and longer than common scale "must have been" assembled with two steel or brass rivets set simultaneously by a (possibly hand-operated) machine made for that purpose. An Estey price list from 1958 offers Common, Philharmonic, Sub-Bass, and Pedal reeds. Chris Brown recalls that Estey had "quite a stock of large reeds, riveted together, but with the tongues not milled out." Apparently large reeds were made and assembled in very few runs of hundreds or thousands, and Estey drew from this stock throughout the remainder of its operation. For example, reeds in Estey two-manual-with-pedal instruments indicate that Pedal Bourdon scale reeds were made twice: in the 1880s and again about 1914.

Philharmonic reeds are the same width as common reeds, but are significantly longer, in order to move more air. Philharmonic blocks were probably made using the "magic" punch machine, but their

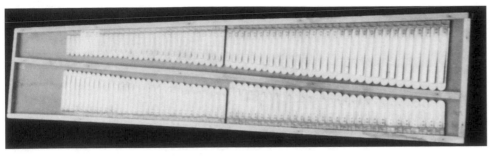

Figure 119.

Reeds from a typical five-octave Estey parlor organ on an Estey reed tray. Top row: Melodia 8' (bass, on the right), Diapason 8' (treble, on the left). Bottom row: Viola 4' (one octave higher and smaller than the corresponding Melodia reeds), Vox Jubilante 8' (which break back one octave to the same size and pitch as the Diapason reeds).

tongues are riveted with two separate rivets (i.e., not by the assembler), the tall heads of which are stamped with a heavy waffle design (figure 117, [18–21]). The reed room must have had patterns for cutting out these scales, especially considering that, as we shall see, Estey made wide, standard, and perhaps all reeds for other reed organ manufacturers. Reeds larger than common scale were drawn from stock and the tops of the tongues milled before they were shipped to a customer or included in an Estey organ.

Examples of unmounted tongues from the factory demonstrate that some tongues were milled out before assembly, and some tongues were milled out afterward. Riveted tongues were milled out on one of two dedicated machines, removing enough material from the central portion of the top to allow the tongue to vibrate (and bring it close to pitch) while retaining enough for it to be tuned (see figures 116 and 118). Small tongues in the top octaves were not milled out by machine, but were carefully thinned by hand.

Reed organ reeds are grouped in sets (or ranks, like organ pipes and soldiers) of one timbre usually numbering as many reeds as there are keys (figure 119). Estey's Child's Organ has three octaves (thirty-seven keys); small melodeons and field organs have four octaves (forty-nine keys); typical

melodeons, flat tops, parlor organs, chapel organs, and two-manual-with-pedal instruments all have five octaves (sixty-one keys); some melodeons and parlor organs have six octaves (seventy-three keys); piano-cased reed organs have seven octaves plus a few notes (eighty-eight keys). Manual reeds also come in half sets for divided keyboards, and short sets—for example, Vox Celeste (forty-nine reeds beginning on tenor C) and Sub-Bass (thirteen or seventeen reeds beginning on CC). Estey pedalboards have thirty or thirty-two keys, and thirty or forty-four reeds per set. Keyboards for one-manual, five- and six-octave organs have F compass, the compass of the vast majority of organs produced by Estey and other American organ builders (see figure 115 and the discussion of harmonium and American organ characteristics in section 1). Two-manual-with-pedal organs and the small three- and four-octave organs have C compass.

Pipe organs for the past two thousand years, and reed organs for the last two hundred, were the first "synthesizers," with which ranks of differing timbres and pitch levels are combined to create composite sounds appropriate for, and changeable with, the moment's music. Each set was scaled and voiced to produce a specific timbre for a specific role in each instrument. As was typical in instru-

Figure 120.
Estey voicing jack (from the collection of Ned Phoenix)

ments from other reed organ manufacturers, Estey's melodeons and small organs have one (rarely two) sets; flat tops and parlor organs have two (sometimes three) sets; chapel organs have two to four full sets and one or two half sets, plus thirteen large Sub-Bass reeds; and two-manual-with-pedal Estey instruments have from five to ten-and-one-half sets distributed among their three keyboards (see figure 117). Photographs exist of an Estey reed organ with three manuals and pedalboard, although no stoplist is available.[41] Mason & Hamlin, Vocalion, Hallman, and others also built three-manual-with-pedal reed organs with many sets of reeds.[42]

The largest Estey reeds were the Pedal 32' reeds, which "measured (at their largest) twelve inches long and one inch wide."[43] The largest reeds usually found are of Bourdon scale in the Pedal 16' stop. The lowest Estey reeds (other than the Pedal 32' reeds) are FFFF—number one in "0" octave, the lowest reed of a 16' set on an F-compass keyboard—which are usually found in Philharmonic scale. The highest, smallest, and rarest are C^5 through F^5 in the seventh octave.

These top note reeds are very difficult to make and tune, and were used primarily in a few chapel organs and the Minshall-Estey, Orgatron,[44] Wurlitzer, and Hallman amplified unified reed instruments.

Newly assembled reeds were packed in sets (chromatically) on reed trays, inspected, and placed on shelves.[45] Blocks were now completed, but tongues had just begun to be worked on.

REED FILING AND VOICING

Estey voicing jacks (figure 120), like the company's other specialty machinery, were made at Estey for their own purposes.[46] Reeds were tested in the voicing jacks; the actual work was done by the reed filers. Both men and women worked at the voicers, which were used primarily to prepare full sets of raw reeds, but also to repair or re-tongue returned reeds or to ready replacement reeds. During the 1930s four reed filers worked at voicing jacks in separate rooms on the third floor of building Number 6.

Three of Estey's voicing jacks are extant, each

set up for specific operations in addition to working on common reeds. Estey voicing jacks have two six-octave keyboards, each with its corresponding set of reed cells and pallets. The top or back keyboard operates the tuned master set of reeds in the back cells. New reeds were slid into the reed cells under the bottom or front keyboard and tested by playing one or both keyboards for each note.

Test blocks for larger reeds are mounted in front of the keyboards. These have ingenious mechanisms that allow one hand to simultaneously hold a reed in place and automatically open (or close) the pallet, leaving the other hand free to work on the reed. Some test blocks have chambers, which develop a more focused sound to better hear low reeds in the noisy factory; others are open to ready access for adjustment and observation of the tongue in motion.

Reed cell blocks from melodeons coupled with cottage organ bellows date Estey's voicing jacks to the early 1860s. One or more of these may have served Estey & Green or its predecessors; the others were most likely constructed in 1865 when J. Estey & Company began its in-house reed-making operation. Although these were originally foot-pumped, suction blowers for small electric organs were installed, probably as soon as blowers began to be used in organs. My voicing jack has a removable (and therefore adjustable) weight to create vacuum instead of the usual pair of reservoir springs.

When riveted to its block, the tongue of a raw reed was a bit too long to pass through the slot—the tip rubbed the end of the slot, or extended onto the block—which ensured that the tongue was not too short. Reeds with tongues shorter than this were scrapped because their sound would be out of character with the set. (Logic may suggest that too-long tongues helped steady or align the tongue for riveting; however, the riveter also assembled reeds of short tongue scale, with inten-

tionally very short tongues that capitalized on this change in character.) When a tray of raw reeds came from the reed room, the reed filer's first operation was to file the tip of the tongue so it would pass through the slot,[47] thus giving the reed its voice and the voicing jack, or voicer, its name. Reeds could then be heard and tuned. When the reed filer completed voicing a set of reeds, each reed was rough-tuned on a test block to match the master reeds.[48] Then all reeds were slid into the appropriate reed cells and tuned from bass to treble in unison with the master set.

After a set of reeds had been given its first tuning, the reed filer arranged the set in order on a reed tray, penciled his or her initials on the lowest reed, and placed the tray on a shelf (see figure 119). Initials identifying each filer's work for production records were also of importance to the tuners, who learned which initials indicated an easy or a difficult job ahead. "Some of the filers were good workers, but some just didn't give a darn," Mel Harris commented. "While I was a tuner at Estey, filers were paid by the hour, not piecework," and their pay was not based on quality. Although essential to the operation and longevity of each reed and each organ's sound, reed filing was the least skilled reed work, mostly done by rote. (Chris Brown remembers that at the Estey factory, "there were a lot of people doing hand work who were skilled but not knowledgeable. Lots of women doing small things for minimum wage.")

BENDING TONGUES AND TUNING REEDS

Tuners chose reed trays from the shelf. If they were unlucky enough to be stuck with the work of a careless filer, before going further they had to complete the filing that the filer did not or would not do, such as thin the tongues down properly. The tuner then bent the tongues with voicing pliers to modify the timbre, to give each set its characteristic voice.[49] In pipe organ work "voicing" is

Figure 121.
Estey common reed. Note
the curved tongue and marks
from filing and tuning. (see
also Figure 114)

the proper term for regulating timbres of flues and reeds, but Estey employees always spoke of "bending the tongues" of reeds; although they bent the tongues with voicing pliers, "voicing" was their term for preliminary operations. When a tuner learned to bend reeds, the head tuner would set the first note of each octave (Fs or Cs), and the novice learned by proportionally curving the intervening tongues. The head tuner also fine-tuned each organ and filled orders for replacement reeds. At least during the 1930s, Mel Harris and his fellow tuners bent the tongues of all the reeds in every organ they tuned. From 1955 to 1960, when John Wessel worked at Estey, Leon Harris bent the tongues of all the reeds; the tuners only tuned reeds in the organ actions.[50]

Tools were owned by the factory and handed down. Some reed filers and tuners had a personal tool kit designed to speed their work, created by them on their own time—that is, during their lunch hours. These tools' wooden handles were of signature design so they would not stray from their owner's bench.[51]

Tuners sometimes worked long hours. In 1938 or 1939, for a rush of a few months before Easter, they worked thirteen hours per day, Monday through Friday, and nine hours on Saturday, for which Mel Harris, a tuner, was paid 40 cents per hour—no bonuses, no time and a half. Starting at 25 cents, he worked his way up to 60 cents per hour straight pay, at which time a per-reed bonus was instituted with which he doubled his paycheck ("I really took a pay drop when I quit"). Estey employees were "paid piecework" during the 1940s and into the 1950s. This piecework incentive prompted a tuners' strike over the EPRO, since it took much longer to tune well than the supervisor decreed, making it impossible for the tuners to earn their usual bonuses. During Estey's last years, employees were paid by the hour.

Mel Harris recalls that during the time he was a tuner, there were six tuner's rooms (along with offices) on the second floor of building Number 6, and, on the third floor, three more rooms for tuners and four rooms for reed filers. The doors were left open when tuners were voicing reeds or setting up a job; doors were closed while they were tuning. In addition to a tablelike bench on which reed trays were set, each tuner had a tuner's table (figure 122). This was a square two-drawer stand on a turned pedestal with a cast-iron tripod base.[52] Easily moved wherever needed, it ensured that tools for tuning and repairing reeds were close at hand. Tools were stored in a rack on the side, and work was performed on the top surface. The top drawer held the tuner's logbook; the lower drawer, in a building covered with slate for fire protection, was for personal items, such as cigarettes.

Reeds must be fine-tuned in their permanent environment. Originally, each completed organ was assembled, then treadled for tuning. At some point before 1935, in each tuner's room in the Birge Street factory was installed a testing table (also called a tuning jack or motor table) with an electric suction unit.[53] An action, with reeds in the reed cells, was clamped to the jack for tuning. Mel Harris tuned small actions on the table, EPRO actions on a special jack, and all other types in the complete organs (which, by that time, had their own suction units). Two-manual-with-pedal organs were attached by flexible hose to a branch of a conduit from a main wind trunk supplied by a large turbine. In addition to relieving the tuner of treadling, these steady, copious supplies of vacuum wind made tuning easier and quicker. The attribute that distinguishes the reed organ (originally called *l'orgue expressif*) is the fact that its wind pressure can be readily altered by the treadler to affect the sound's volume. However, a reed's pitch varies slightly with even a small change in wind pressure. Therefore, expressively flexible "pumping" is wonderful for playing a reed organ, during which the pitch change will not be noticed,[54] but any variance in winding is trouble for a tuner.

New reeds are not easily tamed. After reeds in an organ were tuned, the organ (or action) was set aside while the reeds settled in, optimally for three weeks, when the reeds were tuned again, placed on hold for another three weeks, and so on. Organs were tuned until the reeds stabilized—three to five tunings. The ten sets of reeds in Estey's two-manual-with-pedal reed instruments were tuned until ready—more than five times, if necessary.

A sufficient number of well-timed tunings is an ideal Estey practiced until the Great Depression, but by 1935, according to Mel Harris, two tunings were the maximum, and some 1940s and 1950s Estey organs have only one tuner's number or date, which may indicate only one tuning. Beginning in the 1930s, after bending the reeds, tuners tuned them in their action once, then left the action (or complete organ) in the hall, where the

Figure 122. Estey tuner's table (from the collection of Ned Phoenix)

head tuner would choose organs to correct (give them their second and final tuning) according to the daily order sent up by the shipping department. At that time there was no definite time cycle between tunings, as is attested by label dates one or two days apart.

Labels in Estey reed organs are placed on a horizontal surface, facing up, usually on the chest (one of the back corners) or on the Sub-Bass or pedal resonating box. Several papers and styles were used during Estey's history. Cottage organ labels are the most ornate; labels in small mid-twentieth-century organs are minimalistic.

Labels have the company name at the head, but, as noted above, old labels were used for years after the name had changed, concurrently with new ones. Each organ's serial number is printed in large type, usually in color. Underneath are five lines with initials, as follows (explanations in brackets):

		[date]	[by]	[employee number]
[Set Up]	S.U.	_____	X	_____
[Tuned]	T.	_____	X	_____
[Corrected]	C.	_____	X	_____
[Looked Over]	L.O.	_____	X	_____
[Inspected]	I.	_____	X	_____

The person who set up (put together) the organ "put his number down" on the label, as did the tuners. "Tuned" and "Corrected" (or "Checked") indicate first and final tunings of reeds in their action. In my experience, fewer than half of all Estey organs have both year and day(s) recorded on the label. Even if writing exists, notations are made hastily and lightly in pencil, and dates may be too light to read or covered over with dirt. The full date is sometimes penciled above the top employee number, while the month and day (and occasionally the last two digits of the year) are written on the date line. A date on a label indicates work done and is necessarily different than the date the organ was sold.

Mel Harris said, "Toward the end, I was proud enough of my work that, in addition to putting my number down on the label, I wrote my name and the date on the keys of my organs: 'Tuned by Mel Harris on such-and-such a day.' I was proud of it." He was the only one who did not go back (on principle) after the 1941 tuner's strike, but says, "It didn't seem it at the time, but some of the happiest days of my life were spent over there. For everybody that worked over there it was Old Home Day. Arthur Brasor, a reed organ tuner all his life, told me, 'There isn't a place in the town of Brattleboro that pays less money than this does, but there isn't a place in Brattleboro where you get treated any better than over here,'" a sentiment echoed by just about everyone who worked at Estey.

After the first tuning, actions and organs left incomplete for tuning were taken from the hallway to the case shop for final assembly of case parts, then returned. This may be the "Looked Over" step listed on Estey's labels, but if so, it would be out of order; no specific operation is known for this term. After the head tuner corrected the reeds, the completed organ went downstairs on the elevator to the inspector, who made sure that every reed spoke, then polished the case. From there it went to the shipping room, where it was crated and shipped out.

During Estey's last two decades, when pipe work was slow (and during the 1941 tuner's strike), people were sent from the pipe side to the reed side to help out. Symptomatic breakage of EPRO pedal reeds (beginning in the 1950s) is attributable to inexperienced filing, and may be the product of temporary filers or tuners during the tuner's strike. In the 1950s there was talk of sending John Wessel to teach women to tune reeds, because (contrary to Jacob Estey's former equal-pay policy) it was cheaper to pay women than the men already employed as tuners.[55] This change was never implemented, but John Wessel did tune three-octave Toy Organs. He was required to use a Conn Strobotuner, which slowed his work because to tune by ear was quicker, and, because the Strobotuner's own heat raised its pitch, the machine required frequent recalibration. So he tuned by ear until the supervisor came around, when he dutifully watched the Strobotuner.[56] Wessel also sorted chord actions imported from Italy, many of which were unusable. These had accordion reeds (steel tongues on aluminum frames) that were made and tuned in Italy. The operational chord actions went into Estey's three-octave chord organs, for which Estey made and tuned the manual reeds.

Throughout its operation, Estey sold reeds (individually or in sets) and parts to individuals (Alonzo Hines, for example) who made or repaired their own instruments. Estey also repaired or retongued reeds returned to the factory.

In addition to sales of complete organs to the public, Estey and others bought and sold parts between companies. Everett Orgatron actions and reeds were of Estey manufacture, an arrangement similar to the Minshall-Estey, for which Minshall manufactured only the electronics. The *Annals of Brattleboro* states that "[J. D. Whitney & Son] manufactured over half a million organ reeds a year, which were almost entirely used by the Wilcox & White Organ Company of Meriden, Connecticut."[57] The E. P. Carpenter Organ Company, also of Brattleboro, sold their "organ sections" (actions) with reeds by Whitney or Estey for inclusion in others' cases.[58] Clough & Warren of Detroit sold actions to Karn of Ontario (Gary Schmidt, personal communication). At various times, presumably when they were too busy to produce enough, Estey bought in keyboards (which are generally of inferior quality), fan tremulants, and octave couplers.

All this interfactory trade was dwarfed by Estey's reed business. According to Charles Gunzinger, Estey made all of the reeds for the Mason & Hamlin Organ Company of Boston (see figure 116), probably from its inception in 1854 until the 1920s, when it closed its reed organ division (and dumped its reeds) to continue exclusively as a piano manufacturer.

Mason & Hamlin reeds are distinctive; the most obvious differences in the block's double bevel and are the lack of a reed puller slot (or nick). Some or all of the brass for these reeds is different; some Mason & Hamlin tongue brass is harder than the brass in Estey reeds, and Charles Gunzinger was warned not to use the Mason & Hamlin brass for Estey reeds. In addition to individual voicing traditions, the brass used for reeds has much to do with the tone characteristic of organs from each manufacturer. Mason & Hamlin also used sets of common reeds with square-sided blocks and wide scale reeds almost identical to Estey's Symphonic scale reeds (minus the reed puller slot).

According to Gunzinger, Estey also made Vocalion reeds. Vocalions are known for having reeds with blocks that are much wider than standard, a scale unique in my experience. In sixteen- and seventeen-rank two-manual-with-pedal Vocalions, these wide reeds have tongues of unusual, very effective shapes and scales. Estey retongued Vocalion reeds for individual orders, and may have made some common, Symphonic, large scale, and pedal Vocalion reeds (a 1958 Estey price sheet lists Pedal [Vocalion] reeds, without explanation of source, and no Pedal [Estey] reeds). However, "Mr. Munroe, of organ reed fame, [was] a member of the corporation" started by James Baillie-Hamilton "for the manufacture and sale of the Vocalion."[59] Perhaps Aeolian purchased the Munroe Organ Reed Company in 1892 in order to gain ownership of the Vocalion reed-making machinery, because the unique Vocalion reeds were essential to their "Orchestrelle" roll-playing reed organs, which used Vocalion organ actions.[60] There is no evidence of what became of the machinery when Aeolian ceased its reed operation in 1910, or of Estey manufacture of reeds for new Vocalions.

However, soft and high-pitched reeds in two-manual-with-pedal Vocalions are mostly sized to the standard, common scale. And at the end of the nineteenth century, a third manual scale, with Estey's Symphonic scale dimensions, was

introduced in Estey, Mason & Hamlin, and Vocalion organs (to my knowledge, these are the
only three makers who used this scale). Estey was
tooled up for common and Symphonic scales, and
could have readily provided these for Vocalions.

The Gulbransen Column Electric Organ and
the Magnatone, direct-electric unified amplified
reed organs, used Estey reeds as did the Ketterman organs (Sylvan Ketterman, personal communication). Everett Orgatron reeds were also supplied by Estey. After World War II Wurlitzer
bought Everett's reed operation and for a short
while produced amplified reed organs, for which
they also acquired Estey's spare set of reed-
making machinery. A. H. Hammond & Company
of Worcester, Massachusetts, made reeds for the
trade, as well as octave couplers used in some
Estey organs. The Hammond reed-making machinery was presumably purchased by Estey from
Hinners and sold to Wurlitzer in the 1940s when
Wurlitzer acquired Everett's reed division.

The Hallman Organ Company (J. C. Hallman),
first of Waterloo, then of Kitchener, Ontario,
Canada, built two-manual- and three-manual-
with-pedal amplified reed organs from 1949 to
1965 using exclusively Estey reeds until Estey
closed (George Maurer, personal communication).
Hallman's organs were similar in design to the
Minshall-Estey (and the Orgatron and Wurlitzer
amplified reed instruments), but their design and
sound were better (George Maurer, Gary Schmidt,
personal communication). In most amplified reed
organs currently in use, solid-state amplifiers have
been installed in place of the original tube amplifiers. Hallman used only common scale reeds in
the manual and pedal divisions of their amplified
reed organs. Common scale reeds, also amplified,
were used as pedal bass for their small pipe organs.
Estey shipped raw reeds to Hallman, where
George Maurer and his assistant did all the filing,
bending, and tuning of the tongues.

Hallman employees built a unique voicing jack

(currently extant, with other Hallman items, in a
personal collection). Other manufacturers who
bought in reeds probably built their own voicing
jacks, filed the tongues, and added their signature
bends. For example, Emmons Hamlin claimed to
have discovered bending (voicing) of tongues while
he was a tuner with Prince & Company, and it can
be assumed that Mason & Hamlin voiced the reeds
that are the source of their organs' distinctive
sound. Estey may have provided reeds any way its
customers preferred. Perhaps there exist records,
reed scales, reed-making equipment, or other evidence of these reed-making and -selling activities.

Estey's reed sales diminished as its customers
ceased production of reed organs. Two of Estey's
last reed accounts were with the Hallman Organ
Company of Canada and Yamaha of Japan, both
of which continued reed organ production after
Estey closed. (After Estey closed, Hallman bought
reeds from Renner in Stuttgart, Germany, who
ceased reed making around 1980. At last report,
Yamaha had also ceased building reed organs.) No
individual craftsman made new reed organs after
Estey closed. Reed organ and free reed manufacture in the United States died with Estey.

3. Timbres: Free Reeds and Their Environments

Although free reeds were created with inherent
timbres, the environment within which its reeds
speak has more influence on an organ's sound than
the reeds themselves.

As a vibrator, or sound generator, a free reed,
with its environs, can be compared to your vocal
cords. When you make a sound with your vocal
cords, your throat, mouth, sinuses, and entire body
resonate and modulate that sound; the sound is
you. Your sound can be further modified with your
hand in front of your mouth (or your harmonica or
French horn) or by your environment (e.g., sound-

ing through a closed or open door). Therefore, it is no surprise that everything that surrounds a reed affects its sound as perceived by the listener, including its promptness of speech, timbre, pitch, and volume.

Shape equals sound. The proportions and sizes of resonating bodies and volumes naturally amplify specific overtones in the harmonic series. The amplitudes (sizes) of waves able to reverberate within a shape determine which overtones are accentuated. Not only do reeds produce strong high overtones, but also the small sizes of their reed cells, chambers, and other modulators selectively amplify the smaller, higher sound waves.[61]

Round, full sound, consisting of more fundamental than overtones, is created by round, full shapes; the rounder and closer to spherical (or cubical) the sound generators and modulators are, the closer the sound is to a sine wave. In pipe organ terminology, round tone is flute tone. Thin sound, consisting of many overtones without much fundamental, is created by long, narrow, shapes; the narrower the sound generators and modulators are in relation to their lengths, the more overtones are produced. Thin tone is string tone. Diapason, or organ tone, is scaled between these extremes, and voiced louder. Reed tone, ranging from bright and loud to mellow, is created by wedge, cone, or horn shapes, which develop harmonics characteristic of brass and reed instruments. As with the other timbral shapes, these greater-than shapes may be proportionately thin or wide, resulting in a sound chosen from a spectrum of modulation possibilities. These facts are true for all shapes, including free reeds (see section 2), striking reeds, organ pipes, instruments, speakers, rooms, and all spaces within (volumes).

The reed environment includes the chest (or pan), bellows (sometimes), pallets (or valves), reed tongue, reed block, and method of securing the reed in the instrument (as well as how tightly the reed is secured), and the channels before or after the reed, including reed cells, chambers, qualifying tubes, Scribner's tubes, rank-specific covers, Sub-Bass and pedal resonating boxes, swell shades, Metaphone shades, the tremulant, the organ's case, and the cloth in the expression holes. Suggestions by John Green of London for altering the timbre of his Royal Seraphine (c. 1833) include operating the swell shade, opening the organ's top, and covering the reeds with wood, paper, or cloth.[62] And finally, as with all instruments, much of the success of a reed organ depends on its venue: dead acoustics vacuum up even a fine instrument, while a live, warm space makes anything sound wonderful.

Sound is affected most by density of materials, which is determined by inherent molecular structure, grain, and finished thickness. Materials reflect or absorb harmonics. Density and thickness of materials are chosen to shape the sound by enhancing or attenuating harmonics. (Not all materials are chosen to reflect or amplify sound; reeds in Wurlitzer amplified reed organs were riveted to fiberboard or plastic to minimize their vibrations to other parts of the instrument.) Materials may be chosen for their weight, color, shape, finished dimensions, price, availability, or other considerations; however, when density and thickness are appropriate for production of the desired musical attributes, the type and quality of materials are not important. Successful materials for reeds are found in a range from yellow brass to stainless steel, and in a variety of tempers. Both materials and their tempers are expressions of hardness, that is, density.

A well-fitting tongue efficiently cuts the air as it passes through the slot, creating numerous harmonics. Since free reeds naturally produce many high harmonics, string tone and reed tone timbres are most readily successful in free-reed instruments. The challenge with free reeds has always been to produce good diapason and flute timbres. Width and height constraints of compact reed organ designs limited the roundness achievable

Figure 123.
16' Sub-Bass reeds in a
detached reed cell block

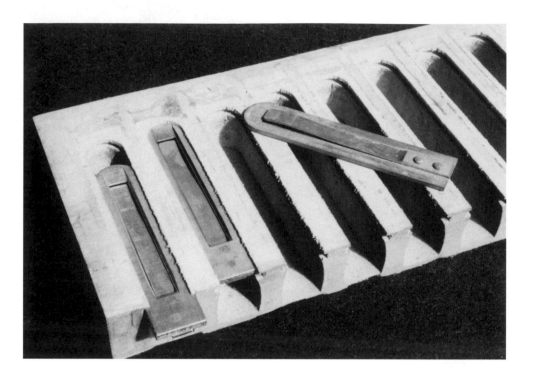

in reed cells and modulators, and thus the roundness of timbres, but skillful voicing compensated
as much as possible to achieve the desired result.
To relieve the harsh (reedy) effect — that is, to reduce production of harmonics — tongues were
curved or bent (voiced). In addition to creating a
rounder timbre, this curved shape leaks air (especially when the tip is twisted or a corner bent
down), and the air noise becomes an inherent element of the reed's sound. To the extent to which
these changes are applied, the result is rounder
and more or less airy, a sound softer in timbre as
well as in volume.

About 1935, Sylvan K. Ketterman experimented
with various materials for reed cells, hoping to replace with a durable, cheap casting a fragile part
that was laboriously manufactured. His quest was
unsuccessful ("Cast iron is the worst! No tone at
all!"), and he concluded that reed cells of pine,
bored in the traditional way, were the best for
creation and resonance of sound.

In American organs, reed cell shapes and sizes

are the first influence on timbres of reeds (figure
123). Widths of common cells are limited by key
width; wide scale manual reeds, Sub-Bass, and
pedal reeds have appropriately wider cells and
actions. Generally, reed cells are small for quiet
sounds and tall for loud sounds, and bulge outward for rounder sounds.

Reed types were combined with cell types for
a variety of timbres. The example at hand is an
Estey Virtuoso, V463, electropneumatic unit
organ, incomplete from the factory (figure 124).
This is but one example of many types and makes
of free reed organs; in total, timbral possibilities
are more varied than is usually supposed, or usually heard. The photo shows the top of the chest,
as if one is standing in front of the organ leaning
over the music rack, with mutes removed. The
lowest three sets of cells pictured are on the Swell
manual; the two Swell sets on the other side of the
reed cell block are not visible. The top two sets are
the Great, which also has two sets on the back
side. The Swell sets are arranged as usual, bass to

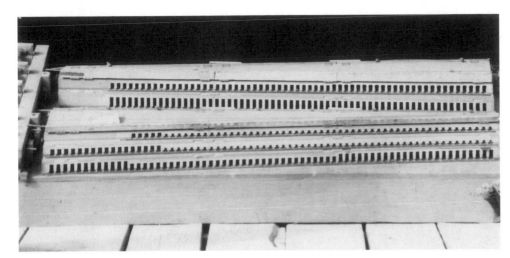

Figure 124.
Estey Virtuoso reed cells.
From the bottom of the
photo, stop designations for
each set are: Swell: Oboe 8',
68 reeds; Salicional 8', 68
reeds; Vox Celeste 8', 56
reeds (from tenor C); Great:
Trumpet 8', 61 reeds;
Dulciana 8', 61 reeds.

treble, left to right. The Great cells are reversed —bass on the right, treble on the left—a space-saving design possible because electrical wires, not mechanisms, connect keys and pallets. The Great has four reeds over each pallet; the Swell has four reeds per pallet in its lowest octave, and five reeds over each remaining pallet.

The Swell Oboe reeds are of common scale from CC to tenor E; from tenor F up they have narrow, full-length tongues. These are coupled with large cells in the bass and treble, and medium-height cells in mid-range, for a bright, not too loud, oboe-like timbre. The Salicional reeds are the same as the Oboe reeds, but their smaller cells produce a quieter sound. The Vox Celeste begins at tenor C, with narrow, short tongues sounding slightly softer than the Salicional in the same size cells. The other two Swell sets are Melodia 8', common scale, wide tongues (with single diamond rivets), reed cells like those of the Dulciana, covered by a half-pipe of zinc with thick felt inside (a very flutey timbre); and Viola 4', narrow, short tongues, reed cells similar to those of the Salicional.

The Great Trumpet has tall cells (to amplify its louder Philharmonic scale reeds) that taper a bit from bass (right) to treble (left). The Dulciana reeds are common scale, with short tongues. Three sizes of reed cells, the largest with rounded tops,

modulate this sweet, mezzo-forte timbre. The other two Great sets are Diapason 8', Philharmonic scale, reed cells as for the Trumpet; and Octave 4', common scale, wide tongues, reed cells as for the Dulciana.

As a reed's sound passes out of its reed cell, it is further modulated by swell shades and boxes. The Virtuoso has louvers on the back of the case, which puts all the reeds inside a very effective swell box for further modulation of volume and timbre. Figure 125 shows, at bottom, an upside-down unattached Sub-Bass reed cell block. The upper assembly (called a Sub-Bass box) shows a cell block attached to its valve board, with Sub-Bass resonating box in place, but slid left to reveal the open mute. The box creates a broader timbre with stronger fundamental ("more bass"), and directs the sound downward to be resonated by the chest. The sub-woofer box for my computer sound system is a modern variation of the Sub-Bass box, which was first used about 150 years ago. Large boxes cover pedal reed cell blocks for the same purposes.

Similar concepts pertain in amplified reed organs, which use reeds as oscillators to generate electrical impulses, rather than for audible sound —that is, the reeds are not actually heard through the speaker.[63] Although the reeds are scaled and

Appendix E: Sound Production with Free Reeds [261

Figure 125.
16' Sub-Bass box and reed
cell block

voiced for each timbre, the modulators, amplifiers, and speakers have more influence on the resulting sound than do the reeds.

Free reeds speak well and sound musical in a great range of designs and environments, from simple toys to meticulously crafted instruments.[64]

The American reed organ industry is an important chapter in the history of the United States and Canada. Continued use of free reeds as sound generators is assured owing to the lure of free reed sound and its modulation and the rising interest in the many aspects of free reed organs.

Pilgrims' Chorus (excerpt)
from *Tannhäuser*

PILGRIM CHORUS, FROM "TANNHÄUSER."

WAGNER.

CALL ME THINE OWN.

From "L'ECLAIR," by HALEVY.

1. Call me "thine own," name fond en-dear - ing, Like mu - sic sweet it falls on mine ear, Tells me of hope,
2. Years may roll on, youth's dreams may leave us, Hopes faint and die that light - ed our way, Tri - als may come,

life's pathway cheer - ing, Whis-pers of home, with thee ev-er near; Call me "thine own" doubt would destroy, For on - ly thro'
sor - rows may grieve us, Friends may depart, or false-ly be-tray; Call me "thine own," all else may fail, With love in our

faith are we se - cure, Mak - ing our hearts strong to en - dure What lies be - fore us, sor - row or joy.
hearts, Heaven still re - mains; Each bond, with time fresh vig - or gains, And o'er life's tempests love shall prevail.

Call me "thine own," thine, thine a - lone, Name fond en - dear - ing,............ Call me "thine own."........
Call me "thine own," thine, thine a - lone, Name most en - dear - ing,............ Call me "thine own."........

NOTES

Preface

1. For a discussion of the uses and functions of music, see A. Merriam 1964, 209–27. "In observing *uses* of music, the student attempts to increase his factual knowledge directly; in assessing *functions* he attempts to increase his factual knowledge indirectly through the deeper comprehension of the significance of the phenomenon he studies" (209).

2. "Each society has a unique musical system related to the character of its culture. But are there not some things about music that all, or virtually all, societies share? Such phenomena are called *universals*" (Nettl 1997, 6–7). For a discussion of music universals, see Nettl 1983, 36–43.

3. Readers should be informed that the body of this work emphasizes sociocultural perspectives, and that they will find relatively few facts on performance techniques (use of stops, for example) or reed organ mechanics (wind systems, action mechanisms, tonal design, etc.). Thanks to the expertise of E. A. Boadway and Ned Phoenix, some of these issues are addressed in the appendix of this book. Otherwise, these matters can best be found in the Reed Organ Society's *Bulletin* and other publications.

4. Eliason 1975; Groce 1982; Larson (AMIS); Sadie 1984; Libin 1985.

5. Reck 1977; Sachs 1940, 1962; Waring 1982; Winternitz 1967.

6. The companion compact disc audio supplement features fitting music, much selected from Estey's two *Organ Methods*, all performed on a variety of Estey organs.

Introduction

1. One of the fundamental principles of the organ family is the use of wind pressure for processing air into vibration. The earliest documented organ in the West is generally agreed to be the Pompeii hydraulis, a type of water organ invented by Ctesibios of Alexandria about 250 B.C. Later representations of organs include a fourth-century Byzantine carving on the obelisk of Theodosius depicting a large bellows-operated organ of eight pipes and an illustration in the sixth-century Utrecht Psalter of a four-man hydraulic organ. A seventeenth-century drawing by Praetorius portrays a typical arrangement for European cathedral organs: the bellows of a large organ were powered by men who literally stood on huge bellows working them in a fashion similar to today's stair-stepping exercise machines. Many varieties of hydraulic and hand- or foot-activated organs were to ensue. For a bird's-eye view of organ history, see Diagram Group 1976, 78–87. For a more in-depth analysis, see various listings relating to organs in Sadie 1984.

2. Two functional distinctions of reed organs versus pipe organs are that free reeds do not necessitate full-sized resonators or pipes, which allows for a more compact construction. Also, flue pipes and striking reeds in pipe organs require a constant wind pressure to maintain pitch and operate properly, whereas free reeds will function under a variety of pressures, allowing dynamic variation from soft to loud without appreciable pitch change.

3. Sadie 1984, 2:219. Essentially, reed keyboard

instruments were called organs simply because they produced sustained sounds, were played from a keyboard, and operated on a differential of air pressures. Some Europeans, especially pipe organ builders and players, preferred to preserve the term "organ" for pipe instruments, with reed instruments called "harmoniums" or another name.

4. Events surrounding the technological breakthrough of using iron bracing to reinforce pianos are a bit confused, with claims of invention being made by various parties. Reports indicate that as early as 1808 John Broadwood of London experimented with adding iron bracing bars to reinforce the wood frame of the piano. During the 1820s numerous designs and devices were developed to further bolster the instrument and permit greater string tension and dynamic range. In 1825 the Boston piano maker Alpheus Babcock was given credit for casting a successful one-piece iron frame. The Chickering and Steinway companies pursued further experimentation in this regard and made many important improvements through the ensuing decades (Sadie 1984, 3:86–87; Gaines 1981, 64–69).

5. See Roell 1989 and the classic Loesser 1954 for a full account of the piano's development.

6. To help orient the reader to the period under discussion, an abbreviated list follows of this era's popular cultural expression, modes that are generally representative of America's Victorian persona: the literature of Mark Twain, Bret Harte, William H. McGuffey, and Horatio Alger; dime novels, story magazines, and weekly newspapers and journals; Currier and Ives and John Rogers in popular art; Dwight L. Moody, Charles Finney, and Henry Ward Beecher for religious revivalism; Chautauqua institutes, Barnum's circus, and big-league baseball; and in theater, light musicals (including ones with scantily clad women), minstrelsy, and comic opera.

7. Ochse 1975, 112.

8. Sadie 1984, 3:223.

9. The name "Harmonium," patented in 1842 by Alexander Debain in Europe for his free-reed instrument with pressure bellows and a divided keyboard, later came into general use for this type of instrument.

10. The word "cottage" took on added meaning during the Victorian era both in Britain and America. "Happy intellectuals, inspired by William Morris, and fortified by a 'hand-woven' outlook, . . . were devoted to [the] country life . . . idealized by the pastoral poets" (Gloag 1961, 52–53). In a phenomenon first seen in England, many of them renovated old farmhouses, filling them with tables and chairs, sofas and sideboards, and bookcases and bedroom sets of their own design; this new, fashionable version of furniture came to be known as the "cottage" style. Small country dwellings were gentrified and furnished in a more or less affectedly rustic style (see Woodforde 1969). Jane Austen describes such a cottage in *Sense and Sensibility* (1811) as having four main bedrooms, two garrets, rooms for the servants, and space enough for Miss Dashwood's pianoforte. By the end of the nineteenth century, weekend cottages might have had as many as eight bedrooms, three parlors, a couple of bathrooms, and room for several servants. The middle classes of both England and America were attracted by the cottage idea; its rustic but genteel connotation implied upward mobility. Though there was nothing particularly rural about the residences or the furniture, prices were relatively reasonable, bringing such symbols of affluence within the reach of bourgeois aspirants. As Austen's description indicates, keyboards were an important cottage accoutrement. Cottage organs (a commonly used label for reed organs during the third quarter of the century) embodied just the right proportion of country and courtly aspects for prospective middle-class "cottagers." Eventually, the term cottage became genericized

to mean all types of frame (sometimes brick) housing with stylish touches of British or European origin (see Schlereth 1991).

11. See Ord-Hume 1986 and Gellerman 1996 for comprehensive lists of organ names, dates, descriptions, and makers.

12. Two early types of reed organs began to appear during the first half of the nineteenth century in America: seraphines and melodeons. Often confused, both generally featured single manuals and only one set of reeds. Seraphines predated melodeons and used a pressure wind system that forced the wind through four or five octaves of reeds; melodeons had a three- to five-octave range and, in contrast, used a suction wind system whereby air was drawn through the reeds by a vacuum generated from the player's treadling. Earlier seraphines and melodeons both looked like small square pianos, but melodeons were also designed in portable styles with folding "lyre" legs (for examples, see Gellerman 1973, 101–2, 106, 113, 124–26, 147–48, 162; Whiting 1981, 16). During the 1850s and 1860s larger "flat-top" models of reed organs gradually appeared that featured larger treadles, two manuals, and an increased number of stops. More-ornate styles of parlor organ with lamp stands, mirrors, and shelves for bric-a-brac appeared in the 1870s and 1880s, and by the end of the century reed organs came in many sizes with a variety of options (Sadie 1984, 223). For more detail, see Appendix D.

13. Richards 1975, 6. The Vocalion was basically a tracker pipe organ design with reed organ chests and reeds with tuned resonators that amplified and modulated the sound.

14. Loesser 1954, 520. Ames 1992, 256, includes an informal comparison, based on trade catalogues, of retail prices of domestic parlor organs and pianos between 1870 and 1890. Specialized models were more expensive.

ORGANS:
Estey & Co., 1874: $160–$400; Packard, 1884: $200–$400; Mason & Hamlin, 1886: $100–$400; New England, 1880: $150–$300.

PIANOS:
Decker Bros., 1873: $400–$1,500; J. & C. Fisher, 1878: $350–$1,200; J. & C. Fisher, 1883: $450–$1,200; Weber, 1880: $650–$1,600.

15. Sears, Roebuck and Company 1902, 180–81. In the late 1890s Sears was selling up to 15,000 reed organs a year under the Beckwith label (Michel 1969, 99).

16. During the 1880s Daniel Beatty, voted mayor of Washington, New Jersey (three terms in a row), was perhaps the most nefarious manufacturer in this respect. Beatty enticed and bamboozled the general public by promising to send absurdly inexpensive organs and pianos to customers who paid the full cash amount within seven to fifteen days (it varied) of an advertisement's date. In return, he pledged to give each order "prompt attention . . . at as early a day as possible . . . and to fill all orders as heretofore." Takers often waited several months with little to show but conciliatory letters. One of many indictments brought against Beatty was for offering to sell an elaborate organ for $50, declared to be worth $100, to a customer who claimed the instrument was worth $15. Perhaps the buyer had purchased Beatty's "Beethoven" model, which bristled with twenty-four stop knobs that, in reality, controlled only two sets of reeds. Records suggest that literally hundreds of customers had similar experiences. Prominent trade journals of the day, the *Musical Courier* and the *Musical Critic and Trade Review*, reported on various inducements Beatty concocted, such as offering free railroad transport from New York to his New Jersey showroom, or providing free dinners and travel expenses for those who purchased an organ while visiting the factory. Such baiting tech-

niques attracted much criticism within the industry. Several magazines launched violent campaigns ("you bold fraud . . . unadulterated foolish ignoramus . . . brute . . .") to warn prospective customers of his tactics; for years, nearly every issue of the *Musical Courier* printed letters from jilted and inflamed customers. In another familiar but questionable practice, Beatty and other businessmen stenciled their company name onto cheap, often shoddy, mass-produced instruments made by unscrupulous manufacturers for quick sale. Though stenciling provided a boon in retail sales for some and was not always synonymous with inferior workmanship, the practice plagued reputable manufacturers throughout the century. Beatty's crooked dealings eventually caught up with him. His creditors and trustees took over the business and promised to end "the fraudulent style of advertising which induced people to send their money to Beatty long before he was prepared to send them their instruments," and to see to it "that a properly made organ was to take the place of the rattletrap he was accustomed to turn out." He was finally convicted of mail fraud and not filling prepaid orders. The industry rejoiced.

17. It is amazing, in fact, how the reed organ fit so well into so many different settings. It quickly became an essential component in most all sacred affairs. Whether seminaries or camp meetings, weddings or funerals, Sunday services or prayer meetings, the reed organ was indispensable. Large congregations might even purchase two or more organs for different parts of their facility. Missionaries' organs were doubtless found in the most varied and exotic settings. On the domestic front, every cottage, house, and mansion had a parlor, drawing room, or grand salon, respectively, that was likely to house a reed organ—each befitting, of course, the status of its owner. And brotherhoods, leagues, unions, orders, societies, circles, guilds, fraternities, fellowships, and other associations used the reed organs (and pianos) found in theaters, schools, conservatories, lodges, clubs, resorts, and hotels for entertainment and ceremony. The reed organ seemingly fit in everywhere.

18. *Harper's Weekly,* Nov. 6, 1875.

19. Loesser 1954, 442–43.

20. Bureau of the Census 1865.

21. *New York Music Directory* 1941, ix.

22. Bureau of the Census 1902.

23. Eliason 1977.

24. Groce 1982.

25. Readers are referred to Libin 1985 for a comprehensive account.

26. Eliason 1975, 1.

27. Bode 1959, 20.

28. See Linn 1991 for a complete treatment of the banjo.

29. Bellson 1973, part 8.

30. Sears, Roebuck and Company 1902, 201–2.

31. "Ukelin" was one of the most common trade names within this instrument family. "Ukelins combine two sets of strings, one group of sixteen strings tuned to the scale of C . . . plus four groups of four strings, each group tuned to a chord. The instrument is meant to be placed on a table with the larger end towards the performer, and while the right hand plays the melody on the treble strings with a violin bow, accompanying chords are played on the bass strings with the left hand using either the fingers or a pick. Each string and chord group is numbered, and sheet music is provided in a special numerical system intended to simplify playing for persons unable to read standard musical notation" (Scott Odell [Division of Musical Instruments, Smithsonian Institution, Washington, D.C.], personal communication).

32. *Leisure Hours,* table of contents.

33. The autoharp became a fad of some note, as attested by a 1890s report about one New York company that manufactured more than three thousand of these instruments per week (Borroff 1995, 161).

34. Libin 1985, 14. It is interesting to note that

with the development of keyed brass instruments, and later, valve technology—featuring more notes, simpler fingerings, an even tone through the registers, and sturdy construction—by 1860 companies had begun to reduce their production of woodwinds, which, for a while, essentially disappeared from many town bands. This was perhaps a result of the popularity of cornet virtuosos during this period and because until American instrument makers began manufacturing saxophones (first produced in 1889 by the C. G. Conn company in Elkhart, Indiana), woodwinds seemed "undervoiced" in the context of a military band. See also Proper 1998, 165.

35. "A number of town and community bands both in the North and South joined regiments during the [Civil] war. . . . Returning Union and Confederate veterans brought home band experiences and music to enliven and inspire local organizations" (Proper 1998, 160).

36. One such full-time artisan was Samuel Graves, an inventor in the true American sense, who reportedly invented a folding bathtub (!) and pulled teeth as a sideline to making instruments (Libin 1985, 71). It was, in fact, at Graves's factory that James Keat, son of a London keyed bugle maker, helped establish one of the country's first musical instrument factories in the 1830s (Eliason 1975). John F. Stratton began building instruments in 1860 just in time to capitalize on the demand for band instruments generated by the upcoming Civil War.

37. "In 1889, *Harper's Weekly* estimated there were 'over ten thousand military bands in the United States.' At that time, there were only two permanent orchestras in America. In many western communities the only music available was that provided by the local military post band. Professional and amateur bands appeared at military ceremonies, parades, civilian celebrations, concerts, amusement parks, seaside resorts, county and state fairs, and national and international expositions.

They entertained their public, and they were ubiquitous. Their repertoires ranged from the ever popular marches, songs, waltzes, and novelty numbers to the classical standards of the day. Most Americans had their first, and typically only exposure to Mozart, Beethoven, Rossini, Verdi, such moderns as Liszt and Wagner, and even staged grand opera through these bands" (Camus 1998, 158).

38. See Mallory 1998, 180.

39. Bureau of the Census 1902, 10:447.

40. Sachs 1940, 63–64.

41. Ord-Hume 1986, 16.

42. As possibly revealed by aboriginal Jew's harps still used in some tribal cultures throughout parts of the Eurasian land mass as well as South and Southeast Asia, Indonesia, and Oceania (Sadie 1984, 2:326).

43. The standard sheng consists of a bundle of relatively small diameter bamboo pipes of varying lengths (traditionally seventeen pipes, some nonsounding, measuring from six to sixteen inches), each with an attached brass reed, anchored in a hollow wind reservoir. Since the relative position and length of sheng pipes have important symbolic import, the actual resonating length is determined by a vent hole on each pipe, acoustically placed for pitch determination. Small finger holes at the base of each pipe are closed, causing the air (inhaled and exhaled through a mouthpiece) to force the designated reed pipe to sound. Today large, philharmonic-worthy shengs, some with keys, are manufactured and played in China.

44. Sadie 1984, 3:219.

45. Sachs 1940, 183; Sadie 1984, 2:692. Besides the Chinese sheng, the most common Asian mouth organs include the Japanese shô and the Laotian khen.

46. Sadie 1984, 3:221.

47. The sheng may have been brought to the West by traders and Jesuit missionaries, but the use of free reeds in regals and pipe organs was

probably already established by this time. The regal was used in Europe from the latter part of the fifteenth through the eighteenth centuries. Several accounts tell of how Johann Wilde (eighteenth-century inventor of the nail violin) learned to play the Chinese sheng, thus allegedly prompting a St. Petersburg physicist, Christian Gottlieb Kratzenstein, and his confrere, an organ builder by the name of Kirschnik, to build an organochordium, a kind of pianoforte–reed organ hybrid, an idea that was pursued again a century later in America and elsewhere.

48. Duga 1968, 24; Sadie 1984, 3:221.

49. For an interesting discussion of the "quagmire of contradiction" that has developed around the term "harmonium," readers should refer to Lewis 1987.

50. Though it is generally recognized that production of reed organs for domestic application never took hold in England as it did in Germany and France or in the United States, Ord-Hume 1986, 30–32, makes a strong case regarding British contributions to reed organ development.

51. Method books for harmonium by important established composers, collections of choral and orchestral transcriptions, and arrangements of ensemble music that included the harmonium, were commonplace in Europe during the last half of the nineteenth century. Composers such as Gounod, Saint-Saëns, Dvořák, Reger, Karg-Elert, Strauss, and Grainger delighted in scoring music for the European harmonium that was generally too difficult for the amateur player (Sadie 1984, 3:225). In addition to European contexts, "the harmonium was widely disseminated, especially by the colonial powers, in Africa and India, where it came to play an important role in local traditions. The harmonium has for a long time been manufactured in India and Pakistan; Palitana, in Gujarat, is regarded as a center for the manufacture of harmonium reeds" (Owen 1988, 242).

52. American builders generally adopted the

suction (also called exhaust or vacuum) bellows system, whereas Continental harmoniums employed a pressure or forced air system. Though the suction system originated in France, it never achieved the prominence in Europe it found in America. Unlike American reed organs, which are idiosyncratic in design and stop designations, European harmoniums featured a standard C compass of sixty-one notes with the keyboard divided between the pitches middle E and F. Mechanical expression devices that made the instrument truly musical were further organized with standardized stop specifications, thus assuring composers that their music would be rendered as they had intended. Harmoniums are mechanically complex and relatively expensive to produce. Consequently, American manufacturers employed the suction system because vacuum bellows were easier and cheaper to make. Likewise, the design afforded reed cells and slide-in reeds, which were also less expensive and quicker to fabricate, assemble, and tune than those on their European counterparts. See Appendix E, "Sound Production with Free Reeds."

53. Bureau of the Census 1902, 10:465.

54. Owen 1988, 242, mentions one such obscure maker, Lewis Awahlen of New York, who in 1832 received a patent for a "Seraphina or harmonicon organ."

55. Libin 1985, 195.

56. Prescott was, in fact, an expert craftsman of many items; today his bass viols are judged as better than most European equivalents. A label inside one of Prescott's rocking melodeon boxes reveals further information concerning his activities: "Abraham Prescott, Manufacturer of Premium Bass and Double Bass Viols, Seraphines and Melodians [sic] and dealer in Musical Instruments, Umbrellas, Parasols, &c., Instruments and Umbrellas repaired at short notice, and Warranted, Opposite the Columbian Hotel, Concord, N.H., Care should be taken in blowing the Melodian to

give a steady pressure, as a sudden motion may injure the tone of the instrument." From 1833 Prescott and his four sons (not all were involved at the same time) established one of the first and most successful reed organ manufacturing enterprises in America. From 1886 to 1912 the Prescotts switched to making upright pianos.

57. Early lap organ keyboards had only two staggered rows of buttons. These were later expanded to buttons arranged in standard piano configuration and finally to actual piano keys. With each advance came an increase in the instrument's range.

58. The celestial import of the word "seraphine" doubtless derives from the root word "seraph" (pl. "seraphs" or "seraphim"), which, according to the 1993 edition of *Webster's Third New International Dictionary*, designates a high order of angels who have access to the presence of God. The implication is obvious.

59. Bureau of the Census 1902, 10:465. As mentioned, the seraphine, like the lap organ, works on a pressure wind system, whereas the melodeon employs a suction wind arrangement, a significant modification.

60. Because of the nature of invention and because (starting with the second session of the First Congress) the government was constantly defining, refining, and revising patent laws, litigation over infringement of patent rights was common in early organ manufacture and American manufacture in general. In the case of Carhart's monopoly, organ builders chafed at the injustice and brought several lawsuits against him. Eventually the Carhart patent was declared void, and use of the suction system became the standard design for American reed organs. Undaunted by his loss of the suction system patent, Carhart continued to invent and in 1856 contributed immeasurably to the development of reed organ manufacture by patenting a machine that efficiently produced reed cells, a noteworthy innovation because it signaled one of the first applications of mass production methods to reed organ manufacture. Carhart was also said to have been the first to apply the term "melodeon" to the American reed organ. The New York company of Carhart & Needham became a large and important producer of reed instruments.

61. A great deal of effort, in fact, went into the attempt to make the reed organ sound as loud as a pipe organ. Some intriguing experiments were carried out using various reed shapes. Instead of single elongated brass tongues, the free ends of individual tongues were made to form crosses, Y's, and forks—thus theoretically increasing the vibrating volume of air moved—while still retaining a single mount. But in the end, though louder, they proved impractical for mass manufacture because the weight of the yokes slowed response (a common reed organ complaint) and caused difficulty in tuning and voicing.

62. If Burdett was the inventor, it is curious that he did not bother to patent his improvement, though there were inventors who felt that their innovations were best served in the public domain. Such noteworthy figures as Eli Whitney, Oliver Evans, and Thomas Cooper refused to take out patents on some of their inventions and actively lobbied against patent laws (though Whitney did patent the cotton gin in 1794). Given Emmons Hamlin's success in business matters, however, it seems rather doubtful that he was of this school of thought. One wonders if Hamlin received the greatest credit simply because his discovery was followed with the most media coverage and because he had obtained the full endorsement of George A. Prince, said to be the leading manufacturer of reed organs in the United States during the 1850s and 1860s. See Gellerman 1973, 8.

63. For a thorough discussion of assembly line mechanization, see Giedion 1948.

64. Strausser 1989, 6. For in-depth analysis of continuous-process production, the reader is referred to Chandler 1977, a seminal work in this field.

65. One of the greatest advantages of production-line assembly was that it lowered costs. On suction reed organs especially, the vacuum bellows, reed cells, and slide-in reeds were cheap to make and easy to assemble. In industries that built highly complex products, keyboards included, some manufactories specialized in the production of single components—piano and organ keys, for instance. Regarding piano keys, the Census Report of 1900 tells of three piano factories in one county in Connecticut that used over a hundred tons (!) of elephant ivory for this purpose, an interesting observation since the reed organ world switched from ivory keytops to celluloid about 1882. Some organ builders, however, continued to use ivory keytops and stop faces for special, large instruments. In other instances, factories, usually those that were located near natural resources, might build only instrument cases. And as product assembly systems became more common in American industry, many so-called reed organ builders did no actual manufacturing at all, but simply assembled purchased parts. Even then, though, assembling a reed organ still required a great deal of hand work.

66. Ord-Hume 1986, 85.

67. Richards 1983, 45.

68. Loesser 1954, 349.

69. *Musical Opinion*, May 22, 1890.

70. "Horatio Alger, Jr. (1834–1899) wrote nearly 130 books for boys, all based on the principle that hard work and resistance to temptation would ultimately lead to wealth and fame. . . . His stories were exactly in accord with the temper of the 1870s and 1880s and in sheer bulk of readers, Alger may well have been the most popular author who has ever lived" (Hoffmann and Bailey 1990, 3–5). "The faith which emerged most clearly in nineteenth-century success ideology, held aloft the example of the self-made man. In the popular imagination, that figure possessed neither intellectual brilliance nor unusual physical prowess; what he had in abundance were industrious work habits, extraordinary moral discipline, and above all an indomitable will" (Lears 1981, 18).

Chapter 1.
The Reed Organ and Victorian Image

1. It became fashionable in Europe and America to designate an era that exhibited distinctive manners, morals, and artistic tastes after the British monarch of the period—e.g., "Tudor," "Elizabethan," "Edwardian," and so on. The term "Victorian" was similarly based on the reign of Queen Victoria (1837–1901), an exceptionally long time period for a European monarch. In Britain, the Victorian era is generally agreed to have commenced in the 1830s and culminated in the 1880s. Victorian hegemony in the United States is mostly understood to encompass the last half of the nineteenth century (though many argue an earlier beginning and more lengthy denouement). The twenty-year lag between Europe and the United States for Victorian fashion is clearly reflected in reed organ development. Remember too that during this era the American Civil War set cultural development back in both the North and the South. Another term often evoked for the last portion of this time frame is the "Gilded Age," generally thought to be from 1865 to 1900 (scholars' opinions differ somewhat), a period of great economic expansion in the United States. Schlereth 1991 and others think the terms "Gilded Age" and "Progressive Era" came from Charles Dudley Warner's *The Gilded Age* (1873) and Herbert Croly's *Progressive Democracy* (1913), and from the writings of Mark Twain. Schlereth's suggestion for the American Victorian time frame is between 1876 and 1915. As we can see, the word "Victorian" is somewhat troublesome. Understanding that history often refuses to fit into neat categories, I will not belabor this issue; generally, the word "Victorian," as used in this study, refers

to the last half of the nineteenth century, when Victorian fashion in America was in full flower.

2. In art history terms, the Victorian Period arose in the latter part of the Greek Revival era (Neoclassicism) and the Gothic Revival. Onto this framework grew Neo-Rococo fashion and several other discernible trends: Louis Quatorze and Neo-Louis Seize, Neo-Elizabethan, Tudor, and Jacobean, Italian and revived Renaissance, and, later, even Anglo-Japanese styles, for example.

3. Bridgeman and Drury 1975, 11.

4. Ibid., 15.

5. Whiton 1951, 325. "It is difficult but not impossible to speculate on the larger cultural significance of eclecticism in the visual arts. Reaching for the legitimacy conferred by traditional symbols (and celebrating their vitality), eclectic designers unwittingly undermined the power of these earlier forms. Uprooting once-sacred symbols from their appropriate time, place, and purpose, the eclectic approach trivialized them—reduced them to commodities in the marketplace of taste. Eclecticism signified the impoverishment of a culture which lacked resources for creating its own symbols" (Lears 1981, 33). As early as 1835, Alexis de Tocqueville succinctly described this American propensity for commercialized culture: "The handicraftsmen of democratic ages endeavor not only to bring their useful productions with the reach of the whole community, but they strive to give to all their commodities attractive qualities which they do not in reality possess. In the confusion of all ranks, everyone hopes to appear what he is not, and makes great exertions to succeed in this object" (Tocqueville 1984, 171).

6. Foy and Schlereth 1992, 54. One home decorator, Mrs. Spofford, even suggested that, "provided that there is room enough to move about without walking over the furniture, there is hardly likely to be too much in a room" (Partridge 1946, 125).

7. Bridgeman and Drury 1975, 26.

8. One rather ostentatious case of mixing historical and international varieties of architecture and interior decor is personified in Henry and Louisine Havemeyer's Fifth Avenue mansion in New York City: "[they] loved to mix styles . . . that drew from Celtic, Japanese, Chinese, Moorish, and Byzantine elements in a house that might, in terms of its general ensemble, be described as American fortress" (Cashman 1993, 182). Besides other well-known New York City mansions, this architectural tendency is evinced by Frederick and Louise Vanderbilt's mansion in Rhinebeck, N.Y., as well as other grand palatial estates located along Bellevue Avenue in Newport, R.I., such as the Château Sur-Mer, The Breakers, Rosecliff, and the Astors' Beechwood. The Winchester mansion located in San Jose, Calif., exhibits Victorianism at its most eccentric. Less pretentious but equally revealing are the thousands of residences located in postindustrial towns and cities throughout New England and elsewhere.

9. Pulos 1983, 133.

10. Garnishment and ornamentation aside, the actual "acoustic resonating space" of both reed organ and piano casing is, of course, ultimately important in the successful blending of their respective reed or string sounds. Stylistically, it is interesting to note that some piano manufacturers criticized the austerity of the piano case and occasionally resorted to putting high tops on their "artistic" models. "The truth is that at the present time the usual upright piano is the least graceful, in fact, the ugliest article to be found in a tastefully appointed drawing room. . . . This is not as it should be, and when some manufacturer shall be found to have enterprise enough to bring out some novelties in piano cases, he will sure to be amply rewarded for his brains and pains" (*Musical Courier*, June 19, 1889, 502).

11. Who were the new American bourgeoisie? Primarily, doctors, lawyers, bankers, skilled craftsmen, well-to-do farmers, ministers, publishers,

newspaper editors, and businessmen. Later, academics, managers, engineers, and sales and service personnel helped to swell the ranks of the middle class. Acquisition for acquisition's sake, which represented success and attainment of a higher social status in America and elsewhere, began to replace acquiring utilitarian items for practical needs and applications. "The inventions and the subsequent industrialization of the latter half of the nineteenth century would not have been possible without the combination of the assured aristocracy of the upper class with the assumed aristocracy of the middle class and the aspirations of the lower class" (Pulos 1983, 181).

12. Bridgeman and Drury 1975, 13. But like the middle classes, the American well-to-do struggled in their own way with the art-as-status syndrome: "As to interior design, not since the heyday of the Venetian Republic had successful commercial families indulged themselves in such ostentatious displays of art as did the entrepreneurs of the later Gilded Age. To enrich their homes and give society notice of their new status, robber barons acquired paintings, sculptures, and manuscripts of great value. The sophistication they could not achieve within themselves by education, they could amass for themselves by possession. The absolute distinction was ownership of a unique object. Ironically, many entrepreneurs who claimed such unique distinction were those whose very wealth came from factories that produced objects, including art objects, that were mass produced" (Cashman 1993, 175).

14. The same industrial expansion that swept England, France, and other European countries in the nineteenth century also revolutionized social, artistic, and economic conditions in the United States. It became apparent in America that the industrial arts—inspired by such landmark innovations as Whitney's cotton gin, Fulton's steamboat, Griffith's clipper ship, and Morse's telegraph—were a manifestation of a new civilization with

technology as its cornerstone. During this period, Irish, German, Italian, Russian, and Balkan immigrants began to exert strong regionalized cultural influences and, as a labor force, affected the overall process of American industrialization. In contrast to the rising industrial tide, the fine arts continued to struggle to establish themselves in a pragmatic society. Though the general cultural environment was stimulating—as evidenced by widespread spiritual evangelism, the development of a body of American folk and popular music, and the literary productions of authors such as Irving, Cooper, Poe, Hawthorne, Whittier, Emerson, and Longfellow—it was considered by some analysts a stagnant time for architecture, painting, and sculpture (see Kouwenhoven 1948). From the beginning, the fine arts had little credibility in a society that placed energy and physical effort at a premium; the arts were even considered by many to be a radical threat to the national future (see Harris 1966). The paucity of art, they maintained, was a sign that the nation was healthy and was successfully resisting the corrupting influences of excessive wealth, blue-blood pretension, and moral decadence. "There was considerable prejudice against intellectuals in general. They were regarded as incapable of making money and therefore incapable of contributing to the development of the country, dangerous because too open to foreign influence, tending to take an 'aristocratic' view of life" (Nye 1974, 189). Finally, from the 1830s to the Civil War, the American artist began to attain passing social respectability. The painter, for instance, through portraiture and landscape painting, reflected a growing nationalistic pride in heritage and homeland. Portraits of the founding fathers, the signing of the Declaration of Independence, the Battle of Bunker Hill, and George Washington crossing the Delaware, all important symbols for a fledgling America, adorned the walls of countless houses. But in spite of greater acceptance and a more fertile artistic atmosphere, the voices of such cultural giants as Horatio Greenough, Walt Whitman, Herman Melville, and Louis Sullivan had to wait for posthumous appreciation. American composers also had to wait for recognition, usually after completing an almost obligatory course of study in Europe.

15. Psychologically, the quality and intensity of our reactions with material objects depends on our capacity first to recognize them as familiar, then to relate them to circumstances which have been stored in our minds, and finally, through sensual awareness, to create symbolic associations. Through these associations, objects become receptacles for people's projected dreams and desires (Ames 1992, 181). The actual significance of this transfer of meaning is naturally dependent on the individual's biological and sexual makeup and on past social and environmental opportunities. And since a greater portion of our reactions usually takes place on a subconscious level, we are not necessarily always aware of subtle aspects of our interactions with people or objects while immediately involved with them. The nature of our interaction is also dependent on the nature of the stimulus: texture, light, pattern, color, shape, mass, timbre, and volume become important input in this regard. The reed organ is an especially good artifact for examination of this sort since it is an object that can be seen, felt, and heard (and, in the case of unrestored antique instruments, smelled). Recollections from turn-of-the-century informants point up various extraordinary social events and strong emotional feelings that they, years later, continue to associate with the family reed organ. Familiar objects and associations are comforting; surrounding oneself with meaningful objects, especially of a kind that are owned and appreciated by others, gives one a sense of status and belonging. Ultimately, they become social tools and are important, consciously and subconsciously, in formulating social strategies.

16. The matter of form and function will be ex-
amined in some detail as we go, but to point out how times have little changed, included here are some quotes from an article in *Time*, the contemporary weekly news magazine: "These days efficient manufacturing and intense competition have made 'commodity chic' not just affordable but also mandatory. . . . When industries are competing at equal price and functionality, design is the only differential that matters. . . . Customers really respond to products that involve new thinking and connect with their souls" (Gibney and Luscombe, Mar. 2000). In the same article, Mark Dziersk, president of the Industrial Designers Society of America, concludes, "This is the principle that began with the Bauhaus: [that] everyone should have access to beautiful things." As we shall see, this principle was actually applied decades before the Bauhaus movement when Victorian Americans formulated, defined, and manufactured symbols of material social status.

17. As with music and the other arts, a unique American creative impulse—call it Yankee ingenuity—first found expression in American folkways. Invention was manifested in countless rudimentary utilitarian items. Refinements of utility objects laid the foundations for a principle that began to characterize American products: functional efficiency, which depended on and resulted in elegance of form. For example, common farm implements from the Old World such as field plows, axes, and manure forks, originally based on English models, were rejected by American farmers in favor of lighter and more functionally designed tools. Axes were balanced and thinned for an easier swing and withdrawal; scythes were lengthened and curved so that grain harvest required less effort with less loss; steel shovels and hay forks made in America stayed sharper and cleaner than their heavy English iron counterparts. Another example, the long-barreled musket, an important tool in the fight for independence, developed in an frontier environment where

wilderness and distance gained new meanings. Men armed with these rifles could not only hunt game at long range but could also hit human targets at 150 yards beyond the range of the best European musket, an important factor in various territorial wars. Designs were frequently made for the designer's own use, and, in contrast with their European equivalents, were characterized by a certain constraint, simplicity, lightness, strength, and economy of line. Ingenuity was freely mingled with functional artistry (see Kouwenhoven 1948, 26–32). Arthur Pulos, the distinguished scholar and industrial designer, cites an oft-quoted excerpt from a letter written by Benjamin Franklin in which the functionalist principle in American design and manufacture was anticipated: "the invention of a machine or the improvement of an implement is of more importance than a masterpiece of Raphael. . . . Nothing is good or beautiful but in the measure that it is useful" (Pulos 1983, 7). Alexis de Tocqueville (1835) noted that "democratic nations . . . will habitually prefer the useful to the beautiful, and they will require that the beautiful should be useful." This native inclination toward simple functional beauty, along with the unconventional yet resourceful and pragmatic spirit of early frontiersmen, was to become the hallmark of the American pioneer; it was a spirit that fostered a national conviction that American society was full of potential creators. This sentiment contrasted with overseas attitudes, since it was decidedly un-European to consider the artist-designer and the practical workman as having much in common. Intellectual and artistic pursuit, after all, was the realm of the aristocrat and the master artisan—their source, as a matter of fact, of power over the populace. Europeans soon learned that while Americans had little understanding of the fine arts, they excelled in the practical arts. While Jean-Jacques Rousseau was formulating his philosophies of a natural, simpler way of life as a remedy to civilization's disorders,

Americans were putting such theories into practice.

18. Pulos 1983, 122.

19. Ultimately, the struggle to establish an artistic identity equivalent to, but different from, that of Europe culminated in an aesthetic eclecticism that coalesced during the latter portion of America's Victorian era: the Gilded Age. Key to the period was an American proletariat that began to formulate and define itself, albeit in hyperbolic terms. Throughout this development, aspiring middle-class Americans, in a headlong dash to establish themselves as a power within the culture, began to cultivate forms of popular art and entertainment that combined the rough-and-tumble realities of the frontier with traditional aesthetic values, still mostly from Europe. As a result, inherited art forms were reworked into modes of expression more representative of the American persona. See Kammen 1999 for a thorough discussion of popular culture in pre-technological America, its progression during the latter part of the nineteenth century, and its twentieth-century transformation into mass consumer culture. Kammen argues that historians too often soft-pedal and oversimplify the transition from preindustrial life to consumer culture. He maintains that the onset of mass media and the commercialization of leisure during the Gilded Age did not cause an immediate or direct shift to mass culture but developed gradually over decades in several overlapping stages, beginning from the 1880s. In spite of the fact that Sears, Roebuck and Montgomery Ward, for example, had begun the move toward a "highly rationalized, bureaucratized, and impersonal proto-mass consumer culture" by 1910, the face-to-face commerce of local communities and participatory aspects of regionalized popular culture still mattered. Issues regarding community stratification, ethnic orientation, mass media, and mass-consumer society (now globalized) continue to be hotly debated today.

20. The fact is that from the beginning, Jeffer-

son and other gentlemen architects of the day relied heavily on popular books from England and the Continent that were filled with drawings and illustrations of fashionable structures; during this period, styles were mostly reminiscent of ancient Greek and Roman buildings, of which Jefferson's own home, Monticello, is an example (Pulos 1983, 19). The same predominance of European-influenced expression continued in American architecture and domestic furnishings throughout the nineteenth century. Pattern books removed the act of project design from the realm of the specialist, acted as a basis for design modification, and eventually created homogeneity of style.

21. One factor in this development was the introduction of balloon-frame house construction, which took advantage of two new products, standardized lumber and machine-made nails. Production of homogeneous low-cost materials begged for application of mechanical techniques. To house designers and furniture builders of the age, abundant decoration was a necessary aspect of beauty and an important reflection of social standing. Consequently, structural carpentry was brought within the reach of many amateur builders who could choose decorative millwork and other enticing enrichments from popular magazines and detail catalogues.

22. Foy and Schlereth 1992, 1–5.

23. Papanek 1976, 23.

24. Ibid.

25. Pulos 1983, 100.

26. Early in American history, the conflict between nature and machine was thoroughly discussed by notable republicans including Thomas Jefferson, John Adams, and even the versatile Benjamin Franklin, who all firmly declared agriculture, not manufacture, as the preeminent American occupation. They maintained that American agrarian self-sufficiency and utilization of this country's abundant resources were to provide the foundation from which a new utopian nation would rise.

Large-scale manufacturing, they argued, was the business of European countries, not America. Unbridled mechanization, as evidenced in England, posed a possible threat to republican ideology, yielding riches for the few and eventual debasement of the proletariat. Doubtless aware of the potential benefits afforded by technology, the leaders' primary fear was that the lure of ever-increasing wealth and luxury, a by-product of progressive manufacturing, might undermine traditional values and republican virtue.

27. Fisher 1968, 228.

28. Veblen 1979. What were the factors that favored consumer affluence and incited a desire for the increasing volume of commodities for the good life? Overall, both the middle and the working classes were better off financially than ever before and (theoretically) had more leisure time, giving them both means to purchase and opportunity to enjoy a variety of the cheaply produced goods that were increasingly entering national marketing networks. More than simply desiring new commodities, consumers began to demand them. Most important, shoppers could act on their preference for one product over another; they were given choices. This unique, unprecedented brand of democratic American consumerism was already causing profound changes in the nation's corporate disposition. With readily available capital, a supportive government, high tariffs, and a large labor supply in the early 1870s, "the country became a businessman's paradise. [The absence of] anti-trust laws, anti-injunction acts, or National Labor Relations Boards. . . delighted the heart of the entrepreneur" (Muller 1982, 232). Expanding industrialization was in perfect harmony with America's increasing population—itself to some extent a result of the importation of factory workers—which rose from four million to thirty-one million people between 1790 and 1860 (Nye 1974, 6), and from twenty-five to seventy-five million between 1850 and 1900. Furthermore, "Veblen erroneously described

'conspicuous consumption' as an anachronistic cultural style confined to a predatory elite. . . . Actually, a broad range of middle and upper class Americans (not merely a parasitic leisure class) was becoming more oriented toward consumption, their outlook affected not only by the democratization of comfort but by the increasingly sophisticated strategies of advertising" (Lears 1981, 37).

29. One effect of industrialized democracy as it developed in United States was the expansion of the middle-class populace, which was estimated to have grown from 756,000 in 1870 to 5,609,000 by 1910 (Hays 1957, 73). With the new privilege of buying and equipping one's own home and the promise of a better life, aspiring consumers became a target for manufactured products. Domestic accessories such as furniture, glassware, floor coverings, wallpaper, clocks, lighting fixtures, and other items were fabricated to meet an increasing demand, and mechanization became particularly linked to the utensils closest to man's daily life, especially furniture. The popularity of machines that could sew cloth, wash clothes, make ice, and sweep the carpet assured inventors and manufacturers that the middle-class home was a prime target for new improved labor-saving appliances. Fundamentally, "mechanization made possible the mass production of culture in the form of consumable objects" (Trachtenberg 1982, 150).

30. Ames 1984, 34.

31. Wallace W. Kimball commenced his music enterprise in 1857 in Chicago and became one of the largest manufacturers of keyboard instruments in the Midwest. In 1880 he began manufacturing reed organs, and by 1922 he had sold over 400,000 of them; in 1888 he began making pianos. He eventually became the largest manufacturer of pianos in the world. Kimball found success in marketing large quantities of organs and pianos at highly competitive prices to small towns in thinly populated areas. By the time he discontinued building reed organs in 1922, he had produced a total of 403,390 of these instruments. His brother-in-law, Albert G. Cone, rhapsodized that Kimball had made available to "the farmer on his prairie, the miner in his cabin, the fisherman in his hut, the cultivated mechanic in his neat cottage in the thriving town the most domestic and the most delightful of instruments, an influence which refines his home, educates his children, and gladdens his daily life like a constant ray of sunshine on his hearth." It was often said concerning Kimball that "there is scarcely a hamlet in the West which has not felt the touch of his gentle influence." The Kimball "touch," however, like that of most successful businessmen, was a calculated one. In the days before newspaper advertising became commonplace, salesmen devised various ways to lure the customer into the sales room or, as was the case for the traveling salesman, to transport the sales room to the customer. One Kimball salesman tells of a common ploy of rigging a wagon wheel so that it would fall off in front of a likely customer's farmhouse. The organ or piano that was in transit would have to be temporarily stored in the farmer's home while replacement parts were acquired and the wagon repaired. The salesman would return in a day or so, hoping the family had tried the instrument and pumped through a few of their favorite hymns and tunes and were in consequence unwilling to part with it. Such shenanigans were common, though with the advent of mail-order catalogues and newspapers, tricks of the trade were reduced more to print.

32. Loesser 1954, 550.

33. *Musical Courier*, Jan. 9, 1889, 34.

34. Libin 1985, 11.

35. Olwell and Waldhorn 1976, 54. The usual procedure for bending wood or making a carved appearance in wood utilizes combinations of water, heat, and pressure.

36. Murphy beds, still used today, are beds that "disappear" when folded against the wall or into a cupboard, thus saving valuable space in an other-

wise cramped apartment or house (Foy and Schlereth 1992, 132).

37. Ibid., 10.

38. Furniture with dual function was widely used for this reason; sofas that turned into beds, beds that looked like chiffoniers, sewing machines that doubled as writing desks, and reed organs that hid within their cabinetry both sewing machines and writing desks were popular with owners of homes with limited space. One report tells of a piano patented in 1866 that turned into a couch and had closets for bedclothes and a basin for washing up. Even the piano stool functioned as a workbox, looking glass, desk, and small set of drawers.

39. Bridgeman and Drury 1975, 22.

40. Pope 1983, 4, says that advertising is at least as old as biblical and classical times. He notes that there are even those who argue that cave wall paintings were a form of advertising. Actually, one has only to visit any village or tribal marketplace in the world to experience the many "advertising" techniques vendors employ in snaring customers. Advertising and salesmanship were not invented in the late nineteenth century; hawking goods is as old as humankind.

41. Strasser 1989, 15.

42. Ibid.

43. Douglas 1982, 21.

44. Pope 1983, 178–79. Even postmasters were said to have exploited and abused their positions by engaging in advertising gambits on the side, a practice now illegal, of course.

45. Strasser 1989, 150–53.

46. "Advertising has been described as an institution, a business, an industry, a discipline, a profession, a science, an art, and a talent. It has been defined as news, salesmanship in print, and mass communication. Some of the best minds in the business, outside the business, and on the fringes of the business have attempted to define and deal with this elusive subject" (Williamson 1980, 3).

Others, at least, are not so equivocal in formulating an opinion on the topic: "Advertising design, in persuading people to buy things they don't need, with money they don't have, in order to impress others who don't care, is probably the phoniest field in existence" (Papanek 1971, xxi).

47. Ochse 1975, 112.

48. Beatty's puffery seemed to have no limits. One representative advertisement begins with the brag: "The most successful business man in the world. More [of] Beatty's celebrated Pianos and Cabinet Organs have been sold during the last four months than nearly all the other manufacturers combined. No wonder they are jealous of his great success. Mr. Beatty commenced business only eight years ago without one dollar, a poor and unknown ploughboy. He is to-day the most successful man in his line in the world, doing a business of several millions annually." He further attributes his success to "attention to business, liberal, judicious advertising, and plenty of pluck" (Gaines 1981, 69).

49. From two 1884 trade journals: *Musical Critic and Trade Review* and the *Musical Courier;* cited in Gellerman 1973, 16.

50. As found, for example, in *Frank Leslie's Illustrated Newspaper,* Dec. 27, 1873.

51. Vermont, like other states and regions in the United States, has its own linguistic quirks, pronunciations, and dialect. In the present case, I am told that in Vermont the word "calmed" would be pronounced "carmed" thus rhyming with "charmed" and "alarmed." Other examples might be "psarm" for "psalm" and "Parm Sundee" for "Palm Sunday" (Ned Phoenix, personal communication).

52. Pope 1983, 48–61.

53. Jane Pavitt, quoted in Tolson 2000, 52.

54. Trachtenberg 1982, 135. Further in Trachtenberg's analysis (p. 138) he states, "The mark or name is a peculiar kind of expression, originating not as a spontaneous act of naming on the part of people discovering a new object in their midst but

as an act from above, the manufacturer's act, sanctioned and protected by the law of copyright: a fiction underwritten by laws protecting what came to be known as 'intellectual property,' the brand name."

55. In regard to merchandising stratagems, the development of commerce on the Internet has intensified the marketing game tremendously. By democratizing information exchange, the Internet provides a powerful medium for exploitation by corporations, media organizations, advertisers, promotional agents, and, for that matter, virtually anyone with the requisite skills and motivation.

56. Ames 1984, 44. Material culture may be examined on two highly contrastive levels. Intertwined with utilitarian use—in the present case, making music on a reed organ—are psychological and expressive functions that are emotional, subjective, and sensual. Evaluation of these realms is a complex task. The perspective of history, however, can aid the analyst, since objectivity often increases in proportion to our distance from the context. Unfortunately, time also distances the historian from subjective reality—that which remains locked in the minds of those who used the object. We are helped by the fact that generally, human beings have similar needs, even though the items used to satisfy those needs change over time.

57. Advertising, usually reflecting more wish projection than reality, may provide less factual information regarding the reed organ's place in Victorian culture than photographic images (which, since they are "real," generally reflect more subtle aspects of life). Many a family portrait was photographed with the reed organ prominently displayed as a point of focus—a sort of domestic shrine. In this context the organ not only becomes a symbol of familial cohesiveness, but, as a material object, transcends the passing of the generations. Examination of selected Estey trade cards clearly shows all generations involved in music-making activity. By the late 1880s photography was available for

home use, thus affording images of private family life unavailable to the professional studio photographer. Though caution must be exercised in the interpretation of photographs as an isolated record, it helps put things in perspective: body and facial expressions, artifacts, and spatial relationships are usually revealing. Photographic analysis in conjunction with other related documentation help present a more complete image of life in the past. The reader will find Moeller 1983 a useful introduction to this subject.

58. Sept. 27, 1873.

59. "In actuality, a pall of choking black smoke and grime emanated from factory smokestacks, hanging over the landscape, to settle as soot on nearby houses. The laborers left their noisy, unsanitary workplace each day to find solace in homes polluted with factory effluent. . . . According to the frequency of illustration, billowing smokestacks were as much a symbol of America as the Statue of Liberty" (Rusch 1990).

60. *Frank Leslie's Illustrated Newspaper*, Sept. 27, 1873.

61. *Riley Burdett v Jacob Estey and Others*, U.S. Circuit Court Testimony, 1876.

62. Douglas 1982, 25.

63. K. Barry 1981, 5. Like trade cards, the calling card portrait offered additional opportunity to exploit the craze for photography. The "carte-de-visite" was first introduced by a Paris photographer, Disderi, in 1854, but it was during the 1860s that Victorian families collected them by the hundreds in specially designed albums. From 1866 to the end of the century the "cabinet card," a larger card resembling the size of the trade card, became a principal format for portraiture. Also popular were depictions in postcard form of famous people and places, as well as more unusual fare including such subject matter as midgets, Indians, scantily clad women, cartoon characters, exotic animals, etc.

64. Until the 1880s "newspaper advertisements

. . . were verbal, informative, and brief, an item on a page crowded with sundry brief items and notices. In the following decade of enhanced production and incorporation, everything changed at once. The new magazines set the pace; by the end of the decade, they carried half- and full-page copy prepared now not by merchants but by new 'advertising agencies'" (Trachtenberg 1982, 136).

65. This trade card depiction is also a favorite of Kenneth L. Ames and is analyzed in Ames 1992, 179–81. Trade cards were invariably in color.

66. This model was depicted in the 1881 catalogue as the 100,000th organ to be produced by the factory. The catalogue boasted: "We have no hesitation in pronouncing this the finest Reed Organ yet manufactured. In its marvelous qualities of tone, it is simply unapproachable; and in its unique and tasteful Case, introducing the highest ideal of architectural design it is without a rival" (Estey catalogue 1881). Strangely, Robert Whiting discovered that the organ bearing the serial number 100,000 (owned by Bob and Diane Yates of Glenshaw, Pennsylvania) is actually of a different cabinet design (Whiting 1981, 39, 147). Regardless, the Salon Organ was one of the more elegant and expensive domestic models sold by Estey, thus making it suitable for the implied theme of this advertisement.

67. Disher 1955, 194.

68. Interestingly, in later renditions of this card, the awkward angle of the chaperone's head was straightened up, and another man, standing primly to the right of the organ and appearing more like a valet than a suitor, was added to the party.

69. In reality, this view of the Estey factory could only be obtained by climbing uninhabited steep rocky slopes on the New Hampshire side of the Connecticut River.

70. There are a number of old mill factories throughout New England, some defunct, some "retrofitted," that feature architecture more char-acteristic of the gothic mien usual to the period, such as towers, patterned slate roofs, vaulted windows, and other idiosyncratic features. One interesting example, the Colt gun factory in Hartford, Conn., though industrially severe, features a huge Turkish radish-shaped dome with painted stars on a bright blue background, a gift from a satisfied munitions customer.

71. In American architecture, early classical and later medieval and gothic legacies are still evident today in the many hundreds of post offices, railroad stations, banks, capitol buildings, and homes throughout the country.

72. Rusch 1990.

73. The capital required to create such a massive edifice allayed possible consumer unease regarding managerial irresponsibility or fly-by-night sales high jinks. The investment in such structures was too great to attract quick-buck artists. In Estey's case, the imposing facade was understood to stand for quality, trust, and good capitalistic intention. Generally, while engineers created functional inner spaces, architects took license in creating "fronts" with far-ranging historical associations and the standard vocabularies of classical, gothic, Moorish, baroque, and Romanesque, designs among others. Though not exploited in factory architecture, this trait is most obvious in city-center buildings such as New York's Grand Central, Boston's Park Square, and Chicago's Illinois Central transportation hubs.

74. Roell 1989, 5–12.

75. "Toward 1800 a literary cult of childhood coalesced, linking latitudinarian Christianity and romantic primitivism in uneasy alliance. By transforming Original Sin into Original Innocence, liberalizing theologians made the idea of an uncorrupted child nature more acceptable to educated Protestants. They began to juxtapose the child's sincerity against the adult's artifice. Romantic thinkers shared the Christian admiration for childlike innocence but added a primitivist stress

on the child's capacity for spontaneous feeling and intense experience. To Blake and Rousseau, freedom from social convention and utilitarian calculation made the child an emblem of a fuller sensuous and imaginative life—a focal point for a potentially sharp critique of the modern superego" (Lears 1981, 145).

76. Tawa 1984, 85.

77. The children-gender-family issue in Victorian culture is a complicated one. "Tensions were particularly severe within the family because nineteenth-century moralists had burdened it with huge and contradictory expectations. Embracing the family as the key agency for internalizing authority in a volatile culture, ideologues of domesticity expected the home to wall off children from a corrupt marketplace and to prepare them (especially if they were male) for success in that marketplace. In the bourgeois imagination, the family was both a haven of social harmony and a schoolhouse for competitive aspiration. On the one hand it encouraged dependence and filial loyalty; on the other it promoted self-assertion and achievement" (Lears 1981, 220).

78. Whiting 1981, 8–9.

79. "Educated Americans sought childlike mental traits from a variety of sources, including Japanese culture. To nearly all Western observers, Japan was a 'toy land' and her people 'in many respects a race of children'" (Lears 1981, 149). "Furthermore, the spirit of cosmopolitanism extended to interest in the arts of the Pacific islands, including Japan. . . . The London International Exposition of 1861 . . . introduced Japanese art to the public in the West and made it popular" (Cashman 1993, 175).

80. Wallance 1956, 2.

81. Though perhaps not in its earlier manifestations, the reed organ later became a product of a developing popular culture between 1885 and 1935. In one of its guises, the reed organ was essentially a "popular" instrument on which one could play "popular" music, and as such contributed significantly to popular culture. As will be discussed in Chapter 2, popular songs and tunes have always been part of the American experience, though we now categorize much of this material as folkloric, instead of popular. In fact, the issue of what constitutes popular culture remains a contentious one among historians; but most agree that it took off beginning in the last quarter of the nineteenth century and continued to gather steam through the first two decades of the twentieth century. As technologies of mass media developed in the twentieth century, certain aspects of popular culture then developed into mass culture. See Kammen 1999, 70–71, for an enlightening perspective on a complex subject. As fate would have it, popular culture was also the reed organ's undoing.

82. Tedlow 1976, 340. By making his catalogues attractive, readable, and entertaining, Sears presaged what merchants now call "shoppertainment."

83. Trachtenberg 1982, 130.

84. Beginning on p. 515.

85. Sears merchandised products mostly bought from other manufacturers, while Estey specialized in the production and sale of his own products.

86. Gellerman 1996, 58.

87. An Estey Hodge & Essex catalogue, London, c. 1890.

88. Estey catalogue 1867.

89. July 28, 1876.

90. Estey catalogue 1878.

Chapter 2. Sing the Old Songs

1. Why were keyboards held in such high esteem? The 1860 Census Report had this to say: "It becomes in all, from the highest to the lowest, a source of innocent and intellectual pleasure and moral improvement. It beguiles the hours of sorrow and alleviates the cares of business, while it diffuses through all classes an increasing taste for the enjoyments of the social and domestic circle,

harmonized and elevated under the influence of music. Even the higher sentiments of religion and patriotism are powerfully stimulated by its aid, as the national and sacred character of the popular songs and airs heard in public and private at all times abundantly testify" (Bureau of the Census 1865, cxlvii).

2. See Chase 1987; Mathews 1889. No other wave of immigrants was to exert the all-pervasive influence of the Puritans. The moral conundrum called the "Puritan ethic"—with its emphasis on labor, industry, and thrift for the common good —permeated the American atmosphere of the eighteenth century. "Puritanism justified wealth acquired through hard work, and it elevated individual effort to the rank of a kind of social service. . . . It was less concerned with theology than with human relations. . . . It reduced mysticism to a vague communion with the divine intended more to improve man on earth than to prepare him for happiness in the hereafter" (Kasson 1976, 36–43). The obvious perplexity inherent in this philosophy —still apparent today—is the moral dilemma of how to work diligently for the public good and enjoy life without succumbing to the seductions of success. The danger was that prosperity, a blessing to the virtuous, might become a source of temptation and indulgence to the ungodly.

3. Contemporary scholarship has put to rest the idea that Puritans hated and suppressed music. "What the Puritans objected to was the way music was often linked to obscene texts, as was the case in some of the popular ballads and song collections which circulated in their day. They took seriously the Biblical injunctions that, if a man be merry, he should sing psalms, which they saw as a Godly form of recreation" (Buechner 1996, 49).

4. Davis 1982, 6; Rublowsky 1967, 12–22.

5. Psalmody is the unaccompanied and unison singing (or speaking) of rhymed metrical versions of the Old Testament book of Psalms to traditional modal folk tunes of fairly simple construction. At-

testing to the importance of Puritan psalm singing in the colonies is the fact that the very first volume printed in this country was a book containing metered and rhymed versifications of lyrical texts from the Bible. *The Whole Booke of Psalmes Faithfully Translated into English Metre*, published in Boston in 1640, came to be known as the *Bay Psalm Book.* (See Kingman 1979, 121–47; Chase 1987, 3–18; Crawford 2001, 23–25.)

6. Owen 1979, 4–5.

7. By the 1720s, after a century of psalmody, two divergent practices of singing had developed: one based on written notation and the other formulated on oral transmission, the latter called the "Usual Way." Few in American congregations, especially in rural areas, could read music, so worshipers had to rely either on their memory or on the deacon or precentor, who "lined out" the psalms for accurate rendition. Consequently, the number of tunes in use shrank, and these were susceptible to variation. In addition, tempos tended to slow down, thus permitting melismatic embellishment of the primary melody by vocally adept singers. Some considered such practices excessive and indulgent, so ecclesiastical musical reform and instruction, promoted as "Regular Singing," ensued. For a comprehensive discussion of these and other related issues, see Benes 1998; Chase 1987; Hitchcock 1974; Kingman 1979; Crawford 2001.

8. The bass viol was called the "church bass" or "God's fiddle" to differentiate it from the "Devil's fiddle," a violin used for dancing, a sinful activity for some denominations. Bass viols were also welcomed in singing-school gatherings, as attested by a personal letter (January 13, 1808) from a General Samuel Fletcher to his children: "'Do not forget to tel William to bring his Base Viol to Townshend [Vt.] for our People are much ingaged in a Singing School at present'" (Ned Phoenix, personal communication).

9. Mathews 1889, 325.

10. Ochse 1975 and Owen 1979 are excellent references for this information.

11. This development was also due to the fact that building pipe organs requires team effort and a formidable amount of knowledge, experience, skill, and a large workshop, whereas early reed organs could be tinkered together by one craftsman at home or in a small workroom.

12. Faler 1981, 100. The first "great awakening" took place in the mid-1700s as a backlash against corrupt church hierarchy; the second great awakening was largely a northern Protestant movement and culminated in the mid-1800s; and the third great awakening occurred between 1890 and 1930 as part of the Progressive movement and New Deal reforms.

13. Ibid. Efforts to establish churches in America were impressive. In the South, churches were built mostly of brick, and in the Northeast, of wood, brick, and stone. In the late nineteenth century church building boomed in the West. Diversity was the rule, both in architecture and in the number of religious sects. The New England churches I visited in search of Estey organs were each architecturally unique, beautifully proportioned, centrally located, inviting (doors were seldom locked), and naturally illuminated (brightness was afforded by numerous windows, white interiors, and high ceilings). One can easily discern why these beautiful buildings were usually located on or near the "village green" or "town common," at the heart of the community.

14. Ogasapian 1983, 89.

15. Ames 1984, 32.

16. Foy and Schlereth 1992, 162–89.

17. *New England Cabinet Organs*, 1880 catalogue, 3. One reason why the home became a focal point for music education was that "in Europe, the layperson's concept of music had been instilled in children by tutors, but in the United States the tutorial system gave way very early, and in addition, the family became a very different social structure.

Even well-to-do mothers raised their own children; governesses and tutors were rare on the East Coast and virtually nonexistent on the frontier. So music in the American living room became a family recreation, as reading aloud was a family recreation" (Borroff 1995, 170).

18. Libin 1985, 199.

19. Cabot 1922.

20. *Musical Courier*, Apr. 16, 1890, 360.

21. Jacob Estey contributed money to the Randolph Baptist Church for the purchase of land. Later, the redoubtable Andrew Carnegie heard of Estey's beneficence and, since the church was still financially poor, wrote J. Gray Estey, Jacob's grandson, about his grandfather's land contribution and suggested sharing the cost of a new organ (a gesture he extended to thousands of churches and libraries throughout the country). So in 1912 an Estey pipe organ was installed in the sanctuary with one-half the payment of the organ borne by Carnegie; Estey replied in kind by writing off the other half of the expense (Laurence Leonard, personal communication)

22. Grubb, *Reed Organ Society Bulletin* [hereafter *ROSB*] 5, no. 4 (Nov. 1986): 25. Beginning with the autumn 1987 issue, the *Reed Organ Society Bulletin* was renamed the *Reed Organ Society Quarterly*.

23. Estey catalogues and brochures frequently included letters from satisfied customers. One typical recommendation came from a Mr. A. C. Wright, missionary of the American Board in charge of the Rio Grande Congregational Training School in Juarez, Mexico. He wrote: "Four years ago my wife received from an uncle the gift of an Estey Acclimatized Organ. It has since traveled more than 2,000 miles, and 160 over the roughest mountain roads; it has endured the great heat and extreme dryness of the climate without injury; it has stood in a house where no spot two feet square could be found without its stream of water from the earth roof, and not a note has refused to sound, nor persisted in lifting up its voice when it should

not; not a screw has come loose; its sound is sweet, soft and strong. From parlor to chapel it has frequently gone, and it sings in Spanish as easily as in English" (undated Estey brochure).

24. Reck 1977, 254.

25. Schulz 1974, 29.

26. To appreciate the considerable power and impressive sonic capability of the reed organ, pick a favorite selection from the accompanying compact disc and turn the volume up to an above-average listening level.

27. Estey Catalogue [1880].

28. A reed organ method book was the owner's instruction manual for learning to operate and play the organ, and for its care and maintenance. The book sweetened the sale and helped assure the owners of continuing success. There were, however, probable confusions, since the various companies' parlor and chapel organs, for which the reed organ methods were written, had similar but nonstandard specifications. Every piece sounded different on every instrument depending on the speaking and mechanical stops available and the manufacturer's characteristic timbre.

29. For more information on stops and their combinations see Appendixes D and E and Boadway's demonstration of stop combinations and effects on the accompanying compact disc.

30. *Vermont Record*, Mar. 16, 1867. A tremulant is a mechanism that creates tremolo. Technically, tremolo, a pulsating effect applied to sustained sound, is *amplitude* modification, in which the volume fluctuates but the pitch does not change. In contrast, vibrato is a fluctuation in the pitch or *frequency* modulation of a sustained note.

31. Estey Catalogue 1878, 4

32. McDonnell 1992, 162–89.

33. Ibid., 163.

34. Grier 1992, 49–74.

35. Grow and von Zweck 1984, 119.

36. Grier 1992, 53.

37. Ibid., 53,148.

38. Borroff 1986, 302.

39. Moseley 1983, 19.

40. Lacour-Gayet 1969, 65–110.

41. Moseley 1983, 21.

42. Mrs. E. Oakes Smith, in an 1851 article entitled "Woman and Her Needs," described the situation most cynically: "The fear that a woman may deviate the slightest from conventionalism in any way, has become a nervous disease with the public. Indeed, so little is she trusted as a creation, that one would think she were made marvelously beautiful, and endowed with gifts of thought and emotion only for the purpose of endangering her safety —a sort of spiritual locomotive with no check-wheel, a rare piece of porcelain, to be handled gingerly—in fact, a creature with no conservative elements within herself, but left expressly thus, that men might supply them, and lead and guide, and coerce and cajole her, as it pleased him best. She is a blind angel, neither adapted to heaven nor earth in herself, but if submitting graciously to man's guidance, capable of filling a narrow, somewhat smoky, and very uncertain nook on this small planet and possibly to win heaven through the perfection of suffering here" (Bode 1972, 81–82).

43. Within a larger historical perspective, the shift from an earlier agrarian self-sufficiency, in which income was generated from within the privacy of the home, to the much more public world of commerce, industry, and factory transformed the nature and function of the American family and the roles of its members. Prior to industrialization, individuals of a family unit each played crucial roles in the maintenance of group physical and fiscal well-being; labor for income was shared more or less equally. As industrialism impacted domestic life, husbands of aspiring middle-class families gradually assumed the role of sole principle breadwinner and were, by necessity, drawn away from the home site, usually to work in a factory; wives were increasingly expected to remain at home and attend to the housekeeping, child

rearing, and other domestic concerns. Through the transformation of roles, women also absorbed responsibilities of principle, namely, the tasks of nurturing the religious and moral virtues of her husband and children. As a result, women, no longer producers, became consumers of newly manufactured goods deemed necessary for a clean, comfortable, and well-appointed home. The intensifying desire of the emerging American middle class for more opulent surroundings, stylish entertainments, and elegant dress helped keep the wheels of factory production turning. Some scholars (e.g., Cowan 1983) view household appliances as having increased rather than decreased women's responsibilities. Where the husband and children (or maids and servants) used to help with chores such as washing dishes and sweeping the floor, now, with the supposed help and freedom afforded by mechanized appliances, women were left to do it all. Whatever help women had before was mostly eliminated as "labor-saving" technology invaded the home. While appliances may have made the labor itself easier, the work was still no less time consuming. Additionally, as household industries (such as making dresses, for example) were taken over by commercial interests, women who used to work at home were eventually forced to search for new ways to be womanly by looking for other productive purposes outside the home, further confusing their function in society. Ultimately, though it provided some amenities, entering the collective labor market did not lessen their obligation to clean house and to cater to family stresses and strains. These are problems yet to be resolved.

44. For an informative account of how mechanization transformed women's household role, see Giedion 1948, 512–627; Cowan 1983.

45. Moseley 1983, 22.

46. Ibid. Further characterization of the model Victorian woman is seen through the artist's brush: "Artists' search for symbols led them to another distinctive form of the American Renaissance, the ideal American woman as a virgin—a symbol of Liberty, Justice, and Columbia. They depicted elegant young women glowing with health but unaware of their latent sexuality. The American virgin can be discerned in all forms of art from highbrow paintings by Thomas Derring to the lowbrow of the Swift Packing Company's Premium Calendar" (Cashman 1993, 196).

47. Trachtenberg 1982, 129.

48. "The family marked the chief arena for the creation of a modern superego, the chief agent of acculturation in a volatile culture. The Victorian domestic ideal pervaded nineteenth-century culture; it was commemorated in the novels of Charles Dickens and Harriet Beecher Stowe, the poetry, prose, and projects in women's magazines such as *Godey's Ladies Book* (1830–1898), and the lithographs of Currier and Ives. The conventional image of Victorian family life—pompous patriarch, submissive and angelic mother, sickly-sweet children—has been the focus for much popular discussion of the family throughout the twentieth century. Nostalgic conservatives have imagined the Victorian domestic ideal to be an emblem of emotional harmony amid disruptive social change; feminists have assailed it as a piece of ideological mystification designed to keep women in their place; social activists have attacked it as the source of 'privatization' which has lured Americans away from public commitments. None of these views gets at the full complexity of Victorian domestic life" (Lears 1981, 15).

49. The early-twentieth-century American music historian John Tasker Howard, in a chapter titled "Our Lighter Musical Moments," formulated a reasonable characterization of popular music in this country: "Most of the popular music of the day has been transitory; here to-day, and gone to-morrow, with something new to take its place. And not always so new, either. Often the latest songs

are old ideas rehashed and modernized. Yet with each generation the type of popular music changes; as people become sophisticated their songs do likewise. . . . If you really understand the popular songs of America, from their beginnings to the present day, you will understand Americans. For Americans, like all other peoples, must have songs to tell what they are thinking about and to extol their heroes" (Howard 1930, 580). Later in the same chapter he sums up his approach regarding the study of popular music: "Always think of popular songs in terms of the period in which they were written and sung. . . . Only when you think of them in their proper setting will they mean to you all that they should mean; for in many respects songs are history" (589). Citing Stephen Foster as an example, Howard insightfully asserts that a certain fluidity exists between folk and popular musics: folk music can become popular music and popular music can become folk music. The difference between popular and folk, according to Howard is that the latter is "the real thing . . . and has endured" (580).

50. Tawa 1984, 2.

51. See Lomax and Lomax 1947.

52. A small sampling of this repertoire must include "Home on the Range," "Git Along, Little Dogies," "Oh Bury Me Not on the Lone Prairie," "The Erie Canal," "She'll Be Comin' round the Mountain When She Comes," "Clementine," "The Yellow Rose of Texas," "Glory, Glory, Hallelujah" ("Battle Hymn of the Republic"), "Dixie," and many more. Innumerable songbooks are available that represent this body of American music. One of the most succinctly comprehensive is Lomax 1975.

53. Hamm 1979, 62.

54. Hamm 1983, 173.

55. The theater, in particular, became a rich avenue for public musical expression. "The majority of all stage entertainments were musicals such as operas, pantomimes, and harlequinades; songs

and solo dances were performed during the intermissions. The number of bandmembers, singers, and dancers equaled or exceeded all other cast-members" (Benes 1998, 8).

56. Clarke 1870.

57. Most of this country's developing (and highly intertwined) folk and popular music histories were established through daily and weekly gatherings. Settings for the enjoyment of instrumental music, dancing, marching, and singing were found in American taverns, meetinghouses, churches, theaters, ballrooms, music halls, schoolrooms, streets, town commons, and homes. "The principal occasions for public music . . . were military and fraternal assemblies, theatrical and social entertainments, and divine services" (Benes 1998, 7). Music was promoted and maintained through formalized secular institutions, including fraternal associations such as the Masons and musical organizations such as the Handel and Haydn and the Philharmonic Societies, which, though not particularly interested in vernacular musics, were committed to forwarding the cause of "cultivated" art music in America. "The fledgling societies flourished much like the . . . lyceums, libraries, bookstores, newspapers, and printing presses [of the day], and in part for the same reason: the democratization and popularization of educated culture" (Benes 1998, 9). See Hitchcock 1974; Chase 1987; Crawford 2001.

58. Hamm 1979, 42.

59. In 1801 William Smith and William Little, together with Andrew Law, published *The Easy Instructor.* They are credited with inventing shape note musical notation. Called the "fa-sol-la" method, the syllables and their corresponding shaped notes (fa = triangle; sol = round; la = square; mi = diamond) helped people sing what they already had in their heads. Though there were many efforts by American composers to exploit this movement, in 1844 Benjamin F. White

published the very successful *Sacred Harp* song-book, which continues to be revised and used widely today. A movement that began in New England and filtered down the eastern seaboard, Sacred Harp hymns are still sung in many southern churches and, in the North, enjoyed largely as a secular recreational activity.

60. Chase 1987, 170–91; Cobb 1989. For accessing the music itself, see McGraw et al. 1991.

61. Chase 1966, 150.

62. The most important movement in this regard was European romanticism, which found fertile soil in America. Foreshadowed by the works of such late-eighteenth-century American songwriters as John Hill Hewitt and Benjaman Carr, texts of a serious sort often reflected America's recent struggle for independence—one of the ultimate romantic events of the age—with its inherent themes of heroism, death, separation, and imprisonment. Even the less formalized songs of Thomas Moore went a step beyond the earlier pleasure-garden songs by describing situations in the first person and emotions from within. Nostalgia became a dominant theme in nineteenth-century song and literature. As exemplified by one song titled, "How That Song Makes Me Wish We Were Back Again Where I Heard It First," a common sense of rootlessness and abandoned homeland permeated the American consciousness. The escape into the past and nostalgia for youth, home, parents, old friends, and lost innocence and happiness reflected in Moore's *Irish Melodies* persisted well into the century and can later be easily seen in songs like Stephen Foster's "Old Folks at Home." Overall, most of the romantic impetus came from Germany, where romanticism flourished earliest and strongest (Hitchcock 1969, 51). Musically, there were few who escaped the passionate influence of Beethoven, Schubert, Schumann, Mendelssohn, Chopin, Liszt, Brahms, Berlioz, Bruckner, and, of course, Wagner. Romantic sentimentalism was the style that perhaps lent

itself most appropriately to the reed organ, a view substantiated by the table of contents in most any reed organ collection.

63. As the nineteenth century continued to unfold, the pattern of cultural imitation continued, and with the immigrants came a surge of European romanticism that began to transform American artistic thinking. Revolutionary ideas of change threatened previously immutable notions of social order (Bridgeman 1975, 29). The romantic muse, American enterprise, abundant optimism, and uninhibited individualism became fundamental to the development of popular expression (Roberts 1963, 169–95). In marked contrast to the Calvinistic assumption that basic human instincts and tendencies were misguided, evil, and in need of repression, the romantic paradigm encouraged full expression of human spirit and capability, seemingly finding a place for everything. The roots of technocracy—that special blend of American democracy, art, technology, philosophy, popular culture, and capitalism—took root during these years.

64. Henry Russell's "Woodman, Spare That Tree" and "Ship on Fire" are judged as songs afflicted with these stylistic affectations. "Ship on Fire," for example, is rife with favorite hackneyed poetic images. After a lengthy pianistic introduction in which some of the themes to be later developed are previewed, the eleven-page song begins dramatically, on a "gale-beaten ship" in foaming seas. A "storm . . . furious and fast" threatens "a young mother [, who] . . . pressing her babe to her bosom of snow," prays to "her God 'mid the hurricane wild" for deliverance. Mercifully, the storm passes, offering a moment's respite for our damsel in distress, who dreams longingly of her "cottage that stands by the shore." There kind friends await to welcome them, and the children, at the end of the long journey, can "sport by the old oaken tree." Then, "Hark! what was that?" Suddenly, a raging fire breaks out on board the ship. Our protagonist,

still with baby in tow and by now engulfed by "thick wreaths" of smoke, "flew to her husband. . . . Oh! there was her refuge, what e'er might betide." Amid the chaos and drama, a lifeboat is lowered into the cold, cold night. They drift away, "alone with destruction, alone on the sea. . . . sad at heart and resign'd, yet undaunted and brave," they pray and persevere. Finally, with a musically melodramatic rising of the sun, comes the cry: "Ho, a sail, ho! . . . Thank God, we're sav'd." Supplementing the highly exclamatory song text is an elaborate, unrelenting piano accompaniment that runs the gamut, as one historian put it, from bombast to bathos.

65. See Davis 1982; Hamm 1979; Tawa 1984.

66. Hamm 1983, 179.

67. William Billings is considered in many ways the quintessential early America composer. A Bostonian, in 1770 Billings published *The New England Psalm-Singer*, the first volume of original music composed by an American.

68. The great success of singing schools was due in part to their recreational and "entertainment" value as well as any musical or religious reward. The following quote by a singing-school participant affirms that they provided a venue where townsfolk could meet with united cause, make a joyful noise, and have fun: "At present I have no inclination for anything, for I am almost sick of the World & were it not for the Hopes of going to the singing-meeting tonight & indulging myself a little in some of the carnal Delights of the Flesh, such as kissing, squeezing &c. &c. I should willingly leave it now" (quoted in Lowens 1964, 282).

69. Tawa 1984, 21–22.

70. Rich 1946, 22–23.

71. In 1849 Hamlin was alleged to have discovered an improvement for voicing free reeds: slightly curving and/or twisting the free end of a reed, which created a less harsh sound by reducing the production of undesirable harmonics. The technique was soon universally adopted. In 1854 he and Lowell Mason formed the firm of Mason & Hamlin, and the ambitious pair began manufacturing their "Organ Harmonium," which featured four sets of reeds and two manuals of keys. This eventually developed, in 1862, into the Mason & Hamlin "Cabinet Organ," one of the most successful reed organs of all time. The company tirelessly touted its cutting-edge improvements: double vertical bellows, self-adjusting reed valves, automatic bellows swell, sounding boards and tube boards, noiseless safety valves, and an improved combination register. Like Jacob Estey, Mason & Hamlin claimed to have "the most perfect of the reed instruments." Judging by the numbers, there is little doubt that this company was in the vanguard of the business. "The production of reed instruments in 1870 probably a little exceeded 20,000, and their value was not far from $4,000,000. Of these the Mason & Hamlin Cabinet Organ Co. (the successors of Mason and Hamlin,) made more than 6,500, of a value of not less than $300,000" (Kettel 1872, 434). For a full overview of the reed organ in America see Gellerman 1996. Information pertaining to industry leaders is found on pp. 19–27.

72. See Proper 1998, 161–62.

73. It must be noted that early in its development, despite the fact that the songs were sung in Negro dialect by performers in blackface, the music of the songs was usually directly derived from European models (Hamm 1979, 110). It is also interesting to note that the portable reed organ was used in Britain and Europe by members of "the cult of burnt cork, banjo and bones," and by French pantomime comic characters called Pierrots, as a favorite instrument for accompaniment (*Musical Opinion*, June 1905). After 1860 in America, only parlor-song arrangements, not the "Ethiopian" minstrel versions, were found in popular collections (Tawa 1984, 92). It is also a little-documented fact that the reed organ was used in early African American music genres, including

the blues (Smithsonian Institution 1973, 17), and, as we shall see in a later chapter, led the way for the electric (especially the Hammond) organ, used extensively in gospel, soul, and rhythm and blues.

74. Intensely nationalistic and aggressively egalitarian, minstrelsy ridiculed the "strange ways" of foreigners and debunked the pretentious. As it entertained, it also served social and psychological functions and in the end actually formed opinion. For in-depth studies of American minstrelsy see Toll 1974; Nathan 1962; Riggs 1986.

75. No doubt some of the preference by the general public for this type of entertainment was because the cost of a minstrel show ticket was a fraction of the price of an opera ticket.

76. *Vermont Phoenix*, January 20, 1893.

77. See Emerson 1997. "Oh! Susannah," "Camptown Races," "Nelly Bly," "Old Black Joe," and many more of Foster's songs have become icons of American music. As one indication of Foster's popularity, his "My Old Kentucky Home" and "Old Folks at Home" were both published in the early 1850s; within four years they had sold 90,000 and 130,000 copies, respectively.

78. Tawa 1984, 24.

79. In addition to the Victorian predilection for Italian opera, blackface minstrel songs, and singing families like the Hutchinsons, a thriving market for all sorts of music and public entertainment continued unabated in America's towns and cities: community cotillions, hoedowns, band programs, classical concerts and recitals, musicales, social dances, church services, and local musical theater. National interest in professional traveling performers was also growing. Circuses and "spectaculars" such as "Buffalo Bill" Cody's Wild West Show (brought east beginning in 1883) lured Victorians from the insularity of their homes and kept them abreast of societal trends. Visiting virtuosi such as Jenny Lind and Ole Bull, along with numerous other cornet-, clarinet-, string-, and piano-playing "artistes," idolized by the American public, helped

raise the standard of performance to such an extent that classical concert music began to move beyond the grasp of the amateur musician seeking simple diversion and amusement. "Popularized" forms of entertainment had unquestionably taken a firm hold on America. But of them all, Jenny Lind, "the Swedish Nightingale," was one of the most successful. Under the management of P. T. Barnum, Jenny enjoyed triumphs in New York, Boston, Philadelphia, Baltimore, Washington, Richmond, Charleston, New Orleans, Natchez, Memphis, St. Louis, Nashville, Louisville, Cincinnati, Wheeling, and Pittsburgh. She gave her adoring audiences a mixture of airs from Italian or German operas, favorite lieder such as "The Echo Song" and "The Bird Song," and selected duets and trios to vary the fare. Invariably she concluded concerts, usually as a final encore, with a heartfelt rendition of "Home, Sweet Home." America loved her.

80. There was much criticism from elites of the indulgent, sentimental song style with its highly stylized, overstated, theatrical decadence. During this time, social-climbing dandies and fashionable ladies, though they did not altogether repudiate popular songs like Henry Russell's or those adapted from European opera, began to prefer imported German lieder and romantic Italian high opera to "trashy" American songs. A rift between the aristocratic and lower classes' tastes in music was finally becoming more apparent. Kammen 1999 points out that this was happening in other areas of activity as well. As "ordinary folks were discouraged or driven away from theaters, concerts, and museums, . . . many alternative modes of entertainment became available to the middling and working classes—an array of leisure-time options from amusement parks to concert saloons, from vaudeville to silent film, from sheet music for communal singing to organized sports. . . . Their new options cost less, were considered more fun and better suited to their educational levels than

the more elitist entertainments and edifications that did not exactly welcome the great unwashed with open arms" (73).

81. It was Charles Seeger who noted two forces in the development of American music: the elitist "make America musical" contingent, whose advocates intended to elevate people's musical tastes through concerts and education courses, and the "sell America music" groups, those with predominantly commercial interests who recognized new opportunities to capitalize on all kinds of music, especially popular forms (Seeger 1957). Richard Crawford observes that two major musical movements in early American music—the singing school movement of the 1720s and early 1800s, and the efforts of Lowell Mason and his colleagues in the 1830s—were in the spirit of social reform. However, the spread of home music making was more commercial in nature and "was different from reform movements, launched in the name of an idealistic prupose and couched in moral rhetoric; it was a business from the start, with producers and consumers" (2000, 221).

82. "Reflective of this aspect of middle-class musical culture was the rapid growth of the sheet music publishing industry, which in America had reached impressive proportions even by the last decade of the eighteenth century and continued to expand throughout the nineteenth" (Hitchcock 1969, 59). Davis 1982 chronicles thirty-one new publishing companies that appeared between 1830 and 1839, thirty-seven during the following decade, and sixty-six between 1850 and 1861 (182). Sheet music began to be produced for home use in 1885. Davis estimates that as much as three-fourths of the music sold was to teachers, who bought their materials wholesale and sold to their pupils retail. Responding to their students' preferences, teachers doubtless included in their lessons the latest fashionable popular pieces on the market. By 1892 the nation's first confirmed million-seller, Charles K. Harris's "After the Ball," convinced songwriters and publishers that big money could be made catering to popular taste. The staggering success of Tin Pan Alley in the following decades proved them right.

83. Loesser 1954, 520.

84. Sadie 1986, 21.

85. It is interesting that Septimus Winner included among his many pseudonyms a feminine name, Alice Hawthorne, instead of a masculine or sexless one (such as Eastburn, another of his pen names) or his own name. He probably felt the more sentimental songs would sell better if penned by a woman songwriter and that customers preferred their bathos from female rather than male sources. Regardless, it is additional evidence of the attitudes toward divided sex roles in the Victorian era.

86. "The music [of 'Home, Sweet Home'] first appeared under the pen of London composer Henry R. Bishop (1786–1855) and was called a Sicilian air. Originally the tune had a different set of words. The text of 'Home, Sweet Home' was by John Howard Payne, who was born in New York City in 1791, but moved to London in 1820" (Schulz 1974, 79).

87. As is sensed from some of the songs in this listing, "for many there was a longing for the past, a sentimental journey through weal or woe, to the simpler days of yore. In some spheres, this emotional symptom took on epidemic proportions. Popular songs of the late decades harped on the goodness of the old days, unfortunately gone forever" (Schulz 1974, 4). On the other hand, Americans had developed enough force of character to create absurd mock portrayals of themselves. Through folk song, comical, sarcastic, ironic, witty, droll, irreverent, ridiculous humor was a way for the citizenry not only to make light of themselves but also to thumb the American nose at an increasingly suspect European civilization. "The tongue-in-cheek brag, idiosyncratic toggery, erratic behavior, and uncouth uniqueness of the American

riverboatman, frontiersman, Yankee peddler, city tough, and black Southern slave and Northern freeman became standard constructs of popular entertainment. However exaggerated were the characteristics of these stock figures, they were recognized by Americans as their own" (Tawa 1984, 141). As the reader may no doubt sense, behind much of this sort of caricature also lay a less humorous element of negativistic ethnic stereotyping. "Us versus them" attitudes, inherited from England and catalyzed by massive immigration and industrialization in the New World, became a characteristic reflection of the eclectic ferment of American society and culture. (For a good case in point, see Slobin 1982, 49–63.) Cultural bias notwithstanding, "from the 1830s through the 1890s notions of popular culture (exemplified by theatrical entertainments, minstrel shows, and affordable writing in booklets and magazines) were strongly tinged by nationalistic hues. That was equally true of tales of Davy Crockett and the Alamo, dime novels about Buffalo Bill's exploits as a scout, and Edwin Booth's cerebral Shakespearean performances" (Kamman 1999, 63). Each figure became legendary in American folkloric culture because of their unique "Americanness" — their identity as a product of a nascent democracy (see Kammen 1999, 62–69).

88. The following listing is taken from the endnotes of Ames 1992: William H. Clarke, *The American Organ or Organist's Parlor Companion* (Boston: G. D. Russell, 1865); William H. Clarke, *Home Recreations: A Collection of New Songs . . . for the Parlor-Organ, Melodeon, or Pianoforte* (Boston: S. D. and H. W. Smith, 1867); C. A. White and Chas. D. Blake, *White's School for the Reed Organ* (Boston: White, Smith, 1875); and H. S. Perkins and Wm. W. Bentley, *The River of Life, for Our Sunday Schools* (Boston: Oliver Ditson, 1873). Other concurrent books include Clark's *New Method for Reed Organs*; Getze's *School for Parlor Organ*; Emerson's *School for Parlor Organ*; Clarke's *Improved School*

for Parlor Organ; Kinkel's *New Method for Reed Organ*; Root's *School for Cabinet Organ*; Clarke's *Dollar Instructor for Reed Organs*; Clarke's *Reed Organ Companion*; Bellak's *Method for Organ*; *Melodeon without a Master*; Mack's *Analytical Method for Cabinet Organ*; Winner's *New School for Cabinet Organ*; Winner's *Cabinet Organ Tutor*; Winner's *Easy System for Melodeon*; *Amateur's Organ Instructor*; Leslie's *Cabinet Organ*; *Cabinet Organ Treasury*; *Young Organist's Album*; and *Organ at Home*. There were doubtless many more.

89. Sears, Roebuck and Company 1968, 539–540.

90. Scholars in other disciplines have made similar comparisons. For instance, the interchangeability of plots and characters in dime novels (a principle on which today's television shows and movies still rely) is analogous to the inventions of Eli Whitney and Elias Howe, who standardized machinery so that parts could be easily modified or replaced (see Trachtenberg 1982, 46). Howe, in addition to making sewing machines, was a maker of musical instruments and wrote an early melodeon method, *Howe's Seraphine and Melodeon Instructor* (1847).

91. Schulz 1974, 41–73.

92. Phelps and Cheney 1882. The full title of Estey's *Methods* is *Estey Organ Method: Containing a Systematic Course of Instruction in the Elements of Music, Illustrated by Numerous Progressive Exercises and Studies, with Choice Gems of Standard Music from the Works of the Best Composers, Ancient and Modern.*

93. Besides the 1882 revised edition of the Estey *Method*, the Estey Organ Company later distributed a completely different publication, *Improved Easy Method for the Parlor Organ* (1886), by W. W. Whitney. The contents of Whitney's *Method* are strikingly contrastive to those of Phelps and Cheney, featuring many dance tunes, no church music, and very few classical arrangements; American songwriters, however, are well represented.

94. Phelps and Cheney 1882, 95.

95. Ibid., 115.

96. Ibid., 148.

97. SATB is a standard choir hierarchy comprised of sopranos, altos, tenors, and basses.

98. Phelps and Cheney 1882, 137.

99. Ibid., 51. "The Last Rose of Summer" was written by Richard Alfred Milliken. Because the rendition found in the Estey *Method* was arranged especially for an Estey organ, it represents "a well thought out and highly successful little miniature for reed organ" (Schulz 1974, 81).

100. Written about 1861, published in 1865, compiled by Suttoni (1981, 67).

101. Phelps and Cheney 1882, 104.

102. "One might well imagine the pious gatherings around the organ where sentiments were especially in tune with the by-gone days and with death. Both topics were exceedingly fashionable in current songs" (Schulz 1974, 84). Schulz substantiates his observation by listing some typical sentimental songs commonly found in organ collections: "Shall We Know Each Other There?," "Take Me Back Home Again," "Far Away," "Departed Days," "Fare Thee Well, Jamie," "A Tress of Mother's Hair (in the Old Family Bible)," and, of course, "Silver Threads among the Gold." And again, it is interesting that the song is written in the key of E-flat major in the Estey *Method* and in G major in Hamm's transcription (Hamm 1979). It is also in G major in *Kimball's New Method for the Reed Organ.* Except for the key, all arrangements are nearly identical. Since there was often some emphasis placed on transposition in most methods, key orientation was probably unimportant, so long as it suited the player and singer. Mostly, vocal ranges were from E-flat on the bottom line of the treble staff to G on top of the staff.

103. Tawa 1984, 26.

104. Ibid.

105. Ibid., 35.

106. Phelps and Cheney 1882, 122–23.

107. Ibid., 128–29.

108. Ibid., 6.

109. Tawa 1984, 7.

110. Schulz 1974, 129.

111. "American ambivalence toward material progress dated from earliest Puritan times. Puritan divines urged diligence and frugality, then fretted over the prosperity resulting from those habits. Wealth was a sign of God's blessing but also an agent of corruption. Freed from adversity, men inevitably sank into slothful ease. Economic success contained the seeds of moral failure" (Lears 1981, 26; this book contains a particularly insightful discussion of the sociopsychological mentality of Americans through the industrial era and into the modern age). See also Trachtenberg 1982 for an in-depth analysis of the industrial/Victorian conflict.

Chapter 3. The Perfect Melodeon

1. An article in the *Musical Courier* puts the number of children in the Estey family as eight: five boys and three girls (*Musical Courier,* Apr. 16, 1890, 360). According to one uncited source, Isaac Estey had accumulated money but lost it all as a contractor for public roads.

2. Legal adoption was unusual. More often, children of destitute families were boarded in the homes of relatives or neighbors who needed extra help, especially during the summer season. Children who were hired out invariably sent wages back home. The term "farmed out" was the common expression used to describe this sort of informal adoption (Richard M. Mitchell, personal communication).

3. *Vermont Phoenix,* May 6, 1887.

4. *Vermont Phoenix,* Apr. 18, 1890.

5. This order of circumstance was not as unusual as one might think and was, in fact, often the norm for teenaged boys. "Some of them were orphan lads, sixteen and even fourteen years of

age, who were running away from apprenticeships and the indifferent treatment of relatives. Others had labored hard to 'buy their time,' and had thus escaped the dreary farm work before the emancipating age of twenty-one" (Stilwell 1948, 210).

6. *Vermont Phoenix*, May 6, 1887, and Apr. 18, 1890.

7. Cabot 1922, 631. The *Musical Courier* reported that Estey secured an apprenticeship with A. M. Knight, not Thomas Sutton (*Musical Courier*, Apr. 16, 1890, 360). The *Courier* is probably in error.

8. Brattleboro is located off the first exit of Interstate Highway 91 after crossing the border from Massachusetts. Hinsdale, N.H., birthplace of Jacob Estey, abuts Brattleboro at the Connecticut River. A small river island called Island Park, situated between Vermont and New Hampshire, was sometimes used by those who plied the Connecticut River in the early days as a place to camp. "For nearly twenty years, beginning in 1909, Brattleboro's Island—a farm in former times and practically non-existent today—was a center of diversion and entertainment for the village and surrounding areas" (H. Barry et al. 1974, 125). The island was developed mostly for recreational use: a baseball grandstand was built, and an elaborate "amusement pavilion" with a ballroom for concerts (Paul Whiteman once played there) and a vaudeville stage for traveling acts were also constructed. Bowling, wrestling matches, circus performances, political grandstanding, boat rides, outdoor movies, and the Brattleboro Pageant all took place on Island Park until around the 1920s, when automobiles allowed people to find amusement farther from home. Eventually "Brattleboro's pleasure garden" was destroyed by a flood; it was never restored. Another minor but noteworthy geologic feature of the immediate area is Wantastiquet Mountain (one of the few places in the region that pays place-name tribute to the first inhabitants), a good-sized foothill in New Hampshire overlooking Brattleboro from across the river. With a lovely aerial vista of the town and the mountains further to the west, various bird's-eye renderings of Brattleboro by artists suggest the summit of Wantastiquet as their vantage point. Today a well-worn hiking path can be accessed from behind the Wal-Mart department store just over the bridge from Brattleboro.

9. In her book of memoirs, Mrs. Levi K. Fuller, daughter of Jacob Estey and wife of Levi Fuller, reminisced about the endless parade of flatboats plying the Connecticut River loaded with freight from Hartford, Connecticut, "for everything seemed to come from that city in those days."

10. From around 10,000 B.C., the Connecticut River Valley area, an Ice Age vestige, was home to countless generations of migratory Indian inhabitants. In the final chapters of northeast woodland native culture, tribal groups such as the Pocumtucks and the Squakeags occupied the southern border area between present-day Vermont and New Hampshire. During the last decades of the seventeenth century, restless immigrant homesteaders began moving from the south into more northeastern areas, thus inciting a major war. The ensuing Indian confrontation, with the French from the north as well as with English settlers, lasted well into the eighteenth century and became the first critical event in determining Vermont's destiny. Soon thereafter the British monarchy was forced to accede to Americans' steadfast commitment for independence and freedom. Though diminutive in size, the states that make up what is now New England harbor a goodly amount of this country's history and to the present day sustain a well-earned reputation for the conservation of traditional early Americana. Countless New England towns, villages, hamlets, and boroughs still emanate a strong sense of America in an earlier age.

11. *Musical Courier*, Apr. 30, 1890.

12. Uncle John Stearns, "bluff, hearty and vigorous, . . . one of nature's own noblemen," was a well-liked citizen of Hinsdale, N.H. His business as a

cattle buyer and dealer, "with all sorts of odd jobs of speculation thrown in in true Yankee style," provided him the opportunity to meet a considerable number of people and spread occasional goodwill (paraphrased from Stearns's obituary in the *Vermont Phoenix*, Dec. 5, 1884).

13. *Musical Courier*, Apr. 16, 1890.

14. At the time, located at the south end of Main Street, close to the mouth of the Whetstone Brook where the old covered bridge crossed the Connecticut River into New Hampshire.

15. H. Barry et al. 1974, 161.

16. Richard M. Mitchell, personal communication.

17. *Vermont Phoenix*, Mar. 21, 1839.

18. Unlike many trades in the nineteenth century, the reed organ business started concomitantly with industrialism. Many occupations were established as trades long before the Industrial Revolution; their practitioners, having already evolved systems of production based on nonindustrial foundations, found adjustment to mechanization and entrepreneurial management difficult. (See Hirsch 1978, Appendix B, for a particularly interesting list of nineteenth-century trades.) In contrast, reed organ builders had little collective identification as a trade until mass production techniques developed. The reed organ owed its very existence to industrial technology, which is why the builders evidently had less trouble than some others adapting to industrialized methods. Also, because organ building was a relatively small industrial enterprise (not requiring large numbers of unskilled workers, compared to the marble, railroad, and garment industries, for instance), it escaped much of the labor turmoil common later in the century. The great majority of organ building firms hired from five to twenty persons. Estey, an exception, was one out of only three organizations in the country to hire over 250 workers (Bureau of the Census 1902, 10:463–64).

19. Past research concerning the development of the Estey Organ Company has been greatly facilitated by the existence of two historical documents: *The Gazetteer and Business Directory of Windham County, Vt.* (1884), compiled by Hamilton Child, and *The Annals of Brattleboro* (2 vols., 1921–22), compiled and edited by Mary R. Cabot. Child's volume, one of the many business directories he assembled in the eastern states, was commissioned by those who could afford personal documentation. Mary Cabot, on the other hand, was a native of Brattleboro who, out of personal interest, found the time to write the now classic account of Brattleboro from 1681 to 1895. Though we are deeply indebted to these chroniclers, the information they provide may be less than totally accurate; Child's livelihood depended on satisfying customers, and Cabot, out of sensitivity to the feelings of her neighbors past and present, naturally wanted to show her subjects in a favorable light. Both accounts were slanted toward the "better" Brattleboro families. Comparison of the two strongly suggests that Cabot used some of the information gathered by Child, thus compounding any inaccuracies that may have existed in the former document. Generally, their documentation, unquestionably valuable, remains the standard history and has afforded the basis for much research on Brattleboro, including previous Estey research and the following chronology. However, though inaccuracies abound here as well, the various town newspapers furnish the most complete description of Brattleboro history. The *Semi-Weekly Eagle*, the *Brattleboro Eagle*, the *Vermont Phoenix*, the *Vermont Record and Farmer*, and the *Brattleboro Daily Reformer* provide a running historical record of the town and have been invaluable in my revised version of Jacob Estey's biography. (See the bibliography for a listing of the relevant Brattleboro newspapers.)

20. As was determined in Chapter 1, anthropologists and cultural historians know that caution must be exercised when interpreting objects based on advertising imagery, for this is how manufac-

turers *wished* us to view their product. The marketing publicity was probably incommensurate with the deeper meanings for users of these items. The true sociopsychological significance of material objects in people's lives is often internalized and transitory and thus difficult, if not impossible, to document.

21. Cabot 1922, 628.

22. Passing mention should be made of William A. Conant, who moved to Brattleboro in 1841 and began manufacturing cellos for Woodbury. The firm was reported to be one the oldest violin and cello makers in the country, and Conant, in spite of the fact that "he could not play a tune" (Cabot 1922, 445), made over a thousand excellent instruments from local woods. All who visited him "received a cordial welcome and [were] entertained with Mr. Conant's inimitable vein of drollery and apt sayings" (*Vermont Phoenix*, Feb. 16, 1894). Most of his instruments were sold to Woodbury, who represented Conant to dealers in Boston and New York. Later Conant worked for six years as an action maker for Estey.

23. Cabot 1922, 623.

24. Early on, reed making was an exacting, time-consuming, somewhat hit-or-miss process. After tongues were sheared from sheet brass, they were hammered to the necessary temper, filed to the required form, riveted into frames, and tuned by hand-filing each reed (Child 1884, 89).

25. In the town of Jacksonville, Vt., I viewed hundreds of holes still exposed in the meeting-hall stage made by the nails in the ends of Alonzo Hine's instrument's four legs, which kept it from "slipping about" while he pumped it for community folk-dance gatherings. It is obvious from this and other accounts that in addition to furnishing accompaniments in small churches, early melodeons were routinely employed in secular capacities as well. Hines apparently made his own melodeon out of parts bought from the Estey factory. The instrument is presently housed in the Historical Society of Windham County in Newfane, Vt. (Ned Phoenix, personal communication).

26. Eliason 1976.

27. *Vermont Phoenix*, Aug. 28, 1845.

28. Cabot 1922, 626.

29. *Brattleboro Eagle*, May 6, 1853.

30. Cabot 1922, 626; also Nadworny 1959, 47.

31. *Vermont Phoenix*, June 23, 1846.

32. *Brattleboro Eagle*, May 6, 1853.

33. *Riley Burdett v Jacob Estey and Others*, U.S. Circuit Court Testimony, 1876, 206.

34. Ord-Hume 1986, 69–71.

35. Nadworny 1959, 47.

36. Gellerman 1973, 7. By the 1820s the artisan class formed the central structure of local society and was a primary source of community values and ideology. These expert craftsmen had the privileges and respect that were later the property of the bourgeoisie. They were generally self-employed, worked in an apprentice-journeyman-master hierarchy, and controlled their own destinies. Highly skilled, they worked through the entire manufacturing process by hand. Though there was no guild system in America, artisans formed a social class in much the same way as traditional European craftsmen did. And unlike European guilds, which guarded their secrets, American craftsmen shared knowledge through societies that began to collect and compile information in public libraries. But this state of affairs was not to last. As the industrial pace quickened, "masters in several crafts . . . expanded their workshops to factory scale. These were rarely mechanized mills; most work was still done by hand, and in many mills the differentiation of tasks was just beginning. But even those 'factories' that were simply large accumulations of craftsmen and raw materials under one roof created a new efficiency in production and marketing, and thus greater profits" (Hirsch 1978, 16).

37. *Brattleboro Eagle*, May 6, 1853.

38. Confusing matters, the *Brattleboro Eagle*

later calculated that by September 1850 Jones & Burditt had made about eight hundred instruments of eighteen varieties, though it hardly seems possible that so many organs were built in so short a time. Eight hundred instruments in four years equals two hundred instruments per year, far above the output estimated in the census report; the numbers may perhaps reflect Jones's and Burditt's combined lifetime totals.

39. *Brattleboro Eagle*, May 6, 1853.

40. But railroads were relatively slow in coming to Vermont. There were difficulties in obtaining capital, and the mountain grades were steep and costly for the engineers to conquer. Exploitive railroad contractors hired penniless Irish immigrants, recently arrived in American and Canadian ports, to do the labor. Later disputes over past-due pay forced confrontations between laborers and local authorities and resulted in some of the first work stoppages to take place in Vermont (Muller 1982, 160).

41. Muller 1982, 162. The growth of railroads after the Civil War was phenomenal. Rail networks expanded from 35,000 miles of track in 1865 to 53,000 miles in 1870; 93,000 miles in 1880; 164,000 miles in 1890; and 193,000 in 1900. In 1865, railroads carried 10 billion tons of freight at a rate of 2 cents a ton per mile of track; in 1890, trains transported 79 billion tons per mile; by 1900, rates fell to three-quarters of a cent per ton per mile (Cashman 1993, 23).

42. *Semi-Weekly Eagle*, Aug. 11, 1851. Cabot (1922, 627) states that Jones sold his interest to E. B. Carpenter in September 1850.

43. Because names and styles of these early organs were still indistinct and freely applied, it is difficult to know how their instrument resembled other manufacturers' "Aeolians" and "Seraphines," which were at this point competing with the earliest styles of melodeons.

44. Libin 1985, 195–96.

45. *Semi-Weekly Eagle*, Aug. 10, 1847.

46. *Vermont Phoenix*, Sept. 13, 1848.

47. *Vermont Phoenix*, Aug. 12, 1848.

48. *Vermont Phoenix*, July 13, 1849.

49. *Musical Courier*, Apr. 16, 1890.

50. After Burditt and Carpenter had moved on, Estey and Green took over the melodeon shop, as evidenced by close examination of the photograph of the shop (figure 34), taken around the mid to late 1880s, which clearly shows a sign over a doorway that reads "Estey & Green."

51. Cabot 1922, 632.

52. Ibid.

53. Stilwell 1948, 212–13.

54. Nadworny 1959, 43–59.

55. Cabot 1922, 632.

56. See Emerson 1997 for the interesting tale that was Stephen Foster's life.

57. Bode 1972, 178.

58. Ibid.

59. Up to the time of the Civil War, much rural commerce was mainly in the hands of peddlers. Some arrived on foot or horseback with tin boxes filled with most anything that might be useful to country folk. Wagons were used for heavier merchandise, especially with the opening of the western frontier. Lore suggests that endless bargaining was the rule and that commercial travelers, hucksters, horse traders, hustlers, mongers, and wheeler-dealers knew all the tricks; honesty was generally not their strong trait. At mid-century native Yankee peddlers were given serious competition by German Jews who had recently immigrated to the United States. The establishment of the general store and more efficient means of transportation eventually outmoded this early form of sales promotion and distribution.

60. *Vermont Phoenix*, Apr. 18, 1890.

61. Cabot 1922, 633.

62. Ibid.

63. Time payment was a strategy pioneered by McCormick with his reaper and later exploited

by the sewing machine industry (especially Singer) and the piano trade.

64. Stilwell 1948, 200.

65. Cabot 1922, 632.

66. *Brattleboro Eagle*, May 6, 1853.

67. *Musical Courier*, Oct. 15, 1890.

68. Gellerman 1985, 20–21.

69. The "Carpenter Organ Instructor" was published in 1883 in Brattleboro, which suggests that E. P. Carpenter had by then resituated from Worcester, Massachusetts. Quite probably Carpenter's company maintained a profitable foothold in the market not in spite of but because Estey was a neighbor and competitor. Having such lively organ making activity within the close confines of Brattleboro is perhaps not dissimilar to the situation today of fast-food outlets, which are clustered in malls or "on the strip." The relationship between Carpenter and Estey was evidently amicable, with competition between the two companies respectfully expressed through friendly bouts of sports.

70. *Vermont Phoenix*, Aug. 21, 1885.

71. According to the *Musical Courier* (June 19, 1889), Carpenter's interest in foreign markets evidently led him to give up the organ business for a while and dabble in a railroading investment in Honduras. Apparently his Brattleboro organ business continued unabated.

72. Cabot 1922, 866.

73. Ibid., 628. Cabot mistakenly calls the company Burdett & Green. There is no record what soever of a Burdett & Green. Though it is verifiable that Burdett was an important figure in the company at this time, it seems Cabot may have understandably confused the company name.

74. Loesser 1954, 520. One measure of increased immigration and rapid westward movement was the growth of agricultural efforts: there were nearly 4 million farms by the 1880s, and a decade later another 1.1 million were established. Centers of commerce were booming: Chicago and San Francisco grew into major cities in one generation

(Schulz 1974, 1). This westward expansion and new settlement provided unlimited opportunity for manufacturers of various products, including reed organs.

75. Estey catalogue 1867. The basic rosewood model had a F-compass keyboard of sixty-one notes and one set of reeds at 8' (unison). Larger melodeons had two or three sets of reeds and often a "Harmonic," the octave coupler patented by Estey & Green in 1857. Each instrument had swell shades operated by the left pedal and a single exhauster controlled by the right pedal. The Methodist church in West Chelsea Hill, Vermont, has a two-rank Estey & Green melodeon with an octave of 16' reeds and a walnut case extending to the floor to cover the bellows. This instrument is a unique survival of Estey & Green's earliest efforts to provide a melodeon really suitable for church use (E. A. Boadway, personal communication).

76. The keys of reed organs were becoming more like piano keys in size. Also, larger bellows capacity permitted easier and steadier pumping and a somewhat higher wind pressure, resulting in more volume.

77. *Vermont Phoenix*, July 28, 1855.

78. "An implicit labor theory of value, that all wealth originates in someone's labor, seemed to assure continuous mobility between the status of laborer and the rank of independent entrepreneur. Its appeal to the majority of workers in the 1850's and 1860's, as the pace of industrialization quickened and factories developed into larger, more demanding institutions, is questionable" (Trachtenberg 1982, 75).

79. Nadworny 1959, 53–55.

80. In fact, much of the information now available concerning the progress of Estey's business was recorded as damage assessment reports.

81. Ord-Hume 1986, 97–98.

82. Dolge 1911, 364.

83. The building in the left foreground of the photograph is the one built by Estey. It is interest-

ing to note that the smaller building in the right foreground, displaying the "Furniture" sign, was probably also owned by Estey, since an artist's rendition of this very same scene shows both buildings' signs emblazoned with the "J. Estey & Co." trademark.

84. *Vermont Phoenix*, Jan. 17, 1861.

85. Mrs. Levi K. Fuller 1928, address no. II, "Some Reminiscences of Brattleboro during the Civil War."

86. The word "cottage," initially referring to the rural homestead, became a fashionable term used by furniture designers of the day (see Introduction n. 11).

87. *Vermont Phoenix*, Jan. 8, 1864.

88. *Brattleboro Daily Reformer*, June 16, 1880.

89. *Vermont Phoenix*, Aug. 9, 1864.

90. Beginning in the 1850s, Chicago increasingly boasted a high concentration of music activity, to a large extent because it was *the* railroad hub in the center of the country. "In 1880, Chicago had fourteen instrument factories; by 1890 there were thirty-one. By 1900, there were twenty-one piano factories (producing 16% of all American-made pianos), nine organ factories (18%), and fifteen manufacturing other instruments. By 1925, over 180,000 pianos were being made in Chicago every year" (Borroff 1995, 165).

91. Nadworny 1959, 47.

92. The famous Chicago firm of Lyon & Healy, highly successful musical entrepreneurs in their own right (see n. 97), became exclusive agents for Estey organs and pianos. Later the company of Estey & Camp (1884–96) maintained a thriving business in the Windy City.

93. No Estey organ with "Chicago" on the nameboard has been found. Likely, all Estey organs bore the "Brattleboro" gilt lettering, regardless of where they were made.

94. Cabot 1922, 633.

95. Owen 1979, 94.

96. Burditt had changed his name to Burdett.

Chroniclers have generally used the new name exclusively, even when speaking of his early life. As the reader has noticed, I have tried to keep the name in perspective. But even after "Burdett" was in common usage, it was not unusual to find the spelling "Burdette" and other variations in trade journals.

97. Lyon & Healy began business in Chicago in 1864, first selling musical instruments and, beginning in 1880, manufacturing plucked stringed instruments (especially the famous "orchestral harp"), pianos, organs, brass instruments, and drums. By the 1890s, in addition to merchandising instruments of other manufacturers, Lyon & Healy was producing more than 100,000 instruments yearly (Borroff 1995, 165).

98. *Vermont Phoenix*, Feb. 20, 1889.

99. See Cabot 1922, 629, for a partial listing of inventions.

100. Duga 1968, 25.

101. Evidently Estey outgrew the buildings at South Main and Bridge Streets and upon completion of the new Frost Street factory moved the "Finishing Factory and Office" to the new location, leaving the "Reed and Case Factories" in the old one (Estey catalogue 1867, 20–21).

Chapter 4. The Estey Organ Company

The epigraph to this chapter is from John Huber, "Over the Edge: When Success Turns Sour," as quoted in *Bostonia*, Apr.–May 1987, 44. The "from humble beginnings" homily is a true Americanism. Later, however, "in the embryonic consumer culture of the late nineteenth century, more and more Americans were being encouraged to 'express themselves' . . . not through independent accomplishment but through the ownership of things. It was a far different and in many ways diminished sense of selfhood from that embodied in the image of the headstrong self-made man" (Lears 1981, 37).

1. Fox, " The Honorable Levi K. Fuller of Vermont," *ROSB* 1, no. 1 (Feb. 1987): 17.

2. Child 1884, 94; Brattleboro Board of Trade 1886, 23.

3. Brattleboro Board of Trade 1886, 23.

4. An 1892 issue of the *Musical Courier* lists a full accounting of the extent of Fuller's tuning fork collection.

5. Fuller was most impressed by the quality of the tuning forks made by Valentine & Carr of Sheffield, England, and Rudolph Koenig of Paris, and was particularly proud of having acquired a set of the twelve chromatically tuned forks used in Koenig's famous experiments confirming the accuracy of the Helmholtz theory.

6. By the turn of the century, Fuller's tuning fork collection was valued at $10,000. Circulated among antique dealers for many years, the remains of his collection were auctioned off in New York City late in the twentieth century.

7. "The International pitch of A = 435 was settled upon in France in 1859, and likewise at the Vienna Congress in 1887. The English retained their A = 450 for many years. The present international standard (which was originally adopted in 1834 by a congress of physicists as 'Stuttgart Pitch') sets Concert A at 440 Hz" (*ROSB* 1, no. 1 (Feb. 1987): 18). A complete table of international pitch developments through 1880 is published in Helmholtz 1954, Appendix XX, 493–513.

8. Dolge 1972, 365.

9. Estey catalogue 1871.

10. One can only imagine the visual impression of Estey's buildings on a Vermont winter's eve, gaslight picturesquely shining through glistening, frosted windows. Viewed from below, it must have seemed as if the Wizard of Oz himself was working his magic atop the hill.

11. *Vermont Phoenix*, May 6, 1870.

12. *Vermont Phoenix*, Sept. 22, 1875.

13. It is extremely important that wood be properly seasoned to guard against the possibility of splitting and warping; Estey's process reduced the moisture content of the wood to an exceptionally low 10 percent.

14. The woodwork in Estey's bellows construction was a form of plywood consisting of three layers of wood arranged so the grains of each layer were in opposition to the one next to it, thus insuring flatness and stability. Intake holes were covered with sumac-tanned sheepskin. Estey's specially made rubber cloth bellows were promised to last a lifetime.

15. *Frank Leslie's Illustrated Newspaper*, mid-1870s.

16. A reed organ's "action" consists of the soundboard, reed cell board, swells and couplers, keys, and stop action. Estey used high-grade felt and soft white leather for valve coverings and quality nickeled brass wire for the springs that held the valves in place, and his "sounding board" was made from New England old-growth, quarter-sawn spruce. The reed cell board—a multitude of small wood chambers, each routed to accommodate tonal requirements and to hold every reed firmly in place thus preventing rattles under pressure—requires precision machining to the thousandth of an inch. The octave couplers are made of bent wires that connected each valve with a corresponding valve—an octave higher in the treble and an octave lower in the bass—thus "doubling" the volume of sound. The swell constitutes a knee-operated shutter that, when lifted, creates a crescendo effect. Estey's keys were made in the factory (many makers bought keys from other companies) from white basswood boards that, to insure dimensional stability, were sawn when the log was frozen, then covered with polished, ivorylike "fiberloid" material. The stop action, mounted through the stop board with slides of hard maple, connects coppered wires to mute strips or stops over various set of reeds. Pulling a stop opens a mute and activates the reeds. (See Whiting 1981, 79–81, for a more expansive exposé, written by the Estey company, regarding the "Details of [Organ] Construction.")

17. *Vermont Phoenix*, Dec. 9, 1870.

18. According to available numbers, it appears that the firm of Mason & Hamlin was outstripping Estey. In 1870 they were recorded to have made more than 6,000 instruments worth $1.3 million, about one-quarter of the entire industry's output (Kettel 1872, 434). Estey had produced only about half that number for the year. However, as noted, Estey's numbers were rapidly increasing.

19. E. A. Boadway, organist and restorer, showed me several Estey organs in and around the town of Claremont, New Hampshire, which was a booming mill town during the nineteenth century. We examined contrasting Estey models in several churches, a lodge hall, a residence, a funeral home, and a school— settings the same as they were more than a hundred years ago.

20. One building was added to each end of the existing rank. Officially, these are designated Number 2 and Number 7 because of their place in the eventual set of eight buildings.

21. Local folklore has it that the chimney stood, "one hundred years long and one hundred thousand bricks strong," until, as some claim, it was declared too much of a temptation for adventurous children and disassembled by the Renaud brothers, who sold the bricks at a profit (Ned Phoenix and Barbara George, personal communication).

22. In addition to displaying his products at the 1876 Philadelphia Centennial Exposition, Estey sent his son's military organization, the "Estey Guards," to parade and thus bring more attention to his product. No doubt Estey realized that the 450 acre exhibition in Fairmount Park, viewed by ten million people, symbolized the nation's love affair with machinery. Trade fairs and grand expositions like the one in Philadelphia provided high-profile showcases for manufacturers' products and, since they were juried by experts, prestige in the marketplace. They also offered Americans "the promise that the industrial arts, in forms that they had formerly associated with an aristo-

cratic style of living, might now be made available to them at affordable prices" (Pulos 1983, 142).

23. Kouwenhoven 1948, 28.

24. Fears that the public would be disappointed were unfounded once the Centennial opened. The Corliss machine was a great attraction, and even its severest critics admitted that the engine looked "much better in motion than it did when standing still." "People said all the fine things that duty required about the pictures and statues in Memorial Hall, but in the presence of the Corliss engine, they were exalted. It stood there at the center of the twelve-acre building, towering forty feet above its platform, not an idealization but an unmitigated fact. Yet to the thousands who saw it, it was more than merely the motive power for the miles of shafting which belted their energy to machines throughout the building" (Kouwenhoven 1948, 28). See also Kasson 1976, 161–64.

25. Though the engine was named after its manufacturer, George Corliss, it is a little-known fact (except to steam engine enthusiasts) that the credit for its design, efficient production, installation, and smooth operation belongs to Corliss's supervisor, Nathaniel G. Herreshoff, a mechanical genius deservedly characterized by his peers as an engineering wizard (R. Merriam 1976).

26. *Vermont Phoenix*, Aug. 19, 1892.

27. Rudyard Kipling lived in Brattleboro for several years toward the end of the century. About local progress he remarked: "Not much more than a generation ago these farms made their own clothes, soap, and candles, and killed their own meat thrice a year, beef, veal, and pig, and sat still between-times. Now they buy shop-made clothes, patent soaps, and kerosene" (Kipling, "Seasons in Brattleboro," cited in Bassett 1967, 101). And this was only the beginning. According to a turn-of-the-century Vermont historian, "The period [to the middle of the nineteenth century] . . . was one of local effort. Grist mills, and saw mills and carding machines and fulling mills and tanneries were

thickly distributed through the State. Shoemakers, blacksmiths and tailors were numerous. . . . Some important industrial changes have taken place during the last fifty years. Several business enterprises begun during this period still continue and have become famous. . . . The local manufacture of boots and shoes has nearly ceased, and men's and boys' clothing is mostly brought from the cities ready made. Many ladies make their selections by samples and purchase their dress goods from the great retail stores of Boston, New York and Philadelphia. These are only samples of changes completed or in progress" (Conant 1890, 153–54, 180–81).

28. "The American fascination with the machine either in its Promethean or in its demonic aspect tended to divert attention from the countless small innovations at the work place. . . . Technological change in these years consisted of vast interrelated pattern of novelty, developments in metallurgy, mining, chemistry, hydraulics, electricity feeding back into each other. The result was new materials —such as hard steel, new lubricants for high-powered machines, new abrasives for grinding, new machine parts such as ball bearings—and improved machines, turret lathes, and milling machines for the precision-making of machines and tools themselves. With steam power prevailing in the 1870's, machines grew bigger and faster, and factories resembled jungles of shafts, belts, axles, and gears to transmit power from immense prime movers. By the late 1880's, industrial applications of electricity had already appeared, especially after the development, by Edison and others, of a central generating source" (Trachtenberg 1982, 55).

29. "Professional, white-collar personnel expanded the size and influence of office and laboratory, both increasingly distant from the shop floor but increasingly pertinent to the daily arrangements and pace of factory life. Calculations of economy and of science developed into professional processes with their own skills and rules, but in the end their effects were felt in the chang-ing relations between human labor and machines, in the steady encroachment of mechanization on the forms of work, of everyday life, and social transactions throughout America" (ibid., 63).

30. The reader is referred to Whiting 1981 for a partial reproduction of this catalogue. It also appears in the 1996 edition.

31. Here the Victorian quest for merging art and science is satisfied through the artistic endeavor of creating variety of sound by scientifically manipulating various ingenious mechanical devices. In this regard, the public was often duped by unscrupulous manufacturers into thinking they were getting something they were not. In extreme cases, pulling a stop knob might do absolutely nothing at all. But "Estey, unlike Beatty [and others], was an honest man. He and his successors never went for gadgetry in the organ. Actions and sounds were straightforward and instruments were well-made and reliable. It is true when advertisers say, 'quality + hype = reputation'" (Ned Phoenix, personal communication).

32. *Vermont Phoenix*, Sept. 19, 1894.

33. The Henkel family immigrated to the United States from Momberg, Germany, in 1850. Records indicate that Charles Henkel, one of four children, worked for Estey in 1860, which, by family accounts, made him seventeen years old. He became an expert woodcarver and designer for the company and signed many of the organs he worked on. Henkel's talents, like those of many craftsmen of the day, went beyond the ordinary. He patented cast-brass revolving hat hooks for use on Pullman trains and an innovative metal cap for chimneys.

34. Known for many years as Vermont National, the bank was recently sold to Chitterden Bank.

35. Confusingly, the firm continued to label organs "J. Estey & Co." well into the 1880s.

36. Trachtenberg 1982, 82–84.

37. Hirsch 1978, 13.

38. Ibid., xxvii.

39. Faler 1981, 29.

40. Between 1881 and 1905 there were close to 37,000 strikes involving seven million workers. The strikes of the 1880s crested in what historians refer to as "the Great Upheaval of 1886, the year of the Knights of Labor's great strike against Jay Gould's railroad in the Southwest, the peak of agitation for an eight-hour day, and the Haymarket riot in Chicago" (Trachtenberg 1982, 71). For an interesting interpretation of the Chicago Haymarket Square riot and its causes, see Trachtenberg 1982, 88–100.

41. Ord-Hume 1986, 55.

42. Dolge 1972, 365.

43. In Vermont the Estey company was compared to two other of the state's successful manufacturing enterprises, Fairbanks in scales and the Proctors in marble.

44. Evidently not connected with the family of Henry Kirk White, who for twelve years worked as superintendent of Estey's tuning department, during which time he taught his three sons the art of reed organ building. After leaving Estey, he figured prominently in the establishment of a number of firms: the Beatty, Cornish, Beethoven, and Gem companies all benefited from White's dedication and expertise. Henry K. White and his sons—James H., Edward H., and Howard—went on to start an organ factory in 1877 with H. C. Wilcox in Meriden, Connecticut, forming the Wilcox & White Organ Company, an enterprise that excelled in the production of "automatic" or self-playing instruments. See Jewell 1985 for a synopsis of the White family's activities.

45. The development and merchandising of "player" keyboard instruments is a fascinating story of invention and salesmanship. One such manufacturer, the George P. Bent Company of Chicago (1881–1949), made a player piano called the Combinola, which consisted of a piano keyboard, one organ manual, and a pedal board. Its distinction was its use of a variety of vibrating, sound-producing sources—hardwood, softwood, aluminum, steel, and sometimes glass, as well as a bass made of buggy springs—that were activated by electromagnets. See Bowers 1972 for a full treatment of this subject.

46. Faler 1981, ix–xii.

47. From a speech by the Honorable J. L. Martin on August 17, 1892, upon the completion of the Estey Company's 250,000th organ.

48. Estey Company Benefit Association.

49. *Vermont Phoenix*, Dec. 15, 1893.

50. Benefit Association pamphlet, 1908.

51. *Vermont Phoenix*, June 16, 1882.

52. H. Barry et al. 1974, 140.

53. *Vermont Phoenix*, Apr. 1, 1887.

54. *Vermont Phoenix*, May 6, 1887. It was important for other reasons for men and women to cooperate, for though it is hard to ascertain, inspection of one of the main structures reveals only one toilet for the entire building! It appears that everyone used the same facility (Richard M. Mitchell, personal communication).

55. *Vermont Phoenix*, Apr. 9, 1875.

56. In contrast to many industrial efforts, building an Estey organ required rather highly skilled labor. Mechanization notwithstanding, the reed organ still demanded a great deal of hand craftsmanship. It was more labor intensive than capital intensive. In industrial terms, rising production numbers did not necessarily mean an increase in production efficiencies. Alfred D. Chandler and other business historians differentiate between "center" firms, those that truly became "big business," and "peripheral" firms like Estey's, those that were unable to achieve the monopolistic oligopolies that distinguished center firms. The center firms were able to actually control their markets, impact the national economy, and make major improvements in production efficiency.

57. *Music Trades Review*, Apr. 3, 1877.

58. Dolge 1972, 364.

59. Child 1884, 891.

60. In 1972 Estey Hall was designated a historic

site by the Historic Properties Commission of the City of Raleigh and is listed on the National Register of Historic Places. In 1976 members of a biracial corporation, the Estey Hall Foundation, collaborated to renovate the building as a multipurpose community center at the hub of Raleigh's revitalized downtown area. Suitable for meetings, offices, studios, and exhibits, the hall also houses a small auditorium, eating area, and gallery space. Today, Shaw University has a twenty-five-acre campus and a population of over two thousand students and is accredited to award degrees in more than twenty-five fields of learning.

61. This interest in institutional development was a common activity among many wealthy American businessmen.

62. *Rutland Globe*, July 21, 1876.

63. The importance of these paramilitary groups in small-town New England life cannot be overemphasized. During this period every able-bodied man was obliged to join and train in the militia and "was expected to supply his own weapon and accouterments [sic] at his own expense and to attend annual muster days for training. The volunteer units began to take on the status of elite organizations. The elitism was often social as well as military. Prominent society leaders were frequently military officers, and these militia units were important participants in all civic and patriotic functions. Music has always been closely associated with military activities" (Camus 1998, 151).

64. *Musical Courier*, Sept. 3, 1884.

65. Child 1884, 879.

66. If a sampling of the neighboring southern New Hampshire area is any indication — there are bands in Hinsdale, Peterborough, Marlow, East Sullivan, East Jaffrey, Keene, and many other towns — New England was teeming with bands during the final decades of the 1800s. "The town band was a typical product of town pride, an object of rivalry with other towns; but it was also entertainment and the exemplar of unity and morale. The town band traveled to other towns as official emissary and in its own town played at ceremonial occasions, parades, reunions, fairs, lodge picnics" (Lingeman 1980, 298).

67. "W. H. Dana wrote in 1878, 'A town without its brass band is as much in need of sympathy as a church without a choir. The spirit of a place is recognized in its band.' Sherwood Anderson echoed, 'What does a band mean to a town? Better ask what is a town without a band'" (Proper 1998, 163–64).

68. *Vermont Phoenix*, January 20, 1893. Social dance helped feed the Victorian desire for music, ceremony, and gentility. "The consumer revolution in dancing and manners was driven by a 'public hungry for self-improvement and for places and occasions to demonstrate their acquisitions and achievements.'" Sociopsychologically, codes of conduct established through "ritualized" social dance were a "fierce attempt by those in power to keep newcomers at a respectable distance" (Keller 1998, 16).

69. *Frank Leslie's Illustrated Newspaper*, mid-1870s.

70. The Constitution of the United States guaranteed citizens protection for their inventions: "The Congress shall have power to promote the progress of science and useful arts, by securing for limited times to authors and inventors the exclusive rights to their respective writings and discoveries." Initially protection was for seven years, renewable for another seven years, until in 1861 the period was extended to seventeen years with no renewal. Patent laws offered the promise of recognition and reward, which effectively spurred the American "mechanic" to sometimes obsessive flights of ingenuity. The middle of the century witnessed the results of such incentives and consequent endless litigation between inventors and manufacturers.

71. U.S. Supreme Court Cases 1883, 109:1058.

72. Cabot 1922, 630.

73. *Musical Courier*, Feb. 5, 1890.

74. Thompson 1967, 58–63.

75. Hirsch 1978, 9.

76. "Measurement of work by units of time was basic to the accounting system of the productive process. Measurement by time represented the transformation of the laborer's efforts, his skills, intelligence, and muscle power, into a salable commodity: his own labor converted into a market value, into wages." (Trachtenberg 1982, 91).

77. The clock on building Number 5 (presumed to be a Seth Thomas) is an eight-day clock and by any measure an antique. The clock fell into disrepair in the 1950s. In the early 1960s Hyacinth Renaud had the clock repaired, but it worked only for a while. "It has an important place in local history," said Renaud. "It ought to be running" (*Brattleboro Daily Reformer*, Oct. 3, 1963). As of this writing, the clock is not in working condition, though there are plans to restore it.

78. Smith 1967, 62. Cashman 1993, 13, reports that there were 37,000 miles of telegraph wire in 1865 and 215,000 miles by 1900.

79. *Vermont Phoenix*, 1896, 106.

80. The development of the telegraph and the ensuing communications onslaught is an enormously complex topic. By the Civil War, transnational and transatlantic news services such as the Associated Press, taking advantage of such inventions as the telegraph, telephone, typewriter, mechanical typesetters, and photoengraving machines, greatly accelerated the gathering and dissemination of news. Manufacturers, ever mindful of changing trends, were quick to exploit the emerging technologies. The connection between telegraph and reed organ—distributed by traveling salesmen, music emporiums, ministers, and mail-order catalogues—was no exception. There were often long delays between ordering a reed organ and its delivery. Relaying "special orders" via telegraph hastened the delivery process considerably. Since the cost of the telegram was based on the word, organ manufacturers such as Estey used short cryptic coded ciphers that described the exact model of reed organ desired. Code names were often a little unusual (examples from Estey include Gigantic, Gloomy, Geyser, Falsetto, Friar, Frenzy, Hatchets, Henchmen, Herbage, Gaudiness, Glandular, Gimlet, etc.) and had little to do with the product itself.

81. Cabot 1922, 615. It seems a little surprising that it took this long for a direct link to the factory, since the first telegraph message was sent from Brattleboro to Boston as early as 1850.

82. As with the telegraph, the telephone expedited the ordering and delivery process of manufactured goods significantly. The important difference, of course, is that the telephone transmits speech. In 1880 there were 54,000 telephones in service in the United States; in 1890, 234,000; in 1900, 1,300,000; and in 1910, 7,600,000 (Bourne 1978, 179). And by 1919 there were 27,298,026 miles of telephone wire connecting eleven million phones that handled thirty million exchanges a day.

83. The typewriter and mimeograph machine revolutionized communication, especially within the business sector. The typewriter was invented by Christopher L. Sholes in 1868 and reached "office size" by 1878. Its effects on the process of doing business are still felt today. (Bourne 1978, 193–94). A. B. Dick invented the mimeograph stencil duplicator in 1884. Like the typewriter, the mimeograph machine greatly facilitated copying and disseminating information, crucial for doing business in a fast-moving world. He sold the idea to Thomas Edison three years later.

84. The increasing number and accessibility of railroad heads and telegraph offices, in fact, acted as "transmission belts which fed goods and information to country stores at rural crossroads[,] . . . significant nodal points in an evolving structure of distribution . . . paving the way for the great mail-order and chain-store invasion of the countryside in the later 1880s and 1890s, the heyday of Sears

Roebuck, Montgomery Ward, and Woolworth's" (Trachtenberg 1982, 114–15).

85. Consult Giedion 1948 for an insightful analysis of how mechanization forever changed the dynamics of commerce in America.

86. *Vermont Phoenix*, May 6, 1887.

87. As attested by an Estey company "Consignment Agreement" dated Aug. 24, 1896: "Agents who handle the Estey Organ Co's goods on consignment, must sell their instruments exclusively, and any deviation from this rule relieves the Estey Organ Co. from any obligation to protect them in territory." Agents were required by contract to remit collections every week and record and report stock on hand each month. At the time, terms gave the agent 40 percent of the sale.

88. Schulz 1974, 100.

89. Some suggest that Estey's distribution system was perhaps modeled on the Kimball distribution system, which was in fact imitated by many firms in the organ and piano trade.

90. Nationally, discouraging figures such as a 95 percent rate of business failure in the 1870s and 1880s, resulting in part from the periodic panics and depressions of this period—in 1867, 1873, 1877, 1884, and 1893—were seen as only the ebb and flow of economic progress. The volatility of the situation is also revealed in a highly fluctuating currency: "In general, prices rose with increases in the money supply and fell with decreases. What cost $1.00 in 1860 cost $2.24 in 1865 (when the money supply was at its greatest) and fell successively as the money supply was reduced to $1.56 in 1870 and then to 99 cents in 1878. This reduction caused slow but grinding discomfort for masses of people, especially in a period when expanding commerce and industry increased the need for currency" (Cashman 1993, 250). Even as early as the 1830s, Alexis de Tocqueville (*Democracy in America*, 1835) foresaw the potential weakness of the American capitalistic system. As predicted, the numerous financial panics of the late nineteenth century,

eventually culminating in Black Friday, 1929, prove Tocqueville's assessment correct when he says, "I believe that the return of these commercial panics is an endemic disease of the democratic nations of our age. It may be rendered less dangerous, but it cannot be cured; because it does not originate in accidental circumstances, but in the temperament of these nations." Remarkably, Tocqueville's insights into such complex issues as national temperament, commercialization, and globalized economics are as relevant today as they were over 160 years ago.

91. An Estey brochure (post-1896) described the acclimatized organ: "All metal parts, such as pins, hooks, locks, screws, hinges, etc., are of brass, thus rendering them proof against rust; that as far as possible glue joints are avoided, but where of necessity they are introduced, waterproof glue is used; that the case is constructed of specially selected oak, prepared in such a manner as to minimize the danger resulting from the attacks of the boring insects peculiar to tropical countries, and that the construction of the case is such as to exclude all insects from the interior of the instrument." Experts agree that much of this description is simply advertising puffery; though these little organs were tough, none of them exhibited all the features described here (John Wessel, personal communication; E. A. Boadway, personal communication; Ned Phoenix, personal communication). Elsewhere in the brochure, Estey promises further precautions: "For shipment abroad our acclimatized organs are packed in a strong box lined with a specially prepared, chemicalized, waterproof paper, or with zinc (depending upon the destination and means of transportation) thus insuring their delivery in proper condition." The standard four-octave Style J. J. portable organ sold retail for $35.00, wholesale for $28.00. The more deluxe Style 2 featured four octaves with additional octave couplers and knee swell. It weighed sixty pounds and sold retail for $50.00. The less portable accli-

matized Church Organ weighed 354 pounds, had one five-octave set of Diapason-Melodia reeds, one five-octave set of Flute-Viola reeds, a two-and-a-half octave set of Violetta reeds, and a one-octave manual Sub-Bass. It sold for $140.00 (Estey brochure, after Dec. 1896).

92. *Augusta (Georgia) Chronicle and Constitutionalist*, Feb. 10, 1882.

93. By now the reader is aware that enormous amounts of wood were processed at the Estey factory. While most other organ manufacturers were city based and had to transport lumber some distance, the accessibility of wood was without doubt one of the reasons Estey remained in the Green Mountain area. Basically, pine, spruce, and maple were used for the action, chestnut for the case frame, and white oak or walnut (or, in less expensive models, birch stained to look like walnut) for the case. Rosewood veneer, used only for Estey's melodeons, was probably imported from either South America or India, and later walnut was shipped in from the Midwest.

94. As time went on, artisans who in the past had followed a piece from inception to sale were increasingly forced to participate in a more stratified arrangement: a team comprising designer, manufacturer, and merchandiser. "The preindustrial master craftsman was designer, maker and seller of his handiwork. Integration of these functions was simple and direct. But changing patterns of production, distribution and business organization have broken up the hitherto united functions which must be integrated in new and often more complex ways" (Wallance 1956, 3). As cooperative approaches to production diversified, hierarchies based on "scientific" organizational strategies evolved: managerial teams, draftsmen, craftsmen, engineers, tool makers, businessmen, accountants, lawyers, promotional agents, sales staff, shipping personnel, and others became part of the production stream. Further expansion led to hierarchies within hierarchies. As confirmation of this grow-

ing complexity of production processes, the final stage on a lengthy production line in Estey's New York piano factory, for example, was subdivided into the varnish department, bellymen department, stringers' department, fly finishing department, finishing department, regulating department, and polishing department. Departmental photographs of Estey employees, sometimes holding tools specific to their task, also attest to this specialization of labor.

95. Though it was mentioned that during his career Estey had the ability to "compel events to work toward his own ends" (*Vermont Phoenix*, Apr. 18, 1890), it is to his credit that there is seemingly no record of public criticism regarding his business methods or otherwise. I comment more on this later in this chapter.

96. *Vermont Phoenix*, June 18, 1880.

97. Whiting 1981, 3.

98. *Musical Courier*, Jan. 16, 1884.

99. Estey catalogue 1886.

100. Perhaps because Jacob Estey generally maintained a low profile, a rumor began in 1886 that he had died. The company quickly circulated a letter assuring customers that Mr. Estey was still alive and active in the business "six days a week," and that genuine Estey organs were continuing to come off the line (letter dated Apr. 12, 1886, signed by Jacob Estey).

101. Though John Boulton Simpson was president, Colonel Estey's sons soon took over a major portion of the responsibility of management (Sadie 1986, 58).

102. *Musical Courier*, Jan. 14, 1887, and Jan. 2, 1889, respectively.

103. Among the old-time songs on Estey's hit list are "America," "Annie Laurie," "Auld Lang Syne," "Battle Hymn of the Republic," "Columbia, the Gem of the Ocean," "Comin' through the Rye," "Dixie's Land," "Home, Sweet Home," "In the Gloaming," "Long, Long Ago," "My Old Kentucky Home," "Yankee Doodle," "Robin Adair," "The

Star-Spangled Banner," "Swanee River" ["The Old Folks at Home"], "Swing Low, Sweet Chariot," "The Last Rose of Summer," "The Blue Bells of Scotland," "The Old Oaken Bucket," and a small handful of other tunes that are less well known today.

104. The Philharmonic Society, begun in 1860 with a cornet, violin, "clarionet," and reed organ, was by this time a sixteen-piece orchestra, from which was drawn a "Philharmonic Quartet." Other music-related activity was evident when, in June of 1886, Fuller presented the town with an attractively landscaped park in Esteyville, which included a bandstand for the newly formed "Esteyville Brass Band." The Brattleboro community, in fact, has a history as rich in performance as in manufacturing. Historically, local talent frequently provided musical recitals, band performances, and theatrical presentations (with Julius Estey often in the lead role). In addition, classical theater troupes, concert bands (including John Philip Sousa's), and traveling shows of minstrels frequently played Brattleboro. More recently I attended several all-night contra and square dances in the 1980s that boasted a spirited "brass band" and numerous talented string bands. Today, the Legion band is comprised of music enthusiasts from around the Brattleboro area, and there is much activity, with both traditional and contemporary forms of music in evidence. The musical traditions of Brattleboro continue to be a vital form of community expression.

105. Fox, "The Honorable Levi K. Fuller of Vermont," *ROSB* 1, no. 1 (Feb. 1987): 17.

106. Cashman 1993, 93. "As labor troubles continued, increasing numbers of affluent citizens grew determined to fight. They armed themselves and their police as never before. President Charles W. Eliot of Harvard . . . began drilling riflemen . . . to defend propertied New Englanders against the eastward spread of rioting workers. Concerned community leaders banded into a number of vigilante 'Law and Order Leagues' during the 1880s. By the end of that decade, massive armories

brooded at the center of every American city— testimony to the official fears of domestic insurrection. Amid such precautions, warnings against the dark designs of labor leaders and anarchist assassins proliferated in the established press, and expectations of apocalyptic class warfare pervaded both fiction and journalism" (Lears 1981, 31).

107. *Vermont Phoenix*, Apr. 18, 1890.

108. "Interlude" was written by a high school student, Marilyn Moore. [*Brattleboro High School*] *Dial*, Nov. 1944.

109. Though Estey's manufacturing effort did not belong in the same category with the monopolistic center firms and the "robber barons" that ran them—Rockefeller in oil, Carnegie in steel, Swift in meat, Pillsbury in grain, Havemeyer in sugar, Weyerhaeuser in lumber, and Morgan in railroads, for example—he probably shared at least some of their character traits as mandated by their roles as leaders of industry. Cashman 1993, 40–42, ventures a portrayal: "The secret of their success lay in their acumen that amounted to vision, their avarice that was transformed into commercial foresight, and their attack that was equal to military strategy. . . . As a rule, robber barons were puritanical, parsimonious, and pious. . . . A new philosophy, Social Darwinism, justified the robber barons and their methods." The phrase "survival of the fittest," first coined by English journalist Herbert Spencer in 1852, described a laissez-faire form of economics that he felt would appropriately favor only the most intelligent, skillful (i.e., ruthless?) participants. Those who did not make the grade were expendable. Though Estey was certainly not of this school of thought, we can surmise that given his extraordinary success, he was capable of a high degree of resoluteness, determination, and pluck when forced to do combat on the marketplace battlefield of the late nineteenth century. Even Jacob Estey, who had as benevolent a reputation as any, must have had to steel a portion of himself for making difficult business decisions that

affected hundreds of peoples' lives. Besides some court proceedings, we know little of these moments.

110. Slotkin 1985, 115. "In factories and bureaucracies of organized capitalism, even the more fortunate workers were being reduced to the status of machine tenders or paper shufflers" (Lears 1981, 60).

Chapter 5. After Jacob Estey

1. *Presbyterian Journal,* Sept. 7, 1892. Special mention of Estey in this Philadelphia newspaper is probably due to representation of the Estey company by E. M. Bruce, a prominent Estey agent in that city.

2. Numbers differ depending on the source. The *Musical Courier,* for instance, reported 700 to 800 employees producing 1,300 organs per month and a monthly payroll of $30,000 (*Musical Courier,* Apr. 16, 1890). Whiting found information in the *General History of the Music Trades of America* (1891) that documented 500 workers producing up to 1,800 organs per month; see Appendix C for more perspectives on production numbers. Estey production tallies reflect a general trend in organ manufacture nationally. The census of 1900 offers a statistical analysis of organ building between 1860 (the previous census that dealt with instrument manufacture) and 1900. Though the results are based on combined pipe and reed organ computations, reed organ manufacture counted for at least 77.5 percent of the total for the two varieties; thus general contours are clearly revealed and retain reasonable validity for analysis of reed organ manufacture alone.

NATIONAL SUMMARY OF ORGAN
ESTABLISHMENTS AND WORKERS

	1860	1870	1880	1890	1900
Number of firms	60	98	171	145	129
Number of workers	716	1,967	4,202	4,608	3,435

It is also interesting to note the breakdown of workers by age and gender. The drop in child labor between 1880 and 1890 was caused by social outcry, the movement for compulsory schooling, and because men wanted the jobs.

NATIONAL SUMMARY OF MEN, WOMEN, AND
CHILDREN EMPLOYED IN THE ORGAN INDUSTRY

	1860	1870	1880	1890	1900
Men over 16	712	1,928	3,948	4,469	3,271
Women over 16	4	28	89	117	28
Children under 16	—	11	165	22	72

An analysis by state (Bureau of the Census 1902, 10:461) shows that the decline in the industry around 1890 occurred more or less evenly throughout the country. For a long time the eastern states claimed the greater part of organ manufacture. But overall Illinois achieved the highest production, accounting for an impressive 42 percent of the total volume (Bureau of the Census 1902, 10:462). This was the result of the general shift of manufacturing from east to west over the last half of the century, as well as Illinois's central location and the cheapness of raw materials in that region. As a railroad hub, Chicago was no doubt the main focus of activity, accounting for 17.6 percent of the total output for the United States. Further examination shows that organ manufacture was essentially a big-city industry—except, of course, for Estey in Brattleboro. In addition to Chicago, we find Boston, Worcester, Philadelphia, and St. Louis among the top-rank organ producers. Surprisingly, New York City ranked comparatively low in reed organ manufacture but was the highest producer by far in the piano industry. Other tables in the 1900 census show that the value of exported organs continued to increase even after the national value began to decrease, though it is not known how long this course of events continued (ibid., 464). Evidently the reed organ export business generally outpaced overseas trade in pianos, since in 1889 nearly twice as many organs as pianos were exported from the United States (*Musical Courier* 1889, 135). Though good pianos were made overseas, foreign manufacture of harmoniums and American organs never reached the production levels of the United States and Canada. By extrapolation (made easy since there were only two large reed organ companies in Vermont, Estey and E. P. Carpenter, compared to, for example, twenty-four in Massachusetts), we find Estey, despite his relative seclusion at the foot of the Green Mountains, among the most prolific manufacturers in the country; only Mason & Hamlin and Kimball approached Estey's level of production. Comparison of Estey's statistics with national averages shows that Estey maintained a high level of production longer than most organ businesses. National data suggest that production at other companies began to diminish well before 1890, whereas the Estey Organ Company seems not to have peaked until around 1894. Nevertheless, the downward trend continued: an Estey company letter dated 1897 expressed hopes that organ trade had "touched bottom" and would soon "take a step upward." As we know, the unfortunate truth was that prevailing taste continued to shift away from reed instruments.

3. Other reed organ manufacturers, such as Mason & Hamlin and Prescott, recognized the increasing popularity of the piano and established piano manufacturing shops. Well into the twentieth century, when Estey was still manufacturing reed organs, those other firms had given up reed organ production, though their reputations with reed organs had helped establish their fame as piano manufacturers.

4. *Vermont Phoenix*, Mar. 7, 1902.

5. Ibid.

6. Ibid. See *ROSB* 8, no. 1 (Feb. 1989): 27, for an interesting overview of the relationship between Julius J. Estey and Dwight L. Moody.

7. Ibid.

8. Whiting 1981, 4. Export to some countries was not, however, always lucrative. A short entry in the *Musical Courier* (Mar. 4, 1885, p. 38) gave an accounting of an Estey organ that had been presented to the Baptist Mission in Mexico City. Perhaps because of the firm's generosity to Baptist churches, the Estey Organ Company sold the organ for $100.00, half the original price. The final accounting, including the consular invoice and manifest, duties and municipal duties, stamps, the commission of 1.5 percent on the invoice value, and freight from Boston to Mexico City, totaled $119.68, or 120 percent in addition to its actual cost. "It needs no additional comment to prove that it is an impossibility to send pianos and organs to Mexico while the present restrictions exist" (ibid.).

9. *Vermont Phoenix*, Dec. 14, 1900.

10. From an Estey brochure issued after 1896, "Estey Portable Organs." There are many such stories and testimonials about the integrity of the Estey acclimatized organ. Another such verifying statement was related by Reverend F. W. Coan, who for twenty-five years was a missionary stationed in "Oroomiah, Persia": "Mr. Parmelee, of Erzeroum, took our Estey Organ out with him twelve years ago. After his return to America we sent to Trebizonde for it. It was brought again over the mountains six hundred miles on horseback, and was seven months in reaching Oroomiah. But with all this rough treatment and subsequent constant use, it has kept in perfect tune, not a reed has failed, and no part has ever needed repairs—save only the pedal carpets and straps—although our climate is a very dry and trying one to cabinet work." Gellerman documents another favorite story about a missionary in Africa who tells of an organ, not so well protected as the aforementioned, that fell into a river when a canoe capsized. After floating around for ten or fifteen minutes, the organ was rescued, but in dire need

of repair. The resourceful missionary writes that unlike organs made by other companies, the Estey organ was very easily restored to its original condition because of its logical and accessible construction (Gellerman 1996, 134).

11. Estey Canadian catalogue, early twentieth century.

12. *Presbyterian Journal*, Sept. 7, 1892.

13. The three-story brick home, named Florence Terrace (also known variously as the "Estey mansion" or the "Stoddard Place," after its builder), was architecturally Romanesque, or as described by one author, an Italian Renaissance Revival villa. The external features on Estey's home were predominantly wood, which was more common than brick in Victorian architecture. Architectural high points consisted of a gable on the north, with a veranda and coach porch, and a portico at the east and main entrance. The porch and portico were garnished with carved Corinthian capitals. The walls of the principal rooms were painted with a sand-hued finish, accented with woodwork of black walnut and oak. In the library, wall decorations were featured in hand-appliquéd relief in tints of gold and olive. Furniture occupying the library and dining room was upholstered in leather. The draperies in the hall and library were of silk plush in the Marie Antoinette style. Carpets throughout the house were described as Brussels, with the exception of one in the parlor by Wilton, a light drab carpet with a crimson border. The parlor woodwork was finished in enameled cream and gold, with the walls and elaborate curtains of silk damask and real lace. The dining room was largely oak, with draperies of flax velour ornamented with flights of birds embroidered by hand (possibly inspired by Julius J. Estey's hobby of raising pigeons). Folding doors between the parlor, library, reception room, hall, and dining room could be opened to accommodate large gatherings. The mansion also boasted "many choice fireplaces" for warmth and comfort during the long Vermont winters. The second-story chambers were furnished in blue, pink, green, drab, and other stylish hues. Servants' rooms were on the third floor and workrooms in the basement. It is also documented that Julius maintained an extensive wine cellar for occasional ceremonial festivities. Within the larger social sphere, the architectural and decorative elegance of Estey's home represented the good taste of the entire community, a fact especially important, for instance, when Julius J. entertained two United States presidents, William McKinley and Theodore Roosevelt. The home continued to be lived in until 1948, after which time it slowly deteriorated, particularly after 1958, when it was heavily damaged by vandalism and looting. In spite of plans in 1964 to renovate and remodel the structure as apartments, the building was unfortunately "shortsightedly smashed to bits in the autumn of 1971" (Richard M. Mitchell, personal communication).

14. The portrait of Estey hangs in Brattleboro's Brooks Memorial Library staff room. It is thought to have been reproduced from a photograph after Estey's death. The artist captured an agreeable likeness of the fabled and venerable Estey persona.

15. Schulz 1974, 116.

16. One result of the new entertainments was that the sentimental nostalgic tearjerkers of the Victorian repertoire were no longer an important part of Americans' musical diet. Personified by the type of popular music that became the stock-in-trade of Tin Pan Alley songwriters, a changing national temperament is clearly manifest in the musical fare popular around the turn of the century. From the Gay Nineties to World War I, songs such as "A Bicycle Built for Two" (Henry Dacre, 1892), "The Band Played On" (John Palmer, 1895), "Ida, Sweet as Apple Cider" (Eddie Leonard, 1903), "Sweet Adeline" (Harry Armstrong, 1903), "Shine On, Harvest Moon" (Nora Bayes and Jack Norworth, 1908), "Down by the Old Mill Stream" (Tell Taylor, 1910), "In the Shade of the Old Apple

Tree" (Beth Slater Whitson and Leo Friedman, 1910), "Oh, You Beautiful Doll" (A. Seymour Brown and Nat D. Ayer, 1911), "When Irish Eyes Are Smiling" (Ernest Ball, 1912), "Too-Ra-Loo-Ra-Loo-Ra" (James Royce Shannon, 1913), and "Margie" (Benny Davis, Con Conrad, and J. Russel Robinson, 1920) plainly indicate a new American self-confidence and joy unknown in earlier times. "People had shifted from a culture of domesticity centered on hearth and home to a culture of entertainment in public places, made possible in wondrous ways by urban electrification at the close of the nineteenth century" (Kammen 1999, 24). With the new technologies and entertainments came new issues. For example, penny arcades and nickelodeons (small storefront theaters named for the five-cent price of admission) had a huge impact on American culture. The invention of moving pictures, pioneered by Thomas Edison and others during the late 1800s, came into its own with nickelodeons (which first appeared in 1905 in Pittsburgh, Pa.). By 1908 an estimated ten million people were paying their nickels and dimes to see the latest films; by 1910, more than 10,000 nickelodeons had sprouted across the entire country; then, around 1914, they began to be replaced by larger theaters that featured longer films (*Grolier Multimedia Encyclopedia* 2000). The popularity of movies led to this country's first major bout of censorship. Moralists, police, politicians, and local censorship boards went overboard in exorcising "objectionable material" from films. They maintained that the masses needed protection from the raw realities of life (mostly sex, violence, and drugs), especially when they were "glamorized" through a movie camera. In a society that protects free speech, such issues remain problematic today.

17. Early vaudeville (a successor to minstrelsy) was largely a "stag" entertainment; by the 1890s it had largely been cleaned up and made more appropriate as a family pastime. See *Vaudeville* 1997 for an entertaining and insightful overview of this important form of American entertainment.

18. Braden 1992, 45–161.

19. Grier 1992, 49–74.

20. "Between 1885 and 1910 the commodification of exercise, competitive sport, and health cures became major manifestations of popular culture in the United States" (Kammen 1999, 52).

21. Schlereth 1991, 166. In the pompadour style, hair was piled more on top, with a treatment that emphasized the front, rather than the back of the head. A marcel, named after the French hairdresser Marcel Grateau, was more elaborate: a curling iron was used to create symmetrical waves that were arranged over the head. Unlike these two styles, the bob, an American creation fashionable after 1910, was close-cropped and straight.

22. Loesser 1954, 521.

23. Called a "piano player," "Pianola," or "push-up," the self-playing piano in its early stages of development consisted of a cabinet with a music roll or note sheet and a pneumatic valve and lever mechanism that, when mated with the front of an ordinary piano and pumped by pedals as on a reed organ, would activate wooden "fingers" that automatically depressed the appropriate keys. By the turn of the century, the apparatus was incorporated within the piano case itself, thus becoming the "player piano." See Sadie 1984, 3:131–33, for more information and resources on player pianos. "For historians, the most important development was the 'reproducing piano,' invented in Germany in 1904 and first made in the United States by the American Piano Company as the Ampico, and by the Aeolian Company as the Duo-Art, both in 1913. The Duo-Art was a player piano whose punched paper rolls captured the subtleties of performance, such as slight variations in tempo and loudness, so that it could personalize performances. The pianists of the day, such as Sergei Rachmaninoff, recorded for Duo-Art and spoke favor-

ably of the capacity of the instrument to present each artist as an individual stylist" (Borroff 1995, 159). Estey made many styles of player pianos and pipe organs but evidently manufactured a very limited number of player reed organs. The Aeolian Company in New York City had "succeeded in capturing probably 90% of the player reed organ market by 1905. What little remained of the market was split up among Wilcox & White, Estey, and a few other makers" (Bowers 1972, 743).

24. Whiting 1981, 100.

25. Wax cylinder phonographs were available to the public in 1903. The Victrola® first appeared on the market in 1906. "At the top of the 1910 Edison phonograph line stood the Amberola, with a sapphire 'reproducing point,' an oak or mahogany cabinet that enclosed the horn and held a hundred records, and a $200 price tag, about a third of a steelworker's annual wage. The lowest-priced Edison sold for $12.50. Each model appeared in the company's 1910 newspaper advertising in 420 cities" (Strasser 1989, 138).

26. "The vacuum tube, which was so important for the telephone, also had enormous impact on radio. Previously treated like, and indeed called wireless telegraphy, radio had the advantage that it could reach places that the ordinary telegraph couldn't, such as ships at sea. Skilled inventors like Edwin Howard Armstrong and Alan Hazeltine built radio receivers which made broadcasting a commercial possibility after the First World War. Although these two men worked largely alone, most of the work in this period was done in university or commercial laboratories. The combined effort brought the radio into increasing numbers of homes: 60,000 in 1922; 2.75 million in 1925; 14 million in 1930; 28 million in 1940" (Bourne 1978, 180).

27. Ragtime, named after its characteristic syncopated, "ragged" rhythm, is the preeminent musical symbol of the Gay Nineties. In the simplest of terms, its development was probably a mingling of the "coon song" and banjo-picking minstrel tradition seasoned with a dose of New Orleans–Caribbean bordello and dance-hall music. Played by "jig bands," the music eventually wandered up the Mississippi via riverboat commerce into the Midwest where it flowered, particularly in St. Louis. Though elements of ragtime had begun to emerge in the 1880s, it was from the 1890s to World War I that ragtime became the rage, especially following the enormous popularity of tunes such as Scott Joplin's "Maple Leaf Rag" (1899). Ragtime was a pianistic music from the beginning, and "the reed organ's inherent characteristics did not make it an instrument congenial with the style. The reed organ was now described as having a 'suffocating' sound, deadly and dull" (Schulz 1974, 115).

28. Schlereth 1991, 193.

29. Baldwin 1912, 8.

30. During the pivotal period from the turn of the century through the 1920s, when popular culture began to fully bloom, the requirements of business, industry, and society became increasingly complicated and enmeshed: commercialization became more intense and manipulative, consumption of contemporary products became a social necessity, and consumerism became an aggressive device of corporate survival. Mass consumer culture was soon to follow. See Kammen 1999 for a full discussion of these issues.

31. Whiting 1981, 46.

32. For several years the Bailey-Howe Library at the University of Vermont in Burlington archived an exceptionally large volume of Estey material pertaining to pipe organs. The thousands of file folders, all that survived as a unit from the office material, which was needlessly destroyed when the factory closed, were brought from Long Island, where they had been stored, to Burlington in a moving van at the expense of the university (E. A. Boadway, personal communication). The archive has since been moved back to Brattleboro

and is presently maintained by the Brattleboro Historical Society.

33. Sadie 1986, 58.

34. The "Haskell bass," a half-length version of open pipes, is still used throughout the world. Refinements in tubular-pneumatic action and electric action (used exclusively after 1930), labial and "reedless" reed stops, and "automatic" self-playing mechanisms flowed from the Estey drafting room until World War II (E. A. Boadway, personal communication).

35. From the beginning of Estey pipe organ manufacture to 1911, the company's instruments featured a distinctive stop configuration invented by Haskell that resembled a standard keyboard arrangement: white keys for "on" and black keys for "off." From a distance, it could be mistaken as an additional, very short manual. After 1911 this arrangement was changed to tilting tablets with names engraved on them (John Wessel, personal communication).

36. *Keene Sentinel*, Mar. 3, 1980.

37. *Vermont Historic Sites and Structures Survey* 1980: section 8-5.

38. *Keene Sentinel*, Mar. 3, 1980.

39. Estey Organ Company brochure, 1923.

40. *Brattleboro Daily Reformer*, May 20, 1930.

41. Ibid.

42. *Vermont Historic Sites and Structures Survey* 1980: section 8-5.

43. "Even before the turn of the century, popular music had become an important business, and songs were written for the purpose of making money. Songs with piano accompaniment were printed in sheet music form and sold in amazing quantities. They were made popular by variety show and music theater performances, piano rolls, and the hardworking song pluggers. In the 1920s, the new recording industry began to assume some of this responsibility. Radio stations played popular recordings in the thirties, but it was yet another decade before radio became influential in deter-

mining the popularity of a song" (Ferris 1990, 126). See also Kingman 1979, 267–71 and Crawford 2001, 714–813; Ennis 1992, 17–99.

44. Howard 1930, 600. From his unique chronological viewpoint, Howard sums up his ideas regarding jazz: "Jazz is American, probably the most American thing we have yet produced. Its Americanism is found both in its sources and in its character. Some of it comes from the Negro; from the blues and the spirituals; from the shouts of the revival meetings. Take these to Broadway and you get jazz. The result is something that reflects the feverish pace of modern life, our jauntiness and our frivolity, and in between, our sentimentality" (591).

45. *Brattleboro Daily Reformer*, Sept. 5, 1930, and Mar. 22, 1932. It is the work of specialists such as Ned Phoenix, of Townshend, Vt.; E. A. Boadway, of Claremont, N.H.; and Laurence Leonard of Laconia, N.H., along with particular members of the Brattleboro Historical Society, who continue to conserve reed organs and collect and archive important historical ephemera, which will preserve for future generations the charm and past circumstance of these important Victorian instruments. In this spirit, a group of citizens are organizing a Brattleboro "Estey Museum" in one of the factory's slate-sided buildings.

46. From an Estey Organ Company broadside (c. 1931) reporting on the "New Estey Visual Instruction Organ." The new gimmickry was invented by Harry F. Waters, general manager of an Estey concern at 642 Fifth Avenue in New York City.

47. In 1941 a Children's Organ cost $25; a Children's Organ with motorized blower cost $40; the Junior Organ listed for $65; and the Junior Organ with motor was $85. Fake walnut or maple finish (not real walnut or maple but stained and finished to look genuine) was the standard. Painted finishes included black with silver trim, black with gold trim, green with buff trim, buff with green trim,

and buff with blue trim—quite a choice for something perceived as a mere toy.

48. Beginning in the 1910s, the Orgoblo, an electrically driven fan blower, was manufactured expressly for Estey by the Spencer Turbine Company of Hartford, Conn. See Whiting 1981, 116, for a diagram and explanation of the Orgoblo, reproduced from an Estey brochure.

49. *Brattleboro Daily Reformer*, Mar. 22, 1932, and Nov. 8, 1932. "The Minshall-Estey design was deemed unsuccessful, and was short-lived (though Mr. J. C. Hallman, of Ontario, Canada, improved the design and manufactured amplified "electronic" reed instruments until 1965, many of which are in use today). Minshall and Estey continued separately in the manufacture of electronic organs with vacuum tubes, not reeds, as impulse generators (oscillators)" (Ned Phoenix, personal communication). In addition to assessing Minshall as a partner, Estey also considered the innovative efforts of a Dr. Jesse Ballinger, who designed series of special transducers he called the "Translator," which could amplify the sound of a reed or pipe organ without distorting the instrument's tone. The negotiations broke down between Estey and Ballinger, and matters were eventually settled in court in 1956. Also see Edward F. Peterson's article (*ROSB* 5, no. 1 [Feb. 1986]) for an interesting account of manufacturers' early attempts to increase organ volume through electronic means.

50. Developed in the mid-1930s by Laurens Hammond and John M. Hanert, Hammond organs are probably the most successful electronic organs ever made. The Hammond "tone wheel" organ received its U.S. patent on April 24, 1934. "In the original instrument, a synchronous motor was used to turn 95 tone wheels the size of large coins. Each wheel was cut or indented differently. Pointing towards the edge of each wheel was a small chisel-shaped magnetic pickup, in which a tiny electrical signal was induced. The wheels spun at a fixed number of revolutions per minute, but their shape determined both the pitch and shape of the waveform induced in the pickup. Hammond designed the tone wheels to produce fundamental pitches (sine waves with no overtones or harmonics) and developed a system of drawbars (control mechanisms) which would enable the player to blend harmonics with fundamentals at varying volumes. The nine drawbars, each with nine possible settings, made it possible, so the manufacturers claimed, to create 253 million different musical tones." (Bacon 1981, 88–89). Like the reed organ, Hammond organs came in a variety of models intended for concert, home, and entertainment application with churches remaining a primary market. "The Hammond organ was purchased by some 1,750 churches in the first three years of its manufacture (a third of all sales). From 1936 until 1938 the company fought a legal battle with the Federal Trade Commission for the right to call the instrument an organ. . . . By the end of the 1930s the company was making about 200 instruments a month. . . . Hammond engineers took out over 50 US patents up to 1945 alone. . . . About 2 million Hammond organs in many different models have been built altogether" (Sadie 1984, 2: 120–21; also 1:690–91). From the 1950s into the 1960s Hammond's domination of the home organ market was continuously challenged by Lowery, Thomas, Wurlitzer, and other organ manufacturers. Compact solid-state transistors and integrated circuits soon superseded vacuum tubes and valves used in electronic organs up to the 1960s thus removing issues of size and reliability. Other keyboard innovation included the uniquely designed Mellotron, in which each note was produced by running a strip of recording tape across a replay head. Its ethereal "pillowy" texture was used by various rock groups including the Beatles, King Crimson, and especially the Moody Blues. Mention should also be made of the Fender-Rhodes collaboration which developed an electric piano during the

1950s and early 1960s using tunable steel tongues or rods which were struck by hammers and amplified by means of electromagnetic pickups, an idea also pursued by Wurlitzer. Rhodes developed several models from the mid-1960s into early 1970s and attracted top-drawer musicians including such notables as Chick Corea, Herbie Hancock, and Josef Zawinul. The idea of struck reeds "is an adaptation of the harmonium percussion action, with which hammers strike reed tongues, imparting an impulse and additional harmonics to the air-blown reed's initial sound. Electric piano reeds have no blocks (which are only necessary when air is used), but their principles are those of free reeds. The electronics for these instruments are modifications of the amplified reed organ concept" (Ned Phoenix, personal communication). The Hohner Pianet and Clavinet were two other electric pianos that gained some recognition during this period. By the 1980s Japanese companies like Casio and Yamaha were beginning to build and import miniature electronic keyboards; these soon accounted for half of all sales of these instruments. Other companies such as Korg and Roland also became dominant players in the electronic and synthesizer keyboard industry.

51. Gellerman 1996, 132–41.

52. Ned Phoenix reports (Oct. 1998): "In the 1970s, I tried to track these down . . . called a few military men . . . heard stories of government quonset huts full of broken, unplaying field organs, rotting on an island."

53. "Of the several hundred American reed organ manufacturers before 1900, by the third decade of the twentieth century only three of any importance survived: the Estey Organ Company; the Hinners Organ Company of Pekin, Illinois, manufacturers of pipe and reed organs, and legally dissolved in 1942; and the A. L. White Company of Chicago, manufacturers of small portable reed organs, and liquidated in December, 1956" (Whiting 1981, 4).

54. Wessel goes on to recount arising difficulties between Rieger and Hancock. As most of the Rieger organs sold in the United States fell apart, they were understandably sent back to Estey, at which point Estey (Hancock) had to refund customers' money. Hancock saw no reason to pay Rieger for organs returned or not yet sold, since Estey had to dismantle and completely restore each one to make them saleable. The interruption of cash flow caused Rieger's owner to complain about Hancock not paying for all the organs Rieger sent to Estey. This situation naturally further crippled the recovery of the Estey enterprise.

55. The Everett Orgatron was "an electric organ whose sound was created by blowing air over metal reeds to make them vibrate and then transforming the movement into an electrical signal with electrostatic pickups. Wurlitzer, the American organ company famous for their ubiquitous cinema organs, took up this principle from the Everett Piano Company and eventually turned this 'piano-to-organ' evolution full circle when they came up with a new design of electric piano using the reed system. . . . Unlike its organ ancestors, the Wurlitzer electric piano uses a simplified piano action to strike the metal reeds, causing them to vibrate. These vibrations are transduced into an electrical signal, amplified, and then fed either to the instrument's own power amp and speakers, or to an external amplification system" (Bacon 1981, 96).

56. Bode's organ was based on a model designed in 1951 that had a six-octave keyboard, one octave of pedals, and twelve oscillators to generate sound (Sadie 1984, 1:720).

57. Apparently the management ordered the workers to economize on nails and other materials, with the result that many of the reed organs came apart even before they reached their destination (John Wessel, personal communication). Edwin W. Phoenix, a worker in the case shop through this period and the father of Ned Phoenix, said that heating in the assembly rooms was also curtailed,

so when hot glue was applied to component parts, the materials were too cold for the glue to take. The result again was that the cases fell apart (Ned Phoenix, personal communication).

58. Bernhard brought in a council of "three experienced executives," M. W. Jacone, H. G. Schaub, and Devereaux Martin, as vice presidents to help buttress the failing company. John Wessel comments, "At least Hancock knew what an organ was." Evidently Bernhard (and his appointed supervisors who ran the factory) had limited working knowledge of the special requirements necessary for manufacturing a top-notch organ. The last half of the 1950s saw a tangle of mergers, dissolutions, shifting management, employee layoffs, and court litigation. The *Brattleboro Daily Reformer* provides the most coherent chronology of these complex events.

59. Estey Organ Corporation (Del.) 1957, 3.

60. Ibid.

61. Ibid., 4.

62. The reeds were actual accordion reeds with steel tongues on aluminum plates.

63. In fact, no such sentimentality occurred. According to John Wessel, a witness to the completion of the final organ, the instrument was erected, tested, dismantled, and shipped without fanfare to All Angels' Episcopal Church, West Eightieth Street, New York City. The three-manual Opus 3261 was broken up when the church was demolished in 1979.

64. At the closing of the factory, three Estey alumni—Elroy Hewitt (who had left in 1958), John Wessel, and Claude Carr—affiliated and continued to build organs in a small way at their homes. In 1964 they centralized their workshop on the second floor of a building (the "Bee Barn") in Guilford, Vermont, which conveniently housed R. V. Anderson & Sons, makers of organ pipes, on the first floor. The collaboration was at that time the only start-to-finish pipe organ manufacturing firm in Vermont. With churches as their principal customers, the trio of veteran craftsmen also covered a large area in maintenance work. Hewitt died in 1966 and Carr a few years later. Wessel continued to build and maintain organs until he retired in 1997 at the age of 75. Mention needs also to be made of Charles H. Gunzinger, who spent most of his adult life working for the Estey company. Primarily a pipe voicer, he also worked with reed organs. Until his passing in 1974, Gunzinger benefited many as a source for hard-to-find Estey items, especially reeds. There were other little-known Estey employees who also did independent general organ maintenance and repair for people after the company closed in 1960.

65. There is some confusion as to various name changes and corporate trading during this period. Another reference (no citation) recorded that in 1961 the Estey Musical Instrument Corporation joined Estronics, Inc. Many of these adjustments might have been an attempt to save the business through manipulation of paper.

66. Two exceptions include the now classic 1925 rendition (*The Smithsonian Collection of Classic Jazz*, 1973 [P6 11891, Columbia]) of "The St. Louis Blues" with Bessie Smith and Louis Armstrong, with Fred Longshaw on reed organ (brand unknown), and a more obscure Fats Waller recording of the "Lenox Avenue Blues" (recorded on Nov. 17, 1926, Camden) on the Estey pipe organ in a church that Victor had converted into a recording studio. Folklore mentions Waller commenting about playing the "God Box," though it is doubtful he was speaking of that particular Estey instrument. It is supposed that further research would turn up more examples of organs in early blues and jazz. With the advent of swing jazz and the high-powered big-band format in the mid-1930s, Americans went dance crazy. Organs simply did not fit in with ensembles of trumpets, trombones, saxophones, and forceful rhythm sections. Benny Carter, Fletcher Henderson, Duke Ellington, Tommy and Jimmy Dorsey, Artie Shaw, Glenn

Miller, Benny Goodman, Count Basie, and Paul Whiteman became tremendously popular during this time. With the early 1940s, overlapping with the end of the big-band craze, came bebop, a small-ensemble music that innovators such as Charlie Parker, Thelonious Monk, Dizzy Gillespie, and John Coltrane took to new levels of abstraction and technical requirement.

67. From the folk-music revival to avant-garde electronic music experiments, the period between 1950 and 1965 was filled with musical innovation. With such diverse landmark musical fare as Elvis Presley's "Hound Dog" (1950); John Cage's *4'33"* (1954); Louis and Bebe Barron's score for *Forbidden Planet*, the first electronic film score (1956); Johnny Cash's "Folsom Prison Blues" (1956); Chuck Berry's "Johnny B. Goode" (1958); the founding of the Columbia-Princeton Electronic Music Center (1959); the arrival of the Beatles (c. 1964), John Coltrane's *A Love Supreme* (1964); and Bob Dylan's "Highway 61 Revisited" (1965), it is easy to understand why the reed organ continued to fall by the wayside.

68. The Hammond B3, introduced in 1955 and phased out in 1974, became one of the great classic keyboards of all time, so much so that computer software is available that can reproduce the B3's distinctive sound—complete with rotating Leslie speaker—with amazing accuracy. As of this writing, vintage B3s are valued at several thousand dollars.

69. Thomas A. Dorsey, Roosevelt Sykes, Fats Domino, Little Richard, Jerry Lee Lewis, and Ray Charles exemplify this blues/gospel/r & b/honky-tonk category of pianists.

70. See Kammen 1999 for a thorough discussion of issues surrounding the development of popular culture in America and its consequent devolution into mass culture.

71. Milton Babbitt and other "experimentalist" art music composers (particularly in Europe) devised various techniques to modify and "shape"

sound, including manipulating magnetic tape (called *musique concrète*) and synthesizing new timbres by plugging into electronic oscillators and altering sound waves through a process of filtering particular harmonics. Much of this music was extremely abstract and overly intellectualized and thus never caught the fancy of the general population.

72. The Moog (rhymes with vogue) synthesizer was one of a generation of analog instruments developed beginning around the mid-1960s. Facilitated by cheap semiconductor technology, Moog's early monophonic model consisted of two short organlike keyboards and three cabinets with panels that contained knobs and jacks similar to a telephone switchboard so that various elements in the synthesizer could be linked or patched to each other. Through skilled programming, manipulation of sound filters and voltage regulators (which modeled sound waves internally), and multitracking recording techniques (single lines of music recorded separately, then mixed), the Moog created new, unusual aural sensations that sounded "bigger than life." Subsequent development of polyphonic keyboards and microprocessing technology from about 1975 into the early 1980s eventually saw markets flooded with progressively more powerful synthesizer "workstations" that increasingly incorporated more digital elements.

73. Walter Carlos's album *Switched-On Bach* (1968, Columbia), consisting of an all-Bach program performed on a Moog synthesizer, was a colossal hit with the public. Patient overdubbing of parts in the recording studio allowed the monophonic keyboard to execute Bach's masterful contrapuntal polyphonies. (Carlos was smart to choose Bach, because no matter what you do to it, Bach's music shines, especially when rendered on what sounds like a gigantic, unearthly, futuristic church organ.) Perhaps more than any other audio production, *Switched-On Bach* demonstrated the marketability and popular potential of synthesized

music and provoked more research and innovation of keyboard-operated synthesizers.

74. Throughout history, cutting-edge technology was always immediately applied to musical instrument development. Thus it comes as no surprise that today's so-called keyboards, already bristling with increasing numbers of "plug-ins" and computer accessory components, will continue to incorporate innovative technologies and attract musicians of all stripes. Computer programming and digital recording hold many new benefits for the music professional—cut-and-paste capabilities, software that instantaneously prints out professional-looking scores in music notation, mechanisms that "burn" (record or duplicate) CDs and DVDs, connections to the Internet, and development of MP3 conventions—and have influenced the democratization and distribution of music to an profound degree. Unfortunately, though, because synthesizers can sound like almost anything and have such vast compositional capabilities, they potentially put scores of musicians out of business: why hire a whole band of musicians when one talented synthesizer player can furnish the same end result? A further discussion of digital technology, computer science, and the role of synthesizer keyboards in a techno-crazed society is beyond the scope of this study. Suffice it to say that industry-wide standardized conventions for audiovisual transmission over the Internet and current consolidation of globalized multimedia networks promise an exciting, if unpredictable, musical future.

75. Ned Phoenix, personal communication.

76. Barbara George, personal communication.

77. In India, the sruti box, a small, bellows-operated, free-reed instrument used primarily as a musical drone accompaniment in Indian classical music, is often played in addition to (or in lieu of) a tamboura, an Indian chordophone uniquely designed for the same purpose. Today small electronic units that simply plug in and emit the ap-

propriate undulating drone pitches are beginning to eclipse use of the sruti box, thus alleviating the need for a person to "play" the instrument.

78. As reported in Owen 1988, 242.

79. Small hand-pumped harmoniums with shortened keyboards are an essential component of Qawwali, an Islamic Sufi form of devotional music. In its most dynamic form, the music features an overall heterophonic texture with driving, highly embellished vocal lines shadowed closely by the accompanying sound of the harmonium. (The recordings of Nusrat Fateh Ali Khan are excellent exemplars of Qawwali.)

80. Roger and Judy Rowell reported in the mid-1980s (*ROSB* 5, no. 3 [Aug. 1986]: 30–32) that reed organs were still being manufactured in Japan, though it is not known whether reed organs continue to be made as of this writing. Recent communication with Lark in the Morning, a West Coast merchandiser of musical instruments from around the world, confirms that China is making small portable keyboard reed organs. Manufactured by the Pearl River Piano Group in Guangzhou, the five-octave, F-compass organs closely resemble Estey's missionary organs, except that the Chinese models do not appear to be foldable.

81. In addition to the usual hand-held variety, the author recently witnessed a large orchestral floor-standing sheng in Hong Kong with button keys like those found on the rocking melodeons of old. The main difference is the absence of bellows: the player activates the reeds by blowing through a mouthpiece, thus allowing musical articulation through tonguing and control of the breath flow. A Western (less sophisticated) counterpart to the sheng is the Melodica, a hand-held miniature keyboard activated by blowing through an attached tube. Used mostly as a music education device in schools at one time, it is now rarely played except by unconventional musicians, including the late jazz master Don Cherry.

82. Several celebrated concert organists, includ-

ing E. Power Biggs, Lynnwood Farnam, Joseph Bonnet, and Fernando Germani, preferred the reed organ for home practice. Biggs practiced on an Estey electropneumatic reed organ until he bought a Schlicker portable unit organ in 1953 (Smith 1988, 19).

83. *ROSB* 13, no. 1 (spring 1994). The Modernistic Organ described has an Action 98, and is number 446,349.

84. With the explosion and exploitation of digital recording technology by professional and amateur alike has come a deluge of popular musical styles and their hybridizations: rap, rave, techno, trance, industrial, world beat, ethnopop, cybertribal, Afropop, ethnopunk, new age, and ambient, to name but a few presently fashionable music types, are indicators of the increasing proliferation and globalization of music of all kinds. Naturally, as with all pop culture, many of these will pass into obscurity while others continue to metamorphose. Furthermore, faster computers with more storage space, enlarged bandwidth for information streaming, component integration and miniaturization, wireless and satellite systems, the development of the MP3 standard and other industry-wide standards to come, and an insatiable consumer interest in electronic devices will increasingly allow virtually anyone to share their audio and video creations with the world via the Internet. The current trend toward a globalized democratization of media will undoubtedly intensify competition among corporate, commercial, and independent interests. Pandora's digital box has only begun to divulge some amazing possibilities.

85. Over a century and a half ago, Alexis de Tocqueville assessed with uncanny accuracy the eventual direction of American media and popular culture (though there were no such terms in Tocqueville's day): "I fear that the productions of democratic poets [i.e., artists in general] may often be surcharged with immense and incoherent imagery, with exaggerated descriptions and strange creations; and that the fantastic beings of their brain may sometimes make us regret the world of reality" (Tocqueville 1835, 184).

86. By now, synthesized organ sounds are not particularly new. "What is different [today] is the quality of the sounds and the speed with which they are being adopted. Proponents say that with the increasingly sophisticated sampling techniques of digital technology, there is virtually no difference in sound between a true organ pipe and its digital impersonator. Any differences, they contend, are outweighed by the savings in money and space" (*New York Times*, July 27, 2000). "But, there is, and always will be, the strong sentiment among organists and organ builders that 'electronic substitutes' are simply appliances, 'toasters,'' and that, no matter the electronic or advertising devices, their sound always comes from *speakers*, it is not generated naturally by and in the air. Thus, true pipe organs will continue to be desired and built" (Ned Phoenix, personal communication). Though there is strong resistance to digital accommodation, many agree that portions of pipe organs in the future will have core ranks of pipes, augmented by digital enhancements for the largest, smallest, and most difficult to maintain pipes.

87. The future bodes well for the reed organ. Though it may never enjoy its past glory and a major revival is doubtful, the spirit of the reed organ will continue to find its way into our contemporary musical consciousness. Things that were of value in the past are often rediscovered, reinterpreted, reinvigorated, and reincorporated in the present, and considering the current interest in antiques and proliferation of various "retro" trends, a reed organ revival may not be out of the question. With so many new musics popping up every year and the endless quest for "cool" sensations, the reed organ will endure, for the sound of the reed organ will forever remain a classic.

1. Roger L. Reid, "Harry Partch, Composer and Instrument Builder," *ROSB* 16, no. 1 (spring 1997): 9–10; Reid, "Chromelodeons: The Adapted Reed Organs of Harry Partch," *ROSB* 16, no. 1 (spring 1997): 11–16. *Reed Organ Society Quarterly* [hereafter *ROSQ*] 16, no. 4 (winter 1997): 19, mentions reed organs played on recordings by Neil Young, Eric Clapton, and the Corner Shoppe (a British progressive rock group). I have restored (and tuned to A440) reed organs of various sizes that their owners play on recordings, as well as instruments for recording studios.

2. Ned Phoenix, "The Free Reed Forever," *ROSB* 11, no. 2 (summer 1992): 29–31.

3. Harmonium history and information may be found in Ord-Hume's *Harmonium* 1986; and Dom Adelard Bouvilliere, "The Harmonium: Its History, Its Literature," *ROSB* 2, no. 4 (Nov. 1983): 1–4; *ROSB* 3, no. 1 (Feb. 1984): 14–15; *ROSB* 3, no. 2 (May 1984): 21–22; *ROSB* 3, no. 3 (Aug. 1984): 28–29; *ROSB* 3, no. 4 (Nov. 1984): 14–15 (reprinted from *Caecilia* 60 [Jan.–Mar. 1934]: 1–3).

4. Opinion of Robert B. Whiting, *ROSB* 2, no. 2 (May 1983): 4. Also see opinions of John Ogasapian, Robert F. Gellerman, Horton Presley, James N. Richards, and John Morningstar, *ROSB* 3, no. 2 (May 1984): 7–9, 15–16; and opinions of Ian Thompson and of Pam and Phil Fluke, *ROSB* 3, no. 4 (Nov. 1984): 9–10.

5. Leonard H. Mauk, "The Tone Quality and Volume Level of Free Reed Operation with Vacuum or Pressure," *ROSB* 4, no. 1 (Feb. 1985): 27–28; Leonard Mauk, personal communication; Roger M. Rowell, "Reed Organ Display Gets Used," *ROSB* 15, no. 2 (autumn 1996): 19; Philip D. Koopman and James P. Cottingham, "Acoustical Properties of Free Reeds," *ROSB* 15, no. 3–4 (winter 1996): 17–23, esp. 20; James Cottingham, per-

sonal communication. See also Gellerman 1996, 89–90.

6. The harmonium's (usually) bright sound was appropriate for the music of its European church, home, and street venues. I feel that there is a psychological reason for American organ tone: those who had roughed the frontiers and fought a bitter civil war desired softness and comfort; therefore, where possible, they smothered all overtones of harshness. Conditions were ripe for the American organ: coincident with the attractiveness of the manufacturing economies of suction wind design, the American organ sound, caused by curved tongues and heavy cases, suited the sentiments and venues of the time and place, as expressed in gospel hymns, unadventurous voluntaries, and other "feel-good" music as heard on the companion compact disc.

7. See Appendix D of this volume and Whiting 1996 for specifications and descriptions.

8. At 8' pitch, the frequencies of a rank of pipes or reeds are the same as the pitches of a piano, violin, etc. Therefore, 32' pitch sounds two octaves lower than piano pitch; 16' pitch sounds one octave lower; 4' pitch sounds one octave higher; and 2' pitch sounds two octaves higher (see figure 115). Free reeds are much smaller than pipes of the same pitch. In addition to reeds, Shoninger Bell Organs, made in Connecticut, had thirty nested bells. Mustel, of Paris, included his Celesta with some of his harmoniums. Many harmoniums have a Percussion stop—small hammers that impart impetus and timbre to the tongue's initial movement. By design or luck, Hammond electric (tube) organs very successfully imitate the sound of harmonium reeds with percussion.

9. William Henderson, "Keyboard Compass, Divisions, and Wind Pressure of the Reed Organ," *ROSB* 14, no. 4 (Nov. 1985): 31.

10. Loesser 1954, 138.

11. Charles W. Landon, "Adapting Pipe Organ

Music to the Reed Organ," *ROSB* 13, no. 2 (summer 1994): 6 (reprinted from *Etude* [June 1915]).

12. Craig Cowing, "An Early Mason & Hamlin 'Organ Harmonium'," *ROSB* 11, no 2 (summer 1992): 14–18; Gellerman 1996, 94–97; *ROSB* 4, no. 2 (May 1985): 30, stop list of a Mason & Hamlin Organ-Harmonium from Ned Phoenix.

13. Also see "Mason & Hamlin Reed-Pipe Organ?" *ROSB* 8, no. 2 (May 1989): 19; reprint of a Mason & Hamlin advertisement from the *Kalamazoo (Michigan) Gazette*, Apr. 12, 1872, p. 1; and Pam and Phil Fluke, "Several Mysteries Solved," *ROSB* 7, no. 2 (May 1988): 20–22, esp. section entitled "Alexandre a la Mason & Hamlin."

14. Robert Gellerman, personal communication; James Tyler, personal communication.

15. Articles on Vocalions may be found in Gellerman 1998 and 1996, in publications of the Reed Organ Society, and in Ord-Hume 1986.

16. Reprint of a Hallman catalogue provided by E. E. Taylor, *ROSB* 8, no. 2 (May 1989): 6–7; Gary R. Schmidt, "Hallman Organs in Canada," *ROSQ* 16, no. 3 (autumn 1997): 9–13.

17. Sylvan K. Ketterman, personal communication. For more on S. K. K., see Ned Phoenix, "A Visit with Sylvan K. Ketterman," *ROSB* 3, no. 4 (Nov. 1984): 16–18; note from Sylvan Ketterman, *ROSB* 4, no. 1 (Feb. 1985): 21; *ROSB* 4, no. 2 (May 1985): 30, referencing an article by Grace E. McGinnis in *Theater Organist* 26, no. 6: 11; Gellerman 1998, 125, 126; Gellerman 1996, 31; and obituaries in the *Muncie (Indiana) Evening Press*, Oct. 26, 1993, p. 7, and the *Muncie Star*, Oct. 27, 1993, B5.

18. Paul Toelken, "Some Former Estey Employees," *ROSB* 7, no. 2 (May 1988): 18–19.

19. Leonard Mauk, "The Production of Tone in the Reed Organ," *ROSB* 6, no. 1 (Feb. 1987): 28–32; Leonard Mauk, personal communication; Keelyn W. Quigley and James P. Cottingham, "Analysis of Two American Reed Organs Using Long Time Average Spectra (LTAS)," *ROSB* 16, no. 1 (spring 1997): 23–30; James Cottingham, personal communication.

20. Gellerman 1996, 19.

21. Gellerman 1998, 69 (entry on Estey), 93 (entry on Hammond), 110 (entry on Ingalls), 167 (entry on Munroe), 171 (entry on Newell), and 263, 265 (entry on Whitney).

22. Beginning in 1901, lead alloy pipe metal for organ pipes was made next door in the casting shed. See Appendix C.

23. Rollin Smith, "E. Power Biggs and his Estey," *ROSB* 7, no. 3 (Aug. 1988): 19; Richard Epler, "The Estey Virtuoso," *ROSB* 12, no. 3 (autumn 1993): 11–15; Wendy S. Coleman, "My Estey Electropneumatic Two Manual and Pedal Reed Organ Apprenticeship," *ROSQ* 18, no. 2 (summer 1999): 6–16; Wesley L. Lewis, "A Reed Organ Recital," *ROSB* 4, no. 1 (Feb. 1985): 13.

24. Placing reeds in organ pipes was not a new idea. See Gellerman 1996, 7–8, 87, 88; and James M. Bratton, "Free Reeds in the Boston Music Hall Organ," *ROSB* 13, no. 3 (fall 1994): 15–17. Free reeds in pipes were used for reed stops in many pipe organs before striking reeds gained precedence early in the twentieth century. I have heard and examined the three remaining German-made, tunable free-reed ranks in the great 1863 Walcker organ in the Methuen Memorial Music Hall, Methuen, Massachusetts, which blend well with the original flue pipes, while its striking reeds, installed during the twentieth century, clash. The free-reed pipes in the 1908 Aeolian player Residential Pipe Organ in Hildene, Robert Todd Lincoln's mansion in Manchester, Vt., incorporate common American organ reeds installed diagonally in the boots of the pipes. Reed pipes in Estey pipe organs had striking reeds. Estey's "reedless reeds," which are overblown string pipes, were invented by Estey employee William E. Haskell, a genius who is best known for his half-length open flue pipes, known as "Haskell basses."

25. American organ reed blocks are all the same width and thickness throughout each scale and set, which is simplest for manufacturing blocks and boring the reed cells into which they fit. Estey blocks are sized in pairs; there are six block lengths for the twelve reeds that comprise each octave.

26. The cutter for hollowing out blocks was changed only two or three times throughout a five-octave set. "Hauling out" was the term, and no noun was used for the result; a block was either properly "hauled out," or it was not. "Undercut," the term in currency today, originated elsewhere.

27. As reported by L. B. Green, "L. B. Green Recalls Visit to the Estey Factory in 1967," ROSB 5, no. 1 (Feb. 1986): 14.

28. Early Estey melodeon reeds have a bump for the reed puller punched upward from the block material in the same manner as the rivets. Estey soon changed to their distinctive and more practical quarter moon-shaped nick (reed puller slot) for its common and Philharmonic scale reeds. Estey's other, larger reeds have rectangular slots (see figure 116).

29. Gellerman 1998, 263–65.

30. Cabot 1922, 633.

31. Gellerman 1998, 263, 265.

32. This chronology is gleaned from my years of restorations and recent research in my collection of reed organs and the collection of the Brattleboro Historical Society and confirms Estey's acquisition of Whitney's improved riveter. In sets of reeds with two rivets the treble reeds have only one rivet of the same small size as the double rivets (figure 117, [11–13]).

33. Worcester, Mass., like Brattleboro, Vt., was an important reed organ town; it may not be a coincidence that Jacob Estey lived in and around Worcester from 1828 to 1834. E. P. Carpenter (son of E. B. Carpenter, who was an early partner in the Estey chronology, including E. B. Carpenter &

Company) made reed organs in Worcester from 1850, and in the early 1880s began manufacturing organs and organ parts in Brattleboro. "The Carpenter Organ Instructor" in my collection, written in 1882 and published in 1883, advertises "E. P. Carpenter Organ Co., Brattleboro, Vermont, U.S.A., removed from Worcester, Mass." and "late Worcester, Mass." See also Patricia Falcone, "Reed Organ Making in Worcester," ROSB 2, no. 1 (Feb. 1983): 4.

34. Cabot 1922, 633.

35. Gellerman 1998, 93, 198.

36. Paul Searfoss, "Free Reeds in Vintage Wurlitzer Electric Organs," ROSB 9, no. 2 (May 1990): 25.

37. Gellerman 1998, 93, 100–101; Edward Peterson, "On the Use of Free Reeds in Electro-Mechanical Organs," ROSB 5, no. 1 (Feb. 1986): 28; and Paul Searfoss, "Free Reeds in Vintage Wurlitzer Electric Organs," ROSB 9, no. 2 (May 1990): 25–30.

38. Estey reeds were installed in all Everett Orgatrons prior to Wurlitzer's acquisition of the Orgatron division of the Everett Piano Company. Two minor differences between Estey and Wurlitzer reeds are that Wurlitzer used a cheaper, yellow brass, and some of their reeds with narrow tongues have very narrow blocks (without reed puller slots, since these were riveted to plastic plates). Also see Gellerman, 1996, 30. For more on Orgatrons see note 44.

39. Edwin Battison, personal communication. This jigsaw is presently stored at the American Precision Museum, where I have seen it. There is currently momentum in starting an Estey museum in one of the slate-sided factory buildings. When the Estey museum is a reality, the jigsaw will return to Brattleboro. Edwin Battison also saw a milling machine with various cutters on its turret that bored reed cells, possibly the large Sub-Bass and pedal reed cells. A friend of Thomas Schaettle,

who visited the Estey factory while it was in operation, was very impressed with a sixty-one-spindle machine that bored five octaves of manual reed cells in one pass. This machine may be different than the sixty-one-spindle drill press that Estey used to create aligned holes in organ keys and keybeds. Estey's stop face embosser, formerly in my collection, is now at the Museum of Reed Organs in Saltaire Village, West Yorkshire, England; see *ROSB* 7, no. 3 (Aug. 1988): 14; and *ROSB* 10, no. 1 (Feb. 1991): 8.

40. Gellerman 1996, 188.

41. Whiting 1996, 144.

42. For specifications of three-manual-with-pedal reed organs, see articles and stop lists in Gellerman 1996, Ord-Hume 1986, and publications of the Reed Organ Society.

43. Information from "Mr. Ernest C. Kendrick, a longtime employee of the Estey firm," *ROSB* 7, no. 2 (May 1988): 2. A reed frame of this size is in the collection of broken reeds and other Estey items that I donated to the Museum of Reed Organs in Saltaire Village, West Yorkshire, England.

44. For Orgatron history and specifications, see Edward Peterson, "On the Use of Free Reeds in Electro-Mechanical Organs," *ROSB* 5, no. 1 (Feb. 1986): 27; "Dr. John Brinkley Selects Orgatron for His Yacht," *ROSB* 8, no. 2 (May 1989): 8 (reprinted from *Orgatron World* 1, no. 10 [June 1939]); Edward Peterson, "Mechanical Operation of Two Early Everett Orgatron Models," *ROSB* 9, no. 3 (Aug. 1990): 23–31; A. Douglas, letter to the editor, *ROSB* 9, no. 4 (Nov. 1990): 2, 22; and Royal H. Akin, letter to the editor, *ROSB* 10, no. 4 (Nov. 1991): 3.

45. A photograph of this operation at Estey is in Gellerman 1996, 189.

46. Another photograph of this voicing jack is in *ROSB* 6, no. 3 (Aug. 1987): 8 (also reproduced in Gellerman 1996, 187). Gellerman 1996, 198, shows a different Estey voicing jack that has been electrified (note original angled bellows supports). Page 188 shows this voicing jack in service at

Estey; the filer is filing a bass reed of Philharmonic scale. A voicing jack not by Estey is shown in Gellerman 1973, 91. A "tuning jig" from the Lindholm factory in Borna, Germany, is shown in *ROSB* 13, no. 3 (fall 1994): 6, and *ROSQ* 17, no. 2 (summer 1998): 21. A voicing jack from the Hallman Organ Company is in a private collection.

47. Logic might suggest that the tongue was bent first and then its tip filed to fit the slot. American organ reeds do not operate on such close tolerances, an attribute that contributes to the sound of the American reed organ.

48. A photograph of this operation at Estey is in Gellerman 1996, 188.

49. The discovery of bending tongues to alter reeds' timbres was self-ascribed by both Emmons Hamlin (while he worked for George Prince in Buffalo, N.Y., after which he cofounded Mason & Hamlin) and Charles Austin of Concord, N.H., but the actual discoverer is more likely Alfred Little, who bent reed tongues while he worked for Charles Austin. See Howard A. Jewell, "Alfred Little and the Lap Organ," *ROSB* 12, no. 1 (spring 1993): 5–9; and Gellerman 1996, 88. Timbres and voices are explained in section 3 of this appendix.

50. Leon Harris may have been forced to retire. According to John Wessel, "he was pushed out because he tuned too well," that is, not quickly enough for the management (personal communication).

51. Ned Phoenix, "Some Comments on Estey Tools," *ROSB* 7, no. 2 (May 1988): 19. In June 2000 I met Deborah Estey Barber (known as Debbie Estey), daughter of Paul Estey, when I bought two wood screws (clamps) stamped "Estey & Co." at the local flea market. She had rescued a box of Estey clamps at an auction, and I rescued the only two she did not keep—a fortunate chain of circumstances.

52. Another photograph of this tuner's table is in *ROSB* 6, no. 3 (Aug. 1987): 8; also reproduced in Gellerman 1996, 187. A different Estey tuner's table is shown in Gellerman 1973, 86.

53. "Ernest C. Kendrick . . . states that from the early 1930's Estey pump organs were made only on special order; all others were electrified." *ROSB* 3, no. 1 (Feb. 1984): 16.

54. Ned Phoenix, Wm. V. Henderson, and Pam and Phil Fluke, "Comments and Reactions to the Question of Pumping versus Electrifying Reed Organs," *ROSB* 3, no. 2 (May 1984): 5-6, 18. Also see Robert F. Gellerman, "The Rimmer Organ Blowing Machine," *ROSQ* 16, no. 4 (winter 1997): 6–11.

55. To save money the heat was reduced in the cabinet shop in 1959, which caused the glue not to set up properly. This resulted in greater expense since it was necessary to remake numerous cases that were returned when they fell apart (Edwin W. Phoenix, personal communication). Delbert Pierce (a Minshall employee who, therefore, occasionally worked at Estey) related that another cost-saving scheme implemented at that time was to weld the pedal key springs onto metal pedalboard frames, which prompted a supervisor "from away" to ask why the springs no longer operated. (Delbert Pierce, personal communication. The conversation actually went: "What do you think is the problem here?" "If you really want to know, it's too many people from the city who don't know anything about organs." "You may be right," the supervisor replied, and walked away.) A new manager wondered why the pipe makers could not make all the organ pipes with the same diameter and "just cut them off at the right heights" (John Wessel, personal communication).

56. George Maurer always tuned with a Strobotuner at the Hallman factory because he found it quicker (Maurer, personal communication).

57. Cabot 1922, 633. Both Josiah Davis Whitney and Henry Kirk White began work at Estey in 1865. Whitney left Estey in 1874 and built his improved set of reed-making machinery about 1876. *The Wilcox & White Reed Organ Instructor* of 1878 states that White was "the head of the tuning department of Estey & Co.," presumably from Whitney's departure in 1874 to 1877. White left Estey in 1877 to immediately cofound Wilcox & White, which bought all its reeds from Whitney when they began producing organs in 1878. Gellerman 1998, 266. See also Howard Alan Jewell, "A History of the Wilcox and White Organ Company," *ROSB* 4, no. 4 (Nov. 1985): 3–12; Alan R. Pier, "The Wilcox & White Co., Meriden, Connecticut," *Silver Anniversary Collection: Selected Articles for the Bulletin* (Musical Box Society International, 1974), 33–50. Cynthia White Nau (granddaughter of Henry Kirk White), personal communication. The Wilcox & White Angelus roll-playing push-up piano player had two sets of American organ reeds that could be heard with the sound of the piano. Screw-top reed organ stools were made by various companies in Meriden, Connecticut.

58. Cabot 1922, 865.

59. "Musical Opinion" (May 1886); quoted in Ord-Hume 1986,144. G. W. Ingalls may have also supplied Vocalion reeds; Keith B. Williams, "The Vocalion and Its Manufacturers: Some History," *ROSB* 8, no. 4 (Nov. 1989): 25–28, esp. 26.

60. Aeolian acquired the Vocalion Organ Company in 1903 or 1905. Keith B. Williams, "The Vocalion and Its Manufacturers: Some History," *ROSB* 8, no. 4 (Nov. 1989): 26.

61. See notes 5 and 19.

62. John Green's suggestions for effecting changes of timbre are reprinted in Gellerman 1973, 3, 61; and in Green, "The Royal Seraphine," *ROSB* 14, no. 3 (autumn 1995): 26–28. In my collection is a reed organ chest of unknown provenance containing two ranks of reeds (8', 4') over which is placed a shallow, rectangular drum with two skin heads. Also see Ian Thompson, "The Soft Stops," *ROSB* 4, no. 1 (Feb. 1985): 29–32.

63. Paul Searfoss, "Free Reeds in Vintage Wurlitzer Electric Organs," *ROSB* 9, no. 2 (May 1990): 25.

64. Ned Phoenix, "The Free Reed Forever," *ROSB* 11, no. 2 (summer 1992): 29–31.

BIBLIOGRAPHY

Books and Articles

Adams, Charles Francis. 1876. *Familiar Letters of John Adams and His Wife, Abigail Adams, during the Revolution*. New York: Hurd and Houghton.

Ames, Kenneth L. 1992. *Death in the Dining Room and Other Tales of Victorian Culture*. Philadelphia: Temple University Press.

————. 1984. "Material Culture as Non Verbal Communication: A Historical Case Study." In *American Material Culture: The Shape of Things around Us*, edited by Edith Mayo. Bowling Green, Ohio: Bowling Green State University Popular Press.

Arnold, Corliss Richard. 1973. *Organ Literature: A Comprehensive Survey*. Metuchen, N.J.: Scarecrow Press.

Asher, Louis E., and Edith Heal. 1942. *Send No Money*. Chicago: Argus Books.

Atkins, Sandra. 1984. *Speaking for Ourselves: An Oral History of Brattleboro, Vermont, in the 1930s*. Burlington: University of Vermont.

Bacon, Tony, ed. 1981. *Rock Hardware: The Instruments, Equipment, and Technology of Rock*. New York: Harmony Books.

Baldwin, A. H. 1912. *Foreign Trade in Musical Instruments*. Washington, D.C.: Government Printing Office.

Barnes, William H. 1956. *The Contemproary American Organ*. New York: J. Fisher and Brother.

Barry, Harold A., Richard E. Michelman, Richard M. Mitchell, and Richard H. Wellman. 1974. *Before Our Time: A Pictorial Memoir of Brattleboro, Vermont, from 1830 to 1930*. Brattleboro: Stephen Greene Press.

Barry, Kit. 1981. *The Advertising Trade Card*. Monson, Mass.: Blatchley's Printers.

Bassett, T. D. Seymour, ed. *Outsiders in Vermont*. Brattleboro, Vt.: Stephen Green Press.

————. 1981. *Vermont: A Bibliography of Its History*. Boston: G. K. Hall.

Beckel, James Cox. 1855. "Amateur's School for the Melodeon." Philadelphia: Winner and Shuster.

Bellson, Julius. 1973. *The Gibson Story*. Kalamazoo, Mich.: Gibson.

Benes, Peter, ed. 1998. *New England Music: The Public Sphere, 1600–1900*. Dublin Seminar for New England Folklife Annual Proceedings 1996. Boston: Boston University.

Berger, John. 1972. *Ways of Seeing*. London: Penguin Books.

Bessaraboff, Nicholas. 1941. *Ancient European Musical Instruments*. New York: October House.

Black, Eugene. 1974. *Victorian Culture and Society*. New York: Walker.

Bode, Carl. 1960. *The Anatomy of American Popular Culture, 1840–1850*. Berkeley: University of California Press.

————. 1972. *Midcentury America: Life in the 1850s*. Carbondale: Southern Illinois University Press.

Boorstin, Daniel J. 1973. *The Americans: The Democratic Experience*. New York: Vintage Books.

Borroff, Edith. 1986. "An American Parlor at the Turn of the Century." *American Music* 4, no. 3 (Fall): 302–8.

————. 1995. *Music Melting Round: A History of Music in the United States*. New York: Ardsley House.

Bourne, Russell, ed. 1978. *The Smithsonian Book of Invention*. New York: Smithsonian Exposition Books, W.W. Norton.

Bowers, Q. David. 1972. *Encyclopedia of Automated Musical Instruments*. Vestal, N.Y.: Vestal Press.

Braden, Donna R. 1992. "The Family That Plays Together Stays Together: Family Pastimes and Indoor Amusements, 1890–1930." In *American Home Life, 1880-1930: A Social History of Spaces and Services*, edited by Jessica H. Foy and Thomas J. Schlereth. Knoxville: University of Tennessee Press.

Bradley, Van Allen. 1957. *Music for the Millions: The Kimball Piano and Organ Story*. Chicago: Henry Regnery.

Brattleboro Board of Trade. 1886. *Brattleboro: Its Attractions as a Home* [public relations booklet]. Brattleboro, Vt.

Bridgeman, Harriet, and Elizabeth Drury, eds. 1975. *The Encyclopedia of Victoriana*. New York: Macmillan.

Brooks, Van Wyck, and Otto Bettman. 1956. *Our Literary Heritage*. New York: Dutton.

Buechner, Alan C. 1996. "Thomas Walter and the Society for Promoting Regular Singing in the Worship of God: Boston, 1720–1723." In *New England Music: The Public Sphere, 1600-1900*, edited by Peter Benes. Dublin Seminar for New England Folklife Annual Proceedings 1996. Boston: Boston University.

Byrd, Joseph. 1983. Review of *Sweet Songs for Gentle Americans: The Parlor Song in America*, by Nicholas E. Tawa. *Journal of American Music* 1, no. 3 (Fall): 85–87.

Cabot, Mary R. 1921. *Annals of Brattleboro, 1681–1895*. Vol. 1. Brattleboro, Vt.: E. L. Hildreth.

———. 1922. *Annals of Brattleboro, 1681–1895*. Vol. 2. Brattleboro, Vt.: E. L. Hildreth.

Camus, Raoul F. 1998. "Military Music and the Roots of the American Band Movement." In *New England Music: The Public Sphere, 1600–1900*, edited by Peter Benes. Dublin Seminar for New England Folklife Annual Proceedings 1996. Boston: Boston University.

Cantor, Milton, ed. 1979. *American Workingclass Culture*. Westport, Conn.: Greenwood Press.

Cashman, Sean Dennis. 1993. *America in the Gilded Age: From the Death of Lincoln to the Rise of Theodore Roosevelt*. 3d ed. New York: New York University Press.

Chandler, Alfred D. 1977. *The Visible Hand: The Managerial Revolution in American Business*. Cambridge, Mass.: Belknap Press.

Chase, Gilbert. 1966. *America's Music: From the Pilgrims to the Present*. New York: McGraw-Hill.

———. 1987. *America's Music: From the Pilgrims to the Present*. 3d ed. Urbana: University of Illinois Press.

Child, Hamilton. 1884. *Gazetteer and Business Directory of Windham County, Vt., 1724–1884*. Syracuse, N.Y.: Journal Office.

Clarke, Donald. 1995. *The Rise and Fall of Popular Music*. New York: St. Martin's Press.

Clarke, William H. 1869. *Clarke's New Method for Reed Organs*. Boston: Oliver Ditson.

———. 1870. *Clarke's Reed Organ Companion: A New Collection of Vocal and Instrumental Music, for Reed Organs, Preceded by a Fresh and Easy Course of Instruction*. Boston: Oliver Ditson.

Cobb, Buell E. Jr. 1989. *The Sacred Harp: A Tradition and Its Music*. Athens: University of Georgia Press.

Conant, Edward. 1890. *Geography, History, and Civil Government of Vermont*. Rutland, Vt.: Tuttle.

Cowan, Ruth Schwartz. 1983. *More Work for Mother: The Ironies of Household Technology from the Open Hearth to the Microwave*. New York: Basic Books.

Crawford, Richard. 2001. *America's Musical Life: A History*. New York: W. W. Norton.

Davis, Ronald L. 1982. *A History of Music in American Life.*. Vol. 1. Malabar, Fla.: Robert Krieger.

Diagram Group. 1976. *Musical Instruments of the World*. New York: Facts on File.

Dichter, Harry and Elliott Shapiro. 1941. *Early American Sheet Music: Its Lure and Its Lore.* New York: R.R. Bowker.

Disher, Maurice Willson. 1955. *Victorian Song: From Dive to Drawing Room.* London: Phoenix House.

Dolge, Alfred. 1972 [1911]. *Pianos and Their Makers.* New York: Dover.

Douglas, Diane M. 1982. "The Machine in the Parlor: A Dialectical Analysis of the Sewing Machine." *Journal of American Culture* 5, no. 1 (Spring): 20–29.

Duga, Jules J. 1968. "A Short History of the Reed Organ." *Diapason* 69, no. 8: 24.

———. 1969. "Reed Organs Revisited: A Glance into the Past." *Hobbies*, April, 24–25.

Dutton, Ralph. 1954. *The Victorian Home.* London: B. T. Batsford.

Eliason, Robert E. 1975. *Graves and Company Musical Instrument Makers.* Dearborn, Mich.: Edison Institute.

———. 1976. "Recently Discovered Information about Graves and Company, Musical Instrument Makers." *Herald* 5, no. 2 (April): 59.

———. 1977. "Oboes, Bassoons, and Bass Clarinets, made by Hartford, Connecticut, Makers before 1812." *Galpin Society Journal* (May): 43–51.

Emerson, Ken. 1997. *Doo-Dah!: Stephen Foster and the Rise of American Popular Culture.* New York: Simon and Schuster.

Emmet, Boris, and John Jenck. 1950. *Catalogues and Counters: A History of Sears, Roebuck and Company.* Chicago: University of Chicago Press.

Ennis, Philip H. 1992. *The Seventh Stream: The Emergence of Rocknroll in American Popular Music.* Hanover, N.H.: University Press of New England.

Estey Company Benefit Association. *Constitution and Bylaws.*

Estey organ catalogues, broadsides, brochures, pamphlets, and price lists: 1867, 1871, 1876, 1878, 1880–81, 1886, 1890, 1895, 1896, 1903, 1905–6, 1914, 1923, 1929, 1934, 1941, 1953. This listing is by necessity limited. Not all catalogues were dated, particularly those in the 1900s. In addition, special catalogues (many undated) were distributed to foreign markets such as England, Canada, and South America.

Estey Organ Corporation (Del.). 1957. *Report for the Fiscal Year Ended February 28, 1957.*

Etzkorn, K. Peter. 1977. "Popular Music: The Sounds of the Many." In *Music in American Society, 1776–1976: From Puritan Hymn to Synthesizer,* edited by George McCue. New Brunswick, N.J.: Transaction Books.

Ewen, David. 1957. *Panorama of American Popular Music.* Englewood Cliffs, N.J.: Prentice Hall.

———. 1977. *All the Years of American Popular Music.* Englewood Cliffs, N.J.: Prentice Hall.

Faler, Paul G. 1981. *Mechanics and Manufacturers in the Early Industrial Revolution.* Albany: State University of New York Press.

Falle, Raymond. 1959. "The Royal Seraphine in Jersey" *Galpin Society Journal* 12 (May): 86–88.

Ferris, Jean. 1990. *America's Musical Landscape.* Dubuque, Iowa: Wm. C. Brown.

Fink, Leon. 1983. *Workingmen's Democracy.* Urbana: University of Illinois Press.

Fisher, Marvin, and Hennig Cohen, eds. 1968. "The Iconology of Industrialism, 1830–1860," *The American Culture: Approaches to the Study of the United States.* Boston: Houghton Mifflin. 228–247.

Flinn, M. W., and Hugh F. Kearney, eds. 1966. *Origins of the Industrial Revolution.* London: Longman Group.

Foy, Jessica H., and Thomas J. Schlereth, eds. 1992. *American Home Life, 1880–1930: A Social History of Spaces and Services.* Knoxville: University of Tennessee Press.

Fuller, Abby Estey. 1929. *Addresses: The Brattleboro Chapter of the Daughters of the American Revolution.* Brattleboro, Vt.: N.n.

Fuller, Levi K. 1894. *Message of L. K. Fuller to the*

General Assembly of Vermont. Montpelier, Vt.: Press of the Watchman Publishing Company.

Fuller, Abbey Estey [Mrs. Levi K.]. 1928. *Addresses*. Compiled by Clara E. Powell. Brattleboro, Vt.

Gaines, James R., ed. 1981. *The Lives of the Piano*. New York: Harper Colophon Books.

Gellerman, Robert F. 1973. *The American Reed Organ*. Vestal, N.Y.: Vestal Press.

———. 1985. *Gellerman's International Reed Organ Atlas*. Vestal, N.Y.: Vestal Press.

———. 1996. *The American Reed Organ and the Harmonium: A Treatise on Its History, Restoration, and Tuning, with Descriptions of Some Outstanding Collections, Including a Stop Dictionary and a Directory of Reed Organs*. Vestal, N.Y.: Vestal Press.

———. 1998. *Gellerman's International Reed Organ Atlas*. 2d ed. Lanham, Md.: Vestal Press.

Gernsheim, Helmut. 1951. *Masterpieces of Victorian Photography*. London: Phaidon Press.

Gibney, Frank Jr., and Belinda Luscombe. 2000. "The Redesigning of America." *Time*, March 20, 69–75.

Giedion, Siegfried. 1948. *Mechanization Takes Command: A Contribution to Anonymous History*. New York: Oxford University Press.

Gloag, John. 1961. *Victorian Comfort: A Social History of Design, 1830–1900*. Trowbridge, Wilts., England: Redwood Press.

———. 1962. *Victorian Taste: Some Social Aspects of Architecture and Industrial Design, from 1820 to 1900*. New York: Barnes and Noble.

Graffagnino, J. Kevin. 1985. *Vermont In the Victorian Age: Continuity and Change in the Green Mountain State, 1850–1900*. Shelburne: Vermont Heritage Press and Shelburne Museum.

Green, John. 1833a. *Airs Adapted for the Royal Seraphine*. London.

———. 1833b. *Concise Instructions for Performance on the Royal Seraphine and Organ*. London.

Grier, Katherine C. 1988. *Culture and Comfort: People, Parlors, and Upholstery, 1850–1930*. Amherst, Mass.: Strong Museum.

———. 1992. "Decline of the Memory Palace: The Parlor after 1890." In *American Home Life, 1880–1930: A Social History of Spaces and Service*, edited by Jessica H. Foy and Thomas J. Schlereth. Knoxville: University of Tennessee Press.

Groce, Nancy. 1982. "Musical Instrument Making in New York City during the Eighteenth and Nineteenth Centuries." Ph.D. diss., Wesleyan University.

———. 1991. *Musical Instrument Makers of New York: A Directory of Eighteenth and Nineteenth Century Urban Craftsmen*. Stuyvesant, N.Y.: Pendragon Press.

Grolier Multimedia Encyclopedia. 2000. [Computer file.] Danbury, Conn.: Grolier Interactive.

Grow, Lawrence, and Dina von Zweck. 1984. *American Victorian*. New York: Harper and Row.

Hamm, Charles. 1979. *Yesterdays: Popular Song in America*. New York: W. W. Norton.

———. 1983. *Music in the New World*. New York: W. W. Norton.

Harris, Neil. 1966. *The Artist in American Society, 1790–1860: The Formative Years*. New York: George Braziller.

Hays, Samuel P. 1975. *The Response to Industrialism, 1885–1914*. Chicago: University of Chicago Press.

Helmholtz, Hermann von. 1954. *On the Sensations of Tone as a Physiological Basis for the Theory of Music*. Translated by Alexander J. Ellis. New York: Dover.

Hirsch, Susan B. 1978. *Roots of the American Working Class*. Philadelphia: University of Pennsylvania Press.

Hitchcock, H. Wiley. 1974. *Music in the United States: A Historical Introduction*. 2d ed. Englewood Cliffs, N.J.: Prentice Hall.

Hoffmann, Frank W., and William G. Bailey. 1990.

Arts and Entertainment Fads. New York: Harrington Park Press.

Holbrook, Stewart. 1961. *Yankee Loggers.* New York: International Paper.

Houpis, John N., Jr. 1973. *Brattleboro: Selected Historical Vignettes.* Brattleboro, Vt.: Brattleboro.

Howard, John Tasker. 1930. *Our American Music: Three Hundred Years of It.* New York: Thomas Y. Crowell.

Howe, Daniel Walker, ed. 1976. *Victorian America.* Philadelphia: University of Pennsylvania Press.

Howe, Elias. 1847. *Howe's Seraphine and Melodeon Instructor.* Boston: Published by the author.

Huber, Richard. 1987. "Over the Edge: When Success Turns Sour." *Bostonia,* April–May.

Jay, Robert. 1987. *The Trade Card in Nineteenth-Century America.* Columbia: University of Missouri Press.

Jewell, Howard Alan. 1985. "A History of the Wilcox and White Organ Company. *Reed Organ Society Bulletin* 4, no. 4 (November): 3–12.

Kammen, Michael. 1999. *American Culture, American Tastes: Social Change and the Twentieth Century.* New York: Basic Books.

Kaplan, Justin. 1968. *Mr. Clemens and Mark Twain.* New York: Pocket Books.

Kasson, John F. 1976. *Civilizing the Machine: Technology and Republican Values in America, 1776–1900.* New York: Grossman.

Keller, Kate van Winkle. 1998. "The Eighteenth-Century Ballroom: A Mirror of Social Change." In *New England Music: The Public Sphere, 1600–1900,* edited by Peter Benes. Dublin Seminar for New England Folklife Annual Proceedings 1996. Boston: Boston University.

Kettell, Thomas P. 1872. "Manufactures: Musical Instruments." In *One Hundred Years' Progress of the United States.* Hartford, Conn.: L. Stebbins.

Kingman, Daniel. 1979. *American Music: A Panorama.* New York: Schirmer Books.

Kouwenhoven, John. 1948. *Made In America: The Arts in Modern Civilization, 1857–1900.* New York: Doubleday.

Lacour-Gayet, Robert. 1969. *Everyday Life in the United States before the Civil War, 1830–1860.* New York: Frederick Ungar.

Larson, Andre P., ed. "The American Musical Instrument Society." AMIS Newsletter.

Lears, Jackson. 1981. *No Place of Grace: Antimodernism and the Transformation of American Culture, 1880–1920.* New York: Pantheon Books.

Leavitt, W. J. D. 1878. *The Wilcox & White Reed Organ Instructor.* West Meriden, Conn.: Wilcox and White Organ Co.

Leisure Hours Folio No. 22. [No date.] New York: Zither Music.

Levy, Lester S. 1967. *Grace Notes in American History: Popular Sheet Music from 1820 to 1900.* Norman: University of Oklahoma Press.

Lewis, Wesley L. 1987. "Semantics Revisited: Some Personal Reflections about Words." *Reed Organ Society Bulletin* 1, no. 1 (February): 7–9.

Libin, Laurence. 1985. *American Musical Instruments.* New York: Metropolitan Museum of Art.

———. 1994. *Our Tuneful Heritage: American Musical Instruments from the Metropolitan Museum of Art.* Provo, Utah: Brigham Young University.

Lingeman, Richard. 1980. *Small Town America: A Narrative History, 1620–Present.* Boston: Putnam.

Linn, Karen. 1991. *That Half-Barbaric Twang: The Banjo in American Popular Culture.* Chicago: University of Illinois Press.

Loesser, Arthur. 1954. *Men, Women, and Pianos.* New York: Simon and Schuster.

Lomax, Alan. 1975 [1960]. *The Folk Songs of North America in the English Language.* 2 vols. Dolphin Books edition. Garden City, N.Y.: Doubleday.

Lomax, John, and Alan Lomax. 1947. *Folksong USA.* New York: New American Library.

Lowens, Irving. 1964. *Music and Musicians in Early America.* New York: W. W. Norton.

Mallory, Steven C. 1998. "Capt. Eliphalet Grover's 'Boon Island Fiddle': The Folk Violin in New England, 1750–1850." In *New England Music: The Public Sphere, 1600–1900,* edited by Peter Benes. Dublin Seminar for New England Folklife Annual Proceedings 1996. Boston: Boston University.

Mason, Henry Lowell. 1983 [1901]. *The History and Development of the American Cabinet Organ.* Deansboro, N.Y.: The Reed Organ Society and the Musical Museum.

Mathews, W. S. B., ed. 1889. *A Hundred Years of Music in America.* New York: American Musicological Society Press.

McDonnell, Colleen. 1992. "Parlor Piety: The Home as Sacred Space in Protestant America." In *American Home Life, 1880–1930: A Social History of Spaces and Service,* edited by Jessica H. Foy and Thomas J. Schlereth. Knoxville: University of Tennessee Press.

McFarlan, Frank G. 1883. *The Carpenter Organ Instructor.* Brattleboro, Vt.: E. P. Carpenter Organ Co.

McGraw, Hugh, et al. 1991. *The Sacred Harp: The Best Collection of Sacred Songs, Hymns, Odes, and Anthems Ever Offered the Singing Public for General Use.* Rev. ed. Sacred Harp.

Meeks, Harold. 1975. *The Geographic Regions of Vermont: A Study In Maps.* Hanover, N.H.: Dartmouth Press.

Merriam, Alan P. 1964. *The Anthropology of Music.* Evanston, Ill.: Northwestern University Press.

Merriam, Robert W. 1976. "The Corliss Engine." *Live Steam Magazine.* Reprinted in "George H. Corliss Day: A Centennial of a Centennial." East Greenwich, R. I.: New England Museum of Wireless and Steam." May 9.

Michel, N. E. 1969. *Michel's Organ Atlas.* Covina, Calif.: Taylor.

Milne, H. F. 1930. *The Reed Organ: Its Design and Construction.* Braintree, Mass.: Organ Literature Foundation.

Minnigerode, Meade. 1924. *The Fabulous Forties: 1840–1850.* New York: G. P. Putnam's Sons.

Moeller, Madelyn. 1983. "Photography and History: Using Photographs in Interpreting Our Cultural Past." *Journal of American Culture* 6, no. 1 (Spring): 3–17.

Morgan, H. Wayne. 1963. "An Age In Need of Reassessment." In *The Gilded Age: A Reappraisal.* Syracuse, N.Y.: Syracuse University Press.

Moseley, Caroline. 1983. "'The Maids of Dear Columbia': Images of Young Women in Victorian American Parlor Song." *Journal of American Culture* 6, no. 1 (Spring): 18–31.

Muller, N. Nicholas III, and Samuel B. Hand. 1982. *In a State of Nature.* Montpelier: Vermont Historical Society.

Nadworny, Milton J. 1959. "The Perfect Melodeon: The Origins of the Estey Organ Company." *Business History Review* 33, no. 1 (Spring): 43–59.

Nathan, Hans. 1962. *Dan Emmet and the Rise of Early Negro Minstrelsy.* Norman: University of Oklahoma Press.

Nettl, Bruno. 1983. *The Study of Ethnomusicology: Twenty-Nine Issues and Concepts.* Urbana: University of Illinois Press.

———. 1997. *Excursions In World Music.* Upper Saddle River, N.J.: Prentice Hall.

New England Cabinet Organs: Illustrated Circular for the Campaign of 1878–'79. Reprint, Braintree, Mass: Organ Literature Foundation.

New York Music Directory. 1941. "New York Packet." In Virginia Redway, *Music Directory of Early New York City.* New York: Public Library.

Niles Bryant School. 1906. *Tuning, Care, and Repair of Reed and Pipe Organs.* Battle Creek, Mich.: Niles Bryant School of Piano Tuning, Music Hall.

Nketia, J. H. Kwabena. 1974. *The Music of Africa.* New York: W. W. Norton.

Nye, Russel Blaine. 1974. *Society and Culture in America, 1830–1860.* New York: Harper and Row.

O'Connor, Kevin M. 1985. "Bloodroots: The Impact of Transportation on the Town of Brattle-boro, Vermont." Honors thesis, University of Vermont.

Ochse, Orpha. 1975. *The History of the Organ in the United States*. Bloomington: Indiana University Press.

Ogasapian, John. 1983. Review of *The Organ in New England: An Account of Its Use and Manufacture to the End of the Nineteenth Century*, by Barbara Owen. *American Music* 1, no. 1 (Spring): 88–91.

Olwell, Carol, and Judith Lynch Waldhorn. 1976. *A Gift to the Street*. New York: St. Martin's Press.

Ord-Hume, Arthur W. J. G. 1986. *Harmonium*. Vestal, N.Y.: Vestal Press.

Owen, Barbara. 1979. *The Organ In New England: An Account of Its Use and Manufacture to the End of the Nineteenth Century*. Raleigh, N.C.: Sunbury Press.

———. 1988. *Organ*. New York: W. W. Norton.

Papanek, Victor. 1971. *Design for the Real World*. New York: Pantheon Books.

Pearsall, Ronald. 1972. *Victorian Sheet Music Covers*. Detroit: Gale Research.

Phelps, E. B., and George S. Cheney. 1879. *Estey Organ Method*. Boston: Printed by J. Frank Giles.

———. 1882. *Estey Organ Method*. Rev. edition. Boston: Printed by J. Frank Giles.

Pomeroy, Rev. Frank T. 1894. *Picturesque Brattle-boro*. Northampton, Mass.: Picturesque Publishing Company.

Pope, Daniel. 1983. *The Making of Modern Advertising*. New York: Basic Books.

Pratt, John Lowell, ed. 1968. *Currier and Ives: Chronicles of America*. New York: Promontory Press.

Pulos, Arthur J. 1983. *American Design Ethic: A History of Industrial Design*. Cambridge, Mass.: MIT Press.

Proper, David R. 1998. "A Joyful Noise, 'Sounding Brass and Tinkling Cymbal': The Late-Nineteenth-Century New England Town Band." In *New England Music: The Public Sphere, 1600–1900*, edited by Peter Benes. Dublin Seminar for New England Folklife Annual Proceedings 1996. Boston: Boston University.

Reck, David. 1977. *Music of the Whole Earth*. New York: Charles Scribner's Sons.

Reed Organ Society Bulletin. Quarterly publication of the Reed Organ Society, Inc., P.O. Box 19, Altamont, N.Y., 12009-0019. Renamed *Reed Organ Society Quarterly* autumn 1997.

Rich, Arthur Lowndes. 1946. *Lowell Mason*. Chapel Hill, N.C.: University of North Carolina Press.

Richards, J. H. 1975. "The Vocalion." *Diapason* 1, no. 16 (September).

———. 1983. "Music and the Reed Organ in the Life of Mark Twain." *American Music* 1, no. 3 (Fall): 38–47.

Riggs, Marlon. 1986. *Ethnic Notions* [documentary video]. San Francisco: California Newsreel.

Roberts, Robert R. 1963. "Gilt, Gingerbread, and Realism." In *The Gilded Age: A Reappraisal*, edited by H. Wayne Morgan. Syracuse, N.Y.: Syracuse University Press.

Roell, Craig H. 1989. *The Piano in America, 1890–1940*. Chapel Hill: University of North Carolina Press.

Rublowsky, John. 1967. *Music in America*. New York: Crowell-Collier Press.

Rusch, Barbara. 1990. "Trade Card Studies." *Ephemera News* [Fall supplement, "Factory Views: Images of a New Social Order"]: 1–4.

Sachs, Curt. 1940. *The History of Musical Instruments*. New York: W. W. Norton.

———. 1962. *The Wellsprings of Music*. New York: Da Capo Press.

Sadie, Stanley, ed. 1980. *The New Grove Dictionary of Music and Musicians*. 20 vols. New York: Macmillan.

———. 1984. *The New Grove Dictionary of Musical Instruments*. 3 vols. New York: Macmillan.

———. 1986. *The New Grove Dictionary of American Music*. 4 vols. New York: Macmillan.

———. 2001. *The New Grove Dictionary of Music and Musicians*. 2d ed. 29 vols. New York: Macmillan.

Schlereth, Thomas J. 1991. *Victorian America: Transformations in Everyday Life, 1876–1915*. New York: Harper Collins.

Schulz, R. E. 1974. "The Reed Organ in Nineteenth-Century America." Ph.D. diss., University of Texas.

Sears, Roebuck and Company. 1902. *The Sears, Roebuck Catalogue no. 3*. New York: Crown.

———. 1968. *1897 Sears Roebuck Catalogue*, ed. Fred L. Israel. New York: Chelsea House.

Seeger, Charles. 1957. "Music and Class Structure in the United States." *American Quarterly* 9 (Fall): 281–94.

Slobin, Mark. 1982. *Tenement Songs: The Popular Music of the Jewish Immigrants*. Urbana: University of Illinois Press.

———. 1996. Introduction to *Worlds of Music*, edited by Jeff Todd Titon. With James T. Koetting, David P. McAllester, and David Reck. 3d ed. New York: Schirmer.

Slotkin, Richard. 1986. *The Fatal Environment: The Myth of the Frontier in the Age of Industrialization, 1800–1890*. Middletown, Conn.: Wesleyan University Press.

Smith, Henry Nash. 1967. *Popular Culture and Industrialism, 1865–1890*. New York: New York University Press.

Smith, Rollin. 1988. "E. Power Biggs and His Estey." *Reed Organ Society Bulletin* 7, no. 3 (August): 19.

Smithsonian Institution. 1973. *The Smithsonian Collection of Classic Jazz*. Washington: Smithsonian Institution, Division of Performing Arts.

Spaeth, Sigmund. 1948. *A History of Popular Music in America*. New York: Random House.

Spellman, Doreen, and Sidney Spellman. 1969. *Victorian Music Covers*. London: Evelyn, Adams and MacKay.

Stilwell, Lewis D. 1948. *Migration from Vermont*. Montpelier: Vermont Historical Society.

Stone, James H. 1956. "The Merchant and the Muse: Commercial Influences on American Popular Music before the Civil War." *Business History Review* 30 (March): 1–17.

Strasser, Susan. 1989. *Satisfaction Guaranteed: The Making of the American Mass Market*. New York: Pantheon Books.

Studwell, William. 1994. *The Popular Song Reader: A Sampler of Well-Known Twentieth Century Songs*. Binghamton, N.Y.: Harrington Park Press.

Suttoni, Charles. 1981. *Franz Liszt: Complete Piano Transcriptions from Wagner's Operas*. New York: Dover.

Tawa, Nicholas E. 1980. *Sweet Songs for Gentle Americans: The Parlor Song in America, 1790–1860*. Bowling Green, Ohio: Popular Press.

———. 1984. *A Music for the Millions*. New York: Pendragon Press.

Tedlow, Richard S. 1976. *New and Improved: The Story of Mass Marketing in America*. New York: Basic Books.

Tocqueville, Alexis de. 1984 [1935]. *Democracy in America*. New York: Penguin Books.

Thompson, E. P. 1967. "Time, Work-Discipline, and Industrial Capitalism." *Past and Present* 38 (December): 56–97.

Toll, Robert C. 1974. *Blacking Up: The Minstrel Show in Nineteenth-Century America*. New York: Oxford University Press.

Tolson, Jay. 2000. "What's in a Name?" *U.S. News and World Report*. October 9, 52–53.

Trachtenberg, Alan. 1982. *The Incorporation of America: Culture and Society in the Gilded Age*. New York: Hill and Wang.

U.S. Bureau of the Census. 1865. *Musical Instruments: Manufacturers of the United States in 1860*. Washington, D.C.: Government Printing Office.

U.S. Bureau of the Census. 1902. *Musical Instruments and Materials: Special Reports on Selected Industries [1900]*. Vol. 10. Washington, D.C.: U.S. Census Office.

U.S. Supreme Court Cases. 1883.

Upton, William Treat. 1930. *Art Song In America: A Study in the Development of American Music*. Boston: Oliver Ditson.

Vaudeville: An American Masters Special. 1997. [Documentary video.] Thirteen/WNET, KCTS/Seattle and Palmer/Fenster.

Veblen, Thorstein. 1979 [1899]. *The Theory of the Leisure Class*. New York: Penguin Books.

Vermont Historic Sites and Structures Survey. 1980. [No publication information available.]

Wallance, Don. 1956. *Shaping America's Products*. New York: Reinhold.

Waring, Dennis. 1982. "The Instrument Maker: With Special Reference to Contemporary Makers in New England." Master's thesis, Wesleyan University.

Whiting, Robert B. 1969. "A Reed Organ Bibliography." *Tracker* 13, no. 3: 9.

———. 1981. *Estey Reed Organs on Parade*. Vestal, N.Y.: Vestal Press.

———. 1996. *Estey Reed Organs on Parade*. 2d ed. Vestal, N.Y.: Emprise.

Whitney, W. W. 1886. *Improved Easy Method for the Parlor Organ*. Brattleboro, Vt.: Estey Organ Co.

Whiton, Sherrill. 1963. *Elements of Interior Design and Decoration*. New York: J. B. Lippincott

Williamson, Elizabeth. 1980. "Advertising." In *Handbook of American Popular Culture*, edited by M. Thomas Inge. 3 vols. Westport, Conn.: Greenwood Press.

Winternitz, Emanuel. 1967. *Musical Instruments of the Western World*. New York: McGraw-Hill.

Woodforde, John. 1969. *The Truth about Cottages*. London: Routledge and Kegan Paul.

Wright, Richardson. 1927. *Hawkers and Walkers in Early America*. Philadelphia: J. B. Lippincott.

Yoder, Paul. 1976. *American Folklife*. Austin: University of Texas Press.

Magazines and Trade Journals

The American Hebrew
Ephemera News
Harper's Weekly Magazine
Musical Courier
Musical Opinion
Music Trades Review
Presbyterian Journal

Newspapers

Augusta (Ga.) Chronicle and Constitutionalist
Brattleboro Daily Reformer
Brattleboro Eagle
Brattleboro Reformer
Frank Leslie's Illustrated Newspaper
Keene Sentinel
New York Times
Rutland Globe
Semi-Weekly Eagle
Vermont Phoenix

INDEX

VICTORIAN SOUNDS ON ESTEY ORGANS: *The Compact Disc*

Twelve different Estey organs, manufactured between 1860 and 1952, can be heard on the companion compact disc. This, however, represents only a small sampling of Estey organ types. The selections were played mostly on small "cottage organs" in homes and churches in southern Vermont and New Hampshire. Overall, production processes were kept to a minimum to maintain a realistic spirit.* Organs were played and recorded on site, with as little pretense as possible, reflecting to some extent the sound and circumstance of performance in mid-to-late-nineteenth-century parlors, lodges, and sanctuaries.

Selections were chosen for their relevance to this study and to provide a representative sampling of various Victorian music genres. Many were taken directly from Estey's two method books—the 1879 edition and the 1882 revised edition (see Appendix C)—while others were selected from the performers' own repertoires. One will find little from the European pipe organ tradition here. The three excerpted vocal pieces from the *Estey Organ Method* are included to help the reader understand and enjoy the analysis of these songs in chapter 2 of the text.

The author is deeply indebted to the talented and patient musicians who so generously contributed to this production: Ed Boadway, Luella Frechette, Carolyn Halsted, Ned Phoenix, and Nancy Reed, organists; and Becky Graber and Jack Reed, vocalists.

The one-manual Estey cottage organ played by Carolyn Halsted was purchased in the mid-1870s by her great-great-great aunt Juliet Haskins, in Belleville, Michigan, and has since been passed through several generations of family to her. Ned Phoenix restored and tuned the instrument on which he performs, an Estey parlor organ now in the collection of Joy Douglass. Nancy Reed plays a one-manual parlor organ presently conserved and housed by the Brattleboro Historical Society. The Estey reed organs played by Ed Boadway are mostly in their original settings in a variety of locations around Claremont, New Hampshire. The pipe organ selections, played on Estey opus 300, were recorded in the First Baptist Church of Brattleboro. The Residence Organ example was recorded in the home of Laurence Leonard of Laconia, New Hampshire.

*Not devoid of charm, each organ has its own particular set of idiosyncracies, especially the unrestored ones: clunky pedals, clattery keys, clamorous stop actions, creaky organ benches, squeaky crank handles, out-of-tune reeds, noisy electric blowers, and other kinetic endearments. We trust the listener will accept these extramusical elements simply as a lively part of restored reed organ ambience, a circumstance certainly not intended by the makers. But considering that many reed organs have had little or no maintenance for well over a century, it is amazing that they work at all. Note, however, that when reed organs are functioning well (new or restored), the wind is adequate, and the mechanisms are silent and do not intrude on the music. Copyrights to all recordings are held by the author. Recorded material was assisted by Gregory Acker and was mastered by Mike Arafeh, Coffeehouse Recording Studios, Middletown, Connecticut.

Selections from the Estey Organ Method

Carolyn Halsted, organist
J. Estey & Co., 1874, no. 49352. Five-octave Cottage Organ, partially restored.

1. Andante from Trio, Op. 1, Beethoven (Estey 1879, 59)
2. Air from *La fille du Madam Angot*, Lecocq (Estey 1882, 50)
3. "Song without Words," Mendelssohn (Estey 1879, 76)
4. Chorus from *Moses in Egypt*, Rossini (Estey 1879, 52)
5. Prelude in C Minor, Chopin (Estey 1882, 93)
6. Pilgrims' Chorus from *Tannhäuser*, Wagner (Estey 1882, 104)
7. National Airs from the *Estey Organ Method* (1879, 137–44)
   England: "God Save the Queen"
   America: "Star-Spangled Banner"
   Russia: "National Hymn"
   Austria: "God Save the Emperor"
   France: "La Marseillaise"

Ned Phoenix, organist
Estey Organ Co., 1898, no. 297262. Six-octave Parlor Organ, restored.

8. *Traümerei*, Schumann (Estey 1882, 86)
9. "Home Waltz" (Estey 1882, 28)
10. "Estey Hymn", Ditmars (Estey 1882, 62)
11. "The Last Rose of Summer," Milliken (Estey 1882, 51)

Songs from the Estey Organ Method

Ned Phoenix, organist; Becky Graber, soprano
Estey Organ Co., 1898, no. 297262. Six-octave Parlor Organ, restored.

12. "I Cannot Sing the Old Songs" (excerpt), Claribel (Estey 1879, 74)

13. "I Love My Love" (excerpt), Pinsuti (Estey 1879, 86)
14. "Call Me Thine Own" (excerpt), Halévy (Estey 1882, 128)

Victorian Parlor Songs

Nancy Reed, organist; Jack Reed, tenor
Estey Organ Co., 1891, no. 235784. Five-octave Parlor Organ.

15. "Home Sweet Home," Payne
16. Stephen Foster medley:
    "Oh! Susanna"
    "Old Folks at Home"
    "Beautiful Dreamer"
17. "The Honeysuckle and the Bee," Penn
18. "Bird in a Gilded Cage," von Tilzer
19. "Drink to Me Only with Thine Eyes," Old English

Music for Church and Lodge

E. A. Boadway, organist
Estey & Green, 1860, no. 7135. Two-rank Perfect Melodeon, unrestored. Collection of E. A. Boadway, Claremont, N.H.

20. "Danny Boy," Irish melody

J. Estey & Co., 1874, no. 45661. One-manual Cottage Organ. Old Trinity Episcopal Church, Cornish, N.H.

21. "Herr Gott, dich loben alle wir" (Old Hundredth), Drischner

Estey Organ Co., 1889, no. 204721. One-manual Philharmonic Organ. Gethsemane Episcopal Church, Proctorsville, Vt.

22. "La Baritone," Leybach

Estey Organ Co., 1896, no. 287018. One-manual Chapel Organ. Community Church, United Methodist, West Unity, N.H.

23. Scottish tune, Anon., published 1877

Estey Organ Co., 1918, no. 411155. One-manual Artist's Organ. Episcopal Church of the Transfiguration, Whitefield, N.H.

    24. "Gegrüsset seist du, Königen," German Catholic hymn tune

Estey Organ Co., c. 1926, no. 439780. Two-manual-with-pedal Studio Organ. Old Trinity Episcopal Church, Cornish, N.H. (hand-cranked by author).

    25. "Piccola Marcia," Mauri

Estey Organ Co., 1952, no. 498541. One-manual Parlor Organ; electric blower. Old St. Mary's Roman Catholic Church, West Claremont, N.H.

    26. Voluntary, Linley

    27. Hymn Tune, "Blaenwern," Rowlands

Carolyn Halsted, organist
J. Estey & Co., 1874, no. 49352. Five-octave Cottage Organ, partially restored.

    28. Hymn tunes from the *Estey Organ Method* (1879, 147–51)

        "Germany," Beethoven

        "Hamburg," arr. Mason

        "Boylston," Mason

        "A Strong Castle Is Our God," Luther

        "Coronation," Holden

Luella Frechette, organist
Estey Organ Co., opus 300, 1906. Three-manual pipe organ. First Baptist Church, Brattleboro, Vt. (donated by the Estey family in memory of Julius Estey).

    29. "Just a Closer Walk with Thee," Traditional

    30. "Come Let Us Sing," Paxton

Mansion Music

Estey Residence Organ with "automatic" self-playing mechanism. 1917 console, pipework from several old Esteys. Installed in the residence of Laurence W. Leonard, Laconia, N.H.

    31. "The Sheik of Araby," Snyder

Estey Organ Tonal Design

E. A. Boadway, organist
Estey Organ Co. Parlor Organ, 1909, no. 370590, unrestored. Choir loft auxilary organ in St. Mary's Roman Catholic Church, Claremont, N.H.

    32. Demonstration of various stop combinations and effects. In its present unrestored condition, it is interesting (and amusing) to hear the organ's internal machinations as stops are demonstrated.

Coda

Ned Phoenix, organist
Estey Organ Co., 1898, no. 297262. Six-octave Parlor Organ, restored.

    33. "Swanee River Swing," Foster, arr. Phoenix

    34. "In the Good Old Summertime," Shields and Evans, arr. Phoenix